C000260899

THE HORSIEMAN

With over ten books to his name, Duncan Williamson was one of the last true, traveller horsemen and the best-known of Scotland's storytellers. This autobiography tells, for the first time, his original story; how the Scottish traveller survived hawking his wares, dealing with local farmers and tradesmen, becoming a family man, creating the world of an unparalleled tradition-bearer. Duncan Williamson died in November 2007.

Linda Williamson, born and brought up in the woodlands of America's Midwest, was educated at the universities of Wisconsin and Edinburgh, and received a PhD in ethnomusicology in 1985. She married Duncan Williamson in 1977 and they have two children. A devotee of Indian philosophy and literary editor of several collections of Scottish stories, she now lives with her son in Edinburgh.

THE HORSIEMAN

MEMORIES OF A TRAVELLER 1928–58

DUNCAN WILLIAMSON

ORIGIN

This edition published in 2019 by
Birlinn Origin, an imprint of
Birlinn Limited
West Newington House
10 Newington Road
Edinburgh
EH9 1QS

www.birlinn.co.uk

Copyright © Duncan Williamson 1994
Preface copyright © Linda Williamson 2008

First published in 1994 by Canongate Press Ltd

Illustrations by Neil MacGregor
Map of Duncan Williamson's route by John Fardell

All rights reserved. No part of this publication may be
reproduced, stored or transmitted in any form without the
express written permission of the publisher.

ISBN: 978 1 912476 40 4

British Library Cataloguing-in-Publication Data
A catalogue record for this book is available
from the British Library

Typeset by Brinnoven, Liv
Printed and bound by Clays Ltd

CONTENTS

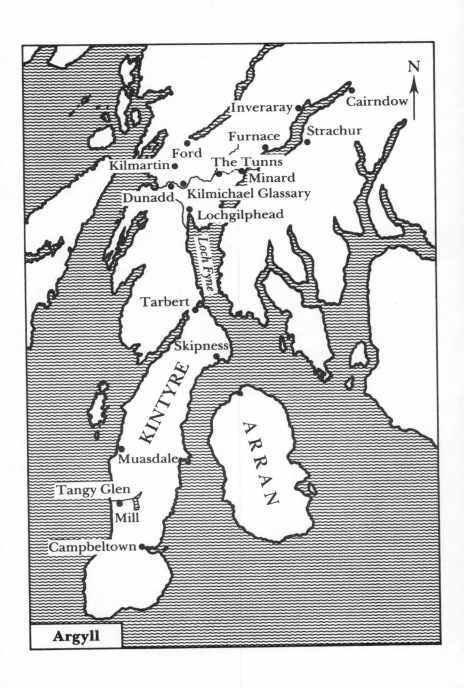

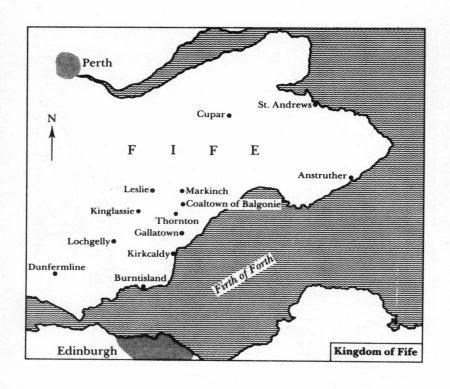

Kingdom of Fife

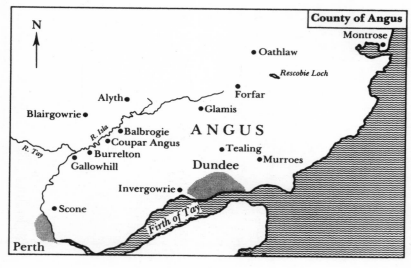

County of Angus

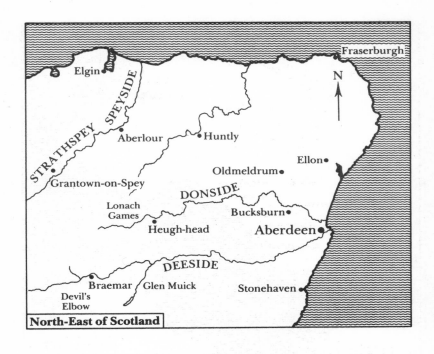

North-East of Scotland

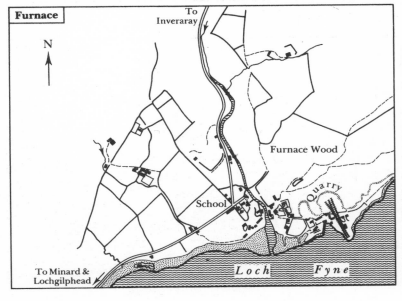

Furnace

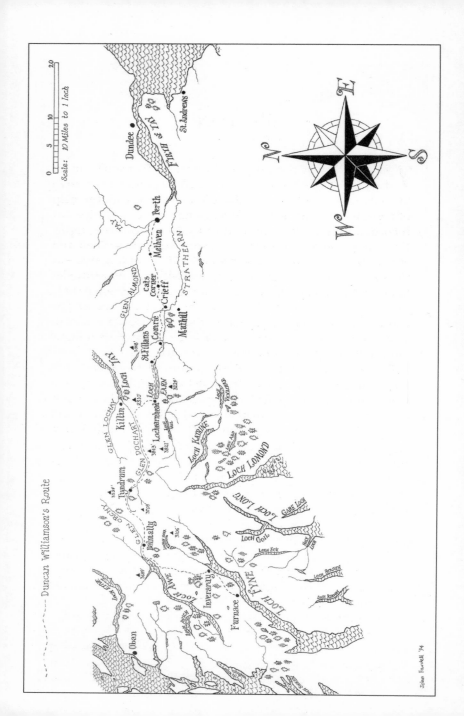

— Duncan Williamson's Route

Scale: 10 Miles to 1 Inch

John Fewkell '94

PREFACE

The Horsieman is the story of Duncan Williamson's life on the road as one of Scotland's travelling people from 1928 to 1958. Composed in late 1980 and early 1981 with the help of a grant from the Scottish Arts Council, the narrative was recorded over thirty hours on to twelve reel-to-reel tapes. These tapes, an oral history testament, were transcribed and edited by myself, Duncan's second wife. Our working title was *Horse Dealing and Traveller Trade*, an exposition of how traveller families in Scotland survived by their wits and traditional skills. The language is racy and laconic, colourful and spirited as Duncan was still very much part of the travelling fraternity in 1980 – working as a general dealer in close touch with many hundreds of traveller friends and relations.

The opening chapter, a brief account of Duncan's early family life, recorded at the request of his publisher, Stephanie Wolfe-Murray, in 1993, differs linguistically from the balance of the book. The narration held more English, less Gaelic and traveller cant; a transformation to which I contributed, that story told below. To help the reader with comprehension, a full glossary of Scots, traveller cant and Gaelic words finishes the book. Supplementing the text of *The Horsieman* are maps of travel routes, camping places, villages and farms where the tapestry of Duncan's life was woven. In the plate section, sketches taken from Duncan's notebook of poems and song show his drawings of traveller tents and the tools of traveller trades, skills now nearly lost and forgotten; we give hearty thanks to Neil MacGregor for helping with these. An oral historian in his own right, Neil has been a constant support throughout the work.

According to Duncan, there could be no real story without a song; and every chapter of *The Horsieman* closes with a poem, traditional song or ballad which Duncan wrote or sang. Wrapped up in these songs is a deeper story, of the writer who is

responsible for all of the storyteller's words in print: a newcomer
to Scotland in 1974, I followed in small footsteps behind the
indomitable Hamish Henderson as a collector of songs and
ballads for doctoral work in ethnomusicology.

The tattie howkers are rained off today and they say I will
find Duncan Williamson here in this potato field near Crieff.
Inside a tent on his knees singing ballads to his traveller friends
I meet him, a widower aged forty-seven. He always said it was
the Broonie, the spirit of a generation and Duncan means
'brown head' in Gaelic, because a year and a half later I marry
him, in 1977. Living the life of the Scottish Travelling People,
we are tented in a gelly – in summer months on Loch Fyne in
Argyll, in winter months returning to Fife, up the Ceres Road
from Cupar to Tarvit Farm. By 1980 our second child Tommy
is in his second year, Betsy is aged three, and from August to
September my mother has been to visit us at Duncholgan near
Lochgilphead, staying in our extended gelly, made a third
longer at the back to accommodate Granny from America.
With heavy rainfall and high winds, Argyll is harsh in the
winter and Duncan has few prospects for hawking, dealing in
scrap metals. His buyer, Davie Band in Perth, is just over the
hill and down the road from Glen Tarkie in north-east Fife.
So, how wonderful to receive the letter from Mr and Mrs Bell
on Kincraigie Farm above Strathmiglo who say 'yes!' Duncan
should come again to help with farm work in exchange for the
cottage beside the bothy at the back of the steadings. Great!
Our first solid roof and floor, and farewell to life on the road, a
decision we make for the sake of our weans, Betsy and Tommy,
after all.

The Scottish Arts Council have awarded us a bursary
(September 1980) to write Duncan's life story. His traditional
folk tales are finding their way into the archives of the
School of Scottish Studies through fieldwork recordings
by various university students and doctoral candidates like
myself; one literary agent and author armed with a handful
of my transcriptions is trying to get an Edinburgh publisher
interested in Duncan's mine of stories. Fife, close to Perth and
the capital, is a good place to put down roots. We begin work
on the autobiography the first week resident in Kincraigie.

Duncan knew in his heart his traveller life was over. His American wife, a thirty-one-year-old academic, had weathered nearly five years as a nomad but the hardships and uncertainties were taking a toll on her health, and with two kids growing like weeds he needed to provide a secure home. Davie Bell, laird of Kincraigie, had been host to his first family of seven since the 1940s. And here in Fife Duncan had become a tradesman, a real horsieman in the fifties. But normal settled life was never going to happen; we would not take charge of our lives, for the world was already keenly aware of the master storyteller, whose recordings had been whirling through the Edinburgh offices of the School of Scottish Studies, stretching into the bowels of the storytelling revival. What began as occasional recording sessions for students from America, Japan, Germany and all the isles of Britain, Canada and beyond soon became a weekly feature of Kincraigie life. Grampian Television, Central ITV and BBC Two camera crews found their way to the rocky hill at the back of the farm where lived the extraordinary tradition bearer who could tell stories for days on end showering guests with his renowned Celtic hospitality. Duncan's life story was shelved for ten years while the Broonie, the hedgehurst, the unicorn, fairies, silkies and woodland elves sprang from his breath into the minds and imaginations of pilgrim storytellers 'from the Alaskan North to the Antipodean South', writes David Campbell, 'all making tracks to Kincraigie Farm.' Publicly recognised as Scotland's living national monument, news spread like wildfire over a short space of ten years and such accolades as 'the greatest living English-speaking storyteller' were commonplace.

From this period comes my favourite horse story of Duncan's.

> I heard this many many years ago when I was just a kid back home in Argyll. It is a very old story. Now once upon a time there was this knight. And he had this horse, oh, what a beautiful horse! It was snow white. And the knight thought the world of it, took it with him to all the battles and every place he went all over the country. And everybody admired this horse. Then one day when he was older, the knight took his horse home and put it in the field next to his house.

Now down in the village there was a bell. And whenever anyone wanted to spread news, because there were no newspapers in these days, if anybody wanted to tell something, they went out in the street and pulled the bell. The bell went; ding dong ding dong ding dong. And all the people gathered round about. A man told what was going to happen, if there was anything going on in the village, if anybody was hurt or anything important! But years passed and things changed, and the bell was never used. It was forgotten about, just like the poor old horse. But the old horse was still in the field only getting very, very little to eat. The knight was now very old and he had completely forgotten about his horse. Then one day the gate leading to the field was left open. The old horse got out.

And he was that weak he could hardly stand. So he just barely managed to wander down the street, right by the knight's house, down through the village till it came to the old church where the old bell was. And all of the old church was covered over with ivy. The old rope that was hanging from the bell, all the creeping vines had gathered round it and the rope was nearly covered – you could hardly see it but the bell could still ring! So the old horse searched about for something soft, because he had no teeth to eat. And the first thing he saw was the vines hanging to the bell. He started pulling them and the bell started to ring: ding dong ding dong, someone has done a wrong.

And all the villagers listened. Some of the old folk in the village who remembered . . . when the bell used to ring when someone had done a wrong, or if somebody had done something good, all came out. Some on crutches, some with staves, old women, old ladies well up in their years, in their seventies and eighties, and they gathered all round the bell. And they stood and they looked.

The old horse was pulling the ivy off the bell rope. It was going, ding dong ding dong, someone has done a wrong. And they saw the old horse. One old man stood up.

'I remember that horse,' he said. 'That was a beautiful animal. It had no other way to come and tell us that its master had starved it nearly to death. Look at it! Its bones are sticking out; its ribs are sticking out of its side, and its hip joints. Look at its tail! It's never been combed for years, neither has been its mane. Its master has done it wrong after all these years, and he will have to be punished.'

So all the people of the village gathered and went up to the knight's big house, knocked at his door and told him to come out. The old knight came out. He said, 'What do you want?'

They said, 'We want you! You've done a wrong.'

And the knight said, 'I've never done a wrong in all my life. I've been a knight to the king all the days of my life.'

The old man said, 'You have done a wrong – you've neglected your old horse.'

'My horse?' says the knight.

'Yes,' said the people of the village. 'Your old horse came down to the village and rang the bell himself, told us that you had done a wrong.'

'Well,' says the knight, 'if that's true, he'll never be neglected again.' So the knight took his old horse back up to his big house. He put him in a warm stable and looked after him, saw that the horse had plenty to eat and plenty to drink for the rest of his days. And that's the last of my story.

It was a special privilege to be able to look after Duncan in the last five months of his life. We spent the previous thirteen years apart, since 1994 when *The Horsieman* was first published, but I never forgot the knight and his steed, or the Broonie! His songs and stories remained an integral part of my own travels, my own story. In July 2007 he taught me the verses of 'The Golden Vanity' closing chapter five below. And asleep in the room at the end of Duncan's house, I dreamed the Night of Peace, our Christmas tree alight with candles under canvas in the woods of Tarvit Farm. On Hallowe'en night after a sweet fireside ceilidh in song with his Ladybank neighbours, Duncan suffered a stroke, and eight days later in hospital my husband died. Now, a soulful legacy, storytellers mourn their loss. Colleague Hugh Lupton pays last respects to Duncan Williamson, a tribute to his artistry:

Everything he heard, saw, touched, smelt, tasted and felt added flavour to the bubbling stew of stories he kept in his memory. He'd lived an extraordinary life to the full. He'd known how it was to be starving hungry, to be kept awake all night by seals with tooth-ache, to fit a cast-off horseshoe, to guddle for trout. He'd experienced loss and love and the pleasures of good company, he'd trodden the roads of Scotland over and over . . . all this fed into his stories, giving them substance, sympathy, humour, a grounding in real places and all the insights that come from a life of hard graft and sharp, humane observation. He might be telling a Jack tale, a silkie story, a joke, but in his imagination it always rested on a solid core of real lived experience that made the story true. Also, through his vast inner store of ballads and poems, through his knowledge of Gaelic and cant, he had a rich and rare vocabulary and a deep feel for the music of language. He was quite simply, the greatest bearer of stories and songs in the Scots and English language.

Excellent recordings of Duncan Williamson's soulful tenor, his ballads and songs, may be heard on the CDs produced by Mike Yates (*Travellers Joy*), John Howson (*Put Another Log on the Fire*) and Pete Shepherd (*FifeSing*). Available from Music in Scotland Ltd are two volumes of *Traveller's Tales*, including 'Closing Our Camping Grounds Down' by Duncan, also known as 'The Hawker's Lament'.

From the Celtic otherworld, the rest is left to our horsieman. May the reader find below something of the profundity and gentleness of the man, as Helen East remembers, 'who did his utmost to make sure we have his stories.'

Linda Williamson
November 2007

Chapter One

Jock and Betsy and the Kids

Some travellers stuck more to one area. But Johnie Townsley, my mother's father, travelled all over. He walked along with a handcart and went to Inverness, Elgin, right down into Ayrshire and down to Dumfries. He travelled all through Fife, Angus and Perthshire – no, not in the wintertime, just in the summertime. But you see, he was a piper and a horse was no good to him. He played his bagpipes in the summertime, by the shooting lodges, big houses, hotels and that. And then he came back home to Argyll and settled down for the winter. In the summertime he took off again with his family.

My mother's mother was old Bella MacDonald. She told me that her grandfather, Roderick MacDonald, used to travel with a pony through the paths to the farms, taking the shortcuts over the hills. Roderick carried his gear, a bundle tied to each side of the pony's back with a couple of kids sitting on, and he led the pony all through Argyllshire and Perthshire. Taking carts through these roads was no good, because the wheels broke and the paths were too narrow.

On my father's side, my grandfather Willie Williamson, born 1851, never travelled at all once he had children, since long before the 1914 war. And I remember my father telling me that his grandfather on his mother's side, John MacColl (whose father was from Ireland) travelled with horses with sackets on their backs. They were pack folk, like the way the cowboys went with pack mules.

John MacColl was born in Kilberry in 1812. His father was a tinsmith, but John liked to work as a coppersmith. He used to go with a one-wheeled barrow, like a wheelbarrow but it had no sides. My mother told me that he travelled the footpaths from place to place because the roads were very bad in these days. He took all the shortcuts across the hills and across the mountains carrying these big sheets of copper on his barrow.

And my mother told me how he came to this farm away in the back highlands of Argyllshire.

The farmer said to him, 'John, that's an awfae bundle you've got on that barra. Would ye no be better wi a bit pony tae pull that bit cart tae youse, instead o pushin that thing across the mountains and across footpaths?'

'It might be all right,' he says to the farmer, 'but I couldna get gaun across my paths across the hills wi a pony.' But he took the pony from the farmer anyway, bought it from him and he threw away the barrow, tied the bundles on the pony's back. He walked with this wee piebald pony through the moors; let it carry his stuff.

But travellers were very poor before they had ponies. They couldn't do much for themselves, and they couldn't carry very much. For the want of carrying more it made them poorer still. Their camping stuff was as light as what they could carry on their backs. It was okay if they had a big family, see what I mean, two-three boys or two-three lassies. Like our family when we went on the move in the summertime. Every one of us carried something of the equipment. But if we'd had a pony, if my father had had a pony, then we could have been a bit better off. Some carried the sticks for the tent, some carried the tent canvas, some carried the cooking utensils and some carried the bed clothes in our family. Everybody had their own thing.

After travellers managed to see the sense of having a horse, getting a pony, buying a cart and harness, they went further afield. They could travel farther. Some Highland families left and travelled into other 'countries', Perthshire, Fife and Angus, the 'low country'. But while it started the travellers and made some of them a wee bit better off, there were some who never bothered with horses at all. They still maintained it was too much bother, especially in Argyllshire among the Townsleys, my mother's people. They bothered very little about horses because they were afraid of burkers, or body-snatchers. These travellers could lift their barras over a fence, lift their wee handcarts or perambulators over into a wood or take them up an old road where they couldn't take a horse and cart – well away from the main roads at night-time. This was handy to them. They didn't keep ponies, because they didn't want to be close to the road when the coaches passed. Before the days of motor cars they believed all coaches were driven by burkers, who took your body and sellt it for research.

My father John Williamson was born in 1892. He came off the Williamson and Burke families (Nancy Burke was his paternal grandmother) who originally came also from Kintyre, whose forebears came from the Isle of Islay. After my father and my mother were married in 1910, they travelled on foot after that around Scotland in the years before the beginning of the First World War. My father was called up in the Army and joined the war in 1915. After he served his time he came back from the Army, and he had two sons Jock and Sandy by then. And he settled in Furnace on the shores of Loch Fyne.

On Loch Fyne, in Furnace wood, my father raised thirteen children. Sixteen were born, but three died in infancy, one when she was just a newborn baby, and she was born in a hospital. Everyone else was born in a tent, apart from Susan, whom my mother had among the heather! I was born by the shoreside. It was early spring. And he put all of us to school in Furnace and took care of us to the best of his ability. My father didn't have a regular job because in these days a tinker was looked down upon, as someone that was socially unfit to work among the common folk. But my father being settled in the one part, and putting us to school, the stigma of being a tinker naturally passed by as most of the folk came to know and understand us. We were called and accepted by the local community as 'the Williamson family'. My father was respected because he'd served his time in the war, and he had come home and registered the marriage to my mother (1916 in Kilmichael Glassary) and had settled down. When a traveller did these things and showed that he tried to make himself part of the community, he gained a little respect from the local folk.

My mother and father ran away together when my mother was only fourteen years old. And my daddy was seventeen. Betsy Townsley was my mother's full name. And she was born in a cave in Muasdale. My daddy was born in an old mill away up Tangy Glen. And the old mill was owned by two old brothers. One of the brothers was blind and they ran the old mill. They left this shed open with some straw in it for the runaway marriages of Kintyre. It was like Gretna Green! And when two people ran away together and spent a night in the mill they were officially married.

But my mother and father lived in the wood together in Furnace. It was a big oak wood in the middle of the Duke's estate. And people tried to get us moved on from that wood, but my grandfather was born there, my mother's father. And of course the old duke, Duncan Campbell in Argyll, my father was a great favourite of his. Because I remember he came with his old car on a Sunday with a big bunch of lollipops, all those different colours you could ever see!

And he said, 'Well, Mr Williamson, I will pay the doctor's bill the next time. Are the children around?' And he wore these plus fours, we call them knickerbockers; and big old brogue shoes, a Balmoral Bonnet and sometimes the kilt. He sat down there and took off his old shoes and we watched him! My daddy strapped the razor on his belt, a big open razor. We wondered what he was going to do. And the old duke took his foot up, put it on my daddy's knee. And his old foot was full of bunions and corns. He was an old man, in his seventies at that time, when I remember him. And Daddy very carefully shaved the skin of his foot, shaved the bunion and the corn with the open razor. And this took away a lot of pressure from it, at the head, the little corn on his foot. Daddy cut it in with his razor and shaved it all right round, and he clipped the nails of his toes with the razor. The Duke wouldn't go anywhere else! But he would come once a month or so, drive his car down. And people would say to the Duke, 'Oh, these tinkers, they're cutting your trees.

'Well,' he said, 'let them cut my trees. They're my trees!'

And of course we used to steal a few apples from people's gardens and we stole a few vegetables. And if we came across a nest of eggs by a hen, we took them! Because the wintertimes were very hard. The summertime was nice because we would run about with our bare feet, and Daddy would take us on a camping trip then. He'd burn the old barricade, the tent we lived in during the winter, and take us on a trip down to Lochgilphead, around Kilmartin among the standing stones. And we would play ourselves there and have fun. We'd thin the turnips on our knees and have a wonderful time because Daddy and Mammy were always there. They would work hard, have a wee dram at the weekends, sing songs and Daddy would play the pipes.

Then he would say, 'Well, children, you've had your holiday. It's time to go home.' And then we would go back to Furnace again, back to the same place. There'd be nothing there, just a piece of ground, hard baked. We built a new barricade tent every autumn in the same place. No grass would ever grow there. Father even used the same holes in the ground, where he'd put the sapling sticks in with the snottum. And he was thirty-seven years in that one little camping place! All his family grew up there. He put them all to the little school in Furnace, so they could learn to read and write.

These summers in the 1920s started early. You got beautiful weather in the month of April. On the tenth of April this year Daddy burned the big barricade and packed all the things he would need for the summer. He got the weans ready, there were six by that time. And my mother was busy expecting. She must have been nine months on the way.

He said, 'Well, Betsy, we'll get the length of Lochgilphead, which is sixteen miles. And if you take ill with the baby down there, maybe they can get you into hospital or something.' She had never been in hospital in her life. Old Granny used to do this, be her midwife. That was my mother's old mother, Bella MacDonald, the old storyteller and fortune teller. But father never went far that day, only about three-quarters of a mile on the first day of the journey. He pitched three little tents, one for the girls, one for the boys and one for himself and my mother just at Furnace shore. And the next morning Mother took ill. That was the eleventh of April, 1928. I was born in the little tent, and Daddy took the other children along the shore for a walk while my granny took me to the world.

I always tell people, 'I was born before my granny!' And my mother took me wrapped in a shawl later that day, for she wanted to show her new baby to all her old friends. And some of the old people kept a diary of my mother.

They said, 'Betsy, which one is this?' Some of the old ladies in the village, maybe old spinsters she visited who never had any children of their own, or maybe some with their children grown up, said, 'Well, Betsy, which is this one?' My mother was only a young woman at that time.

'This is my seventh,' she said.

Now the villagers of Furnace knew the time had come, that Daddy had burned his barricade and we were going for our summer's trip. 'Oh,' they said, 'there'll no be many eggs stolen again for a while!' And of course, every one of my mother's friends knew my mother was pregnant. And they probably wished the baby would be born in Furnace, like some of the other ones.

But this particular day a dear friend of my mother's died, the same day in 1928 I was born. Duncan MacCallum. He died with TB, tuberculosis. He was a great shinty player. His brother Archie had heard that my mother had had a wee baby. And his mother and my mother were great friends. He cycled from Furnace down nearly a mile to the shore to the tents. And he told my mammy and daddy that young Duncan had died. Somebody had spread the word, somebody was out on the road that morning and had said, 'What's wrong? Johnie's walking with the weans. Oh, Betsy's haein a wean.' And the word spread back to the village. Betsy had never got to Lochgilphead. Betsy had the baby at the shore, at Furnace shore. And Archie took his old bicycle and cycled down. My granny by this time had tidied me up and rolled me up in a bit of cloth or something, whatever it was, and had tidied up my mother. And Archie came to the fire at the front of the tent. Father had a wee fire there with the door of the tent pulled down for my mother to have a little privacy.

He said, 'Duncan has died.' Duncan was only twenty-four.

And my mother said, 'What's that? Duncan has died!' Because she knew Duncan had been ill.

And he said, 'Have you a boy or a girl?'

She said, 'It's a wee boy.' And my mother cried out, 'Well, I'm going to call him Duncan!' And she called me Duncan MacCallum Williamson. And Duncan MacCallum had died two hours before I was born. And she said, 'Well, we're going to call him Duncan after Duncan MacCallum.' And of course Archie was really chuffed, really proud. And they were good people. Soon my mother was up and she walked to old Katie MacCallum, young Duncan's mother and showed her the baby – me! And Mother told her she was going to call it after Duncan. They were quarry workers who stayed in Furnace. And of course they were so pleased that Duncan's name would be carried on for years.

My father stayed for a week at the shore after I was born. By then my mother was a little stronger – she was a strong woman after having all these children. And we shifted. She took me and showed me off to all her friends, all round Minard. My father stayed there for a few days. Oh, that was the idea! Handsel the baby, give the baby a silver coin, a sixpence or threepenny piece or a shilling. My mother would collect several shillings, a lot of money! She'd say, 'Oh, Mrs such-and-such, this is my new baby!'

'Oh, I'll have to give the wee baby something.' And she collected seven or eight shillings in a day. In 1928 that was worth a fortune to you. And they made their way to Lochgilphead. And he had friends there, and this was Betsy with her new baby! I was a kind of pension to her for the first three months of my life. And Father cut a little hay, tied a little corn, and worked on a few farms till the days got shorter. Then he made his way back to Furnace again, put up the barricade once again and sent the children to school – Sandy, Jock, Bella, Betty, Willie and Rachel. My mother took care of the baby, walked back to Furnace and showed me to the rest of the old friends who had never seen me yet.

And then the cold winter nights, Granny went into her little compartment, tent, in the barricade, and it was storytelling. I was very young then, but I remember my granny well. There were wonderful stories told round the little fire. I remember my daddy sitting around the fire in the middle of the floor, just a stick fire in the middle of the tent, a hole in the roof and the smoke going straight up through the hole. A little paraffin lamp, the cruisie turned down, home-made by my father.

Granny would tell a story, Father would tell a story. Maybe a few travellers passing by would stop and put their tent over in the 'Tinker's Turn', a place across the burn from the wood where we stayed. My father's cousin Willie Williamson, old

Rabbie Townsley and some of the old travellers, Sandy Reid and others would come in. They would also tell stories and have a little get-together. Our tent was a stopping place for travellers who came down to Argyll, and there was always time for a story.

Now Granny would stay with us all winter in that big barricade with her little compartment. Her son Duncan was there as well. He helped my father to get firewood, and they'd go fishing together, catch a few salmon and snare a few rabbits. Granny went hawking with my mother through the houses in Furnace and Minard. But also some days Granny took off on her own and it was our love to go with her. Granny was wonderfully good to us. Whatever she got, something tasty, she would always share it with us. In the summertime when the days got warm, my father would dismantle the tent, the big barricade; and Granny would move her little tent away from our big one to have some privacy of her own. Just because it was so warm.

Now Granny was an old lady, and every old traveller woman in these bygone days never carried a handbag. But around their waist they carried a big pocket. I remember Granny's – she made it herself, a tartan pocket. It was like a large purse with a strap, and she tied it around her waist. It had three pearl buttons down the middle, no zip in these days. Granny carried all her worldly possessions in this pocket.

Now, Granny smoked a little clay pipe. And when she needed tobacco, she would say, 'Weans, I want you to run to the village for tobacco for my pipe.' And she'd give us a threepenny bit, a penny for each of us and a penny for tobacco. The old man used to have a roll of it on the counter, and he cut off a little bit for Granny for her penny. We came back and our reward was, 'Granny, tell us a story!'

She sat there in front of her little tent, and she had a little billy-can and a little fire. We collected sticks for her, and she'd boil this strong, black tea. She lifted the can off, placed it by the side of the fire and said, 'Well, weans, I'll see what I have in my pocket for you this time!' She opened up that big pocket by her side with the three pearl buttons. I remember them well, and she said, 'Well, I'll tell you this story.' Maybe it was one she'd told three nights before. Maybe it was one she had never told for weeks. Sometimes she would tell us a story three-four times; sometimes she told us a story we'd never heard.

So, one day my sister and I came back from the village. We were playing and we came up to Granny's little tent. The sun was shining warm. Granny's little can of tea was by the fire: it was cold, the fire had burned out. The sun was warm. Granny was lying, she had her two hands under her head like an old woman, and her little bed was in front of the tent. By her side was the pocket. That was the very first time we'd ever seen that pocket off Granny's waist. She probably took it off when she went to bed at night-time. But never during the day!

So my sister and I crept up quietly and we said, 'Granny is asleep! There's her pocket. Let's go and see how many stories are in Granny's pocket.' So very gently we picked the pocket up, we took it behind the tree where we lived in the forest and opened up the three pearl buttons. And in that pocket was like Aladdin's Cave! There were clay pipes, threepenny pieces, rings, halfpennies, pennies, farthings, brooches, pins, needles, everything an old woman carried with her, thimbles . . . but not one single story could we find! So we never touched anything. We put everything back inside, closed it and put it back, left it by her side. We said, 'We'll go and play and we'll get Granny when she gets up.' So we went off to play again, came back about an hour later and Granny was up. Her little fire was kindling. She was heating up her cold tea. And we sat down by her side. She began to light her pipe after she drank this black, strong tea. We said, 'Granny, are you going to tell us a story?'

'Aye, weans,' she said, 'I'll tell you a story.' She loved telling us stories because it was company for us, forbyes it was good company for her to sit there beside us weans. She said. 'Wait a minute noo, wait till I see what I have for you tonight.' And she opened up that pocket. She looked at me and my little sister for a while, for a long time with her blue eyes. She said, 'Ye ken something, weans?'

We said, 'No, Granny.'

She said, 'Somebody opened my pocket when I was asleep and all my stories are gone. I cannae tell ye a story the nicht, weans.' And she never told us a story that night. And she never told us another story. And I was seventeen when my granny died, but eleven when that happened. Granny never told me another story, and that's a true story!

Life was very hard for us as a travelling family living on the Duke of Argyll's estate in Furnace in Argyll, because it was hard to feed a large family when times were so hard. We ran through the village and we stole a few carrots, stole a few apples from the people. Some of the local people respected us, some didn't want their children to play with us. We were local people too, but we were tinkers living in a tent in the wood of Argyll. And of course we did a lot of good things forbyes, because we helped the old folk. My brothers and I sawed sticks and we collected blocks along the shore for their fires and we dug a few gardens. If there was a little job for a penny or two, we would do it for them. We did things for the people that the other children would not do. And we gained a good respect from some of the older folk where we lived. As the evening was over boys would get together, and we'd climb trees and do things, but we never caused any trouble or damage. But some of the people in the village actually hated us.

I went to the little primary school in Furnace when I was six years old. It was hard coming from a travelling family. You went to school with your bare feet wearing cast-off clothes from the local children that your mother had collected around the doors. And of course you sat there in the classroom and the parents of the children who were your little friends and your little pals in school had warned them, 'Oh, don't play with the tinker children. You might get beasts off them, you might get lice.' You were hungry, very, very hungry in school. You couldn't even listen to your school teacher talking to you, listen to her giving you lessons you were so hungry. But you knew after the school was over you had a great consolation. You were looking forward to one particular thing: you would go home, have any kind of little meal that your mother had to share with you, which was very small and meagre, but she shared it among the kids. Then you had the evening together with your granny and your parents. The stories sitting by the fire, Granny lighting her pipe and telling you all those wonderful stories. This was the most important thing, the highlight of your whole life.

We were the healthiest children in the whole village. We ran around with our bare feet. We lived on shellfish. We didn't have the meals the village children had, no puddings or sweet things. We were lucky if we saw one single sweet in a week. But we hunted. If we didn't have food, we had to look for it. And looking for food was stealing somebody's vegetables from somebody's garden or guddling trout in the river or getting shellfish from the sea. We had to provide for ourselves. Because we knew our parents couldn't do it for us. Mammy tried her best to hawk the doors, but you couldn't expect your mother to go to the hillside and kill you a hare or a rabbit. And you couldn't expect your mammy to go and guddle trout. So, from the age of five-six-seven year old you became a person, you matured before you were even ten years old. And therefore you were qualified to help raise the rest of the little ones in the family circle. You could contribute. Because you knew otherwise you wouldn't have it. You didn't want to see your little brothers and sisters go hungry, so you went to gather sticks along the shore, sell them to an old woman and bring a shilling back to your mother.

The epidemic of diphtheria hit the school in 1941. Diphtheria then was deadly. Now you had to pay a doctor's bill in these days. And by this time there were nine of us going to the single little school, all my brothers and sisters going together. But because there were so many children actually sick with diphtheria, they closed the primary school. Now we ran through the village with our bare feet. 'Little raggiemuffins' they called us in the village. Our little friends, five of them went off to hospital with diphtheria. Two of my little pals never came back.

My mother had good friends in the village, but some people wouldn't even talk to us. One particular woman, a Mrs Campbell, had two little boys. She was one who wouldn't even look at you if you passed her on the street. She wouldn't give you a crust. After the school had been closed, I walked down to the village this one day in my bare feet. She stepped out of the little cottage.

And she said, 'Hello, good morning.' I was amazed that this woman should even speak to me. She said, 'How are you?'

I said, 'I'm fine, Mrs Campbell. I'm fine, really fine.'

She said, 'Are you pleased? Are you enjoying the school closure?'

I said, 'Well, the school's closed. We're doing wir best to enjoy wirsels.'

She said, 'Are you hungry?'

I said, 'Of course, I'm hungry. We're always hungry. My mother cannae help us very much.'

She said, 'Would you like something to eat?' Now I didn't know, I swear this is a true story, that her two little boys were took off with diphtheria and sent to Glasgow to hospital. She said, 'Oh, I have some nice apples. Would you like some?' Now an apple to me was a delight. She said, 'Come in, don't be afraid!' And she brought me into that house for the first time in my life, into the little boy's bedroom. And there was a plate sitting by his little bed full of apples. He was gone. And she took the apples from that plate and gave them to me, three of them. She said, 'Eat you this, it'll be good for you.' I didn't know what she was trying to do. Because I was too young, only thirteen. And she was trying to contaminate me with the diphtheria because her two little boys were taken away. Because none of Betsy Williamson's children ever took diphtheria. And that school was closed for five weeks. And everyone was saying, 'Oh, have you got a sore throat?'

Then they began to realise, why were the travelling children so healthy? And they used to say, when my mother walked round the doors of the village, 'What was Betsy Williamson – oh, Betsy Williamson must have superior powers. She must be collecting herbs or something in the woods and looking after children.' You see what I mean? And some would say, 'Oh, she must be some kind of a witch.' And things were never the same after that, never the same.

We were nine children going to school. But if you were a mother with only three, and you lost two with diphtheria; and your neighbour next to you, all her children survived, you would feel very, very envious. You're going to feel very broken-hearted that some children should survive and some children should not. And that woman who gave me that apple, she never, never spoke to anyone again as long as she lived. Not even me, not my mother, nobody. She never spoke to anybody at all, she went kind of crazy out of her mind. She lost her two little boys and went completely crazy. Her man about four years later fell over the quarry and was killed. Some said he threw himself over.

When my brothers and sisters and I were in the school we had to stand torment from the children and static, the teacher saying we were little tinker children. She didn't pay as much attention to us as she paid to the rest of the kids in school. We weren't even second class. We were just there – she had to teach us because we were there. She couldn't have cared a damn whether we were or not. But we did not stay off school. Some of the local kids stayed off, when they took flu and sneezes, colds. But even though we were not feeling very well and we were hungry, we still went to school. The only reason we went was to get 250 attendance marks, each of us, so that we could get away with our daddy and mammy for the summertime. We got two attendance marks per day, and we did about five months in school, from October through till February. The more we attended school, the sooner we could get away. Once our Daddy knew we had got our attendance quota, he knew we could take off. He burned the big barricade and packed up the few things which we children could carry. Each one of us carried something. And this is what we looked forward to all year. We weren't interested in getting our education in school. Education began when we left school: hunting, guddling for trout, camping by the seaside, cooking shellfish and having a long summer to go with our parents, go hawking with our mother round the doors and going round the fields with our father cutting a little hay. It was an exciting time.

We travelled all Loch Fyneside, down to Lochgilphead, down to Tarbert, up Kilmichael Glassary, round by Oban. We had the time of our life. Father would get a little job in a farm and we put our tent in the field. In these days the fields were full of rabbits and the burns were full of trout. But one thing Father was against was the standing stones, the Pictish stones. We were allowed to look at them, admire them. But we could not even put a hand on them. He wouldn't even let us touch them. We were not allowed. It was a belief that had passed down from his generation, from his parents as a kid; he was taught to leave these things alone.

But I didn't believe my father, so I climbed one of the stones.

Right up to the top of the standing stone. I sat there in the
sun. The camp was beside the stone. He wouldn't put the tent
too close to it, just within looking distance, about thirty yards
from the stone. He admired the stones himself. I've seen him
standing there with his hands at his back for hours looking at
that stone. What he had in his mind I wouldn't know. Looking
at it for hours on end, staring and imagining. But then I sat up
on top. Oh, I was the king of the castle, you know!

He said to me, 'Boy, would you come down off of there!'

I said, 'Why, I'm no doing any harm!'

He said, 'Come down off that stone at this moment or
something bad's going to happen to you.' This was the month
of June. It was a warm summer. Father was cutting a little hay
with a scythe. 'Come down from there, boy,' he said, 'at once!
And don't you ever try that again.'

But anyway, I obeyed his order and I came down from the
stone. 'Now,' he said, 'when I get my hands on you, I'm going
to put my belt across your backside.' So I was a wee bit afraid. I
wandered away. And the young corn was coming up. I sat down
in the corn, next to the field where we stayed. And then I must
have lain down, because I got sleepy. And the sun came up . . .
and I was sun struck. They searched far for me. They thought I
had fallen in the River Add that passed by. They thought I was
lost. They shouted and cried. But I heard nothing. I was struck
with the sun. And for two long months, June and July . . . it was
the beginning of August, time to leave and go back home to
Furnace again, get the tent built up and get us back to school.
But my mother hurled me in a little pram. I can't remember
that; she only told me later. I was completely lost for exactly
two-and-a-half months. Struck with the sun, and I was about
seven years old.

Then, just before we came home to Furnace my brothers
George and Willie were catching gulls. They never hurt them,
but caught the white gulls that flew around. They had a piece of
bread on a string. They tied it and scattered bread all around.
The gull would come down and swallow the piece of bread tied
to the string. There were no hooks or anything, so it wouldn't
hurt them. As the gull swallowed the piece of bread, within

seconds he pulled in the fishing line and caught it. You petted the bird, looked at it and then set it free.

So I was lying out there in a little pram my mother had for me. I couldn't walk, was completely lost, brain burned out with the sun. My legs were paralysed. My father and mother blamed it on the standing stones, the curse of the standing stones. The boys were catching gulls, and I saw this gull with a piece of line in its mouth. My two brothers were pulling the gull in, nothing to hurt it, pulling . . . And I opened my eyes. I looked up and saw them catching this gull. Pulling it in, and that's when I came back to my senses. After two long months. George was two years older than me, Willie was two years older than George. Nine and eleven they were.

Father had said, 'These stones belong to your people, your people a long time ago. They put them there for a purpose, so that you would remember them. These stones are there for you to remember your people by, not to deface them, not to climb them, not to touch or do anything on them. Respect and love them, that's what the standing stones are for.' And Father would always make sure he would camp not far from some of the great standing stones. He would have no fear of burkers, no fear of ghosts or spirits that many people had in these days. He felt safe, as if that giant stone were looking over, guarding us children. The stone was looking over us. In the summer. And we always went back to the same place in the summertime.

Years later I was to spend time under the Pictish cairns by myself. But it was the lesson Father had said to us, 'They'll never hurt you, they'll never touch you. Leave them alone, they will guard you, you will feel no fear. You won't be afraid.' Respect and love for these stones had been taught to him down through the ages. It was magical.

The end of October, that's harvest time. Father would finish the corn cutting, and that's when we went back to school. We came back a week before the end of the October holiday. You had to build the barricade tent, help Daddy get the sapling boughs for the frame, patch the covers, collect stones for the base to hold the covers tight. We had to build a winter home for ourselves in the wood. And Father needed all the help he could get. We had to go to another wood, cut saplings, build the barricade all over again. He couldn't do it on his own. It took two weeks, and we came home in the middle of October. He knew once he had the tent up and everything fit for us, then we could go back to school.

He said, 'Now, weans, it's up to yourself. If you want a holiday next summer . . .' I remember getting up in the mornings in winter. Mother and Father lying sleeping in their bed and we going to the burn, washing our faces, with our bare feet. No tea, no breakfast, nothing and we went to school. All because we needed that 250 attendance. But my daddy and mammy knew they were giving us an education we were never going to get in school, because they knew we were never going to go off to any high school or things like that. They knew what they were teaching us was going to stand us good in our lives to come. Now we could leave home: I ran away from home first when I was thirteen and by the things I learned travelling with my father and mother around Lochgilphead, I was able to cope with my life. I knew the farmers, I knew how to work on the farms, I knew how to cut peats. If I hadn't done that 250 attendance in school, I would never have got the experience – freedom to learn from my parents.

But there was also the law that children were taken away from their parents if they did not attend school. If we had left school without the 250 attendance, we would have been arrested. It was law. The School Board would have come along, the Cruelty Inspector.

He said, 'Have your children been in school?'

If Father had said, 'No, they've never been in school.'

'Okay, then, just a moment.' The Inspector walked to the first old traditional phone box. He phoned up a taxi. And then you were gone! You never saw your parents again, never. There were hundreds of children taken off, some went to Australia, some to Canada, some went around the world, no one ever saw them again. And parents were never informed. They were taken to Industrial Day Schools – not only traveller children. But they were worse against the travelling children. If you were in a settled community you would be able to attend school some days in the weeks through all the school terms. But the travelling people travelled to find work, and never sent their children to school most months of the year. And anyone over the age of five without the attendance quota was taken off – you never saw them again. I had cousins who were taken away, whom I never saw again. My Aunt Nellie's lassies.

Well, my father loved and respected his children, and he wanted to teach us to grow up to be natural human beings, learn the basic things of life he had learned as a child. He taught us about the standing stones, how to work in the fields, and gather stones. Oh, he couldn't read or write himself, and he wanted us to be able to have these skills. But the teacher couldn't care less whether we learned to write or read. And we didn't wait till the school broke for a holiday. Once we got the attendance quota, we were off! Sometimes it was March, sometimes February. And this was the basic thing; Father knew the moment he took us off the school, we learned how to put up a tent, how to pick good dry grasses for our beds, how to gather firewood. When he got a little job, we went along and helped him with it. All the kids went and helped their parents every way; girls went with their mammies hawking round the doors.

We used to go up in the hills. Well, there's a shortcut that takes you from Minard over the hill to Kilmichael Glassary, a twelve mile cross. And there in the middle of the hill is a sheep farm known as the Tunns. Old Duncan Stewart and his brother Hendry and sister Annie owned the farm. And we stayed there for a week, sometimes a fortnight. Mammy scrubbed the stairs and Daddy helped with the hay, cutting it with a scythe and building up little stacks. The Stewarts kept a couple of cows, and they had mostly sheep. And we would have the time of our life! There were fruit trees in the garden, and we cleaned old Annie's garden. And she would bring us each big bowls of porridge. We slept in the byre, sometimes if the nights were cold. And she would sit there and milk the cow in the morning, 'zing, zing, zing' into the zinc pail, us lying in the stall among the straw, warm as pies, you know what I mean! And the big River Add ran beside us. We could guddle trout or poach an odd salmon. Daddy would dig the garden, cut the hay and trim the trees. He clipped the sheep with old Duncan and Hendry.

Mammy scrubbed the kitchen floor. And they looked forward to this!

Old Annie would say, 'Och, Betsy will soon be coming.' And Annie Stewart kept a diary on every child that my mother had. And the sad thing was, even though Annie loved us all, Mother never called one of her children after her. And she always wanted one of Betsy's kids to be called after her, old Annie Stewart. Mother called the children Susan, after another farmer's wife, and Nellie, after someone else. But never 'Annie'. Annie was her dearest friend. And Annie always looked forward to Betsy coming in the spring to clean the stairs and scrub the landing, help to clean up the kitchen and things like that. Because in these days things were really rough. It was a sheep farm away out in the countryside. And of course Hendry and Duncan waited until my father came before they started clipping the sheep. He helped them because he was a great clipper himself, rolling the wool, bagging it and doing all these things. But we never caused any problems around the farm, no way in this world.

It was a highlight for us visiting the farm, but it was always a highlight for them! Mother gave them the news. Because it was eight miles to Minard. Mother walked round the doors of the villages with her basket and she would talk to Mrs MacVicar or Mrs such-and-such and say, 'Somebody's ill', and 'somebody's died' and 'the gamekeeper this' and everything. She would bring the news to Annie. And she and Father would sit in the kitchen, have a wee drink together. They would have a wee talk and a wee ceilidh.

Mother would tell the news about Lochgilphead and Loch Fyneside.

And Annie would say, 'What's the next wean you have now, Betsy?' She'd write it down, the date of birth, where it was born. But I was sorry my mother never called one of her nine lassies after old Annie. They practically reared us while we stayed there for two weeks. Because my father smoked a pipe, my mother smoked a pipe and Duncan and Hendry smoked tobacco. They used to buy the whole roll of tobacco so that the whole farm was self-sufficient. You had eggs, you had milk, you had porridge, you had tatties, vegetables, fruit from the trees, fish from the burn. You didn't need anything else. And Father might work there for three weeks, and they gave him about five shillings a day. Then we'd move down to Kilmichael Glassary and Father would buy himself a half bottle of whisky. He'd take out his pipes and play a tune. Granny would tell us stories. It was a wonderful way of life. Hard sometimes but wonderful.

If my father came at night and was too late to put the tent up on a farm where he worked, he never disturbed the farmer. He just walked into the shed, which was always full of straw, full of hay. Maybe he went into the byre. He had the freedom to go into the sheds and sleep. And Mammy could go the next morning with her big teacan and go to the farmer's wife, get it full of tea made in the house and a big heap of scones. Then she would come and we'd be asleep in the shed. But what we hated was to hear the rain battering on the tin roofs – when we had to get up and go on our way! Oh, it was murder! Lying warm in a dry stall and the cow across from me, the cow chewing all night long. It lulled you, you know, chewing its cud, lulled you to sleep. We were so comfortable, just wanted to stay and lie on, you know. We'd have a couple of stalls in the byre full of hay and a couple of blankets, maybe a couple of shawls or something. Mother would have them thrown over us and we would lie there cuddled up. Father and Mother had another wee place by themselves. That's when we were walking late on the road and we couldn't see to put the tents up.

But when we came to a farmer who had a job for my father, he'd build us tents, one for himself, one for the girls and one for us, little bow tents. And we'd argue and fight, nip each other and pick each other. He would say, 'Now behave yourselves, children. Tomorrow we don't know what's going to happen.' Having a big family, you had to cope with them. But they were kindly persons, my parents, very kindly. They never beat us, never argued with us. My mother was a jewel. She was a great woman. And so was my father, and he was a big man. We had many wonderful times together. He knew he had a large family, and he knew he had to cope with it. But the most important thing was, teaching us things that he had known himself when he was young, what he wanted to teach us.

He knew that someday we would leave and have to go out in the world and do our own thing. And he made sure that we were qualified to do just that. I could clip sheep when I was ten years old, because my father had taught me. I could cut peats when I was only twelve. And he had shown me, 'Now do this way, laddie!' I could make a basket when I was five years old. I could make heather scrubbers or make a besom, which has nothing to do with farm work. And he would always say, even though you had made a bad job, 'Oh well, that's not too bad. You've done well there. Keep it up. Do it again.' Even though it wasn't very good-looking. The first basket I made was twisted and out of line. He said, 'You've made a wonderful job!' So this was our education, what you couldn't get if you went to school. Because once you stayed in school all the time, your whole culture changed.

If I had been in school all my life from the age of six till fourteen, I should never have known about the curse of the standing stones, the love of walking, and the stories. And this travelling education was the most important thing: you knew the names of all the wild flowers, the name of every insect. You went to the anthills, were warned not to touch this, not to touch that and leave things alone. Not to take too much fish from the river, don't eat and take too much shellfish, leave some for another day. It was schooling in a way. Because down through the ages the old traveller people in their lives had never been in school; but they became wonderful people, and knew many wonderful things that scholars didn't know.

MY WEE MAGGIE

'O my wee Maggie's a humph and a proochen
A bu'n wood sprachen, my wee Maggie.'

Johnie with the bundle, Maggie with the can
Up the glen tae the auld blind man,
'Up the glen tae the auld blind man
And we'll feek wir weed in the morgan.'

Johnie said tae Maggie, 'O, bing into the shed,
I will shake the strummel and you can make the bed,
For this is the place where your naismort she was wed
And we'll bing doon the glen in the morgan.'

[Traveller courtship cong, translation from cant:

'My wee Maggie is a strong carrier and a natural speaker
With a bold, undaunted tongue.'

Johnie carries the blanket, Maggie the teacan
Up Tangy Glen to the mill owned by the two brothers,
        one of them blind;
'And like travellers before us, we'll get our tea in the morning.'

Johnie said to Maggie, 'O come into the shed,
I will make the mattress and you can sort the bed
For this is the place where your mother she was wed
And we'll go back home in the morning.']

                                        Traditional

Chapter Two

The Soldering Bolt

We had our schooling and my father did his best for us. In these days back in the early 1930s work was hard to get. There were all these small farms round about the district and they only employed one person, maybe two. And you maybe got a day's work here and maybe a half day somewhere. But my father was a tradesman. He was a basketmaker and tinsmith. He could cope by his own way of working. But it needed my mother to sell his wares. He could make baskets and he was a fine tinsmith. And there was a demand in these times, just before the Second World War and after the 1914 war for his wares. And he could cope – with the people buying his stuff. My mother only sellt his wares in a small area – she had Inveraray and Furnace and Minard and Loch Gair. That was as far as she travelled on foot. And these people through the years who had used his products knew how good they were. They would say to whatever travellers passed through, and there were many who came to Argyll in these days, travelling through trying to sell baskets and selling tinware; 'Oh no, oh no-no, we dinnae want nothing frae you. We've got wir own man who makes all these things fir hus. Betsy Williamson supplies us wi as much as we need. And we're only sorry that we cannae buy something from her every day.' You see what I mean? This was the story! And my father could supply everything that they needed because he could make kettles, he could make pots, he could make pans, he could make toasters, he could make baskets, he could make everything. He made them from tin. Now this was done to keep us at school. And he cut his wands for baskets from the wild willows in the woods, which he cut first the one year and then again the next year and so on. He knew every bush, he knew every tree, and he knew where to go to cut them, to pick them up. And he made scrubbers, or reenges for the pots, from the carlin heather. So this is how we were reared up.

Traveller men and women were always busy making and trading their home-made wares – until the mid 1940s when the demand for tin dishes fell away with the coming of aluminium goods to the market. Before the end of the Second World War my father buried all his tinmaking tools, which had belonged to his father. He wouldn't show us where he'd buried them, because he felt they were too precious to be lost or destroyed. The following is a description of the various tools and accoutrements for some of the many different types of traveller trades in which both men and women were engaged.

The Tinker Man The tinsmith required a box of tin sheets, three feet by three feet; an anvil, made especially by a smith for making tin, which was portable; wooden mallet for taking wrinkles out of the tin; raisin hammer, which didn't mark tin because the head was raised, used for shaping out or making bulges, and there were three types with iron, leather and wooden heads; snaps, to cut the sheets of tin; scutcher, a piece of wood for making seams; rivet tools, long pieces of iron with different sized holes for making tin rivets; rat stick, for measuring, it was a long piece of steel with a sliding tongue of tin; soldering bolts, three of differing sizes, one for corners; bar of solder; resin to make the solder stick; block of pitch to make pitched handles on the pans; copper wire to go round the mouth of the tin jug or pan for support; roll of hoop, thin strips of iron for making ears on pots; spirit of salt, dip to help solder take effect; flat hammer, for making corners; snottum or 'pot stick' for hanging pots and kettles over the fire.

The Hawker The accoutrements were a hank for carrying and displaying the tinware, a circle of thick wire which hung on the wife's shoulder as she carried the goods from door to door; inmated milk cans,* basins for settling milk, made for farmers; square kettles, pots used for boiling tatties, soup, tea, making any food or drink; pans and big jugs; tea jugs, like enamel cups but made of tin; fish turners, spatulas; graters; toasters on legs which slid back and forth on the front of grates; milk cans, for carrying milk; sieves, for straining milk; sauce pans and flat frying pans.

The Spoon Maker This set included a pot for boiling horn;

---

* inmated milk cans – pails with metal sieve inserts

six knives; files for sharpening knives; rasp, a large file for smoothing horse-hoof bones; selection of horn – sheep, cattle and cow; spoon set – iron spoon moulds for setting horn, which was first cut and soft boiled.

The Basket Maker Equipment included a bundle of split hazel for making tattie creels or baskets; bundle of cane weighing about fifty pounds, split to make creels for holding tatties, feeding beasts, holding coal, kindlings and other domestic usages; bundle of wands weighing about twenty-five pounds, for making small message baskets; three–four knives; pliers; slipe, a hand-made wooden tool for peeling bark off willows.

The Cheeny Feeker He was a mender of delph or porcelain. He used a feeker's bow and drill, a bent stick with a leather strap, like the early caveman's fire starter; wooden drill in the centre of the strap for drilling holes in broken delph; a turn on the strap which was pulled back and forth to activate the drill; wooden drill-shaft with head of steel; steel clamps put in the holes of the delph to hold the pieces together.

The Tiger Hunter He or she was a mender and maker of mats. She needed a roll of stack rope, coconut matting for door mats; large sack needle; ball of strong string for mending mats.

The Pearl Fisher A traveller used a long hazel rod, six feet, with an end split and a ring for gripping the freshwater mussel shell; pearl jug, large with glass bottom to see through; sack for shell, once it has been collected; canvas boat (sometimes).

The Scrubber and Besom Maker The tools used were a spool of wire, copper was best; sharp knife; long boots or stockings, for protection against snakes in the heather.

The Mush Feeker He or she was an umbrella mender and they used a bundle of steel staves; roll of black cloth; roll of ribbon; box of ferrules, steel rings; umbrella ends, steel with rubber points; bone fringes for ends of staves; box of needles; knife; spare handles, made of deer horn, bone or wood.

The summer of 1933, when I was five years old, my father got a wee job from an old man called Duncan MacVicar in Achnagoul. It would be about the month of May. The old farmer sent word down, 'Will you tell Johnie to come up and gie me a wee bit help at making the hay?' My mother tellt my father. And my father was dying to get a few days' work.

'Oh aye,' he said, 'Betsy, I'll go up and get two-three shillings, and help you get a bite to the weans. I'll go up the morn.'*

So that night, anything Daddy wanted, we children were going to get it. All for the sake of going with him to this farm! He wouldn't take the lassies, any of my three older sisters. And Willie was a bit too old. But my brother George, or Dodie, and I were going to get Daddy anything he asked. I said, 'Daddy, what do you want? Do you want me to do anything for you? Are you wantin sticks?' But finally he promised me he would take me with him the next day. And when he made a promise, you'd better believe it, he would keep it.

He said, 'Brother, I'll take you with me tomorrow. Tae Achnagoul. Are you sure you can walk?'

'Oh,' I said, 'Daddy, I'll walk – I'll run all the way with you.' And I remember holding on to his jacket, a wee totie† laddie. It was five miles. He wasn't old in these days but he was a big man. Six foot odds. I'm holding on to his pocket, running all the road. And we got to the farm and we travelled up.

This was the first time in my life I'd ever been in this place. But my father took me up and into this house. And this is the first time in my life I'd ever been in a house! The old farmer and his two aunties lived here. They brought us in. It was an old-fashioned house. And I was to spend many years in that old kitchen later on. There was a big table and a big fire, with a big iron kettle hanging on the swey at the front. What fascinated me were the two old sisters, to me like two old witches! Oh, they had these long dresses on them, buttony boots and their hair hung down their backs. There was this big old wooden table, with no tablecloth or anything. And these two big collie dogs sat in front of the fire. The old farmer and his two aunties knew my father very well.

'Oh, come in Johnie and have a wee cup of tea.' It was these old-fashioned clay mugs. And I mind on my father blowing the tea and giving me a wee sip out of the cup. I was just a wee shaver. Father says, 'You sent for me to come up to the hay.'

'Aye,' said old Duncan MacVicar. I was to spend many years

---

* the morn – tomorrow
† wee totie – tiny puff of a

with him later on. This is where I gained my education. He said, 'Aye, Johnie, I want you to cut me some hay.'

'Oh,' my father said, 'aye, I'll cut your hay.'

'Well,' he said, 'that's the field down next to the main road.'

Father said, 'All right.'

He said, 'The harness is in the stable. And the horse is in the stable.' Now that was all he tellt my father, not another thing. He said, 'I'm gaun awa to the hill.' It was lambing time.

Father came down and he opened this door. There were two big horses standing in the stable. 'In the name of God,' I said, 'what is my father going to do with these horses?' I had never given it a thought before. And all this harness hanging up on these stacks along the wall pole and a bar across. And he takes a big leather belt, belts it up to the horse's collar. He takes the other horse, puts it in the same way on the other side of the pole. And he belts this cross bar to the other horse's collar. And he takes a long chain, cleeks it on one side of the machine, and another chain to the other side of the machine. He takes the four reins for the two horses down, two on that side and two on the other, and ties them in a knot. There's a big handle – he wraps them round the handle. I'm amazed at this. Now there's these two big metal wheels, and a big blade going out. All these wee things like fingers of your hands are sticking out the sides of this big blade.

'Now,' he says to me, 'brother, I want to tell ye one thing; keep away fae that thing – it's awfae sharp!' The old farmer had tell him he'd sharpened it beforehand. There were two seats on the machine. He said to me, 'You sit on that seat and I'll sit on this one.' Now he jumped up on one, and I jumped on the other. Now he said, 'Haud on!' But there was no place to hold! You had to hold on to the seat like a chair. And I'm sitting. 'Chuik', he clicked to the horses, and the two horses go forward. Away goes the machine!

But we had a wee bit to go to the field. We went down this wee hollow and around to the foot of the field. He pulled the machine in close to the hedge, as close as could be. Now he said to me, 'Brother, are you sitting all right?'

'Aye,' I said, 'I'm sitting fine, Daddy.'

He said, 'There's gaunna be an awfae noise.'

I said, 'How a noise? The're nae noise off it yet.'

'Ah, but,' he said, 'wait! It's no workin yet.'

I said, 'What do ye mean? Oh, it's no workin . . .'

'Now,' he said, 'I haena put it in gear.' There was a way, when the horses pulled it, you could put it in 'free' or you could put it in gear.

So he pulled this lever and I saw this big blade going down, lowered into the grass – it was not grass, it was hay! And the hay was that height, about three feet high! He lowered the blade close to the fence. He turned a wee handle, and he chuiked the horses. And then it went, it started, bhrrrrrrrrrr, bhrrrrr. And I'm sitting down here on this seat. And he's in that seat driving the horses and watching the drive shaft. It's going bhrrrrr bhrrr, like a thousand grasshoppers. The cutter blades are going back and forward like that, and the beautiful hay was getting cut. It was lying in rows, lying in rows. Right round the field, right round the field, close into the fence he stopped. I'm sitting watching these horses, and their two ears are going forward, you ken! And they're walking, together tied to this pole. This to me was out of this world. I never was as happy in all the days of my life sitting on this thing! And he knew what he was doing. He went round the field twice. Now this, I was to learn later, was a reaping machine, an old Wallace reaper for cutting hay. And I'm so happy sitting beside him on this seat. So, round and round and round the field we go. Round and round and round. The farther he was going round, the more hay was getting cut, the centre of the field getting closer.

All this hay was getting cut. Oh, we must have went on for about three hours. He looked up.

He said, 'We'll stop now. Thon's the old woman wavin to us. Old Morag.' Morag and Chrissie were their names, the two old aunties. 'She's waving,' Father said. 'It's dinner time.' Father lowsed the two horses, lowsed the pole off their necks, took the harness off in the field. I was to learn later this was a thing the country hantle* never did. Only travellers. The country hantle hadn't got the idea. This was my father's idea. Because the horse was wet, sweating under the harness and sweating under the collar. By the time he had walked it to the farm and

---

* country hantle – settled community

it stood for an hour and it walked back, the sweat was dry. But if he had walked it to the farm with the harness on, it would not have got a chance to dry. So he took off everything but the bridle. Because these collars were split. And he dropped them, put them beside the old reaping machine. He took the two horses with the reins over his shoulder and he walked them. And I'm walking.

He said, 'Are you wanting up on the horse's back?'

I said, 'No, Daddy, I'm feart, I'm no gaun.'

He said, 'You'll no faa!'

I said, 'I couldna sit.' I never was on a horse's back in my life.

He said, 'Come on, I'll put you on the horse.'

I said, 'No, no, no! I'm no gaun on the horse's back, no way in the world.' He coaxed me. It was for my own good. But no. I said, 'Gie me a haud o the rope.' So he never actually gave me the rope. He held the rope and he gave me the bit that was on the other side of his hand. I was only a wee totie boy of five, and I'm holding this bit of the rope. I was thinking I was doing the work! So we led them up to the stable.

He put them into the stable and he took an old bag, and he rubbed them down. He went to the big corn kist with a lid on it and he got a scoop. He filled it full of corn and put it in their two troughs. And I remember to this day . . . it must be exactly forty-eight years ago, nearly half a century, and I can remember it just like this moment.

We walked up to the farm and it was up three steps to the house. The grass was growing on the steps and round the back there was a stick shed. And then there was a door for the hens going in, and a door for the cows going in. We went in the same door as the cow, two milk cows went in that way and turned right. And we turned left into the kitchen. My father took his bonnet off. I had never seen this show of respect before. He held his bonnet in his hand. He walked into the kitchen.

By this time the old farmer was back from the hill. And these two old aunties, two old sisters, oh, they were like witches to me! Things I had seen in story books. They were bustling about and they had this big metal pot sitting on this big fire. And this frying pan. It was a new experience, I had never seen this

before. I was only new from my father's tent, never in a house
before. And they took this bowl and put it on the table. And
these chairs round the table. They put a chair up for me. And
these two collie dogs were sitting there looking at me. There
was a reddish one and a black and white one. I'm sitting in this
chair, same as my daddy was. And the farmer himself is sitting
at the other end of the table. This old woman put a fork down
beside me and a spoon, and a plate. My mother had given us
a plate and a spoon, but we always held it on our knees. I was
never at a table in my life, never knew what a table was. There
was no cloth on it, just a bare wooden table. And this collie
dog's sitting looking at me. I remember fine, it was some beef
and some tatties on this plate. Oh, the old women were good
to me. They were kind.

They said, 'Are you all right, wee laochan?' They spoke in
Gaelic. 'Are you all right, sitting there, laochan? And your
daddy. Did you enjoy yourself today?' I wasn't wanting to speak
very much, I was kind of ashamed, you ken.

And my father said, 'Oh aye, he's all right. He's a good laddie.
He's Duncan.'

'Oh, he's Duncan. Oh aye, just like wir own Duncan.' Duncan
MacVicar was the name of their nephew. And when they knew
I was Duncan, that was it. The two old aunties, Chrissie and
Morag, I was to spend many years later with. 'Oh Duncan, is
the meat okay?' And they fed me this meat and tatties. Oh, this
was a good dinner. I'd never had a dinner like this before in
my life. And a spoon and a fork and a plate. I'm sitting and I
also had got this bone on my plate. I didn't know what to do
with it, you see. I had picked it clean and I didn't want to put it
on the table. And these two big collie dogs were sitting. I could
see the saliva running down – the dogs were watching me! And
the farmer was sitting on the other side. He was eating wee bits.
They were awfae rough, from what I know now. And he was
flinging anything he couldn't eat . . . sluuuuurp, and the dogs
were just, sluurrp, golloping the bits up. I didn't want to do
what the farmer was doing, but I slipped my hand down canny
beside the chair, down beside the table. And this big red collie
was sitting beside me. I put the bone down canny to the dog.
And slurrp. Oh, the dog was contented. He lay down at me feet,

see? This is fine. So, my father was watching me. This was my
first experience being with non-traveller folk.

Oh, we'd had the best of meat to eat with my mother and
my father. But we just sat with the plate my mother gave us on
our knees at the fireside. There wasn't a table in our tent. But
anyway, I saw the idea and I was slipping the bits of meat I didn't
want in below the table to this dog. And I mind my father, God
rest his soul in heaven. After the meat, the aunties brought us
a big mug of tea, scones and cheese. And my father lighted his
pipe and the old farmer lighted his. They both smoked and were
sitting cracking about the hay and their good crop. 'Oh, and
how's Duncan getting on?' And 'he's just fine,' this carry on.

My father said, 'Well, we'd better go away again, brother.
Time to go.

I said, 'Right.' This was dinner time finished. Back down to
the stable.

He said to me, 'Did you get plenty to eat? Are you hungry?'

I said, 'No, Daddy, I got bings to eat.'

He said, 'The flesh was moich. Brother, the flesh was
moich.'

I said, 'Moich? What?'

'The flesh was moich,' he tellt me. He meant that it was off, it
was bad. You see, the farmer had killed a sheep. I didn't know
in these days. He had killed a sheep and hadn't cured it right,
kept it too long. And the old craturs, the nephew and these two
old women, they'd put it in a barrel with salt. But they had no
freezers or anything to keep it right. They'd kept it for maybe
a fortnight or three weeks.

'I ate it, Daddy,' I said.

'Aye, I ken,' he said. 'You gied it to the dog.

I said, 'No, I didna gie it aa to the dog.'

They'd cut their chops, you see, a rough cut with the ribs and
left an awful lot of meat sticking to them. Maybe there were
three ribs together on each plate. They'd stewed the mutton
and put the tatties in beside it. And the old craturs were doing
their best, you know.

He said, 'Did you get plenty?'

I said, 'I'm not hungry.'

'Well,' he said, 'we're gaun oot to cut more hay.' So, back

again. And he led this horse out. 'Noo,' he said, 'look, you tak one and I'll tak the other.' He took this big horse out of the stable and he gave it to me. 'Noo,' he said, 'watch your feet, in case they tramp on ye!'

I said, 'Aye, Daddy.' I mind I had on a wee jersey. A wee brown jersey and a tie. You got these jerseys and ties combined. And my mother tied the tie in a bow across my neck. And I had short trousers. There were no long trousers on the laddies in these days. It was a shame for laddies to wear long trousers. And my bare legs, no stockings. And these wee bits of shoes. I don't know what kind, but they were bits of shoes on my feet. They weren't sandals or sandshoes. Maybe they were two old shoes belonging to my mother with the heels chapped off. But my bare legs into them.

He said, 'Brother, watch it disna tramp on yir feet!'

I pulled this horse out, oh, this was a great big monster horse! I was to own bigger horses later on in years. But it was the typical horse of Argyll, a crofting horse in these days, a garron horse, fourteen hands, maybe heavy built. It wasn't a Clydesdale. They didn't have big heavy Clydesdales with their big hairy feet in these days in Argyllshire. I was to see these horses later. But I was daft, moich on these horses. Just to even handle the rope, and pull the horse behind me was something I was never going to live down, you see! And this time Daddy actually gave me the rope itself. This horse had a moustache on its lip. And it's stepping out, ken, stepping canny. And I'm turning my back to it, pulling it over my shoulder. And then now and again I would turn round to look at this horse.

My father said, 'Are you gettin on aa right?'

I said, 'Aye, it's comin fine, Daddy.' We walked down this wee hill, down by this place called Baby's Byre and down the brae to the field on the flat. He backed the two of them into this machine again. Yoked them up into the machine. I jumped up in the seat, but I never jumped up till he got them yoked. Oh, I was fly enough for that! And he shoved this lever forward, put it in gear. Pulled the four reins up, clicked the horses round the field again, clickety-click. Rippita rippita rippita, round this field and round this field. Round, round this field till four o'clock in the afternoon. And cut it all, cut the lot.

He said, 'That's it finished, brother!'

'Aye,' I said, 'that's fine.'

'Finished it,' he said. Now I'm happy as a lark, see! Cut it all. Pulled the machine in close to the fence, and left it. And lowsed the two horses out and came back up. Took the harness with him this time. He never left the harness because it was getting on towards night. We put the two horses in the stable, took all the harness and put them back on the pegs. Got a bag, cleaned the sweat off the horses' necks, cleaned the sweat off their backs and gave them a wee puckle corn, filled their hecks full of hay and shut the door. Back up to the old women again. Now this time we didn't go into the house. It wasn't dinner time. We knocked on the door and one old woman came out. And then the old farmer came out.

'Oh, you're finished, Johnie!'

Aye,' he said, 'I'm finished, Mr MacVicar. That's it finished.'

'Well,' he said, 'ye'll be wantin to go awa hame noo.'

He said, 'Aye, I've got to go hame noo. Ye'll manage noo.'

'Aye,' he said, 'I'll manage fine.'

So my father says, 'Betsy says you were tae gie me, to ask you for a bottle of milk.'

'Oh aye,' he said, 'ye'll get a bottle o milk.' And the old woman went into the house and she got one of thon old-fashioned whisky bottles, a three-cornered bottle. It had a net wire round it. It was full of milk, beautiful milk. And he gave it to my father, and also the money, five shillings. 'There ye are, Johnie,' he said. 'But I want you back to help me with the corn, cut the corn.'

And my father said, 'Ye any tatties?'

'Oh aye,' he said, 'I'll gie ye some tatties.' So he went and filled him a wee bag of tatties. My father put this bottle of milk into the tattie bag, and he put it on his back. He took me by the hand.

I said, 'Daddy, can we see the horses before we go hame?'

'See the horses – they're away to their bed, brother,' he said. 'They're away to bed mair the night.* They're hungry, they're tired.'

I said, 'Daddy, I want to see the horses before we go back.' We had to pass by the door of the stable, you see.

_____
* mair the nicht – for the rest of the night

He said, 'Laddie, are ye moich on horses?'

'Aye, Daddy,' I said, 'I like horses. These big beasts, big animals.' And he opened the stable door, pressed the latch down with his thumb and shoved the door. I was to work in that stable, take the horses to my own contract work years later. And once he'd opened the door, I heard crunch-crunch crunch-crunch. The two horses looked round at me. And this one had a white blaze on its face.

He said, 'Are you pleased now?'

I said, 'Aye, Daddy, I'm pleased noo.' And he shut the door.

He said, 'We'll go hame.' So we started the five miles back, walking down through the field, through the cut hay. And the smell of the hay would take your breath away. Soon we reached the road. It was a long bit from Achnagoul to Furnace, but oh, I'm running along all the way. I wasn't hungry, no way, because I'd had bings of haben.* We landed home and I'm thinking about these horses. My father gave my mother the five shillings, the bottle of milk and some tatties. She cut across the wood to the shop. But I couldn't get away from the idea of these horses, you see.

'Noo,' I said, 'Daddy, are you finished wi the horses? Are you no goin back to work, to the fairm nae mair?'

'No, brother,' he said. 'The old man doesn't want me. I cut the hay for him because he was gaun to work among the sheep. But he wants me back to cut his corn.'

I said, 'Daddy, will ye tak me wi ye when ye go to cut the corn?'

'Aye, brother,' he said, 'I'll tak ye wi me.'

'Can I sit in the seat?'

'You cannae sit in the seat, though,' he said. The farmer'll have to sit in the seat, brother, because he'll have to make the sheafs of corn.'

But my mother got the messages for the night. She came back from the shop with plenty to eat, tobacco and things for my father. And she made our tea.

Two months passed by and it came again – my father's going back to Achnagoul. It must have been about August. Old Duncan had sent a message down with the post. The post

* bings of haben – plenty to eat

collected the letters from all the farms. And Mr MacVicar had tellt the post, 'Will you go up and tell old Johnie to come up the morn, I've got a wee job for him?' We never got any mail, except a postal order we'd receive when my father would send away a parcel of rabbit skins to Glasgow, a fur trader. My mother had collected them from the houses. That's the only mail we ever got. But the post always came up and tellt us if he got a message. The next day we had to go up to Achnagoul because the man was wanting us to cut the corn. I would have nothing in the world,* but I was going to greet and carry on if I didn't get to go with my father! So, it was a bonnie day.

I said, 'Daddy, you promised to take me with you.'

'Nah, brother,' he said, 'nah! Ye cannae, ye cannae come wi me this time. It's too far to walk. Wi your bare feet it'll be sore.'

I said, 'Look, Daddy, you said you would!' I gret and I gret and I gret. I wanted to and I carried on. I said, 'I want to see the horses!'

'All right, come on then,' he said. 'It's yir ain fault, yir ain fault! If ye cannae walk, it's yir ain blame. I'm no waitin on ye. Come on!' So he finally took me with him. We walked up the field to the old farm once again.

When we landed up, the old farmer was out. And his two old aunties were out. They were tying poles together with pieces of rope. And they had corn rakes, and they had forks. They were tying these three poles together with pieces of rope.

My father said, 'Well, Duncan, it's a nice day.'

'Aye fine, Johnie,' said Mr MacVicar, 'fine day.' I was with him and I saw the two dogs. But I never saw the horses. They were in the stable. And I mind the old red dog's name was Sam. I liked old Sam, he was a good old dog, a big red collie. He wouldn't touch a mouse. I used to pet him, ken. But his tongue always hung out the length of my finger. And he was always hungry!

'Oh,' the farmer said, 'Johnie, you go doon and yoke the horses, put the harness on. I'll be doon wi ye in a minute.' And my father went into the shed and he took two forks out, two-pronged ones with spikes on the points, and a hand rake with teeth on it. He took them down, put them on his shoulder.

---

* I would have nothing in the world – nothing meant more to me

And he went down to the stable. He put the harness on the two horses again.

I said, 'Daddy, can I catch one?'

'Aye,' he said, 'noo watch your feet. Watch they dinnae tramp on you!' Now this field that the corn was in was just close at the back of the stable a wee bit. This was a beautiful field of corn, you know, big corn straws about three feet high! And the heads of corn . . . the horses were reaching over and trying to bite the corn. My father's ay pulling their heads up with the rope, rope reins he had. And I'm pulling these big corn straws, holding them up to the horses. They were gobbling them, especially the one with the moustache. This was the whiskery one with a white blaze on his face. He was puckering up his lips as I'm holding the corn straws. You were amazed how fast these straws could disappear in the horse's mouth! The farmer had brought up the cutting machine before we got there, the reaper with two seats. My father yoked the two horses on, the same way he had done for the hay. And then I saw the farmer.

My father says, 'Here's Duncan coming!' And he had this thing, a board with a lot of wee strips on it, and a wee wheel. He was pulling it after him.

I said, 'Daddy, what has he got?'

'Oh,' he said, 'that's the tilting board.'

So I said, 'Daddy, what are ye gaunna do noo?'

He said, 'The farmer's coming with this board and we'll put it onto the machine. And you cannae sit on the machine, brother, because the farmer's got to sit on it. He puts his foot on this wee board, and makes the sheafs of corn. But if you walk behind, you might get a rabbit that's got its feet cut off with the machine!'

After the farmer had got the tilting board belted on to the side of the reaper, he said, 'That's it ready, Johnie!' Now you can imagine, this machine cut to the left. There's only one way it cut. So they couldn't walk in among the corn and cut it, or the horses would have to walk among the corn. So they had to go up to the end of the field and turn and come back. And the horses had to walk close in to the fence while this blade and machine was into the corn. Now this was the best part! So they circled the field right round about with the blade on the outside. And my father turned the horses. I'd never seen this done before. He had to turn the opposite direction; they couldn't go up and down the one side. The field wasn't big, maybe three acre. It was a big corn field to my standard as a wean. But I could have cut it my ownself in a couple of days with a scythe when I was a teenager.

So Father was the steerer, he drove the horses. And this farmer sat and had this rake in his hands. And he's sitting in my seat, my hay seat! And I'm a wee bit envious of him. But my father tellt me, 'You'd better walk behind.' But walking behind this reaping machine was better than actually sitting on it. Father came up, turned the horses at the top of the field. And he reached down and put it in gear. I knew how to put it in gear, I could have done it myself! You lifted this wee lever and put it over, and this was a wheel drive. When the horses pulled, the wheels drove the blade. And this blade went back and forward. And I wouldn't say it was a bad noise . . . it was the most fascinating noise you ever heard in your life . . . bhrrrrrrrrrrr. That's the way it went! And I saw this old farmer – he lay back and he's in this seat – and he put his foot on this board.

Now the reaping machine was cutting, and there was a pulley and a belt. When the blade cut the corn, it all fell back. And it travelled up, when it was cut, along the board. And this wee board the farmer had, had a double canvas onto it, and the canvas ran round.

It brought the corn up all the one direction. The farmer held his foot down till he got a lovely sheaf of corn! And then he put his foot up, and the sheaf fell off.

'Ah, dear me!' I said. And he went and gathered again with his foot till he thought the sheaf was big enough. Then he put his foot up, the sheaf fell off. And he was going along, dropping the sheaves of corn. But they weren't tied – just sheaves of corn loose. And my father and the farmer went right to the end of the field and stopped.

My father says to me, 'You watch the horses – they dinnae walk awa!' Now along this row, which would be about 150 yards long, the farmer had dropped every three yards a sheaf of corn. There must have been maybe twenty-five sheaves of corn lying in a row. Beautifully made. But they weren't tied!

So my father got up and the farmer walked back; they each pulled a wee handful of corn out of the sheaf. They bound it round and they twisted it, and they put one end under the tie. They flung the sheaf aside. And they tied another one. And he tied the whole lot. I'm amazed at this.

I said, 'I could learn to do that myself.' So next time we came down I said, 'Daddy, the horses'll no go awa . . . I want to see how you tie this corn.'

And the farmer said, 'Come on, Duncan, you can dae this.' He was a Gaelic speaker with a real Highland accent. 'Come on now, Duncan, I'll show you what to do. You pull a wee handful of the corn out like this, and see it is straight.'

I said, 'Aye, I'm watching.'

'Now lift your sheaf of corn and put it in below and bring it up and give it a wee twist and shove it in the back.' But he showed me three or four times. And I tried it myself. But the first row was a mistake. I couldn't do it. The second one was worse! The third one was bad. It only took my father about three seconds to tie a sheaf of corn. But I was to get good at this in later years. I could nick a row myself in minutes. You took a band of corn, twisted it round, and you shoved one end in below. Tight. And you threw the sheaf off, so's it would let the reaper pass the next time. But I went up the row. For the full row of corn I still couldn't succeed. I never what you call 'bund' the sheaf. I never bund one single sheaf in that row!

So they turned the horses and I followed behind the reaper again. Back down again, bhrrrrrrr. And I loved this noise. I'm watching these horses. They were walking that slow with their big broad feet. And now and again they were leaning over and having a wee snap of corn with their teeth. But it was the inside one. The one next to the corn could ay get a mouthful, but the outside one never. But I made sure he got these when he went into the field, because I always pulled these corns from the root. I was ay sure he got a handful. I've seen him walking up, and these corn straws hanging down his chin, and he was chewing all the way. The farmer never bothered me. He knew it wouldn't do him any harm. Because it was ripe. The sun was hot and the corn was rattling dry.

We came to this dip and it was a big mess. The corn was all

knocked down. My father stopped the horses. And the farmer got up. He pulled the corn up with his hand, because it was flattened.

And I said, 'How did this happen?'

My father tellt me, 'The deer. The deer were in here last night and they flattened the corn.' The machine couldn't cut it.

'Well,' old Duncan said, 'if the bugger comes back tonight, he'll get a surprise!' I didn't know a thing about this. I was only a wee boy. They lifted the corn up with their hands, and the heads were all eaten off it. It was a wild mess. But we managed to get it up so's the machine could catch it. But they did another row, and I'm trying again. But no, still no success. But by the fourth row I began to get into the idea. And I tied some, and then they loosened again. My father tied them over again. But that wasn't all the idea! Once it was tied and bund, you had to put it in stooks! They cut away all day and they stopped about three o'clock. They lowsed the horses out. Then they started. But this was my favourite part.

You picked up four or five sheaves and you put them together, built a wee hut with them, like the three pigs' house. This was my glory! I could run and give them the sheaves, and they would put six together. Two each side, six in a row, and they built the wee stooks of corn. After it was up it looked beautiful. And you could creep in – I used to creep in between them, you know, see if I could knock them down!

Father said, 'Watch it noo, laddie, dinnae knock the sheaves doon.' But it took us through the next day before we'd finished this field of corn and it was all stooked. Before we went home my father said, 'I'm gaun roond to the back of the fairm. The man's gaun to gie me a bit deer.'

I said, 'What?'

He said, 'He's giein me a bit venison. Ye mind that bit corn yesterday? He got him last night!' Unknown to me, the farmer had sat all night with a shotgun. And a big stag came down. It was knocking down the corn. And he shot the big stag with the gun and killed it. And he cut it up. He gave my father this big lump of venison, a big deer's leg. And we carried it home with us. But first I bade goodbye to the horses.

We had only worked the two days. They wouldn't give you

more than one or two days. And it was the same thing again – I
wanted to see the horses before we left, pet them. Now I was
well acquainted with them. But I went home with my father that
night and the same rigmarole started again. Oh, I was good,
I was with my daddy working all day. I was respected. I was
better than everyone. And he gave me a penny. I mind, God
rest his soul, he gave me a penny. And he said, 'Ye can go wi
your mother to the shop.' I was in his good books. He came in
and he had this big lump of stuff wapped up in this paper, and
it was wet in below his oxter. It was the deer, venison.

He said to my mother, 'Betsy . . .'

'Oh,' she said, 'that's good. That'll make a lovely meal to the
weans.' She went to the shop and I went with her.

My mother used to wear an open apron, a braty, tied round
her waist, with a bit in the front and a bit in the back. She had
two pockets in the front and she put the money in one. I'm
following with her. I took off my shoes and was in my bare feet.
There was a wee shortcut across through the woods. She went
through the path. But I had my penny in my hand. And she
bought her messages. I went in and got one of those cakes of
McCowan's toffee, with a big Highland cow on it. A penny for
a bar of McCowan's Highland Toffee. There were eight blocks
in the bar.

She said, 'Noo, dinnae eat it aa yirsel, bring a wee bit back
and gie yir brithers and sisters a wee bit.'

I said, 'I'll gie them a wee bit when I go back.' It was hard,
you could break it like glass. And if you chewed a block, you
could chew for ever.

So Mammy got the messages and back we go. Daddy had to
go for sticks for the fire. Oh, I had to go with him, because I
had been with him all day. I gathered all the wee sticks and
put them in a heap. And I had my own bundle of sticks on my
back. He got his bundle, and we came home. But it was happy
times in those years.

THE OLD SOLDERING BOLT

O I was a piece of copper
As shiny as a star
A lovely piece of copper
Cut from a copper bar.
I was taken and battered
Battered and hammered and rolled
And made by the hands of an old tinkerman
Into a soldering bolt.

O he was a fine old tinsmith
He knew all the tricks of the trade
He knew how to solder a skillet
And how a toaster was made.
O happy were the days I spent
With my head shiny with tin
And handsome was the little bag
He always kept me in.

I remember the happy days I had
With a cruisie burning overhead
While beside me sat the good old wife
A-baking oatmeal bread.
Then as we wandered the old cart roads
After doing a job or two
From a little hole in his bag
I tumbled and fell through.

Now here I lie upon the grass
I am getting green with mould
My handle's getting rusty
I am no more the colour of gold.
Will ever I see another fire
Or mend another pot?
Or must I lie here for ever
Among the grass to rot?

But I hope some day in the future
I will be found again
And hung in a place of honour
In somebody's but and ben.*

Duncan Williamson

---

* but and ben – a two-roomed cottage

CHAPTER THREE

MY MOTHER'S PENSION

No later than the end of March, the beginning of April, and every year until 1940, when the war was under way, my father burned our winter tent and we all went travelling on foot round the villages and farms along Loch Fyne. Minard, Lochgilphead, Ardrishaig, Kilmartin, Tarbert, down Kilberry side, Tayvallich, up to Ford, Kilmichael Glen and up to Inveraray, round by Cairndow and Strachur. We worked gathering stones off fields, thinning turnips, helping with the hay and the corn harvest. My father built us a simple bow tent to sleep in, and my mother cooked over an open camp fire. The bow tent was a traditional construction for the summer and my father carried eight camp, or tent, sticks with him, usually hazel, five foot each and peeled of their bark. He also carried the riggin stick, which was bored with holes to hold the camp sticks in place at the top of the tent.

The snottum, home-made from iron, was probably the most important piece of camping equipment. It was used to hold kettles and pots with handles over the fire, for cooking or boiling the tea; and it was used to bore holes in the ground for the tent sticks. It was also a deadly weapon, kept by the door of the tent at night-time. The tent was covered with canvas or other waterproof materials, and held down with stones around the bottom.

At the end of September we always returned to Furnace wood where my father built a large barricade and tents for the winter. It was huge by comparison with the bow tent, but we had to live inside it during the long winter nights. The most important difference from the bow tent was the inside fire, built right on the ground inside the door of the tent. There was no chimney to contain the reek, or smoke. But the main compartment of this barricade was peaked, to draw the smoke.

For light we had a wee cruisie, a home-made lamp. My father used to screw a bit cloth into it, make a wick out of a bit cotton.

It had a wee handle on it and he hung it up inside the tent. It just burned the open flame, but it made a good light. On either side of the fire were smaller, lower tented compartments. These were the sleeping areas. My mother and father had one tent, and the older lassies had theirs. The younger children had another one. The central area was like a big chamber. This was the kitchen, the living room. We had no carpets. The floor was like concrete, swept for years! Hard packed. It was stourie, but very dry. The fire in the centre was built with stones and a hole in the top of the tent drew the smoke. My mother kept a box on one side for her dishes and things. The cases for the weans' claes, the school claes were right at the back of her tent. Oh, it was tidy enough!

During the war years 1939–45 my father could not take us away for the summer months, because of the restrictions on camp fires at night. So we lived all year round in the barricade. My own story starts now, when I was about ten or twelve years old. By this time my brother Sandy, the oldest, had got married. But Jack, he had joined the Territorials, and went into the Army. Sandy was two years older and he joined the Navy.

I wasn't much interested in school and I started to look for bits of work to myself. From the time I was nine years old, I was awfae clever round the houses. If I got four pence working gathering sticks along the shore or washing and gathering jeelie jars, selling them for pennies, or helping an old woman dig her garden, I never forgot my father. If I had four pence to spend, before I would spend it on myself, I would always buy my father a bit tobacco. When I was nine years old, there was no such thing as me buying sweeties. It was tuppence for a wee tin of Nestle's Milk, because some of the weans at home might be needing a wee taste milk. If I went for a message or helped an old woman by digging her garden, if I got a penny, I always made sure I spent it on something that was essential. And my father and mother knew this. If there was anything on the go, I was the favourite. Till the day my mother went to her grave, I was her favourite. She never seemed to have the same respect for the rest of my brothers and sisters, even the youngest of them. Because if I went to the town and a woman gave me a job, I always got my mother shoes and I got overalls for her and I got everything . . . these were begged or swapped for my doing errands and odd jobs. All the wee bits of work along the way I would take. I always had a burning ambition to get something for my mother, to help her out. That was my idea. My ownself I had no feelings for.

Mother and I used to walk to Minard and she hawked the houses. I walked along the shore and I went to the farm cowps and the cowps of the houses. And I collected jeelie jars. I had this wee go-chair, a wee pram. And I gathered all these jars, some of them were green with fog, grass growing in them! Now this old grocer, he gave you a penny for four wee anes, the half-pound jars. And if you got the big anes, they were two for a penny. My mother called the houses, sellt her scrubbers, begged a puckle tea and sugar and a puckle tatties, maybe some herring or anything. But she always depended on me for tobacco and paraffin, because these were the main essentials – a light and a smoke for my father.

Now she could beg, or sprach, or get tea and sugar. And she got our clothes for us, things from the houses. But they wouldn't give her any money. You couldn't expect the folk to give her money, because the non-traveller men were only working for a wee wage themselves, maybe some men only getting two pounds a week. She never asked them for money. But I always could get money for her, oh, little as it was. I would gather these jeelie jars. Sometimes I had two dozen. Sometimes I had three. And I used to take them, we always stopped at the burn right at the doctor's before the grocer's. I used to go in there – I suffered some cold days – I had to wash them all, you see. And be careful I didn't break them. Get the green mould out of them, some lying for months and years! What I couldn't beg, and I'd never steal them, I would find some jars on the shore. I found them in the middens, I found them at the backs of houses. Anybody could gather jeelie jars. There was a great demand. And I would maybe get her ten pence, eight pence, a shilling, one and tuppence, eleven pence, whatever, for my jars ! Now she could go to a shop, get half an ounce of tobacco for my father, or a bottle of paraffin. It was tuppence. For our wee cruisie, a teapot made into a lamp. Maybe she was short, didn't have enough bread for the night. She would buy, spend tuppence for a half-loaf or maybe four pence for a tin of condensed milk. I didn't smoke then. And I was her pension. I was a pension every day she went with me. It didn't matter what direction we went, I had to get these jars.

But this old man, his name was Dan MacDonald. And he had this wee shed next to the shop. This is a pantomime! There was a chain on the door, a cleek on the door, and he had a big staple and padlock onto it. It was a wooden shed. Dan used to set all these jeelie jars on the floor, right back to the wall. And one day I was stuck. I had nothing. Cleaned up with jars, couldn't get a single one. And my mother was at home.

She says to me, 'Laddie, do you no think, mebbe, you could get a couple of jars, and get yir father a wee bit tobacco? He hasnae got a smoke.'

I said, 'Mammy, I'll go and look for the price of tobacco to my father.' But I said to myself, 'I wonder if there are any jars . . .'

Now, there's a high dyke round the back of old Dan MacDonald's shed. I said to myself, 'Maybe somebody forgot about it.' I went round the back of the shed. I touched this board . . . and the board was loose. I pulled the board back and I keeked in! There the jars were sitting in dozens, see! It was a klondike! It was like going into the back of Fort Knox. I pulled this board back and gasped for breath. See, the man used to come and collect them from Dan once a month with a van from Glasgow. And they were all sitting on top of each other in there, clean. And I only pulled back the board. The hand in – they were sittin in hundreds! I said, 'I'm made!' So I said, 'In the name of creation o God, how am I gaunna get this many at once?' Now I tried to fill my jersey. I put them up my jersey . . . I said, 'That's nae good.' I couldn't cut my jacket. So I took my jacket off. It wasn't much of a jacket, a wee blazer. And I put my blazer down. Now there was a high dyke at the back, and nobody could see me. I started taking the jars out through the loose board. Two dozen. I got them in my jacket. The ones I went for were, you ken, the old clay jars, the ones that weren't easily broken, the Kellar Watt jars. He gave you a penny for them! I picked two dozen and I got them in my wee jacket. I tied them, put the board back and went down to Dan MacDonald.

He's busy cutting ham. I come in. I had my jacket full of clay jars, big Kellar Watt ones. He liked them best! There was an awful demand for these jars.

I said, 'Dan, I've some jars.' Oh, they were all bonnie and clean. He put his hand down round the mouth of a jar, looking for dust, see! I put them all on the table. He counted them out, twenty-four. Oh, twenty-four, penny for two. He gave me a two-shilling bit in my hand. That was fine.

I said, 'Dan, ye'll no manage. Come on, I'll help ye, I'll carry them oot.'

'All right,' he says. He was old, you know, about sixty.

I said, 'I'll gie ye a wee carry wi them.' I wanted to oblige him. He had an old sister cried Leezie. She was as mean as a church mouse and she was bent like that – nose touched her chin.

'Wait till I get the key!' he said.

So he got the key. I took a dozen in my oxter and he took some. He could catch – big hands he had. The way he catcht them he could take four or five in each hand. He put his fingers in the jars like a waiter carries so many glasses. But I had to pack them all this way in my oxter to get a dozen. Big clay jars. My brother Jack used to keep them for his tea for years and years and years. Kellar Watt jars. They're antiques now. And he got the big old-fashioned iron key and he turned the lock. He opened the padlock. He opened the shed, and there's all these jars lying on the floor, see!

And I said, 'Dan, there's no much room. We'll put them at the back.'

'Okay,' he said, 'put them at the back.'

What did I do? I built them back in the same place where I took them out! So's there'd be easy access to get them again, ken! I didn't want to put them in front of the door, because if I pulled the board back I couldn't reach them.

So I said, 'Here! There's bings o room here, Dan. I'll put them at the back.'

'That's fine, laddie,' he said, 'That's fine, a bhalaich.'* He turned one upside down and put one on top of it; turned the other one upside down, put one on top of it. So they would sit.

---

* a bhalaich – laddie

And I put them right back close to the board. He never kent the
board was slack. I built them to the back, the clay jars.

I said, 'That's fine.'

'Thanks very much,' he said. 'These are good anes.'

'Oh,' I said, 'I got them from Mrs Sinclair,' or Mrs such-and-
such, tellt him a lie, ken, where I got them.

'That's okay!'

So here I go, feel like a lark. Nicked over to the shop. I got
an ounce of tobacco, four pence. Two loaves for my mother, tin
of milk, half pound of margarine, and what I could get for my
two shillings. You got an awful lot for that amount. I wouldn't
buy sweeties of no description. Not if I thought I was denying
my mother one single penny. I wouldn't do it, no way in this
world. And I came back up. I was a hero. They were all sitting
in the tent. Maybe they were very hungry. Maybe they didn't
have very much. Father didn't have a smoke. And I had kept
tuppence for a whisky bottle full of paraffin oil. That burns for
about four days in the wee cruisie. But I had a pension. I knew
I had it made and I wasn't worried.

Father says to me, 'Where'd you get the money, laddie?'

I said. 'I had some jars. I got some jars. I begged some jars.'
So this was it. And I was thinking about it in the morning again.
I couldn't wait to get back again, back again to the same shed.
Now the ones I'd sellt, I built them right back to the board
where I'd lifted them, so's the next day I could take the same
dozen back out again. He never catcht me! And I wouldn't tell
God Almighty.

If my brother Dodie went with me or some of the lassies, I
would never go near it. Or if I were with the country laddies
I wouldn't go near it. No, it was my secret and I wouldn't tell
anybody. And, he also had lemonade bottles. He gave a penny
for these lemonade bottles with a naked man and a wire on
the top, like old gin bottles. He had them stacked in the corner
and I could reach out my full arm's length, and I could only get
two or three sometimes. They were built in crates and everyone
had a wee space. But I couldn't reach the crate. I made up my
mind I was going to get some of these crates close to the hole
some way in the future.

The next day I went down again and I looked all around.

There was the high dyke, and the wee path at the back of the shed. I pulled the board back, and out with a dozen clay jars, the same dozen I had built in! Back again to old Dan with them.

'Oh,' I said, 'Dan . . .'

'Oh aye,' he said. I never went back with him this time. I wouldn't take them back to the shed every time. I had only taken twelve this time. I left some for myself again. I wasn't going to be too greedy. He gave me a shilling. And a shilling, I'll guarantee, it was as good to you then as five pounds now. If you spent it right! So I took the shilling. I put the wee board back into place and shoved a stone against it with my foot, so's nobody could find it was slack. And back up to my mother.

I said, 'Mother, a shilling.'

She said, 'My laddie, where'd you get the shilling?'

I said, 'I was gatherin blocks along the shore.' These were roots that came in with the tide, blocks of stick wood.

There was an old woman, Mrs Gordon, and she was crazy on blocks, tree roots washed in by the tide. I used to walk for miles along the shore gathering all the driftwood and putting it up to dry. And God upon anybody that stole them – brother Dodie used to steal my sticks often! And I used to build up the sticks on the shore off the tide mark. Then, when they were kind of dry, I gathered all the wee ones, or if I could, break the big ones in two. Mrs Gordon was awful fond of blocks to put in her fire. It was the old-fashioned grates. And if they could put an oak block on the fire with a wee bit firewood, it burned the whole fairin night! I used to put my blocks out to dry on the shore. I had two directions – away along the low shore, and the other way around by the pier. But they were never good by the pier, because the dykes were too high. The sticks were always waterlogged, never got washed up far enough. The beach was the best.

Now I had three different things; some women liked kindlings and some women liked blocks; some women liked bits of sticks. You always had plenty to do! So you kept your bits of sticks till you got a bundle of thick bits, and you left them to dry. You kept your blocks and separated the wee bits that came in with the tide, for the old women who liked kindlings. Old Mrs Gordon wouldn't take them, she had plenty kindlings. I charged tuppence for a wee bundle of sticks. They would always take them from you! And along with the sticks, you would always say to them, 'My mother wants a bit kail.'

The old woman would go to the garden and take two big twists of kail for you. Or if she was digging tatties she would give you the wee ones out of the garden. But I had my beach, and I used to go along the shore and gather my sticks. Now I was thirteen and needing to go back to school for another term. This was February.

I was a good sized laddie for my age. The school's high up the brae, and I was down on the shore. It had been a heavy day of rain. The burn was in spate. And all the sticks that came down with the burn got thrown out in the tide, and then the tide would wash them on the shore. And I was busy gathering sticks along the shore, putting them up to dry. I looked up – here's three big laddies from school, the three biggest laddies from the master's, Mr Campbell's class, sent to bring me in! I had absconded for a month, on the run!

You see, my father and mother weren't worried. I could read and write enough and I could count. I was a better scholar than the rest of my brothers and sisters, and the village children who were in school. My parents weren't worried, because I was a source of income to them. They kent fine if I got a penny or a shilling, tuppence or thruppence, I wouldn't waste it on any rubbish. My brother Dodie would buy a bar of McCowan's toffee, climb a tree and sit till he ate it before he would bring a penny home. But I wasn't like that.

So the three boys were sent, the schoolmaster sent them to arrest me. But I didn't see the boys until after they had come down the banking. They had short trousers on. I was thirteen and I could fight like big guns! I wasn't heeding about the three of them. And I had my day planned. I was going to get my sticks out, now I had more dried along the shore. I had Mrs Gordon, Mrs Beattie and Mrs Harrison, I had them all in mind what I was going to give them. I had every day laid out for myself. And I kent which was which and who was getting what. And woe be to anyone who was in my territory! It was worse than a robin in the snow. Dodie daurstna touch them, no way! Touch my sticks – it was murder, because I'd have had him killt.

I'm just at the burn and I saw this big stick coming down

with the burn. I said, 'He might go away to the tide, go across the sea. I'll never get him.' I unbuckled – off with my boots. I'm going out to catch him before he goes too far – big lump of stick that came down the burn. But I left my boots on the banking. I waded out, to keep my boots dry. When I got back to the boots, who was standing there? Here were the three boys waiting on me. Now it's about eleven o'clock, playtime. Oh, I'd been on the run for about a month . . .

And the lassies, my sisters were all making excuses for me. But they kent! I was running wild in the village, going along the shore boiling whelks, begging the houses, robbing the gardens – but not doing anything destructive, mind ye! No bad turns. My father and mother didn't mind because they kent every penny I got was for their sake. And my father kent – I used to sit and read Western stories to him, cowboy books at night-time. 'Well,' he said, 'I cannae dae nothing with him.' He wouldn't hit me. My mother wouldn't touch me. Now I was only waiting on one thing, when she would go to Minard till I got my jars. And I robbed the shed at night and sometimes through the day. But I made my mistake going back at night-time. I got too greedy. I took a box of bottles, and the next day I went back– there were fifteen big nails in the back of the shed! That's another story, though. But he didn't know it was me!

Anyway, the three boys came to arrest me for to take me to the schoolmaster, to the school. I said, 'What is it, boys?'

They said, 'We've got to take you to school, Duncan.'

Now I kent I wasnae good enough for all three of them. I put my boots on. 'Well,' I said.

He said, 'Mr Campbell said we've got to take you in. We're takin you! We were sent for you and we're takin you in.' By force they were going to take me in to school.

There's nobody in the world is going to take me to school, no way in the world! I wasn't fourteen till April, you see, when I was legally free to leave. I had a couple of months to go. I was telling them in the school that I was older than I was.

I said, 'Look, boys, I've left school. I'm fourteen. I was fourteen in January.' But there was an old woman in the village who was close to the schoolmaster. She had a record on every wean my mother had till the day my mother died. And they kent our age as good as what we did. So I had put my boots on, just bits of boots slipped on my bare feet. 'Well, boys,' I said, 'there's nothing for it. I'll have to go to school.' Now the burn's in a good spate, and I had it planned. When the minute they mentioned it – I had it planned – up in my head right away. 'All right,' I said. 'I'll go with youse. Nae arguin about it. I'll go to school. Wait a minute, I've got to wash my face.'

Now, I had a wee bit jacket on me. This was for holding my jars and my eggs and my vegetables. You know, the lining was all torn out. I turned the sleeves, for the inside of the sleeves was the only bit that was clean. I turned the jacket outside in and left it down on the banking.

They said, 'Okay.' As long as I left my jacket, they believed me. And this bloody lad, I mind on him yet!

I said, 'I'll have to wash my face. I'm no gaun to school without washin my face.' So I got down in the burn and they're standing on the bank. I waded in the burn. I was trying to wash my face, and I waded out a bit further. I knew they wouldn't wet their feet! My jacket was still on the banking. I was supposed to dry my face with it, with the sleeves. And when I got a good wee bit in the burn I cut right across! Right across, to the waist. And they flung stones after me. Now they wouldn't come in, I knew they wouldn't. And I crossed the burn to the other side. This laddie catcht my jacket, my wee bit jacket, and he flung it right out into the burn. It went away with the spate! I shook my hand at him.

I said, 'Ye'll no catch me! You'll no get me!'

'We'll get you,' they said, 'when school's over. We'll get ye the night-time, when school's over.'

I said, 'Ye'll no catch me!' But that's my jacket gone now. And God knows where I was going to get another. Do you know where I got my jacket? Four days later coming in with the tide! It went down with the burn, out in the sea and in with the tide. I took and put it on a stone to dry. I waited another four days for my jacket to dry. And I still never went to school!

After the boys had gone back to school that morning, I had waded back across the burn. It was nothing to me going in to the waist. I didn't worry about water. I was like a duck. Now, I had kent, it was eleven o'clock. They were back in school –

playtime was passed. And they tellt the master the whole story what happened, how I'd made a fool of them. Now I'd shamed them, and they were making a plan to give me a touching up, give me a beating. But they never gave me any beating; I got them one at a time after that. And I frightened the life out of the three of them. I was thirteen, sister dear, I was like nails! There was nobody in the world could do anything to me!

I'll tell you what records I held with the laddies in school: now I'm not exaggerating! I held the record for the highest jump, jumping over the high banking, because I jumped over the Furnace bridge into the water. And there was nobody would follow me! That was one record. I had the record for climbing the highest tree, up to the top, well you couldn't go any further. No laddies would follow me, you know! See, if you had the record you kept it, nobody could beat it. And I hold it yet! For going over the bridge. And I climbed to the top of the school building, the chimney. And I sat at the back – this is where I was gotten – and this is the story.

About two days after the attempted arrest, I got kind of wearied. I kent my mother had two-three shillings, so I went to the school. I used to go up and play with the laddies all the time on the school playground, carry on with the lassies, and when the school went in I cut away. I wouldn't go into school. So it was dinner hour and the weans were out. Somebody was speaking about climbing.

I said, 'Right.' I went up at the back of the school, right up to the top of the building, up the side of the wall, climbed the roan pipe up to the roof, over the roof and right up to the chimney pots. As low as your father and as low as my mother, I'm telling you the God's truth – I sat on top of the chimney pots. Who came out but Miss Crawfurd! And this wee lassie who used to like me, she stayed on a farm. This laddie shouted, 'Duncan's up!' The lassie held her hand across his mouth, but before she could get her hand across, the teacher looked up and saw me on the pots. She made me come down. I came down, and she put me back into the class in school.

And I'm sitting, I'm wicked! Now I've been two months out of school. It was like taking a wild weasel and putting it in a nest of rabbits! I'm looking for an escape. I'm no interested in what she's speaking about to me. I'm looking for a way out. I was really wild. I mean, no bad, nae way. I wasn't bad, wasn't violent. I wouldn't hurt a wee wean or anybody, I wouldn't give anybody cheek. But there was nobody could catch me! And there was no way in the world anybody was going to tie me down! No way.

The teacher tried to keep me in school. I asked out, to leave the room. No, she wouldn't let me. Now, they had blinds down on the window. It was late on in the afternoon. The teacher had a big lamp lighted on the roof. She filled the blackboard with writing. And then she wanted the piano shifted from one room to another. This was the God's truth. She picked the biggest laddies because she always had it shifted back and forward.

'Come on,' she says, 'you can help tae.' Miss Crawfurd. She had glasses on. In her own way she really liked me! I think she envied my freedom. And she says, 'Come on, Duncan, you'll help too!'

I said, 'Aye, all right, I'll help too.' This is the school room here, and there was a long passage going through to her room. And there were the toilets in there and the washhand basin, and there was a door out to the gate, see! And you had to pass by the main door to get into the master's room, where there was a big room on your right and then a partition for the wee five-year-olds.

So, we got the piano. Three laddies at the front, three at the back and a laddie at each side. And we put down the lid. Miss Crawfurd was working with the blackboard. The boys are all shoving the piano. I waited till I got level with the door – feesht – and I'm out and off! I never saw that piano again. That was my last time. I only spent about an hour and a half in that class from that time she got me till the minute she shifted that piano. I got rid of her, I was out, over the dyke and off. Off to the shore. And that was me, I never went back in school again. Nobody kent where I went. It was a waste of time trying to tie me up. You couldn't do it, no!

So I went away, cut to the shore, begged two or three matches. Down along the shore I tore a wee bit of my jacket, lighted it, gathered wee sticks and kindled a wee fire. I got limpets, got whelks, had my wee fire, sat and ate my meal. Roasted limpets, boiled whelks, and I never used a pin! I got a sharp stick, sharpened it with my teeth, and picked the whelks out of their shells. That was my dinner. I had a tin I'd hid in a bush with a wee wire handle. I held it on the fire with a wee stick and I waited till it came to a boil. Salt water, you boiled them in salt water. My own lonely fire on the shore. And I could kindle a fire, sister dear, you've no idea, I could kindle a fire in the middle of the sea! I had this knack, I could kindle a fire on a day of heavy sleet or snow or storms – it was no difference to me. And I could kindle a fire along the shore in any circumstances in any way! I could get things to make a fire where nobody in the world could get them, wee bits of driftwood washed under a rock; or I'd lift a stone and get dry grasses in below. To get a wee blaze started! Once you got a wee blaze, you fed it till it got into a flame. I didn't have a pot; I had my wee wire, a circle made on the end of it. I put the limpits sitting in the circle and held them over the fire so they wouldn't fall off.

And then one day, it was just about a month before I was fourteen, my mother said to me, 'Are ye comin wi me, Duncan? I'm gaun up to Adie MacCallum's. He wants me up to plant a wee puckle tatties.'

I said, 'Right, Mammy, I'll go wi ye.' Oh, I was glad to get away. Now she had got me a pair of long trousers from the jeweller in Lochgilphead. Long flannels. The first long trousers I ever had in my life. She had been down in Lochgilphead and the jeweller's wife had given her some rags. In among them was this pair of flannels. He was about my size and they just fitted me to a tee.

We were just on the road to go up to Adie's at Auchindrain when we came to the bridge. There's this man sorting the dyke at the roadside. Now my mother smoked a pipe, she carried a wee cuddy pipe in her pocket. And she cracked to the man. Neil she cried him. He smoked a pipe too.

She said, 'Gie me a wee bit tobacco fae ye, Neil, tae fill my pipe.' He kent her for years since she was a wean.

'Aye,' he said, 'Betsy, I'll gie ye a bit tobacco.' He gave her a bit. 'Man,' he said, 'that laddie's fairly growin.'

'Aye,' she said, 'that's Duncan. He's comin on fine. We're gaun up tae Adie's tae plan . . .'

'Aye,' he said, 'he hasnae much.' Neil was building drystone dykes along the side of the road.'

She says, 'Ye're makin a good job there, Neil.'

'Aye,' he said, 'I'm makin a good job. It'll be all right.'

'Man', she said, 'hoo do ye manage these big rocks, liftin these rocks?' My mother was only a young woman; bonnie, short, blonde curly hair.

'By God, Betsy, it's no so easy,' he said. 'Sometimes it's no so easy.

She said, 'Could you no get somebody to gie ye a help.'

'Whaur am I gaunna get onybody? I cannae afford nobody tae gie me a help.'

She said, 'Duncan'll gie ye a help if ye're needin him for a day or two. If ye show him what tae do.'

He said, 'Do ye think so – would ye let him come and work wi me?'

'Well,' she said, 'I'm sure he's better daein something as knockin aboot Furnace. There's no much work fir him doon in Furnace. Ye could aye gie him something fir giein ye a wee help. Suppose it's only liftin stanes to ye.' My mother was always like that, willing to help.

'Man,' he said, 'I could dae wi the laddie to gie me a wee bit help.'

'Aye,' she said, 'I'm sure he'll gie ye a wee help. We'll no be long with Adie, about half a day.' Adie had about thirty drills of tatties.

Now Neil had a wheelbarrow for hurling the stones. He had a spade and a graip for picking up small stones, and a reel with string on it for measuring the level of the dyke. And he had his wee can for boiling his tea. And his web of cloth to keep things dry. Also a graip and a rake for tidying up. But he hurled it all in the barrow wherever he went. This was his job.

'Duncan, would you like to come and give me a help?'

'Aye,' I said, 'Neil, I want to gie ye a help. I'm no doin nothing else the noo.'*

'But, Betsy,' he said, 'I'm no wantin him, mind, fir nothing. I'll gie him half a crown a day.' Oh, sister dear, half a crown!

---

* the noo – at the moment

Back she tellt my father, 'Duncan got a job. Johnie, Duncan got a job today!'

He said, 'Wha wi?'

She said, 'Wi Neilie.'

'Oh, wi Neilie the mason,' he said, 'aye.'

'He got a job fir buildin the dykes,' she said, 'on the road.'

'By Christ,' he said, 'that's a good job! Watch yirsel wi snakes!' my father tellt me.

The next day I went up. No piece, no nothing, no flask, no tea. Just a wee taste o black tea in the morning from my mother. Eight o'clock I went up. My father wasn't working. He was off, had nothing to do.

I tellt Neil, 'I want my half-crown every night because my mother needs it.'

'Duncan,' he said, 'you'll get your pay.' He kept a wee saddler's purse. I mind on Neil fine, God rest his soul in heaven. He had a wee purse with a flap on it, kept pounds on one side and the change in the other. He always had money. He was good to me, God bless us. I started the next day and I had a knack for this job. The minute I started with him till the day I left him, it was the same as I had done it all the days of my life. I was only with him for about three days and he said, 'You take the one side and I'll take the other.' The same as I was born into it, drystane dyke building.

And then my brother Sandy came back to Furnace with his wife Betsy. I had stayed working with Neilie all that winter on to the next spring. Now I was fifteen. My brother Sandy put his wee tent into my father's barricade. He was back from Perthshire and he had two weans. Together we went to fish the tip, the granite quarry causeway along from our camp. We had to dig worms on the shore, and Sandy started to tell me the cracks about the horses, the travellers, Blairgowrie in Perthshire and other travellers and their horses. Laddies my own age with a pony.

'Ye're a big young laddie. What dae ye think,' he says, 'ye cannae stay here all the days o yir life! Are ye no better comin away tae Perthshire and gettin a job tae yirsel?' I was fifteen exactly. This was the month of April, 1943. Sandy says, 'Me and Betsy is gaun tae Forfar tae work on a farm. There's an awfae guid gadgie, and aa the broon hares in the world's sittin there.'

He coaxed me like a lamb of God. I wasn't wanting to go. I was never away from Argyll in my life. Never more than a few days' walk away from my father, and mother.

He says, 'Brother, I'm gaun awa – if ye'd like to come along wi me . . . ye can come wi me for a wee while.' And the stories he tellt me, the way he built it up to me, I had this picture in my head about all these travellers with horses.

He said, 'It's no rare to see seven and eight horses in one camp at one time!' And I made up my mind, I was going to go with my brother Sandy to Perthshire. For the first time in my life I was going to leave my father and mother, and Argyll.

THE TINKERMAN'S FRIEND

Well I've been east and I've been west
I've travelled this far country
And the finest friend I ever had
Was a tinkerman to me.

He's taught me things I did not know
About my ain country
And the finest friend I ever had
Was a tinkerman to me.

He makes his home with canvas small
As comfortable as can be
And he will lie on his bed of straw
Like any king could be.

Now I've got money and I've got land
And I have mansions three
But I would gie them all tonight
If a tinker I could be.

I'll give away my money, I'll give up my land
I'll sell my mansions three
And I will go on the road tonight
For the tinker I must see.

I'll travel east, I'll travel west
I'll wander far and free
And I will go on searching
For the tinker I must see.

Duncan Williamson

CHAPTER FOUR

SANDY WAS AN ORIGINAL TRAVELLER

I knew that life at home in Furnace with the old folk would be dull after hearing these stories my brother was telling me. The fantastic tales of travellers dealin and swappin, and the laddies of my age ownin ponies o their ain, which I didn't believe, but was later to find out was the truth! So I told my father and mother, 'I want to go wi my brother to Perthshire for a while, see the country for masel.'

My mother and father weren't very happy about it, as mothers and fathers aren't when their son goes away from home for the first time in their life. I was only fifteen. But when you're fifteen years of age among travelling folk you're qualified to take care of yourself, and there's little the mother and father can really do about it.

Now my father had travelled the country as a young man himself, all through Fife and Perthshire and Angus. But after he got my mother, and got some family, he never left Argyll. My brother Sandy was a great worker and he liked to work on the farms, and worked all year round sometimes. By 1943 he had made the trek two or three times from Perthshire to Argyllshire back and forward and he knew all the roads. He had a couple of kids, a lassie Susan, and a laddie, Charlie. It was the spring of the year and he said he was going to make his way back to a place called Balbrogie Farm outside of Balbeggie on the other side of Scone by Perth. There he was going to stay for a while.

Now Sandy didn't have a horse. He never had a horse in his life. He had this old twin pram he had converted into a kind of handcart. He put shafts on it, so's he could pull it with his bits of stuff on, which was very little. Some sticks for the tent, some canvas, some cooking utensils, a snottum for the fire for boiling the kettle, some clothes for the weans, a basin for washing their faces and some clothes for himself and for his wife. That was all he needed. And his dog! He always kept his dog for the rabbits – for the pot.

So, we set off on a Monday morning. Now we had to walk all the way. Sometimes we put one of the kids on the pram and hurled them when they got tired, give them shot about. But we couldn't make much speed, maybe ten or twelve miles a day at least. He had all his camping places set out along the road and he knew the distance he could go each day, like from Furnace to Inveraray, and from Inveraray to Dalmally, about fifteen miles. And he always left the roads to travel in the spring when the days were getting longer. You never hardly did it in the wintertime because the days were too short, you couldn't go that distance.

We left Furnace and travelled on to Inveraray, spent the night on the shore. Sandy was a good traveller and he could build a good tent and take care of things. He knew what he was doing and I just strung along and helped him in every way, all I could for company's sake. His wife Betsy made paper flowers. I never saw anybody in my life who could make paper flowers like what she could. She'd made them since she was a bairn at school. She was born and schooled in Tarbert on Loch Fyneside, reared with her granny. Seeing these flowers she made at a distance, they were just as if they were natural. And Sandy would make baskets. In the spring of the year the willows began to peel, but it was quite easy cutting willows along the roadside as you went and carrying a few with you. We always made a basket at night.

I'd been in Inveraray often enough, but I'd never been past Inveraray in the Dalmally direction. So we travelled on and we managed to make fifteen miles that day. We camped at this railwayside by Dalmally, about twenty-five feet from the track, a single track going to Oban. And I'd never seen a train in my life. I was excited. When it got dark we had this big coal fire, and while the kids were in bed we sat, cracked and made tea.

Sandy said, 'Here's another one comin!' When the train was coming up the hill the fireman flung on coal, and the sparks were fleeing way up in the air off this train. I was fascinated.

I said, 'Can you go on them trains?'

'No,' he said, 'that's a goods train. But you can go on a passenger train.' I promised myself someday I was going to go on one.

So we pushed on the next day. And this dog Sandy had, Jackie, he'd reared since it was a pup. It was a lurcher, between a collie and a greyhound. It was just a matter of Sandy taking him over to any place. There was no myxomatosis in these days – any wee piece of wood or any wee piece of field, anything – it was just rabbit while you wait! You just stood and said, 'Go on, Jack!' And away he went, scented the rabbit out, just killed it, brought it back and dropped it at your feet. Kill and carry! He was a great dog. So we never wanted for any rabbits along the way. And pheasants! He stood with his nose pointing at pheasants with his paw up, and then he dived. He snapped the pheasant, gave it a shake and that was it. And hares – he was great on the hares. But there weren't so many of them. I had never seen any brown hares, there were none on Loch Fyneside. Plenty were in Kintyre, but I'd never been as far as Campbeltown at that time.

As we were walking I said to Sandy, 'You were tellin me so many stories about horses and carts, and so many travellers . . . why do you no keep a horse? It would be handy. The bairns could get a hurl and your wife could get a hurl when she gets tired. You wouldn't need to worry about pullin any barra.' When we came to a hill we both had to pull it up, and both of us had to hold it back going down the brae. It was a hard thing to handle, kind o heavy.

'No,' he says to me, 'brother. I cannae be bothered wi a horse. In no way. I never had one and I'll never bother wi one. They're all right for people who likes them. But for all the traivellin I dae, maybe back to see my mother and father in the summertime, I like to stay in the one place. I like to work on the farms. But you're interested in horses – you'll see plenty when we go on, maybe two or three miles further on the road.'

So that day we got the length of Tyndrum. The night before Betsy had made these beautiful flowers. I remember it fine. Red and white paper roses she made– beautiful. She took her two dozen and I took two dozen.

I said, 'I'll go to some o these houses wi you and gie you a help tae sell them.' Six pence each for these flowers. I remember fine I went up to this house and knocked at the door. This old woman came out.

'Oh my goodness!' she said. 'Flowers! Aren't they early? I've never seen them so early as this.'

'I said, 'They're no early, ma'm, they're made o paper!'

She said, 'I don't believe you.' Now when Betsy made the flowers, she put a green stem and a green bud on them and two wee leaves made of green paper. And to stand from here over to that corner, if you held one in your hand I couldn't tell the real thing from the truth. She really was good. And the woman came over and felt them. 'Well,' she said, 'they might be paper, but they're the most beautiful flowers ever I've seen. Who makes them?'

I said, 'My sister-in-law makes them.'

'Well,' she said, 'I'll take six of each.' And she took six red ones and six white. 'You know,' she said, 'I'm goin to tell you something probably you don't know. The next time you go sellin flowers, don't put white roses and red roses together.

I said, 'Why this?'

'Well,' she said, 'some people are a little superstitious o havin white and red roses together in the same bunch. But not me. But for the sake o yirsel sellin them, it would be better if you put some more coloured ones among them.'

So I had no bother selling my flowers. I sellt two dozen in no time at all. It was no a big village. I came back and I had twelve shillings. I wasn't an hour getting them sellt.

Sandy said to me, 'You're good at the flooers.'

I said, 'I'm no as good as what your wife can make them. Tell me something. That old woman I was speakin to down there, she tellt me it's unlucky tae have red and white roses together.'

'Ach brother,' he said, 'that's an auld supersitition. That goes back a long, long time. That's no the first hoose that tellt my Betsy that. It goes away back tae the days o the battle o the War o the Roses. Some folk fought for one side and wore a red rose, and if you fought for the other side you wore a white rose.'

So we got on pretty well. We never stayed more than one night in a place as long as the weather was good on the road. It was good fun to me steppin oot, pushin this pram on the level. Sometimes I had Charlie on it and sometimes Susan on top. I hurled them along the road. And Sandy and Betsy were just walkin linked to each other along the road like lovers. But I noticed the farms were getting bigger, and I could see the bigger ploughed fields. I remarked about this to Sandy.

'Och brother,' he said, 'you've never seen nothing yet. This is only wee crofts here yet. Wait till you get down to the Lowlands and you'll see right farms and right horses! Big horses.'

'Well,' I said, 'they're big horses – in that field.'

He said, 'They're no the right big horses. Wait till you get down to Angus, down to Forfarshire to see some farms with fourteen and fifteen Clydesdale horses, real big anes. The farm I work on has got twelve horses onto it.'

I said, 'I'd like to see it some day.' So, we travelled on and the next day we got the length of Lochearnhead.

He says to me, 'We'll go along to the shore and kindle a fire. Sister Betsy'll go back to the hotel and she'll maybe get a piece tae make some tea.'

Now hotels in these days were awful good for giving a handout. Women just went round and they gave the maids, the lassies at the back of the hotel or the cook some flowers or a basket or something. And I remember what she gave Betsy in return. It was a pike, a cooked pike, full-sized with the head and tail off it. It was steamed. She brought it back and we had a good tea.

He said, 'It's hardly worth it . . .' It was early in the day. 'It's hardly worth us staying here overnight' cause we've got a good bit road to push on. I think we'll go on tae St Fillans. It's no far, only seven mile. And that's a regular camp fir traivellers. Ye'll see some traivellers and mebbe a wee yoke. There's always folk gaun away North, away up by Glencoe or that in the summertime, the beginnin o spring onyway. And you might see some traivellers.'

So we pushed on to St Fillans and sure enough when we landed, we saw the smoke. He says, 'There's somebody campit here.' We pulled in. He said, 'I'm no gaun nae farther the night.' It was about six o'clock, still clear. 'We'll camp in here.' So I came with Sandy. There were two tents, two bow tents and a fire in the middle between them. This young man and his wife and two laddies. He knew my brother Sandy well.

'Come on in,' he says, 'and put yir tent up at the fire.' Sandy had met him before and camped with him. 'Come on in, he says.

I gave Sandy a hand to get the tent up and we went for sticks. We were just close to the river. We used the water out of the river, it was quite clean.

Sandy says, 'This is my young brother here. One o my brothers. He's gaun with me for a while in the summertime. He's never been ower this distance afore. And he's awful fond o horses, gaun to see all these horses I was tellin him about.'

'Oh, ye'll see plenty o horses there, laddie,' the man says to me. 'Good anes and bad anes and all kinds.'

But I didn't want to speak very much, because me being reared with the country weans in the village of Furnace, I had the same kind of Highland accent as had the local weans I went to school with. The Highland tongue.

So we made our supper. And it still wasn't late, so they put on another fire and some more tea. Then they sat and cracked about things, about farms and about travellers, who they saw and who they never saw, persons they'd never seen for years. The way the natural travellers' crack went. And I mind the woman made some tea and gave us something to eat. Then she put the wee-est laddie to bed. We sat and cracked till, oh, it was late on at night-time. Then it started to rain.

Now Betsy, she always went into the front of the tent and half pulled down the flap. She lighted a candle and made her flowers inside the tent. The woman was in watching her making the flowers. They were okay, so we were sitting cracking at the fire.

The traveller man says to me, 'You like horses, laddie?'

'Aye,' I said, 'I like horses, mister. I'm awfae fond o horses.'

He said, 'I've got a horse. A wee pony there. I use it for pullin the wee bit tent aboot. Ye'll see it in the morning.' And up against the side of his tent, so's it would shield the fire and act as a kind of wind break was this wee cart, a float. He said, 'I have a wee Shetland pony.'

'Oh,' I said. Now I'm dying to see this pony. But they all made up their minds for to go to bed, so we did.

The next morning it was still drizzly. Now flowers are no use when it's raining. But Betsy was fly, as fly as a fox. She always kept a big packet of candles. She put them in a skillet and melted the candles. Then dipped the paper flowers into the wax. And this made them more real. With the candle grease the rain couldn't do them any harm. So she and the traveller woman went away back to call the houses in St Fillans. The rain kind o faired up. But it was still drooky wet.

The man said to my brother Sandy, 'You'll no be shiftin the day. You cannae take yir tent doon wi that rain, laddie.' The man would have been in his forties.

'Ach well,' Sandy said, 'the weans are needin a rest onyway. They've had a lang step fae Inveraray. I'd be as well tae bide the day till the rain fairs up onyway.'

Betsy and the woman hawked the houses, sellt their flowers and got as much as they could get. Whatever kind o coppers they got they bought some messages. But there was no bread or milk in thon wee village, so when they came back the laddie came up to me.

He said, 'I want to go to the shop tae Comrie. For something for my mother. Are ye wantin anything fae the toon?' he says to Betsy.

She said, 'Aye, laddie, get me a pint o milk and a packet o fags.'

He said to me, 'You comin wi me?'

'I'll go wi ye,' I said. 'Is it far to the toon?'

He said, 'It's only aboot five mile.'

'Oh,' I said, 'that's a lang walk.'

'Ah but, I'm no gaunna walk the five mile.' he said, 'I'm takin the wee pony, the wee yoke.' He was a laddie about fourteen. He went over and pulled this float out, like a big barrow with rubber wheels on. In below on the axle was this set of harness, the loveliest wee set ever I'd seen. You could lift them in your hand. And a wee collar and hems on it. I'm looking all around for this pony, couldn't see it. He went over the back of the bushes where there was a bit of green grass, and he took up this pony. I wish to God you'd seen it! I guarantee it was no more than twelve hands high, fat as a wee pig. But the colour of it, like a piece of coal, as if it was cut out of coal, and its mane and tail were near hanging on the ground. It was bottle black, shiny like a craw's wing.

I said, 'I've never seen a pony like that in my life!'

He said, 'That's what you call a Shetland pony.' Its wee hooves were polished like black oak.

I said, 'Can you manage to drive it, can you work it all right?'

'Ach, I can work it all right,' he said. His father never even looked the road he was on. It was just as if he was going on a bike. In two minutes he put the saddle on its back, and on with the collar, the bridle, bit in its mouth, buckled on the reins, pulled up the wee float, backed it in. He put on the traces for clicking onto the cart, fastened the breeching straps. He says to me, 'Jump up on the other side!'

So he jumped up on one side, I jumped up on the other. And he pulled the reins, and this wee thing set off along the road. I wish you'd seen it go! I'm tellin' ye, its wee mane and tail was flying in the wind. You couldn't see its feet! They were no sooner down to the ground when they were back up again. It was just like playing a rhythm with drumsticks, on a drum with its feet. Round the corners and bends as fast as you could go – I was feart it would fall. But no! The wee laddie's sitting holding the reins as if they didn't exist. It wouldn't bother about motors or anything. He drove right into Comrie and pulled up at this shop.

He says to me, 'You comin into the shop?'

I said, 'No, I'm no goin into the shop.' He looked at me as if I had done something wrong. I said, 'I'll watch your pony.'

'Ach, dinnae worry about hit. It'll stand itsel,' he said, 'stand there all day if I want it to.'

Now I noticed these big windows and fruit and everything. They were different from the wee shops I had been reared with. I told him, 'This is a guid lump o place.'

He said, 'This is no a big place at aa. This is only a wee village. You want to see Perth or Dundee. That is a real big toon.'

I said, 'You been in these toons?'

He said, 'I've been in them aa. I've been in Inverness, Aberdeen, Dundee, Perth – in them aa with my faither. I like to go with my faither to the markets, to the horse markets.'

I said, 'Horse markets?'

'Aye,' he says, 'Where the folk sell and buy the horses. But are ye no comin in?'

'No, I'm no goin into the shop,' I said. Now he wondered at me. Because if traveller weans, suppose they've only got a penny to spend, they'll go into a shop just for the sake of getting a look around. Suppose they never buy anything. Curious to see what's inside the shop.

'Oh well,' he said. But he wasn't long in, about five minutes. He came out with a wee box of milk and bread and things, put it in the back of the float. Whirled the pony around on the main street and it set off like a shot from a gun, back up the other side of the road the way we came. Ah, it was no time till we were back home. It wasn't late in the day, no more than three o'clock. So we had something to eat, some tea.

And the traveller man says to my brother, 'Come on, we'll go and have a game of quoits. Me and my laddie will play you and your brother as partners.'

I said, 'I cannae play quoits.' I'd heard about quoits, but never played.

'Aye, ye'll soon learn,' the man says to me. Away they go to a burn. And they pick these flat stones, about a pound weight. Brother picks two and the man picks two. They chip them, make them all nice and round. Later I met travellers who carried their own stones with them from place to place, to play quoits. So, they step out twenty-five paces and they stick a stick in the ground, and a tin on this stick. They do the same at the other end of the pitch, a tin on a stick.

Now my brother and the traveller man stand at one end, and the wee laddie and I stand at the other. You've got to fling these stones underhand, as if you are playing cricket. If you hit the tin you get three points. If you put it in close to the tin, you get one point. Or if you can get two close to the tin, you get two points. The game is 'twenty-one'. You change sides at twelve. They who get the first twenty-one are the winner of the game.

So, it was the two men's turn to start off. Now my brother and the traveller man had played quoits before. And they were out to give me and the wee laddie a lickin – show us how good they were. So they did! Because I couldn't play it any! I couldn't get the idea, how to fling the stane, to get the tin or fall near it. So the wee laddie showed me. 'Fling it this way,' he said. Oh, and he must have got a good score his ownself. By the time he got eleven or twelve, I got nothing. They won the twenty-one. They played two or three games. I was lost. I shamed my brother

Sandy. My father could play quoits but he never played with us, no. I had never seen it played before, but I kent all about it with folk cracking about the game. I was to play it many, many times later on in years to come. I saw traveller men down on their knees and measuring with a wee straw to get one extra inch just for the sake of the game. I saw one traveller man near tears, greetin because he got beat at quoits, at Cupar at the berries one time.

So the rain began to kind of smoor off,* and ach, we got fed up playing. It was a one-sided battle. I couldn't help him much. But me and this wee laddie, we got to be awful good friends. He said, 'Come on, we'll go and shift the pony tae a bit green grass.'

I said, 'That's a bonnie wee pony you've got.'

'Ach aye,' he said, 'it's all right. But it's too wee. It does for my wee brother gettin a hurl along the road and my mother sometimes when she gets tired. But me and my father cannae get a hurl, cannae sit up and drive on when we want to, come to a waste road. I like the big horses the best.'

I said, 'If I had that wee horse I would never part wi it.'

'No,' he said, 'you would think too much o it! But I cannae dae that. If I thought too much o that wee horse and came to like it too much, and my father kent that, my father wouldnae gie it awa. He would be only torturin hissel, because we couldnae keep two horses. He'd need to get another big ane, and we couldnae keep two. So I just work it for him, treat it to the best and like it . . . I like every horse.'

I said, 'So div I. I like every horse. How long have you been among horses?'

He said, 'I dinnae mind when my father hadnae got a horse. I cannae mind. Sometimes he swaps and deals, and sometimes we've got three different horses in the same week. He never keeps them very long. But he'd never be withoot ane. He always gets ane before he puts ane away. Probably the next travellers we meet, he'll probably swap this ane awa and get another ane. That's the way it goes on. But it'll soon be the market in Perth. And we'll probably go up the length o Crianlarich and back doon in by Callander, and back roon in by Perth.' That was the

---

* smoor off – dampen down, diminish

way they went. 'And if somebody doesn't get it on the way, he'll probably take it into Perth and swap it awa.'

The rain kind o faired up. And we all went for a bundle o sticks apiece. That's one thing I could dae. I hadnae sense o much else, but I was sensible enough to get sticks. So we climbed across the road. And me and him got to be good friends.

He said, 'I wish to God my father would turn back wi yese and go back by Perth, but he'll no do that. We've just come up that way. So if you're makin doon that way, you'll probably see traivellers. You'll have to go through Perth, the way you're brother's gaun tae get to Scone and Balbeggie.' He kent all the roads! He was only fourteen tae.

I said, 'My brother Sandy was tellin me there are a lot of horses at the berries.'

'Oh, the berries,' he said, 'see, we never miss the berries. We always go, my father goes to the berries every year.'

I said, 'Do you mak a lot of money?'

'Nah,' he said, 'we never do. But it's good fun, plenty laddies, lassies, and folk like yirsel to play wi. My faither has plenty o folk tae crack tae, and he gets plenty swappin and dealin. We aye make a few shillings, the four o us pickin.'

So we sat and cracked till well on tae night-time, cracking about everything under the sun. They start speaking about burkers and about ghost-haunted places they'd camped in. And old David Johnstone, he was a great old cracker, great crackin man. He was telling my brother about the haunted camps, things he heard he could never explain. His wife was awfae quiet, an awfae quiet woman. She and Betsy got on fine. So while we were sitting cracking, Betsy was busy sitting making the flowers from crêpe. She bought paper every day. Whenever she sellt her flowers and got two-three shillings together, the first thing she did, go into the shop and buy a packet o fags and three packets o paper. It was only six pence for a big roll. Sandy had made her an oval basket for holding her flowers. Charlie and Susie were in bed. We cracked on to twelve o'clock at night. I didn't say much because I was feart o embarrassing Sandy wi speakin about things I didnae ken very much aboot. He was a bit fly for it the next day on the road. It must have been late when we went to bed. But the rain faired up.

The next morning we packed up and had our breakfast. By the time we had got up, the man had his tent down, his wee float packed all nice and tidy and the green cover folded over the top. You couldn't see a thing under it. And he'd gathered up the two or three stones holding down the cover for his tent. Oh, clean, tidy-goin folk they were. And the wee horse was standing with the harness on it. But he wouldn't move till he saw us packed up too. So we packed up this pram thing that Sandy had, and we pulled out on the road. We spoke for a few minutes and bade each other 'good morning'.

The man led his wee pony and his two laddies said, 'Cheerio, we'll see you again sometime.' They went away up by Lochearnhead and we travelled on right down to Comrie.

Sandy says, 'What do you think o this big toon?'

I said, 'It's a good size.'

'Aye, it's bigger than Furnace anyway,' he says to me.

I said, 'Aye, it's bigger than Furnace.'

So the shops in these towns were awful good in these days. Especially a butcher's. They didn't have fridges or anything to keep food. And you could go with a sixpence into a butcher, just tell the man to give you something for that amount. You could get big lumps of beef, and any shop would give you a big lump o ham end for tuppence or thruppence. And I was very good at this, 'pitchin the fork' they called it. I wasn't embarrassed in this way, no. Because I'd done it all my days for my father and mother when I was back home. With just about a shilling I was through the shops in two minutes. Asking the woman for a bit ham end to make a drop soup. And into the butcher's and the baker's, telling the woman – did she hae any stale cakes or anything she didna need. You could get a big box full. So, we had plenty to eat. But we travelled on.

I said, 'Hae we far to go tonight?'

'Well,' Sandy said, there's a wee camp we call Monzievaird doon here. And it's your chance tonight to get the rabbits for the pot.' Sandy had to have rabbits every night. He says, 'It's hivin with rabbits!'

Now Jackie, the dog, Sandy always kept on a chain all day and kept him tied to the side o the pram, the side o the road. Jackie. And he had a white chest. He was a good old dog. After we got our tent up at Monzievaird – it was a wee layby off the roadside – got some sticks and water for Betsy, made our tea, he says, 'Come on brother, we'll take a walk and get a rabbit for the pot.' Sandy just killed them and skinned them right away, when they were warm. That's what he did, and put them in the pot right away. He gutted them as soon as the dog killed them.

He said, 'I dinnae like the mothers. I like the halflings.' If he got a milker, he flung it away. Even if they were young he wouldn't use them. But getting on to the end o April there were wee halfling rabbits. He says, 'We'll no kill very many, two or three'll dae us for the pot.' He used to pull them, skin them and wash them, pop them in the pot, tatties and neeps in with them. Make a good pot o slutter. And what we didn't eat at night we had for breakfast the morn.

We went away over the back of this place, and what rose but a hare, a broon hare, a halfling. Now it takes a good dog to kill a halfgrown hare. But Jackie was only about three years old and there never was a halfling hare that rose that he couldnae kill! I'd never seen a broon hare before. White ones with the black ears, mountain hares, I'd caught plenty o them. So Jackie carried it back.

I said, 'What's that he got?

'Brother,' he says, 'that's a marlech. That'll dae, that's enough.' We brought it back. 'Ach,' he says to me, 'these things cannae run. Ony dog can catch them.' He was pulling my leg. That night he cooked the hare and we had a good supper. We sat and cracked all night. 'Now,' he said, 'tomorrow morning we'll push on. You'll see the real big farms fae noo on. We're makin on tae the borders o Crieff.'

But just before you go to Crieff there's a big field at the roadside. And sitting in the middle of the field was a broon hare, a big one. As we were walking along Sandy said, 'Thon there's a hare, brother! Brother, I bet you a pound you could catch thon nae bother! You could catch thon nae bother yirsel, never mind a dog. They cannae run very fast.'

It never really bothered me very much, the tricks my brother played on me. Because I knew in my own mind he was trying to educate me the best possible way. By another field he told me there were ducks, and that I should go and catch some.

He said, 'Brother, you'd better go and see if you can get a couple of those ducks for the pot.' When I landed in the field it was turnips the farmers had put out to the sheep. I had never seen farmers putting turnips out in the fields. And they really did look like ducks to me. It was me who suggested they were birds. Back where I was born and reared, if a farmer had two-three drills o turnips, they put them in a shed, never spread them through the fields. But anyway, Sandy just laughed and I took it all in fun.

Now he says to me, 'Brother, you must remember, you will meet a lot of travellers going into Perth.'

I said, 'How far is it to Perth?'

'Well,' he says, 'we'll have to go to Crieff, and frae there it's about seventeen miles to Perth. We'll have a couple of stops along the way and we'll probably make it by the weekend.'

I said, 'Is there any place we can stay there?'

'Well,' he says, 'we'll have to go through the town and find a place to stay on the other side.'

We pushed along our way and I was shoving this cairt. Well, as I tellt ye, a converted pram. Camp sticks, covers, dishes and two kids sittin on top. And he always walked with his sleeves rolled up. Sandy never wore a jacket. All the days o his life he never wore one. Bare shirt. And Betsy, she always walked along the roadside. Sometimes they were hanging on to each other and sometimes they were kissing along the road – you know they were the two happiest people ever I saw in my life. I took care o the pram with the bairns. We travelled on.

We came to the other side o Crieff and he said, 'Brother, there's an auld road here – we can stay for the night.' The camp was called 'Cat's Corner'.

I said, 'Right.'

So he says, 'Are you wantin to stay with Betsy and sell some flooers, or do you want to go on and help me with the camp?'

I said, 'You can manage yirsel. Put up the camp. What's the sense o me goin on wi you?' He had his camp sticks tied on the barrow in case he came to a place where there were none. I said 'You go and put the tent up on the auld road wherever you can. Kindle the fire and boil the kettle and I'll go and help Betsy.' Betsy knew the road. I didnae. This is my first time in Crieff.

The night before we had made these paper flowers and we had gone up to this house, asked an old woman for the privet.

On the hedges, these beautiful long stems o green. Betsy had her flowers in a cardboard box. The woman had said, 'Oh, help yirsel to some privet!' So I'd broken the long thin stems and Betsy twisted the wee bit copper wire that held the flower together onto the privet. I had told her, 'I dinnae want all the one colour.' We had about three dozen o paper flowers. And at six pence each that was eighteen shillings. In Crieff in these days for eighteen shillings you could have bought as much food that would do you for a week.

I said to Betsy, 'Gie me a dozen and a half, and you take a dozen and a half.' I remember it just like yesterday. It was yellow and red flowers she had. And they were beautiful! I never saw a person in my life who could really make flowers like Betsy. Now I said to her, 'I dinnae want to loss ye. I want to keep wi ye. So instead o goin up the main street, we'll take the back street.' She went to one door and I went across the street. I kept my eye on her so's I couldn't lose her, because this was strange to me. Betsy was a very queer kind o person, very soft spoken, very quiet.

She just went to the woman and asked, 'You needin any flowers?'

And the woman said, 'Well . . .'

She said, 'They're made o paper, you know, and . . .

Betsy hadn't got the idea o the 'go'. See, I could see this. It was up to the woman whether she bought them or no. Betsy never persevered. I went to this other woman. An old lady her hair full o curlers. And her garden was full o beautiful flowers. I knocked at the door. I always went to the back door, never to the front. I went down three steps into this old-fashioned house in Crieff, up the back road just before you go to the high road. And this old woman came out to me.

'What is it?' she said.

'Well madam,' I said, 'you needin any flowers?'

She said, 'Did you come up by my garden?'

I said, 'I did.'

'And did you see all these flowers growin in my garden?'

I said, 'Yes madam, I did.'

And she said, 'Aren't they beautiful?'

I said, 'Yes, they're beautiful. But they're no paper flowers, madam. Your flowers are real, but mines is made o paper.'

She says, 'Don't go and tell me that!' This is the truth now, I'm no tellin you a lie. 'Don't you tell me that!' she says to me.

I said, 'Yes, my dear, ma'm, they're paper flowers. And I'm sellin them, me and my sister-in-law. We're just on the road, we're travelling people, and this is what we do. From town to town. We cam away up from Argyll.'

'How far did you come from?' she said.

I said, 'From Inveraray.'

'Oh, I know Inveraray well!' she said. 'What do you charge for them?'

I said, 'Six pence each.' She hemmed and hawed* for a while.

'Well,' she says. 'Give me half a dozen.' So I gave her half a dozen. And in twenty minutes my flowers were gone. I sellt them nae bother. So, I had nane left: two or three more houses and a woman took two, another woman took three, another took two or three. They always took two, never less. So I came across to Betsy.

I said, 'Gie me another two-three flooers.'

She said, 'How'd you get on?'

I said, 'Look, they're all gone. I got on fine.' Anyway we sellt our flowers. But to make a long story short, I said, 'There you are, get me a packet o Woodbine.' Tenpence-halfpenny for twenty Woodbine. That was all I wanted. I didnae need anything else.

So she went into the shop and got her messages, and she said, 'It's a good wee bit doon this auld road.'

So down we go to the old road. When we landed, Sandy had the tent up and the fire going, and he had the kettle boiling. Well, it wasn't a kettle, it was a can. Sometimes he put on the pot for tea. Whatever was cleanest he used. If the can was too dirty, needed scoured out, he would use the pot. Tea out o the soup pot. If it was clean they would put it on and boil some tea. When the can got too dirty with making tea too much in it, travellers always took it to the river and scrubbed it with sand to make it clean.

---

* hemmed and hawed – dithered

So he says to me, 'How did you get on, brother?'

I said, 'Oh, I got on fine. I had a great day. Flowers, I could sell flowers for evermore!' This was really fun to me because I had never done this in my life before I'd set out with them.

'Well,' he says, 'we'll stay the night here and tomorrow we'll go to Perth. Now there's not a camp between here and Perth we can stay on, and it'll probably be late. But we're goin right through Perth. I know all the back roads. I want to get pushin on, I want to go tae Balbeggie.' This farm was the other side of Scone and wanted to get there as soon as possible. 'Aye,' he said, 'you'll be meetin up wi yir ain folk shortly. Aa yir freends.'

I said, 'I've got nae freends – aa ma freends is back hame in Argyllshire.'

'Aye, I bet ye,' he said, 'tomorrow ye'll see all yir freends when ye get to Perth.'

But I had noticed that the place I was born in, Argyllshire, was a different kind of country, a different world from this country – this was Perthshire. There were farms, fields for evermore. And the haystacks were like ones I'd never seen before. Corn stacks in hundreds sitting along the roadsides. And horses, big Clydesdales running in the fields. I had stopped with the pram when I came to a field, because the farmers had maybe fifteen and twenty horses in the place. Sandy had told me the ones running and used in the field one day were given a rest the next day. And they used the other ones. I had stopped to admire these horses.

Sandy would say, 'Horses! You're moich on horses.'

I said, 'Of course I am.'

He said, 'You'll see plenty horses before you lea Perthshire and Forfarshire.' Now he was going to take me to Forfar to the farm where he used to work for years and years. So, we sat and we cracked all night. He was telling me about Perthshire and about other travellers. Telling me how to behave myself and not get into any trouble. He was trying to educate me. But he never played any more tricks on me!

The next day we got up early. I always got up first, kindled the fire, made some tea. I used to lie in the front o his camp at the front o his door. We just made a bed o straw and covered it up wi a bit cover. The next morning we just packed up the

tent, set fire to the straw and the place was as clean as the day
we came. That's an overnight short stay. There were no more
travellers on the old road that night, not a soul.

The funny thing was, you could tell . . . travellers were a queer
race o people. I mean, when you came to a camping place,
suppose it was empty and not a soul on it, the travellers could
read the camping place. They knew who had been there! You
think this is hard to believe, but this is truth. There were people
who were clean and tidy, and people who left a mess. People
who built their tents in such different kinds o manner. And you
got accustomed to this. My brother would say to me, 'There's
naebody here but there were somebody here about three days
ago. I know who they were.'

I said, 'How do you ken who they were?'

'Well,' he said, 'I ken hoo, the way they built their fire and
hoo they had their tent, how they shaped their tent, how they
cleaned up their tent.' He measured the holes, he would ken by
the way they put their sticks in the ground if they were original,
good travellers who carried their sticks. Or somebody who just
cut sticks for the night, ken what I mean. Travellers could read
all these things. They were like Indians! And Sandy would ken
if the travellers had two tents and a big fire in the middle.

He would say, 'Well, there was a couple here. It was just a
couple and a couple o wee weans.'

I said, 'Brother, how in the world do you ken these things?'

'Well, he said, 'look, there's the mark o one bow tent and one
wee fire. Look across frae that fire – if that had been a crowd
o folk there'd be another tent on the other side and a mark
o that other tent. There'd hae been a great big monster fire
in the centre. It was only one family that was here. Now they
didnae have no horses.'

I said, 'How do you ken?'

'Well,' he says, 'the grass is no etten up the roadside and there
nae mark of horse's dung, and there nae place where the horse
was tied. Or, they didna hae a dog.' He even kent this!

I said, 'How do you ken?'

'Well, if they had a dog,' he said, 'you would see a bit fur or a
rabbit skin lyin aboot where the dog was playin or something
the dog was playin wi.' He kent that.

I said, 'That's queer to me, how these people learns these things.' But I was learning anyway.

So next day we pushed on and we travelled all day. Now it was all downhill. We had gone over the mountains. It was level going. We came into Methven and we sellt some flowers. Sandy went out with his pram and he waited at the end of the village. He never kindled a fire. We took the kettle with us, sellt some flowers and Betsy got some things in the shop. I mind Betsy made a kettle of tea along the roadside – it was what you call a short stop. She'd just put some tea and sugar in the kettle and went to some house, got hot water in it. Saved us from kindling a fire. We travelled on, and by four o'clock we reached Perth.

Now my brother spoke a lot of cant. Sandy was a great man for the cant and he taught me a lot of the language. He spoke it to me suppose there was nobody around. I mind his words, God rest his soul, he says to me, 'Brother, this is a big gav' (meaning a big town). 'And we'll have tae get through it before it gets too late.' It was the end of April. 'Not only that, we've a good bit to go through the gav tae the other end, about six mile on the other end o Perth before we get a place for the night.'

'Well,' I said, 'You're walkin.'

'Aye,' he says, 'I know I'm walkin. I'll push, and never mind, I'll push the pram. So I'll take you all the back ways through the toon.' He knew Perth very well. And he made his way round the cobble streets, round this way, back this way. It was strange to me. I was seeing all these people and all these people were looking at us. But I didnae feel nae shame or nae embarrassment in any way. There were hundreds o people in the streets we went through. And on the cobbles the old pram was doubling, reetle-rattle, the wheels o the pram were liltin. Charlie and Susan were sitting on the pram. They were just wee toddlers. The rattle o this old pram going through the streets, and dog Jackie tied to the handle – anyway we made wir way through Perth.

Sandy says to Betsy, 'Dinnae stay in the toon. Come on wi us, come straight through. And we'll make our way to the campin place.' So we travelled on right through Perth, over the bridge, the river. Biggest river I ever saw in my life. I stood on the top of the bridge and looked down on the top o the banking.

He says to me, 'That's the River Tay. That comes from the

mountains, from Loch Tay near where we cam doon.' I was used with wee totie burns away back in Argyllshire. You could stand across them. I was wanting to watch this beautiful river a wee while, but Sandy wouldn't let me. He says, 'Come on, we've a good bit to go!'

We travelled on and to the other end o Perth on the Scone side. The road said 'Blairgowrie'. He took this road and Sandy said, 'I'm going out to a wee place they call the Knock Camp. There's an old road, and there'll prob'ly be traivellers, cousins o yir ain. This is a great camp wi yir cousin, yir uncle's laddie.'

I said, 'I've never seen my uncle.'

'No,' Sandy said, 'you'll no see him. He's dead and buried. He died when the war started. But there two laddies and two lassies, and they stay wi their mother. If yir cousin is anywhere aboot Perth, this is where he'll stay. Perth is where they haud the market, the horse market. It's Monday morning.' In these days it was every Monday, and this was Friday. 'There'll be a big market. When it starts the traivellers come fae all parts and all over! Some of them are on the road frae Friday night makin their way fae Aberfeldy, fae Dunkeld to catch this market. This is where they dae their dealin and their swappin, where they change their horses.'

'Brother, how do you no bother wi a horse?' I said. It'd be awfae easy . . . what about that family we seen away back there at St Fillans. Look how easy they went!'

He says to me, 'Brother, what was I goin tae do wi a horse? Look, I never had a horse and I'll never hae one. I like to work and when I gae oot workin in the one place I work all day, come home at night. And I like to read my paper, fill my coupons. I would forget aboot it. It would prob'ly dee wi hunger. I wouldnae even look after it.'

'Ah well,' I said, 'every man to his own. But I'll tell ye something, if I ever get married and get a wife, I'll never hae nae barras like that. I'll have a horse.'

'Well,' he said, 'you keep on the way you're daein, you'll get a horse! Go to Blairgowrie, go to the berries, You'll prob'ly get a horse and get a woman an aa alang wi it!'

'They tell me how great . . . about these Blairgowrie berries,' I said. 'What's so good about it?'

'Well,' he says, 'the traivellers comes fae all over the world, all over Scotland to the berries. This is where they see each other and where they swap. They deal and they swap, they trade and dae everything under the sun. They see each other for wonst a year. Probably a man losses his wife. There probably a woman gets a man or a man gets a woman. Dinnae believe they just change horses! I've seen many's a poor man loss in his wife at the berries. Many's a wife lossin her man at the berries as well as their horses.'

'Ah,' I said. I didnae believe him. But it was true. He was telling me the truth.

'And it's fine for the young anes,' he says, 'tae get in among their ain folk. There fights and there quarrels tae forbyes. And it's a dangerous place. Ye could get yirsel killt! You could get yirsel robbed, you could get yirsel stabbed to death. You could get a good horse or you could get a bad ane. But it's up to yirsel. I'm only tellin ye tae look out. But anyway . . .' This is the cracks Sandy tellt me walkin along the road to pass the time.

And Betsy, she's walking away behind smoking the fags. She smoked all day, she smoked nonstop. And she had this red hair away doon her back! She was a beautiful woman, beautiful when she was young. She wore this red hair and tied it with a ribbon at the back. But she was very soft spoken. She was Highland spoken and she was one of the greatest singers you ever heard in your life. Oh, she could sing like a bird! She sang everything under the sun, old Granny's songs, old ballads and old things that she . . . see, to go back a wee bit.

Sandy and Betsy were full cousins: Betsy's mother was my father's sister, and Betsy's father was my mother's brother. Well, my mother's brother was called up; he joined the Army in 1914 and was only eighteen years of age. He left his wife with one wee baby, only a year old. He joined up from Campbeltown in Kintyre. After his training he was taken to France, and he only landed in France when he was killed. Now, Betsy's mother was only a young lassie. She had a wee baby and her man was killed in action. To this day you can see his name on the stone in Furnace where I was born – Charles Townsley. A brother of my mother's. So Betsy's mother married again. But the old granny, my granny and my grandfather who took care o the baby when her father was killed in France, wouldnae let the child go wi the mother when she married again.

And the mother and father say to her, 'If you're goin to go wi another man, right, you're no gettin the baby.'

So Granny and Grandfather, they thought so much of the baby, they kept Betsy. Betsy was reared with them and they put her to school, taught her everything. And not only that – they had another two sisters there in Tarbert who had lost their husbands years before – my two aunties who stayed with their father and mother forbyes. Nellie and old Jeannie. They too loved the wee lassie. She was a wee totie lassie, two years old, and they wouldnae part with Betsy when her mother remarried. And everybody had to bring Betsy back something every day from the village. They only had to walk a short distance where they stayed in Tarbert. And they were well known, you know. He was old Willie Williamson, Uillium MacUillium, that's what they called him. And he spoke the Gaelic. He mended the floats for the fishermen's nets and he was a tinsmith. And he was a mushfeeker, a champion umbrella mender. He stayed on the rubbish tip and took care o the tip for thirty-seven years in Tarbert. He never got paid for it, but the laird let him stay there in the one bit wi his tent.

Now his wife, my granny, was only a young woman then when she had her family. You know what like travellers are, they have their family very quick: all in a minute they're young, and all in a minute they're old and grown up. My granny and grandfather were just a young couple, I would say in their late thirties, when my grandfather got this umbrella to mend. A brolly for Mrs Campbell in Tarbert.

She says, 'Willie, you'll take this umbrella home and you'll mend it for me.' Now it just shows you what like travellers were. This is the way the story went . . .

'All right,' said old Willie, 'I'll take it home.' And he was the most beautiful wee man you ever saw! He wasn't very big, but he had some big sons. He was only about five foot two, and he had red rosy cheeks, fair curly hair, and he wore this fisherman's jersey and a blue jacket. And he went up with this umbrella after he'd fixed it. He put a slide into it, new stems in it and fixed it beautifully. He went up with it to Mrs Campbell, gave her the umbrella and she was pleased about this! Umbrellas weren't easy things to buy in these days. And my granny, she's waiting at the road for him coming down. To mend an umbrella then was about two shillings. But she thought he was taking too long. Mrs Campbell asked old Willie in for a cup o tea. So he naturally went in. Not to insult the old woman he went in and took a cup o tea from her. Now Granny, she's waiting on the road. She waited and she waited and she waited, waited for about half an hour. No Willie. He was still in the house.

Now she believed in her mind there was something between Mrs Campbell and my grandfather. And when my grandfather finally came down, she flew at him like a bat from hell, told him that he was having an affair with Mrs Campbell. Now this was the story I'm going to tell you. Betsy was only four years old at this time. That was 1918. She was born in 1914, was four years old just when the war was finished. And I remember my granny and grandfather in 1937, that's when George VII came to the throne, I wasn't very old. And from that day in 1918 on to the day that she died my granny never slept with my grandfather again. She came home and built another tent to herself. She stayed across from him, she made her own meals and he made his own meals. And they sat and talked and they cracked, put young Betsy to her bed. She said, 'Good night, MacWilliam.' That's all she called him, all the days o her life she never called him anything else. 'Good night, MacWilliam, I'm off to my bed.' From that day on, and she was seventy-eight when she died, she never slept with him another day.

Now, to let you understand how Betsy was. Betsy was reared with these two old folk and put to school. And when she was eighteen my brother Sandy who was two years younger, only sixteen, came down to visit my granny and grandfather from Furnace to Tarbert. And he fell in with Betsy, and the two of them ran away together. Now, that's the story how it happened to them.

LADY MARGARET

O Lady Margaret she sat in her high chamber
She was sewin her silken seams,
She lookit east and she lookit west
And she saw those woods grow green.

So picking up her petticoat
Beneath her harlin gown,
And when she came to the merry green wood
It was there that she let them down.

For she had not pulled one nut, one nut
One nut nor scarcely three,
When the highest lord in all the countryside
Came a-riding through the trees.

He said, 'Why do you pull those nuts, those nuts?
How dare you bend those trees!
How dare you come to this merry green woods
Without the leave of me!'

She said, 'Wonst on time those woods were mine
Without a leave of yours,
And I can pull those nuts, those nuts
And I sure can bend those trees!'

So he took her gently by the hand
And he gently laid her down,
And when he had his will of her
He rose her up again.

She said, 'Now you've had your will of me
Come tell to me your name!
And if a baby I do have
I will call it the same.'

He said, 'I'm an earl's son from Carlisle
And I own all those woods so green,
But I was taken when I was young
By an evil Fairy Queen.

But,' he said, 'tomorrow night is Halloween
And all those nobles you can see,
And if you will come to the five-mile gate
It is there you can set me free.

O first there will come some dark, some dark
And then there will come some brown
But when there comes a milk-white steed
You must pull its rider down.

O first I'll turn to a wicked snake
And then to a lion so wild,
But hold me fast and fear me not
I'll be the father of your child.

And then I'll turn to a naked man,
O an angry man I'll be,
Just throw your mantle over me
And then you will have me free.'

So that night at the midnight hour
Lady Margaret made her way,
And when she came to the five-mile gate
She waited patiently.

O first there came some dark, some dark
And then there came some brown
But when there came a milk-white steed
She pulled its rider down.

O first he turned to a wicked snake
And then to a lion so wild,
She held him fast and feared him not
He'd be the father of her child.

Then he changed to a naked man
O an angry man was he,
She threw her mantle over him
And then she had him free.

Then cried the voice of the Fairy Queen
O an angry queen was she,
Saying 'If I had hae known yesterday
O what I know today,
I'd took out your very heart's blood
And put in a heart of clay.

So Lady Margaret on the white-milk steed
Lord William on a dapple grey,
With the bugle and the horn hanging down by their sides
It's merrily they rode away.

                                        Traditional

CHAPTER FIVE

GIE ME A HAUD O YIR HAND!

We had some messages in the pram and I had fags, and Betsy had fags. Sandy said, 'The best thing we can do is push on and get the tent up for the bairns. But there'll be a lot of traivellers there on the old road, and prob'ly we'll no even get a place for wir tent.' Now I thought this camp was only going to be a wee bit beside the road. I'd never met many travellers in my life.

But we landed and came into this camp. Sure enough, the first thing I saw was two gellies sitting. Now in these days the travellers built gellies summer and winter. The old travellers a long time ago built the barricade, like my father had – a round structure with a big place inside where the family could sit, and a hole in – the top and a fire in the centre; with wee tents or sleeping compartments built off to the sides. But after the war the travellers who came from Skye introduced the chimney, the fire can or 'tank and lum' inside the tent. There was no more need for this big high structure because a chimney drew the smoke. The gelly, so called for its shape like a ship's upturned galley, came into use – a straight tent, lower and longer with less room than the barricade. It caught less wind, had less headroom and the chimney came up through the centre. Now I had never seen one of these gellies before this time with my brother. There were two sitting together in the Knock Camp. Smoke coming up the chimney and the door in the centre. Up the road a little bit further were another two, with two carts sitting nearby, and another cart further down.

Sandy says to me, 'I ken that's yir cousin. That's yir cousin and yir auntie in that camp ower there.'

I said, 'Hoo do you ken?'

He says, 'I ken. And that's Hieland folk up the other road.'

He called them Hieland folk because they came from Skye or from Inverness-shire. They were great Gaelic speakers, and they had Gaelic cant forbyes. They had a different culture, a different way of life all together, different customs and different religion. The only thing was, they would never speak Gaelic among themselves if you were talking to them in their tent. I'll tell you a wee bit o what happened to me a short while after that.

While we were staying on the Knock Camp I went up to that Hieland folk's tent. There was a wee boy about two years old playing with a ball at the door of the gelly. I came up to crack to the folk, and they were mangin Gaelic back across to themselves. The wee boy flung the ball out and I caught it, threw it back to the wee boy and I said, 'Seo'. The boy caught it. And from that day on till the day I left that place, those people never mentioned another word o Gaelic. They thought then if they said anything, that I would be able to understand what they said. They knew, me being Highland-tongued like themselves, I was a real Gaelic speaker. They were ashamed, thought I may have known Gaelic better. They were very sensitive, believed if they said a word and didn't pronounce it right, maybe I knew it better.

So anyway, we pulled in and my brother says, 'We'll just put wir tent up there.' But we hadn't got the pram in and the dog tied to the fence – we tied old Jackie to keep him from going in the road – this was our livelihood, old Jackie, he was the boy for the pot. You had to take care o him. And here comes this young lad walking across. I'd never seen him before in my life. And Sandy introduced him.

'This is your cousin John,' he said to me. So the laddie shook hands with me. I noticed he had a bad eye, it was discoloured. Oh, the laddie was about the same age as me. He gave us a hand to put the tent up and in two minutes he and I went for sticks. We got the fire going, we sat and cracked and Betsy made some tea.

Then he says to me, 'You comin ower to see yir auntie?'

I felt kind o shan, ken, kind o droll. I said, 'Aye, I'll go and see my auntie.' So I said to Sandy, 'You've anything else you want?'

'No,' he said, 'brother, I'm okay. I'll get a pail o water to your sister Betsy.' He called her 'yir sister Betsy'. 'You go and crack to your auntie,' he said. 'I'll be ower later.'

So I said, 'Right, I'll come ower.' And I walked over. I felt a wee bit ashamed. I never had much to do among travellers really, except back among my own folk. So I came in, into this gelly. Oh, it was long, a good big tent! There were two sides in the tent, a table in it, and the thing that amazed me was the fire can in the middle with the chimney going up through the top. There were a heap of logs beside the fire. But there were no carpets; it was just the ground, grass. Because they were only going to stay for a short time. The grass was fine and dry with the heat of the fire. I thought it was really beautiful inside. They had a lamp, a Tilley lamp going. So John introduced me.

He said, 'This is your auntie. This is my sister and this is my brother.'

There were two brothers and two sisters, a family of four. My auntie had lost her man in 1939 and she took care o all this family herself. He took rheumatic fever with fishing for pearl, and he died in Dundee when he was only thirty-three. And his baby daughter was only nine months old. But my auntie, I looked at her for the first time in my life. She had long, dark hair away down her back. She looked to be like something out of a gypsy picture. She wasn't dark in the skin, but to her last days she was a beautiful woman.

But anyway, we got talking and cracking, and she asked me how my mother was and how my father was. 'How many brothers and sisters have you got noo?' And she tellt me, 'It's a long time since I've seen your mother and father. The last time I was there we'd only the oldest laddie there, Charlie. He was only an infant. But I always promised to take the boys tae Argyll for a summer to see their cousins.' She was my mother's cousin, forbyes she was my mother's brother's wife.

I said, 'That's right enough.' But me and my auntie hit it off very well. We got on very fine and I felt at home with her. We sat and cracked and had some tea.

My cousin said to me, 'Come on, I'm going up to shift my horse.' Oh, now this is more in my line!

So we go up the old road, and there were three horses. John's horse was tied to the fence. Beautiful chestnut pony, nice. It wasn't big but it was beautiful. And then there was a white horse and an old thick, fat horse.

He says to me, 'Do you like horses?'

I said, 'I like horses. Horses is my life.' I started to tell him the story about back home, the wee farms in Argyllshire and the horses my father used to work. I said, 'How long've you had horses?'

He said, 'I cannae remember when I didnae have a horse. I've had them all the days of my life.' And he was horsie moich. He cracked and tellt me all these stories about horses. 'And that one there, that's Hieland folk's fae Skye, that old white horse. But that old thick horse, that's a guid auld horse. But he's old.' Little knowing that he was going to own it very shortly. 'But,' he said, 'whaur are ye makin fir?'

'Well,' I said, 'cousin, I'll tell ye. This is the first time in my life I've ever been in Perthshire. And my brother Sandy tellt me all aboot Blairgowrie.'

'Ah,' he said, 'it's a long time till Blairgowrie yet.'

I said, 'Are ye goin?'

'Oh, I always go,' he said, 'for a wee while. For the odds o seein it, to say I was there. But, brother, there's an awfae travellers there, an awfae horses and swappin and dealin. And fightin and arguin all hoors o the night. You never get much peace. My mother disnae like it very much. She's too feart o us gettin into trouble.' But he was an awfae nice laddie and I liked him an awful lot. He says, 'Come on back doon.'

We went back down and we sat in my brother Sandy's camp for a while. Then he says, 'Come on ower to my mother's for a while. You're no goin to yir bed yet?'

'No, I'm no going to bed.' I said, 'Bed disnae mean nothing to me.' So we sat and cracked and talked. I was telling him about Argyllshire and fishing and hunting for shellfish, and all this carry on. He was telling me these cracks.

And Auntie says to me, 'Can you read?'

'Oh, Auntie, I can read all right!' I said.

She says, 'John can read.' But he had a wee bit hesitation in his speech, a stutter. 'But,' she said, 'the rest o them cannae read. You wouldnae care to read me a wee bit story?' she said to me.

Oh I felt shan! I said, 'What kind o story?'

'Well, that laddie,' she says, 'that cousin o yours is mad on cowboy books.' Westerns. 'And,' she said, 'he reads me a bit sometimes. But you wouldnae like to read me a wee bit story?'

'Oh,' I said, 'Auntie, I'll read ye a wee bit story all right.'

So she went up, and stuck in the tent cover was a blue book. I remember it fine. It was a hard cover, a cowboy story. She says, 'I'll make some tea.'

So I sat and read and read, read out loud to her. She really enjoyed it. She made me tea. Oh, that was done a lot among the travellers. See, they didn't have any wireless or anything in these days.

Auntie says, 'You're a good reader.'

'Ach well, Auntie, I'm no really good.' I said. They thought you were a good reader, ken, because she couldn't read or write herself. So I read on till about twelve o'clock. This story was *Smiling Frank Orio,* and she really loved it, about two twin sisters who owned this ranch and both of them were in love with this boy. I read on till everybody got sleepy, and I took the book and stuck it back up. 'I'll come back tomorrow night and finish it for you,' I said. And she thanked me very much.

By the time I got over to our tent, my brother Sandy was in bed. And his two wee kids were asleep. Betsy was lying smoking. Before she went to bed she always made her flowers. She never missed a night! Come hell or high water, she'd get these flowers made. And she could make that paper stretch like nobody else in the world could do it! Now me, I'll take a sheet of paper, and clip it the full length. But no her! She could cut that paper, and she knew what one sheet could make. If she was out one flower, she knew she had made a mistake.

The next morning Sandy was up early. He could see I was very interested with my cousin and his horse. My cousin John had tellt me he was going to the sale on Monday. While we were shifting the pony the day before we had talked.

John said, 'Look, do you ken where Balbrogie is? Brother, that's an old waste farm where your brother goes. And he stays in an old mill. It's an old house right enough. But, brother, it's miles frae the road. And it's two mile to the nearest shop. And you'll never see a soul. He works there. It's all right for him, but you're going to be bored stiff if you go there.'

I said, 'I've nae other choice. What can I dae?'

He said, 'Come along wi me. You can stay with me and my mother for a while.'

I said, 'I cannae dae that.'

'Aye,' he said. 'Be my mate for a while. I like your company. Come along wi me. Tell your brother Sandy you're no gaun.'

I said, 'He's gaunna be kind o upset. He's older 'n me.' But we made this plan up. I was going to tell Sandy the next morning I wasn't going to Balbeggie.

That next morning Sandy said to me, 'Well, brother, I'm making off, on my way to Balbeggie.' He took his tent down, packed his pram, got his things, said goodbye to his auntie. He always came by to say goodbye to his aunt when they were at a camp together.

He said to me, 'You gaun?'

I said, 'Brother, I'm no gaun.'

He said, 'What?'

'I'm no gaun,' I said. 'I'm gaunna stay wi my cousin John here for a while.' He was a bit upset.

'Well, you ken I promised your faither,' he said, 'I would take care o ye and bring ye back safe.'

'I can take care o masel,' I said. 'I'll come and see ye for a while later. John kens where ye are. I'm able to look after masel noo.'

'Well, look,' he said. 'Will you make me a promise before you go?' He never tried to keep me back, but he wasn't very well pleased. He said, 'If you're hame before me, back in Furnace. I'll prob'ly no be back till the summertime again, next summer. Or, prob'ly Betsy's gaunnae hae another wean before that time.' And he made a wee laugh about it . . . but it really did happen. Because every baby Betsy had, she would go back to Campbeltown to have them. It didn't matter, suppose she was in Aberdeenshire, she would go back to Campbeltown. So, Sandy told me to behave myself. And he said, 'You know you're only a wee laddie away fae your father, and I promised to look after ye. Noo you're leavin me, and if you get back hame before me, mind and tell your father that you left me; I never left you.'

I said, 'Okay, brother, I'll dae that.'

'But stick wi your cousin John,' he said, 'and I'll tell you, what you dinna ken about horses, he'll learn ye. That laddie was among horses since he could creep.'

So we parted the best of friends. I said to Sandy, 'I'll come and see ye.' He went on his way to Balbrogie Farm. I was looking forward to the market on Monday. The market meant a great trade to the travellers.

Some travellers the week before had bought a horse, a young horse in the market. They broke it in, made it work and brought it back in the market to sell, swap or deal it away a week or two later. If they were kickers or biters, or they were lame, travellers fixed them up the best way they could. Maybe they had bought one ruined with worms; they cured it. If it was lame they fixed its feet. If there were anything wrong with it, it wasn't pleasing them, they took it back, cured it. It's the same idea today with motors. Only in the 1940s there were no regulations on horses. Anyone could buy a horse, own one. You didn't need to register it.

Cousin John really became my good pal, for all the years I knew him. We had our bit fight later, but he was a great friend to me and taught me an awful lot. So I felt ashamed, but it made my auntie quite happy those nights I was there to read her the stories. That Saturday night I sat and read the book to her the whole fairin night and finished it. She was quite happy. The next day, Sunday, John and I walked up the road to see the Highland travellers.

John said, 'Come on, we'll have a crack tae these Hieland folk.' There was a man in his late sixties and his son-in-law, and they had two gellies. They had a couple of good ponies. But they didn't have floats. It was Aberdeenshire spindled carts. John said, 'They're good carts. These folk'll no have floats because they dinnae like the rubber tyres.' When they got a puncture they couldn't fix them. Rubber tyres weren't very common in these days. The old man had a white horse and his son-in-law, a young man a wee bit older than us with a couple of kids, had an old, thick garron with a short tale. It was fat and it was smart-looking. John said, 'That's been among the travellers for a long, long while. That's a guid old horse that.' So we cracked to them for a while and they asked where I came from.

I told him, 'Argyllshire.'

And oh, the old man kent Argyllshire fine, 'Oh, years ago,

laddie I was doon that way,' he said. 'And round Fort William, roond by Oban and that.' The old man talked about Oban to me and I'd never been there in my life at that time. They came from Inverness. And Inverness to me then was foreign. But they were very nice folk. John asked them if they were going to the market.

'Oh,' he said, 'we'll go to the market all right. But we'll just go and see, we're no takin nae horses wi us.' But anyway, time passed by.

Monday morning. Cousin said to me, 'I'm takin my horse into market today.'

I said, 'Are ye gaun to sell it?'

'No,' I'm no goin tae sell it,' he says. 'I'll prob'ly swap it awa if I see something that suits me.'

So we yoked it up. Oh, I gave him a help and put the harness on it. Funny how light the harness was compared to the one I used to work with on the farm horses. John jumped up on the float, tellt me to jump up beside him. We drove into market. And his mother was coming, she was wanting off at the shop. We left her in the town. She said she was going to take the bus back. So we drove right into the main street. This wee pony could fairly go. It was as fat as a pig. It had a silver tail and mane and could fairly trot. It wasn't big, about thirteen hands. He went up these side streets and through this street, past the buses. Oh, I was amazed how he could handle this pony in among the traffic. We landed into the market. There was this big, long passageway and a big place on each side. It's still a market today, for sheep. Even the ring where they sell cattle today is still the same old horse market. In the 1940s horses came from all over. There were horses came on a Friday, Saturday and a Sunday from Inverness, from Killin, from all over the country. They came by truck. And there was a special man in the market who fed, watered and took care o them over the weekend to be ready for the sale on Monday. And then the men came to buy horses for slaughter. Nobody would give a damn, ken. You could buy it and send it for killing just as if you were killing a sheep or a cow at this present moment. There were no restrictions of any kind! Some of the most beautiful horses you ever saw went for horse meat. John tried to explain this to me.

I said, 'There should be a law against it.'

'No,' he says to me, 'you can dae nothing; there's nae law against it.'

You could buy them at six a penny and sell them, turn them over in the same day for slaughter. And they were killed, young horses, foals, colts, anything went for meat. I felt ashamed at this. I wished I could have bought the whole bloody lot. So we loosened John's horse out and he tied it up, took the harness off and flung it on top of his wee float. It was early, nine o'clock in the morning.

He said, 'They'll no be many folk in yet.' There were a couple of travellers with ponies, but they were standing cracking to each other. John said hello to them. But I didn't speak to anybody I didn't know. So John says, 'Eh, I'll have a walk up tae these pens.' They were like cattle pens full of ponies! There were stalls of ponies downstairs and upstairs, double-decker. There were piebalds and donkeys of all description. Then there was a part just for the Clydesdales, colts and then mares – I never saw so many horses in all my life! So he says to me, 'I'll have a walk here and see if I can see onything that suits me. You have a walk up. The sale'll be startin in a wee while.'

So I walked up and down and I came back to where John's pony was tied. It was okay. He had flung a handful of hay to it, it was eating off the top of the float. And here's these two traveller men. They must have bought a carry-out, because the pubs weren't open. And they were standing trying to deal with each other. Now I didn't want to interfere.

I didn't know the men from Adam, but I wanted to listen to see what they were doing. This one was a wee bit older than the other, a man maybe in his fifties. And the younger one would have been in his thirties. But I kent they were travellers the way they carried on, with their weather-beaten faces and their clothes a wee bit disorderly.

He says, 'Come on then! Jump up and gie me a bit hurl and see what it can dae.' I stepped back. Now he had this pony yoked into a wee float and he jumped up on the float and pulled the reins up! The other man jumped up on the other side and he drove it away up to the top of the pen, whirled it round and drove it right back down. He stopped, jumped off.

'Now,' he says, 'does that please ye? Wha' dae ye think noo?'

'Oh aye,' the man says, 'it's no bad, no bad. But, he, it's a wee bit wee for me.'

'Aye, it might be a wee bit wee for ye, but it's young,' he says, 'and I'm needin the money.' And then they started arguing. I could hear some of the words but not them all. 'Well,' he said, 'are ye interested or are ye no interested? Tell me the truth – dinnae waste ma time.'

The young man says, 'I'm interested in it.'

'Well, come on, hoo can me and you deal?' he said. 'I'm needin the price o a drink!'

'Well,' he said 'ye've seen mine.' Now I'm standing against the wall, you see, smoking this fag. And the men thought I was maybe a country laddie.* They never paid attention to me, because I was clean and tidy. I always went that way when I was young. There never was a day I didn't wash myself and keep myself clean. I always carried spare clothes.

The old man said, 'Gie me a haud o yir hand then, laddie!' And the lad held out his hand. This is a pantomime, funny to me. Now I'd have given the world if my cousin could have come, so's he could have translated to me what was going on. I couldn't see him, no way. But I'm listening. He said, 'Gie me a haud o yir hand!' So he catcht the young man's hand. 'Come on. If ye're really interested,' he says, 'in this, I'll tell you what I'll dae wi ye. [SLAP] Gie me five pound and yir yoke fir mine, straight through, one for each other.'

'No,' the laddie says, 'no! I couldnae dae it, I couldnae gie ye five pound.'

'Well, let me hear ye!' he said. 'A biddin man's a buyin man. Let me see, what do you think?'

'Well,' the young man said, 'I havenae much money, but I'll tell ye what I'll dae wi ye. Haud yir hand! I'll [SLAP] I'll gie ye three pound aboot, and yokes.'

The old man says, 'No. No, no! No, it's nae good.'

'Well,' he says, 'that's aa I can dae. I cannae go another penny, I havenae got it.' The old man walked up and he hemmed and hawed again. And I saw by the way he was walking up and down he definitely had something on his mind. So he walked back

---

* country laddie – non-traveller young man

again and they stood and cracked. And they started arguing about some problem. I didn't want to get involved.

But then the old man catcht him, 'Come here, then!' he says. 'Come here, dinnae go awa like that. You bid me three and I asked you five. Come on [SLAP] gie me four pound and we'll call it a deal!'

The young man said, 'No, I never gied a man in my life what he asked for.' He said to the old man, 'Haud yir hand.' Now this is queer to me. I was as if at this present day sitting watching television, all exciting to me. I had never seen this before. He said, 'I'll split the difference wi ye – I'll gie ye three pound ten and I wouldnae gie ye another penny as a swap aboot and yokes! One for each other.'

The old man says, 'Right. Put it there!' [SPIT] And he spit in his hand. [SLAP] And they made a deal. Now,' he says, 'come on.'

He paid him three pound and across the street to the pub. It was just opened and they walked across.

'Well,' I said to myself, 'I never saw something like that!' Now I want to tell my cousin about this. But by the time I walk up here I meet him at this pen, and he's aside this pony. He was looking around this pony in a wee pen to itself. It wasn't a heavy-built horse. It was light made, but it wasn't thin. He's lifting its feet and chapping its feet with his hand. I came up and leaned over the top of the gate. The gates weren't very high, just so the horses couldn't jump out. 'Well, did you get something that you fancy?' I said.

And he looked up. 'Oh, it's you.'

I said, 'Aye.'

He said, 'Whaur were ye?'

'I was doon there. I saw a couple of travellers and they were swappin horses.'

'Ach, they're always at it,' he said. 'You've never seen nothing yet. It's no started yet.

'The queerest folk in the world,' I said, 'John.'

He said, 'What was queer?'

I said, 'They were slapping each others' hands, spittin and slappin.'

'That's their dealin,' he says. 'That's their deal. These folk, that's their bond. They cannae read or write and there nae pen and paper with them. The're nae bill o sales or nothing. That's what they dae. Once their deal's made that's it! There's no comin back with them. He'll prob'ly go into the pub and drink that three pound ten.' I had tellt John about the deal. He said, 'I hope you didnae interfere with them.'

'No-o-o,' I said. 'I didnae interfere, I didnae ken nothing aboot them, what they were doin. I was only a bystander.' In fact, I wasn't even supposed to be listening to them. See, travellers are a queer lot. It they were having a deal with each other they hated anybody to listen in, especially if you owned a horse. Because if you already knew how much the man had got and what the horse was costing him, then it was unfair if he tried to swap you this horse to yours. So it was a policy among travellers if you saw somebody dealing, you turned your back or walked away, didn't interfere. It was none of your business. That's why they actually pulled each other aside. It's the same at the present moment. If you're going to deal with somebody about a motor you don't deal in the open, but quietly, so's nobody's going to ken. If somebody overhears what I buy a thing for, they're not going to give me a profit onto it. But they weren't so hard against country folk,* a traveller man and a country man dealing. Travellers liked to see them dealing, although they wouldn't interfere. They liked to see the reaction of the country man against the traveller, and the traveller pitting his wits against the country man. I've seen many's a time when two men could not reach a deal. A traveller man standing by would come up.

He'd say to the man, 'Well, are you finished?'

He would reply, 'Well, I could dae nothing with him.'

Now he would say, 'Are you sure you're finished?' He would ask twice.

And the traveller man would say, 'Well, you go ahead. I'm finished wi him, I can dae nothing with him.'

Then the other traveller would come in and say, 'Well, if you cannae deal with him, how about me and you haein a bit trade?' It started all over again. That could go on for five or six folk before a deal was made.

---

* country folk – non-traveller people

But anyway, I said to my cousin, 'You got something?'

'I like this horse,' he says, 'an awfae lot. It's no very old, but it's been workin. I think it's broken in. But I ken the man that owns it. He's been at me once or twice, but I haena seen him yet. He's prob'ly knocking about.'

'Oh,' I said, 'I wouldna ken him.'

'No, you'll no ken him,' he says. 'But were you up at the ring? I think the sale's started.'

I said, 'No, I wasn't up at the ring.'

'You go up there and take the first door to your right, and,' he said, 'gae in there. You'll see a big ring full of sawdust and you'll see all the folk, and a lot of seats. Go in there and pass the time. I'll search and listen to them getting sellt. You've never seen a horse getting sellt?'

I said, 'No, I've never seen a horse gettin sellt before in my life.'

'Eh, and I'll have a wee bit walk up, aboot,' John says. 'This is what I'm interested in, this horse here. I'll no be buyin naething in the ring. If I dinnae get this ane I'll prob'ly keep my ain. Did you see plenty horses noo?'

'Oh,' I said, 'I've seen plenty horses, you've nae idea.'

'Pro'bly half of them you've seen today'll go for slaughter,' he said. 'Half of these beautiful horses . . . But dinnae be too long because I'm goin for a cup of tea. Come back in a wee while. If I dinnae see you I'll come lookin for you.'

I said, 'Right.' So this is strange to me. I walked up and I met this man. He had this hankie tied around his neck. I didn't know he was a dealer. He had red boots on him and a whip in his hand. I said, 'Eh, whaur are they sellin the horses, mister?' And he looked at me. 'Whaur are they sellin the horses aboot?'

He said, 'Are ye interested?'

I said, 'Aye, I'm interested.'

He said, 'Can I sell ye something?'

I said, 'No. I want to see where they're selling the horses in the ring.'

He said, 'Go in that door to your left there, first door, gae in and you'll get the ring.'

As I walked in the people called 'runners' were running the

horses around the ring. A young laddie went to the stall, took the horse out and ran it round the ring so's that everybody could see it. There was a big high railing all around. The horse couldn't get near you, or you near the horse. The seats were high up, built like a picture hall. But the seats were built behind each other so's you werenae in each other's road. You could also stand round the railing in the front to get as close to the animal as possible. There were women in riding breeches, there were lassies and there were men, old men, people with books in their hands with catalogues, with all the horses listed and all the numbers. There were horse dealers and travellers galore, all round this ring watching these ponies getting sellt.

As I landed in, in came this horse. Oh, it was a beautiful pony. I didn't know much about horses then, but it was a pony about fourteen hands, a piebald, black and white, a mare. And this laddie was running her round. I wished I had had money. Now the auctioneer sat up on a high stool and he had a wooden mallet. There was a form in front of him and a table. Now I had never heard an auctioneer selling horses before in my life. I got in, I crushed into this wee space close to the fence. And I'm leaning over. This laddie about fifteen or sixteen ran this pony round, trying to make it run.

Then the auctioneer started, 'Come on now, ladies and gentlemen, now! Here we are. Here's a nice four-year-old piebald mare. Warranteed sound. Free from vice, free from all road traffic. Work in single or double harness.' It was really broken in for everything. 'And very quiet with children, and quiet in the saddle. What am I bid for her, then? What am I bid? Any advance on fifteen pound?'

This old man I was watching had a newspaper in his hand. He held up the paper, ken, that's what they did.

'I'm bid sixteen pound. Sixteen pound I'm bid, sixteen pound. I am bid sixteen pound.'

And another man in another corner, 'Seventeen pound.'

'Seventeen pound, seventeen pound I'm bid. I'm bid seventeen pound.' And then he went on from seventeen to eighteen, 'Eighteen pound I'm bid, eighteen I'm bid, any advance on eighteen pound? At eighteen pound!' Chap with his mallet. 'Sold at eighteen pound.' And that was dear at eighteen pound.

I'd wished I'd had that money, I'd have bought that horse. I thought to my ownself, when I worked on the farm back in Argyllshire it would have taken me nearly six months at half a crown a day to get eighteen pound. So I watched more ponies getting sellt and I'm fascinated. They're all ponies. The dearest horse there that day was about twenty-six pound. There were mares and foals, there were Shetlands, there were donkeys. They were going for very little, but it was a lot of money then.

So I said, 'I think I'll go and look for my cousin John.' I walked back out the door and down I went. I met him standing with this wee gadgie, a man. He wasn't very big, about five foot. He had the clearest blue eyes I ever saw in my life. He looked straight at me and John introduced me.

'This is my cousin from Argyllshire.'

And the wee man said to me, 'Have you any ponies?'

'No,' I said, 'I have no ponies, sir. I've nae ponies.'

'No,' John said, 'this is the first time he's ever been in market in his life. He disnae have any ponies.'

He says to me, 'How are the ponies selling? Were you in the ring?'

I said, 'I didna ken hoo they're sellin. They're no very dear. They're goin very cheap.'

He said, 'What do you call cheap?'

'Well,' I said, 'I saw a beautiful pony gettin sellt for eighteen pound.'

He said, 'That's kind o dear.'

John tellt him, 'This is my cousin from Argyll, and this is his first time in the market. Eh, he disna ken very much about horses. He's stayin with me for a while.' So he and John talked. But he was the best looking wee man ever I saw in my life. And he was so civil and so nicely spoken. You could take to him right away. And he had this hankie, this tartan, what they called a 'muffler' tied across his neck. But he wasn't a traveller. He was a country gadgie.

So he said to my cousin, 'Are ye interested in that pony?'

And he said, 'Aye, I'm quite interested.'

He said, 'Ye still got that wee chestnut yet?'

'I still have it yet,' he said, 'it's doon there.'

He said, 'Is it aye as good as it was, aye as fat as it was?'

'Aye, it is. Ye ken I always look after it,' he said, 'it's ae as fat as it was.'

'Well, this beast is no very old,' he said.

John said, 'I ken it's only four year old. Is it broken in?'

'Aye, well, it's workin onyway.' That's all he said, you couldn't guarantee any more than that. 'So eh,' he said, 'If you're interested, I'll prob'ly see ye after the sale. I've got a man to see. I'll prob'ly see you later on.'

So John says to me, 'Come on, we'll go down and get a cup o tea.' So we walked out of the maket and we had a cup of tea and a pie in a wee place further down. He says, 'What do you think of the sale noo then?'

'Oh, wheesht speakin,' I said, 'you've nae idea! It's fantastic. I've seen mair horses than I've ever seen in my life. And they're so cheap. If I had money I'd buy the whole bloody lot, everyone of them.'

He said, 'It'll go on tonight till about eleven o'clock. Most of those horses you've seen all go to get killed. These dealers come. But come on – we'll go back up and let me have a look, see what's gaun on.' So we go up to the ring, in through the same door. And by luck we got back to the same bit where I had been. Straight across from where we were was this man with a weather-beaten face. He was dark skinned. His hair had never been combed for weeks and he had this raggie coat on him. And every pony that came in, up goes his hand! He was bidding on every one, but he never bought any.

So I said to John, 'That gadgie ower there, John, he seems to be tryin to get a horse.'

'Brother, he's no tryin to get nae horse.' He said, 'I ken him well. He'll bid on every single pony there. He's jeein them up tae other folk. He kens what the owners o these horses want for them. You notice when it makes a certain price, he'll drop out. And he'll no pass that. That's what the owners want for the horse. If they want twenty pound, he'll drop out at eighteen, and he'll dae that aa day. After the horse is sellt the body belongin to the horse'll prob'ly gie him a pound, maybe ten shillings. He'll make hissel mebbe eight or nine pound for his day's work.'

I said, 'Is that no against the law?'

He said, 'It's no against the law, but if he's catcht at it he'll be banned from the sale. Naebody never seems tae bother.' So we sat and watched two or three horses getting sellt for a while, and he says, 'Come on. It's gettin kind o late. I'm no interested in nothing here onyway.' It was about one o'clock in the afternoon, and he said, 'I'd better go and see that wee gadgie.'

I said, 'You really gaunna put your pony awa?'

He said, 'I ken we've had it a while, and I could dae wi something a wee bit bigger.' So we came down back out, and when we landed by the stalls there were about fifteen or sixteen yokes o travellers all lined up. You never saw so many travellers in your life! Some of them were drunk, some women with horses, laddies with horses and lassies. And they're running them up and down, up and down. The old men standing with whips and they're hitting the horses, welting them up and down, not touching them, just cracking the whip to keep them running, so they could see that their legs weren't lame. Running them up and running them down and they're swapping and dealing, hitting hands. [SLAP] And they're out and in, back and forward into the pub.

I said, 'This is a pantomime!'

John said, 'This is their day! This is their life. This goes on every Monday. And this'll go on till late hours at night, and some of them start, come in here wi a good horse and they'll go home wi nothing. Some of them will come in here wi nothing and they'll go home wi a good horse. They'll swap and they'll deal and tomorrow morning they'll be sadder and wiser. But they'll still keep it goin, they'll still never forget. Some of them'll be burnt, some of them'll be roasted, some'll have a bad deal, some'll have a good deal. Some of them will fight, some o them will drink, some will have an argument. But tonight it will all be discussed back over the camp fire again. And some of them come from miles away to get here!'

So we came down, right at the pen where this pony was. Here was the wee man, this country gadgie, this horse dealer again. John spoke to him.

He says, 'Come on then, let me have a look at your pony. See if it's as good as ever it was the last time I seen it.' Now I didn't want to interfere. And the wee man said, 'Well, what do you think?'

'Well, I could dae wi your pony,' John said, 'and you could dae wi mine. I ken you could.'

'Well, how can we deal?' the wee man said to him.

My cousin said, 'Mine's in workin order. I dinna ken so much about yours, and it's kind o young, kind o poorly. It's no thin, but it's poorly. And I think I'll need five pound aboot fae ye.'

'Heh-heh-heh,' he said, 'no laddie! I doot no. You'll no get nae five pound aboot fae me.'

'Well,' John said, 'what do you think?'

He said, 'I was thinkin I'll gie ye three pound. Ye asked me five, I'll gie ye three.'

'Nah,' John said. 'No, I think mine's valuet a bit more 'n that.'

'Ah well, there nae harm done,' the man said. 'That's twice I've been at you for it, but I see you're no keen on puttin it awa. But I'm tellin you, that's a good pony. If you get it and keep it, it'll come into a good pony.' So they hemmed and hawed and they cracked a while longer.

Then John says, 'Come here. I'll tell you what I'll dae wi ye. Look, you bid me three; gie me four pound and we'll call it a deal!'

The wee man said, 'I'm no wantin yir cart and harness. I've got plenty at hame. No! I wouldnae gie ye four pound. Haud yir hand oot! Now this is the first time!'

I said, 'Here it goes again!'

He said, 'Come on, I'll gie ye three pound ten [SLAP] and my horse for yours.'

John says, 'Right, haud yir hand [SLAP] – done!'

'Noo,' he said, 'how're we going to work this?'

'Well,' John said, 'I'll tell ye what I'll dae wi ye. I'll take this pony, it's yir pony now and put it in your pen.'

The wee man said, 'Look, I've got a man to meet and I'll have to go, boys.' So he took the money out of his pocket and paid John three-pound-ten. And he said, 'Just put it in the pen where ye get yir ain ane oot.'

So John took the wee pony up, took out the other one, and put this one in. Then he pulled it. It wouldnae walk very easily; it wasn't walking very well. I came behind it and I hit it wi a bit rope on the hip, but it didn't seem to take any effect.

I said to myself. 'I doot yir gaunna be kind o slow, kind o lazy.' Because I began to understand then, I had a good idea. When I hit it on the hip, it pulled its bum into it, pulled its tail in. 'Oh,' I said to myself, 'you're no wicked, you're no a kicker nae way.' But I said to John, 'What do you think?'

'Oh,' he says. 'this is a good beast. It's a good pony. I've been after this pony for a while.' But it had the longest neck I ever saw in my life, a neck like a goose. But it was a good beast. He put the harness on it in two minutes. We yoked it up, put it in the cart, backed it in, pulled the float out and fastened it. He said, 'We'll lead it a wee bit through the toon in case it disna rein right.' So we led it down through the back streets out over the bridge on the main road to the camp.

He says to me, 'Jump up on the other side! And we'll see what it can dae.' So I jumped up beside him and he took the end of the reins. He skelped it. But nah, nah! It did a wee bit trot, ken, deedle-doddle, deedle-doddle, deedle-doddle, trotted on and on and on. It wasn't as fast as his other one. But he kept bragging, telling me how good it was and admiring it. I knew he was only building up his own idea. But it went fair enough with him. He went into the shop, bought me twenty fags and twenty fags to himself, and a book with the ten shilling. He kept three pound to bring back to his mother. But we made our way back to the old road, and we had to pass by the camp on the road coming in. His mother was in the tent making tea, boiling tatties or something. John tried to pull the pony's head up and hit it with the reins, make it prance coming to the camp to give it a good show. We never saw the two traveller folk, the Hieland man and his good-son in the sale, in the market. But John had introduced me to bings of travellers, people I had never seen before in my life. 'Some of them are yir ain relations,' he was telling me. And I had an exciting day. I'd seen things I never believed existed. I thought on my brother Sandy's words. And I really liked the market an awful lot. I made up my mind some day I was going to go back there when I had money of my own. But the thing was, all those years I was among horses for close on thirty years, I never bought a horse in a market in Perth. I bought them in Aberdeen and in Glasgow markets.

So, as I tellt you, we landed back to the camp, and it wasn't very far off the road where the tent was and his mother. She never even came out. She heard the horse's feet on the road. We pulled in, we loosened it out, took the harness off and we took it up to the front of the camp.

He says, 'Mother, come and see, what do you think of this?'

That's what she said, 'It's a nice pony, laddie, but I'll tell ye something, it's lazy.' She knew just by hearing its feet on the road. And John knew himself it was lazy. This was its complaint. That's why he only had it one night.

I'd like to tell you about this place where we were staying at that time. It was an old road about six miles the other side of Perth on the main road to Blairgowrie. It was owned by a farmer there and it was a right-away to his fields. But it went right up, if you followed it, an old cart road, an old drove road at one time going up to Scone and the aer'drome. The travellers had been staying there, och, for close on a hundred and fifty years. And there were four generations of this family who owned the farm. The travellers used to tie their horses to the fence, there was no place else. And you know when a horse has been tied up to a fence it pulls against the rope and slackens the posts, and sometimes they tangle up in the wire.

Somebody had remarked to the farmer at some time, it was told to me by someone, 'Why is it you tolerate these traveller people or tinkers on your old road up there, the access to your fields?'

'Well,' he says, 'they've been camping down that road before my time and I suppose they'll be there after I'm gone. But man, ye ken something, it would be a dull day for me if I would wake up some morning and look up that old road and never see a camp on it for a week. I'm so accustomed to seein tents on that old road that it would feel funny to me if they bypassed it.'

I think he really had a wee bit in mind, that if travellers did pass it by, it would be unlucky. There were certain camps that were open for travellers to stay on, but the travellers passed them by and said they were unlucky. Prob'ly he had got that idea in his head at one time, or his father before him.

So my cousin and I took the pony up the old road to tether it. The grass was beginning to come. It was late spring and the horse was able to pick enough to keep itself alive. In the two other camps were the family of Highland Stewarts with their two horses, a white one and a garron. We walked up the old road and the old man came out. He spoke to my cousin, but I never said much.

And he said, 'You got a strange face, laddie?' That's what they called a new horse.

My cousin said, 'Aye, I got a bit o a beast there.'

He said, 'It's a nice young horse that.'

And my cousin said, 'Oh aye, he should do well if he gets a bite o grass for the summer.'

We walked further up and tethered the pony in the best bit. The grass was eaten up with the folk shifting their horses up and down the old road. But the main thing was, when the grass was short you had to shift your horse more often. There were plenty of places, the road was long and it wasn't very broad, a fence on each side and access to the farmer's fields all the way up. So we walked back down and we looked at the two horses on the road passing.

I said, 'That's no two bad ponies.'

'Aye,' my cousin said, 'the old one, the old thick horse there would dae anybody's turn. But I'm not sae fond o the white ane.' It was still early in the evening. We came back and got some supper from my auntie. We sat and cracked for a while. John says, 'We'll go back up again and shift the pony. I always like to keep in touch wi a young horse, or a strange horse in case it gets its legs tangled up in the rope, because it might no be broken into the tether.' We walked up and shifted the pony. On the road back down the old man came out again from his camp.

He said to my cousin, 'Can I see you a minute? Youse busy, lads?'

We said, 'No, we're no busy, just shiftin the pony.'

He said, 'Eh, I ken you've only got that pony the day, but I took an awful notion tae it.'

And my cousin said, 'Were you no in the market yirsel?'

'Aye, I was in, but I didna stay very long.' He said, 'I just went in and cam back on the bus.' The buses passed every half hour on the road to Perth. 'But I've an awful notion tae that pony, laddie,' he said, 'and you wouldnae be puttin it awa would ye?'

'Ah well,' my cousin said, 'I only got it today but I'm no married tae it.' None of the travellers ever refused a deal. They never refused.

'Well,' the old man said, 'you've seen my pony there, that white pony. It's a bit poor, but if it was fattened up on the grass it would be a good horse.'

'Well,' says my cousin, 'you ken the old saying: no disregards to your horse, but a white horse is only worth white money.' And they laughed. This was all new to me. The old man didn't feel insulted in any way, he just took it as a joke.

'Well, laddie, I've got a notion tae your horse,' he said, 'how can me and you swap?'

'Old man, the best way we can! I've seen your horse and it's comin up a fair age.'

'Oh,' the old man said, 'it's nae youngster, but it's a good horse, it's a soond horse.'

'Ah,' my cousin said, 'a soond horse, aye, I can see that. Well, if you're willin to gie me, willin to have a deal, I'll take ten pound aboot fae ye and yir horse.'

'No,' said the old man, 'that you'll no dae!' So they talked and they hemmed and hawed for a bit, but there was nothing else. John stuck to his word and maybe he wasn't wanting to deal with the old man anyway, because he didn't like the white horse. They didn't barter much. The old man said, 'No, laddie, it's too much money for me. That ane I've got there's costin me too much, but I've got a guid float and harness.'

John said, 'A good float and harness never made a good horse.' Oh, he was up to all the tricks of the day, though he was only a young laddie. He knew it. He knew all the patter. But we were just standing cracking after that. They couldn't deal anything. Then a young man came walking up. It was the old man's son-in-law and he spoke a wee while, spoke about the market, asked us what the prices were. I never said anything because I didn't want to say something out of line.

He said to his father-in-law (and must have planned earlier between them, that the old man was going to have a deal), 'Do youse two no mak a bargain at all?'

'No,' the old man says, 'we cannae come to terms. He's askin me too much tae deal. But I like his pony.'

'Well,' John said, 'I asked him fair enough. That pony cost me a good bit masel.' And he tellt the young man, 'I asked him ten pound aboot.'

The young man said to him, 'You've seen my pony haven't you?'

'Aye,' John said, I've seen your pony. It's seen a few travellers.'

'Aye,' the young man said, 'It's been among a few travellers. It's been among wir family for a while too, for a long while. Well, I'll tell you what I'll do wi ye. You asked the old man ten pound aboot. I'll gie ye ten pound and my horse for that young horse you've got!'

'Well,' John said, 'you've never met a gamer man in your life! Ane horse is like another to me.' And before you could say 'Jack Robinson' the two of them hit hands [SLAP] and that was the deal made.

So the young man says to him, 'I'll just lea it where it is the noo.' But they had dealed horses and harness: he said, 'I'll need yours because my harness'll no be able to fit that.' it was heavy harness the lad had. 'But, mind, they're no a great set o harness.' My cousin's set was light and they wouldn't fit the big horse. It was a good, thick pony, a garron.

So he says, 'All right.' Old harness was cheap at that time, easy to pick up. You could pick up a set for about twenty-five shillings or two pound. So John said, 'I'll hae a look at your harness onyway.' So the lad took us down to his tent and his young woman came out. She was tall and had long braided hair down her back. She asked us for tea.

'No,' we said, 'we'll take a cup of tea, but we just had wir supper.' We didn't want to refuse the lass a cup of tea because it was a bad policy refusing a cup of tea from folk. They thought that you were thinking it wasn't good enough. She had a couple of wee weans running about. And the lad had his harness lying in below his cart.

So my cousin pulled them out. They were a workable set but not up to high standards. The old man had walked down with us to the lad's camp, and we'd kent by this time the young man was married on to the old man's daughter.

And he said to my cousin, 'Well, you finally got the old faithful.'

'Aye,' John said, 'I've got him.'

'Well,' the old man said, 'laddie, I'll tell you something, you'll never be stuck wi him. There's nae road lang enough for him. He'll tak you ony place you want to go. That's been along among wir family for a number o years, that old horse. And I fetched him doon fae Inverness masel.'

So my cousin said, 'Och, he'll dae me fine. We're on wir way. I was thinkin o movin tomorrow doon by Dundee anyway. We're goin down there for the summer. And prob'ly I'll no hae him that long anyway.' But, his words were wrong. Because John did have him for a good long while after that. He had him all that summer, all that winter and kept him till the following summer again.

The old man says, 'Well, we're thinkin o movin away up by Alyth and back by Blairgowrie. Knock aboot there till the berries is started.'

John said, 'It'll be a while afore the berries yet!'

'Ach, but,' he says, 'we'll get something tae dae.'

So John tellt the young man, 'Just lea the harness; I'll get your harness in the morning, but I'm keeping ma float.'

'Oh,' the lad says, 'I want to keep my ain wee cairt. I like my cairt best. Fine and handy for the bairns, they cannae faa oot with these rails roond the side.' A float was only flat, and the bairns might fall out. So we cracked for a long while about everything and we bade the laddie good night. We tellt him we'll see him in the morning.

So we came back home. We had some more tea in my auntie's place and I sat and read the Western book to her. And she was quite happy.

John tellt me, 'We're goin to Dundee. I heard that my auntie you've never met, my Uncle Sandy and Aunt Katie and them, they're aa bidin at the Hoolet's Neuk* at Dundee. We're movin doon there for a while. You'll have some o your ain friends there too.' He knew that wee Sandy Townsley was a cousin to my mother and also a cousin to my father. He said, 'You'll like it doon there fine. And you'll see plenty o horses there. The dealers come drivin up every Sunday for the sake o gettin swappin and dealin wi the travellers.'

---

* Hoolet's Neuk – Owl's Corner

So I felt good about this. I would have liked to see, get in among some other travellers for a while. Because I'd never had any opportunity before. But anyway, we got up early next morning. By the time we'd got up, the two Highland families had their tents and their carts packed and ready for the road. The horses weren't yoked, but they were standing with their harness on them. And I noticed that the old man had the young horse that he had tried to swap for that night before! And the son had the white one. But my cousin never asked any questions or anything. So we walked up to get his own horse, to get his harness.

And the old man said, 'We're pullin oot, but we didnae want tae go without biddin youse laddies good morning.' So they yoked their horses and pulled out on the road, bade us 'good day'. Away they went. And I never saw these folk again.

So we weren't long a-taking the old horse down. And oh, it was fat. It was really fat and strong. We put the old harness onto it. It just fitted his float and we packed it, covered it tip with the canvas cover. His two wee sisters jumped up on the side of the float and we walked along the road. I walked beside John and the other two walked behind the cart. Oh, this garron could travel. It was as fast at walking as some horses could trot. You couldn't hardly keep up to it.

My cousin said to me, 'Look, if you get tired . . .

I said, 'How far is it to Dundee?'

'Oh,' he said, 'we'll no prob'ly go the length o Dundee tonight. We'll go the length o Invergowrie. It's a good bit along the road, anyway.' There was no bypass then. You had to go right through the village and in the middle was a great big green. The travellers could stay there. For twenty-four hours you were allowed to camp. So he says to me, 'If you get tired, you can aye jump up and get a hurl . . .'

I said, 'No me, I wouldnae feel fit to sit on the top of the float.' So we travelled on and we stopped along the way and made some tea. We travelled on to Invergowrie and stayed on the green. The next day we made our way to the Hoolet's Neuk.

The Golden Vanity

'I have a ship, she sails on the sea
And she goes by the name of *The Golden Vanity*
But I doubt she'll be sunk by a Spanish galley
As I sail by the lowlands low, low,
I sail by the lowlands low.'

Up stepped the cabin boy, a well-spoke lad was he
Sayin, 'Captain, o captain, o what would ye gie
If the Spanish galley would trouble ye no more
As you sail by the lowlands low, low,
You sail by the lowlands low?'

'Great gold I would gie, and silver in store
My pretty little daughter who waits by the shore
If the Spanish galley would trouble me no more
As I sail round the lowlands low, low,
I sail round the lowlands low.'

Straightaway the cabin boy bared his breast and dived in
He held in his hand an auger sharp and thin
He held in his hand an auger sharp and thin
He went swimming in the lowlands low, low,
He went swimming in the lowlands low.

He bored and he bored, he bored once or twice
While some were playing cards and some were playing dice
The water it rushed in and it dazzled in their eyes
And he sank them in the lowlands low, low,
He sank them in the lowlands low.

He swam and he swam crying 'Captain take me in,
I am drowning in the lowlands low, low,
I am drowning in the lowlands low.

Throw me a rope, a rope,' cried he,
'O a rope, o a rope, you will never get from me
For you have sunk the dark girl, the Turk of Admiree
You have sunk her in the lowlands low, low,
You have sunk her in the lowlands low.'

He swam to the starboard side crying, 'Messmates take me in,
I am drowning in the lowlands low, low,
I am drowning in the lowlands low.'

They threw him a rope, his messmates brought him in
Then they wrapt him in that old cowskin
Then they wrapt him in that old cowskin
And they sank him in the lowlands low, low,
They sank him in the lowlands low.

                                        Traditional

Chapter Six

The Hoolet's Neuk

I'll always remember that time, that journey to Dundee with my cousin and his mother and his little family on our way to the Hoolet's Neuk. Especially in Dundee, the largest town I'd ever seen. The thing that excited me most of all was the tram cars. When they started hissing along the main street it seemed strange, something out of a dream. Then there were the horses, so many horses, coalmen's carts, carters of all description, rag-and-bone men, stick carts and fish carts.

I asked my cousin, 'There must be an awful travellers about this place?'

'Well,' he said, 'in the toon itself there's a lot of travellers. But they're mostly all dealers, horse dealers.' In the early 1940s there must have been between one hundred-fifty to two hundred in Dundee. They weren't all travellers. They swapped and dealed with travellers. When a traveller was needing a deal he just drove into Dundee. If he went to one dealer and didn't get a swap, something to suit him, all he needed to do was go two streets down to someone else.

I said to my cousin, 'Have we far to go?'

'Well,' he says, 'we could take a roundabout, but seein you huvnae seen much o a big town, I'll take you right through. Because I'll prob'ly be leaving my mother in the toon. She'll stay in Dundee and then follow on.' That was the usual thing among the travelling people. When the women came to a town they never went on to the camping place. They stayed behind and did their bit hawking in the town, saved them making a double journey.

So we travelled through Dundee, and this was great, tram cars, horses and men selling brickets. I swore to myself someday I was going to go on one of these tram cars – how they used to flee along the street with the sparks coming from the wire at the top!

I asked my cousin, 'Did ye ever travel on one of these things?'

'Aye,' he said. 'They're cheap things to travel on.' And this railway, the lines were on the street, and all these streets were cobbled. 'But,' John says, 'these cobbles are no very good on the horse's feet, because if a horse stays too long on them it gets cobble-beat, sore feet. I've got them often and they go lame with walking too much on the cobble. Once they're a while out in the country, get on the grass, it goes away.' The horses hooves were stunned with walking on the hard cobbles steadily. It affected the tendons in their feet. There were many's a dealing man made an excuse.

If a horse was really sore and he tellt you, 'Oh, it's just cobble-beat. It'll be okay, laddie, once it's away a while off the cobbles.' But it could have had a real complaint. They were always up to all these tricks! Anyway, we had our journey to make, through the main street of Dundee, right up the hillock Hilton, right out to the place they called the Hoolet's Neuk.

'There,' my cousin says, 'we're going to stay for the winter. There's a farm where they've got a lot of work.' Travellers shawed the farmer's turnips and he gave them a camping place for the winter. While they were working they could put their horses in the farmer's field. But the reason travellers gathered there was that all the horse dealers came up from Dundee on the weekends. There they swapped and dealed on Sundays among horses.

If a dealer was needing a swap he would just say, 'Och, we'll drive out to the tinkers' camping place and see what they've got about them.' I remember one Sunday later while I was there, five horse dealers came out wanting swapping and dealing. Each dealer kept seven, eight, maybe nine horses at a time. He didn't keep them in his stables; but had them in fields further along. Maybe he had one or two on hand and hired a field from the farmer, kept nine running outside. Every dealer had his own wee bit of farm where he could run the horses he couldn't stable in his place.

We travelled right out to a place called the Murroes, then through Moncraigie and on to the Hoolet's Neuk. This is the first place I ever met my mother's cousin Sandy Townsley, wee Sapps. He and his wife, my auntie's sister, were there. And then there was my auntie's other younger sister and her son. He had lost his father when he was young too. And he had a white horse, a beautiful pony, the first horse I ever drove. But that's later on in my story.

So we landed on the Hoolet's Neuk that night and everybody made us welcome. There were about seven camps, seven gellies, for seven families, and everyone had horses. Wee Rabbie Townsley was there and Galen's grandfather, John Townsley. All their horses were running loose in the field. They were all working at the turnips. This farmer didn't have work for everybody, but he didn't mind if you stayed on his ground if you went to work for somebody else. As long as somebody was working for him, he didn't bother. Actually he didn't own the camping place, but we could stay as long as he didn't complain to the police. In these days, far different from now, the landowner just had to phone the police and then you were shifted right away.

I said to my cousin, 'This is a nice place to stay.'

He said, 'Aye, we'll stay here for a while.' We put up our gelly and we drove down to the farmer for some straw. That was the thing most hard to get in these days, straw for your bed. You carried a big tick with you and just filled it with straw to make a mattress. Because you couldn't carry a mattress in a wee cart. And even suppose you did carry one, and then put it on the ground, once it was soaking, the next day it'd be no use to you. You'd have to chuck it away. So the travellers in these days just got fresh straw wherever they went from place to place; they filled a new mattress which was little trouble to them. All they needed to do when they shifted the next day was just shake it out and put a match to it.

After I gave my cousin a help to put up his tent, got the horse tethered out, got some sticks and did all our bits of work around the place to make it ready for my auntie coming home – she came home on the bus later from Dundee that evening, after she had got her messages in the town – I wanted to go round and speak to everybody. I was excited! When I was back home I'd never seen many travellers in one place. So I went round all the traveller camps, one after each other and got to know everybody. And in turn when they went to see their horses I went with them, admired and inspected – there were black horses, white ones, big ones and wee ones, Shetland ponies, about seven or eight. The most interesting person I met there was my mother's cousin's boy, just about my age. He had lost his father when he was only five or six years old. Charlie (Buggy) Reid and I got off just like two peas and later I was to spend at least seven years with him.

The next day, Sunday, was when the dealers came up from Dundee. This was their main day, their great day because they knew they would get all the travellers in. Nobody was working or doing anything. What the travellers used to do there on a Sunday, and they knew the dealers were coming; apart a good bit from the camps, away from where the women were cooking or washing the bairns or sorting the clothes or anything, they would kindle a big fire. And then all the men would gather round this big fire, crack about things. Then when a man drove up with a horse and cart he would loosen his pony out, and instead of going to the camps he would come to the fire! And stand and crack or talk at the fire. Maybe somebody would invite him in later for a cup of tea to one of the tents. He knew he wouldn't be hungry being there all day. I've seen them coming up and staying the whole day, the local country men. I've seen one coming up with a horse, swapping that horse away, and he'd get one of the travellers' horses. Then somebody else would swap him and he would get another traveller's horse! Then somebody else would swap him again and he'd get another horse. There was always a few shillings changing hands. And as sure as heavens before he landed home that night, he was back with his own horse before he left! So this is where the dealing went on, round the fire. Perhaps he came for a deal and he couldn't swap, couldn't get a deal. But then, an hour later somebody else would drive in, somebody from the other end of Dundee who wasn't a traveller at all, and these two men would deal at the travellers' fire! It was a meeting place for the whole area.

Now these travellers didn't keep their horses just for swapping and dealing. A tinker's horse had to work. In these days travellers used the horse for hawking. They gathered rags, but they never gathered much scrap iron with a horse. Very few gathered scrap. But they hawked handmade baskets and flowers. And the thing was, in the big towns you could sell anything in these days. There were second-hand shops where you could sell clothes and boots and even books. There were so many of the local cadger folk in the town of Dundee itself, who hawked the town and sold to these small premises, that the people in the town were completely cleaned out. They didn't have anything else to give. This is where the traveller gained an advantage. They had their horses and could yoke a pony in the morning, drive to Forfar and drive away down to Letham. And they could hawk the country and collect all the junk in the country, bring it back and sell it in Dundee at the weekends. They never actually hawked Dundee itself, because there were so many small hawkers around it wasn't worth their while. It was nothing for a man to rise in the morning, and his wife, yoke a pony and drive twenty miles in the morning and twenty miles home hawking that way. She hawked the houses and he did too, and they collected every single thing. They collected dishes, they collected boots and books, and they sold flowers, they sold baskets and they sold scrubbers. There wasn't any tin-making at that time there. The tin-making finished just as the war started. Tin was very scarce to get and that stopped all the tinsmiths. But the horses were most important.

If a man was broke and he didn't have any money, but he had a horse, he said to his wife, 'Well, there's nae use o you gaun oot the day. I'll go doon tae Dundee and I'll maybe get a deal.' As long as a traveller had a horse he never was broke, never stuck. This was always a trade to them. But the thing was, he never would sell it outright. But he would swap, swap to anything as long as it could walk on two legs. Because he knew there was always somebody would give him one that was worse than his. And he would always have to get some money along with it, money to boot.

And travellers loved their horses, but they never got really attached to them, like you would a pet. They were kind to them, treated them on the best. At that time I did think to myself, 'If I ever own a horse, the first horse I get I'll never part with it; I'm going to keep it all the days of my life.' But when I got my first horse I only had it about twenty-four hours till I swapped it away again.

It was also the way with travellers that they would not swap with their relations, their own family. If the horse had something wrong with it, he wouldn't give it to you if he thought it might not work or might break down in another couple of days. But they would give it to the dealer because the dealer would do it on them. They didn't have any feelings for the dealer, but they had feelings for their own traveller folk. You wouldn't give a horse to a traveller with a couple of kids, who might have given you his last penny about. Then he might try to yoke it, and it's going lame with him, and he's going to shift the next day. You had horses that wouldn't pull, horses that would kick the cart or horses that would run away, horses that couldn't eat, and you had some that wouldn't lie down and they were always tired. The travellers knew all these complaints. And even suppose they knew that these horses had complaints, they would still swap to get them! (Because they knew in their own mind they were going to pass them on to somebody else.)

The very next day after arriving at the Hoolet's Neuk, my cousin said to me, 'It's all right for them there, they've all got a wee bit something to dae. But how about me and you goin lookin for a bit job?'

I said, 'Fine! That would be all right.'

He said, 'We'll go and look for some turnips to shaw.' In these days shawing turnips by hand was a great thing among the travellers. They did a lot of this work, picking up the turnips, cutting the shaws and the roots off, putting them in rows so the farmer could lift and drive them out for the cattle. Now it's all done by machine, but in the 1940s it was all done by hand. So we went and got a field of turnips from this farmer. And you made a bargain.

The farmer said, 'Well, what can I do for ye?'

'Well, sir,' I said, 'we're looking for a bit job o shawin turnips.'

'Oh yeah, oh that I'm needin. Can you shaw turnips?'

'Oh aye.'

'Where are you stayin?'

'We're staying up in the tents in the Hoolet's Neuk and some o wir friends is workin tae the farmer there and there no enough work for everybody, so we're huntin for a bit job of wir own.'

'Oh yes. Have you shawed neeps and turnips before?'

'Oh, we've shawed turnips all wir life!' And the farmers knew the travellers were the greatest at this job because they'd done this all their days. But it was a bargain. Yellow turnips which had a small root, you did them a penny cheaper. And then you got the swede turnip, they had a big root and you got a penny extra for doing these. So the travellers were cute.

The farmer would say, 'Well, what do you charge?'

'Well, we usually do them by the hundred yards.' At that time we were getting four pence, so you had to do three hundred yards for a shilling. If you put four hundred-yard drills together and made a row of turnips, then the cart could come up the side and the farmer could load them in. But the bargain was, 'We'll do them for a shilling if you give us some hay for the horse!' You had to get the hay.

The farmer would say, 'Okay, we'll give you some hay for your horse.' Now in these days there were no balers for baling hay. There were stacks of hay all over the place. Every field was filled with the best of hay. The farmer would tell the travellers, 'Oh, yes, there a stack, go and help yourself. Take some hay!'

Now they would go and take some hay. But they wouldn't go back again and take any more of this hay where they got permission. They would go to another farm where they weren't working at night-time and help themselves to as much as they wanted – steal it! And feed their horses. Oh, I've done it myself!

Then if anybody, the police came and said the farmer missed his hay, somebody was stealing it, we'd say, 'Oh, we didn't steal any hay.'

'Where dae you get yir hay for yir horses?'

'We get it on the farm where we're working. As much as we want.'

And the police would drive down to the farmer and say, 'Are you missing any hay? Are the tinker people, travelling people stealing your hay?'

'No,' he says, 'I gev them permission tae take hay, and there been nobody here since they came. I tellt them to help theirselves, and they've hardly ever took a drop o hay frae me. It's there for them if they want it. They work for me and can have as much as they want.'

But what sense would it be taking all his hay when there was so much going about for nothing, for the taking of it? We could have taken his hay, as much as we wanted. But these other farmers wouldn't give you any at all, they wouldn't even sell it to you! We never made too much of a good thing. We did take some of his hay now and again for an excuse, in case the other farmers we took it from would kick up hell and phone the police. But remember, keeping four or five horses off one stack of hay would soon have gone down, got finished in very little time. Where would we have been then? And we did share it out with those who didn't have enough.

So my cousin and I started shawing turnips and we shawed all week. The farmer was very pleased and he gave us plenty of hay! My cousin then said to me, 'I'll have to go to Dundee. I would like to have a walk down through the rest of the dealers. Do you want to come along?'

In 1943 when I was there in Dundee there must have been, at least, close on four hundred horses on the street, four hundred people working with horses. The co-operative had horses for the delivery of milk. Then there were the coalmen, there were people selling brickets, people selling firewood and there were others who just kept horses for dealing alone. There were rag-and-bone men. There were people collecting, hawking in the streets in Dundee. And it was nothing to see, going into a rag store in an evening, fifteen, sixteen or eighteen horses yoked, lined up tail to nose waiting to get served. All these horses and all these wee dealers in the town. They came from all neuks and crannies. And my cousin took me to all these places. He said, 'We'll go to such-and-such a place, we'll see such-and-such a man here.' He took me all these wee back places, the wee stables at corners – you've no idea the corners and hideouts where they kept their horses! They had loose boxes in here and wee stables in this place, and round these corners, up these wee streets – all had these horses. Some had two, some had three. They had one for work and the orra one for swapping and dealing with. This is what brought all the travellers here. Because it didn't matter what kind of horse you took into Dundee, you could have a deal before you went back that night.

I remember wee Rabbie Townsley. He had a pony, a fat

Shetland. It was as broad as it was long. But it was lazy, lazy as could be! And this man came up on a Sunday and he had a beautiful horse. It was a hackney, a trotting horse. And everybody saw it coming – you could see up the road in the distance because it was a long strait before you came to the camping place. There were no hedges or anything. And the idea was, when the dealers came near the camps, they put the horses going as hard as they could so the travellers could see.

They looked and said, 'God, there's a horse comin. Look at the way that can go, the way he's goin! And he's comin in here.' They would say to themselves, 'Well, if I can have a swap for him, I'll get hit!' So this man came in, and his horse, head in the air. He was pulling it back on the reins, a high stepper. He drove into the camping part.

'Well, boys!'

'Aye.'

'Nice day!'

'Oh, yeah, great day.' Oh, this great big fire, camp fire going outside.

He looked all around, 'Ye got many beasts aboot yese the now?'

'Oh, we've two or three here.' Then they swarted to swap. Everybody wanted this horse! But no. Some of them offered money, five and six pounds with their horses. Some of them tried to deal with him. But no. He had a look round every horse that he came up to. And wee Rabbie Townsley had this fat Shetland pony. It was like a block of wood. And I knew Rabbie in his own mind thought there was no way in the world this man was going to take this Shetland from him. So everybody tried their best to get a swap and deal with him; nobody could deal. This fast trotting horse. And the travellers liked a trotting, fast horse, because it was a means of getting there and getting back! Cousin John tried. No, he couldn't have a deal. So Rabbie was standing near the fire and he had this wee horse. Black Shetland.

So the dealer turns round and says, 'Wha belangs tae the wee bit Sheltie, the thick Sheltie there?'

'Oh,' we said, 'that wee mannie there, that chap, his tent's up the road there.'

'Man, that's a braw bit o beast that,' he says. 'It's a braw Sheltie.'
You wouldn't see it, was that small! He must have needed it for
some purpose. He had a mark for it. 'Man,' he said, 'I like that
wee pony.'

'Well, if you like it, there's the chap belangin to it.' Wee
Rabbie came wandering over, his pipe stuck in his mouth. I
can remember him fine. When Rabbie was young he had the
bonniest head of curly hair you ever saw in your life. Beautiful
curls! Rabbie came, smoking his pipe, walked over to the man
by the fire. And he was admiring this great trotting horse that
everybody had tried to deal for.

The man said, 'Is it you that belangs tae the bit Shelt, Rab?'

'Aye,' he said, 'it's me. Aye, that's my wee bit pony there. It's
no much, really, an old dottlin thing.'

'Aye,' he said, 'I dinna ken, it's a braw wee Sheltie. What would
ye be seekin for the likes o that? What kind o money would ye
be wantin in it?'

'Oh,' Rab said, 'I couldnae sell it. I couldna lea masel stuck
without a horse. I wouldnae sell it. I would swap, but I wouldnae
sell.' And swapping Rabbie's horse was like swapping a mini for
a Rolls Royce. And all the travellers were there. The man had
turned down some good horses. But he wouldn't take any else.
This was a surprise to everybody.

'Well,' he says, 'what do ye think o that beast I've got there?
That's a guid bit o trottin horse, that would dae ye a turn. It's
quiet and it can trot for fun.'

'Oh,' Rabbie said, 'maister, I ken by the looks o it, I've seen it
comin in the road there. It can really trot. That's a guid beast
that. I could dae wi a beast like that, but I could never, I'd never
hae the money tae buy that.'

'Well,' he says, 'maybe we could hae a bit o a deal.'

'Oh,' Rabbie said, 'no, maister, I couldnae deal wi you, no wi
the horse I've got. Ye'll be needin too much for that.'

'Nah, man,' he says, 'I wouldnae be sayin that.'

'Well,' Rabbie says, 'what kind o deal will ye want? I've nae money
tae gie ye. And I ken yir horse is a lot better than mine.'

'Well,' he said, 'I've taken a notion to that wee beastie o yirs,
man.' This was a man Kelby from Dundee. 'And I think, how
do you say, we'll take one for each other?'

Well,' Rabbie said, 'fair enough. If that's what you want, I'll gie ye one for each other. But I've nae money aboot to gie ye. I'll gie ye a level swap.'

'Well,' he said, 'we'll call it a level swap,' and they [SLAP] hit hands and that was the deal made. So the man went and got Rabbie's beautiful wee pony, fat and thick, but it was young, yoked it on his float. And he went away walking with it home to Dundee. Now all the travellers were gathered round Rabbie.

'Rabbie,' they said, 'by Christ, you've got, by God you've got a horse this time, Robert! That horse can trot. Did you see the way it was comin in there?'

'Oh,' Rabbie said, 'it's a guid beast, a guid horse. That man must be a wee bit moich, giein me a horse like that for that wee bit Shetland. Well, them that wants it noo can hae it. I can swap onybody here that wants it noo!' But no, he never had a deal.

So next morning Rabbie couldn't wait to get it yoked. And he made all the excuses to go for sticks – there were plenty of sticks at the camp already – but he wanted to drive with it. And he put the horse in the cart. It couldn't walk! It was that lame it couldn't even take a step. It was beautiful, a topper o a horse. Whatever way the dealer had doctored it up, its two front feet were just as if they were boiled – it had founder in both feet. Rabbie should have known right away. But it was standing in the long grass when the man bragged it up. And poor Rabbie lost his pony that day. Rabbie could have checked on it. Everybody was so excited, but everybody was fooled.

A horse that's foundered, if you start off with it, it goes lame till it heats up. Once you go for a couple of miles the pain goes away from its feet. But once it stands the night, the next morning it can't walk.

If travellers went to a yard for a swap and they saw the horse that interested them . . . you see, travellers in their own minds were very, very cute, especially among country folk, among the country dealers. The average non-traveller dealer thought he was cute, but the travellers could buy and sell them at every corner! Especially when they went into a place where a dealer had three or four horses, and they wanted a special one. They had a look around and the minute they saw the horse – they were like Indians – this horse they would never go near, never try to swap for it. They would pick some other one, and try and barter or deal for it. And when they couldn't come to a deal they'd turn round and say to the man, 'Well, what about this ane here?' The one they were interested in would be the last one they would come to, even suppose there were six horses in the stable.

Some travellers bred horses themselves. They kept mares, a special one and they bred foals off it. But the only snag that bothered travellers was when a mare foaled. They had to stay in the one place with this mare until the foal was able to walk. A young foal couldn't walk on the road, and the mother full of milk. She couldn't work and couldn't walk on the road because the foal needed to have a suck every now and again. So the natural thing was to take the mare to a farmer's field and let her run there for about four or five months till the foal's feet got hard. When a wee foal is born it's feet are only soft. You couldn't expect it to walk on the hard road, wear its wee hooves away.

And travellers would sit up with a mare the whole night when she was going to foal. They would kindle a big outside fire and tie the mare as close as they could. They would sit up till it foaled. The least disturbance, the least movement the mare would make, they would go up to her. And they would keep this great big fire on.

Other travellers again wouldn't take a mare in foal, no way, because it was too much burden, too much bother. I mind on one traveller man getting a mare in foal, and when the mare foaled, he put it in a bag and drowned it. Like a pup. He couldn't do anything else. It was illegal to yoke the mare when it was foaled. You could work it right up to the end till it was just about foaling. But after, you had to get some place to put the two horses.

But oh dear, dear, dear, the dealing among them! Some of these non-traveller dealers, the country folk did nothing else but deal in horses. That was their trade. And it was a great thing in their life to burn you. They took enjoyment out of getting the best of a deal. It's not that they held any animosity against you, and they didn't want to be tricky against you. But it was a code never to get the worst o a bad deal. And these non-traveller horse dealers tried their best to get the best of the traveller. I've been through it, I've had my burns as well as the rest of them. I've paid for my learning along the way.

I mind a wee tale about this old traveller man who went to the market with this horse. He met this well-known dealer. And it was a nice horse he had, a beautiful horse. But these two had always been at each other for having a deal every time they met, and they always tried to get the best o each other. So they finally had a swap, and they had a deal on the road. This old traveller man gave this horse dealer his horse, and he got a horse and got some money to boot. So after the old traveller man had the deal, one of the men came up to the dealer.

He says to him, 'By God, Bob, the old tinker finally fixed you today. You finally had a bit swap with him, he finally set you back today a bit.'

'What do you mean about that?' he said.

He said, 'You didnae get the best o him the day anyway.'

'Ach aye, I got the best o him, man!'

He said, 'It's no a bad bit beast you got, but you didnae get the best o him!'

'And what makes you think that?'

He said, 'I ken that horse you got fae him.'

'Dae ye?'

'Aye, I ken it.'

'Man,' he said, 'I got a good pony there. The ane I gied him is blind in the ane ee.'

'Aye,' he said, 'I ken it's blind in ane ee, but that ane he gied you is blind in baith! Now that the God's truth! I've seen that horse. That's a pit pony. That horse is blind in baith een.' It was stone blind. That was big Bob Forsyth. By Christ he got him on that one!

And they walked about, this gold watch and chain across their breast, ye ken, this gold eldrin hanging down. They always had this whip in their hand, the horse dealers. And this scarf had to be tied. It didn't matter who it was, this hankie was tied to the side of their neck, like a cowboy's bandana, but folded in like a scarf. The horse dealers never went without a red polkadot bandana around their necks. God, they were queer! just common men, family folk, the natural everyday man. But that was their life, horse dealing. And they would go far and near. It was the patter, the tale they built up about this beast and what it could do. Where they got it and what it came off. You've no idea! Who had it before them and how it could trot, all this carry on. Oh, I ran in with some of the best of them.

Old Mickey from the Star of Markinch. He could look through a horse, x-ray it with his eyes from tail to head. Some of them were really good, you know. You couldn't cheat them, no way. They could look at it, just see it standing or walking, and every complaint the horse had, ringbone or spavins, any complaint it had from tail to end they could tell you. I knew Mickey for about thirty years. He was ninety when he died. I spent a lot of time with him and I had many's a deal with him. He told me a wee story.

He told me he left Fife, where he stayed all his days, and went to Aberdeen to the sale. In these days there weren't lorries or transportation to take horses back. They walked any horses they got all the way back by road. And he bought nine in the Aberdeen sale. Now it takes a bit of doing to walk nine horses from Aberdeen to Fife. And he put them into a field at night. (Any farmer would let you turn your horses into a field for the night.) And he had a coat on, it was the summertime, he just lay down in the hedge. Then took them on the road next morning again. And he came to this old man and woman, a tinker's camp at the roadside, a wee bow tent. It was the morning, he had just come out of the field. Between Aberdeen and Stonehaven, Old Mickey tellt me this himself, and och sure, I could let you hear it with his son!

Mickey said, 'I was hungry. I would have given anything for a cup o tea, for a drink o tea. So I came to this wee camp. There were an old man and his wife, and they had a donkey and float. The old man came out. He'd seen me coming with these nine horses. They tied them tail to nose, led them all along the road. He stopped me on the road.'

He said, 'Ye're kind o early on the road Mister Mickey.' He kent him.

'Aye,' he said, 'early on the road.'

He said, 'By God, you've got a handful there.'

'Aye, a wee handful. I've got a long road to go, I've got to go to the Coaltown of Balgonie in Fife. But I'll tell ye something, has your wife ony tea?'

'Well, Mister Mickey,' he said, 'I'm just getting the fire kindled. And I'll come, I'll gie ye a hand wi your horses.'

'So we took all the horses and tied them to the hedge. And he took me in to make me some tea. I was badly needin it tae. And this bloody donkey! He had this bloody donkey, was a curse to me! So he gied me a good breakfast, a good tea. But he wanted a swap wi a donkey. So I had a braw wee pony, a wee Sheltie, the wee-est one of the lot. He had nae money. But I kent the old soul well. So he wanted a swap to the donkey. Noo I could barely refuse him after him giein me such a good breakfast in the morning. But havin a donkey wi eight horses on the road wasnae for me! Well, I said, "Look," I tellt him straight, "you keep yir donkey! And tak that wee horse for the tea."'

Aye, old Tam told me that. He gave him his horse for his tea. But fifty shillings, three pound, five pound was the price of them then. I remember myself, I went to this farm over at Lochgelly, and all the money I had was fifteen pound. And I bought a two-year-old Clydesdale colt. And I knew I needed a pound for my messages. I got in touch with this farmer. I turned my pockets outside in to him and gave him a story. I left with that Clydesdale colt, and I had it for five years. I reared it up and it came into a beautiful animal.

I said, 'Look, there all the money I have.' I had one pound hidden in my shoe, for I was needing it for my messages that night. I said to him, 'Look, if you find another penny in my pocket . . . you can have everything I've got for that horse.' Now it took me about an hour to deal with this farmer. I said, 'You can have everything that I've got within my possession if you'll give me that colt!'

And he says, 'It's a deal.' And his foreman was with him. I turned my pockets outside in. I counted my money, I had fourteen pound. He says, 'Laddie, I couldnae dae it for fourteen pound.'

His foreman said, 'Look, you tellt the laddie you'd take every penny he had, and he's giein ye everything he's got!' And honest to God, I got it. Five years I had that horse. I took it to the market after that and sold it for thirty-six pound when I was finished with it. I used it, kept it a long, long time. And it was the only horse in my life I never tied up, wherever I went. It belonged to Edith, she was a wee lassie at that time, my first-born daughter. That's why I hung on to him so long. Edith could do anything with him. I'd sellt my pony the day before that for sixteen pound. I'd spent a pound for some messages, and I had the fifteen to go looking for a horse the next day. I got this beautiful colt, but it was unbroken, never was harnessed. Edith was about three years old, that was 1952.

But that winter when I was fifteen was one of the best I've had in my entire life. In the Hoolet's Neuk in 1943. We wanted for nothing and there was plenty work to do. You had plenty camps to visit and plenty ceilidhs, plenty cracking and storytelling going on. Rabbie Townsley was a masterpiece at telling stories. It was good times there. And then you could walk to Dundee if you felt like walking for the pictures at night-time. But we never bothered going very often. Then there were the horses, the most important thing. You could go and yoke a horse anytime you felt like it and go for sticks. So I'd say, 'Lend me your horse till I go for some sticks.' Or if somebody yoked up and they were going some place, driving up to a cowp for sticks or driving to the town, going out hawking, you just jumped in the first cart.

I remember the first day I got to go with a horse myself. It was my mother's cousin Jeannie, her laddie. Charlie had a white horse and everybody was away out hawking. He and I were left and we didn't have any fags. I thought 'If I had a horse . . . it's a good bit.' The first wee shop was down in the Murroes, about three miles away.

He says, 'Take my horse and go for fags.' Now I could yoke a horse or drive a working horse, but I had never had the experience of driving a trotting horse on the road myself on a gig or a trap. And it was a trap with high wheels. We yoked this white horse and he lent it to me to go to the shop.

It was about three months from the time I'd left my father and mother at Furnace, from the time Sandy tellt me about traveller laddies having their own horses, driving their own horses on the road. And I was really interested because I wanted a horse. A horse to a traveller laddie then was just the way a car is for a boy nowadays. Having a horse of your own gave you the feeling that you were growing up, you were getting somewhere. But Charlie really used the horse to shift with his mother, for his mother's stuff, because he stayed with her and his sister. I was to spend another year with him after that. And he and I became great pals, great friends. We still are to this day.

And then I had to get a shot of Charlie's horse again to go for sticks. And every time I wanted to go somewhere, I got a loan of it.

I was gaining the experience, because someday I hoped to have one of my own. Everyone there at the Hoolet's Neuk had a horse, as I've said. They were all running in the fields, and you could go and help feed them, groom and brush them. And there were always other strange folk coming in with horses at the weekends looking for swaps and dealing. Not that you'd interfere when anybody went to have a bit swap or a deal, but we always gathered round this big fire and you heard what went on.

So there was plenty work to do there. It was a great winter, you always had a few shillings. You shawed neeps to the farmer. And the women were making a good living with the wooden flowers. These were a great go then and I learned to make them. You cut the elderberry into short lengths and peeled it, then heated it in the fire. Then you got an awfully sharp knife and made petals on the pieces of wood. The heart of elderberry is very soft and the women used to sit in the evening and make two or three dozen. The men would give them a help sometimes if there were nothing else to do, but it was mostly a woman's job to make these flowers. Some were really good at them. They were white, like carnations.

The women would get dye, put it in a pot with hot water, and then dip these flowers. Sometimes only the petals, the points of the flowers, and sometimes the whole flower. Then they'd put them in a basket to dry, and they carried them in the basket to the town. They went to some house or a woman in the town.

They said to her, 'Can I have some o yir privet?' The green privet. They picked the long stems and stuck the points into the soft hearts of the flowers. They just looked so real.

Well, there was such a good trade with these flowers. There's some folk making them yet. The sale of these flowers is as good today as it was then. Even with the plastic flowers in the market, all shapes of them, a lot of folk prefer the wooden flowers.

Then they would yoke their horse and drive for elderberry. You had some places you had to steal it, because the forests were private where the elderberry grew. You had to be careful where you cut it! It wasn't good for anything, only a bush! And the travellers would never destroy bushes. They would cut the wee straight bits in the middle of the bushes. They wouldn't slaughter the plant to get this elderberry. And the people who had houses in Dundee would come out to the country, some cycled out with a wee bag on their back to get elderberry for making flowers. The traveller women were getting six pence each selling them. I've seen them going to the town with five dozen apiece. Well, sometimes they gave them away for things too. It depended. If they wanted to they would sell them fast for money. Six dozen at six pence each, you could imagine how much foodstuffs you could buy for that eighteen shillings then!

And the thing was, the women bought the same amount each time they went to town, see what I mean! The average woman today may say, 'I bought enough of this thing yesterday so I don't need it today.' But the traveller women never did that. Seven days a week they bought the same thing. It doesn't matter how much was left, how much they bought the day before. Whatever was left at home, the kids who were at home or the men could use it up. That was it. And they had to wait until the women came home the next day.

Well, sometimes they bartered. They went through these second-hand shops. In these times we had rationing for five years after the war finished here in this country. And a lot of things were scarce. Clothes weren't scarce, but you needed coupons for them, and you only got a certain amount. So the traveller women traded the flowers for clothes and for old shoes. They collected them for about two or three hours, carrying them. And then they went to a certain place and picked all the best of them, put them in pairs. They had a brush and they gave them a bit clean up. Then they would go to a cobbler and sell the shoes, all in one day! Well, you see, two or three women always went together. If they camped together, maybe five women left the camp in the morning. They never took any buses or anything. They walked to the village. Maybe a man would walk with them for company if it was a wearying road. He maybe brought back a couple of pints of milk or a pack of fags to them who were at home. Because when they left in the morning about eight or nine o'clock, it was four or five o'clock before they came home at night.

If they had a big family, one of the older grown-up weans watched the younger children and the men went out and hawked with the women. The father went with his cart and hawked. But he would prob'ly save his stuff up for the end of the week. Well, the women never went anywhere on a Saturday. The man would prob'ly drive to the scrap store on a Saturday morning and sell his quota, whatever he got. And he would give her enough money to see her over the weekend. He kept the rest in his pocket. And she started on the Monday again. The women always supplied the foodstuffs, unless times were hard. If they were on the road moving, shifting, and the women had to stay on the cart and look after the weans, well, when it came late at night the man would give her a couple of pound for messages. Only in an emergency would he give her money. If she was able to look for it that day, she had to go and do it. She either had to sell baskets or sell laces, it was up to her to take care of the family – provide messages and things through the week, get food and get clothes. But not every woman! There were some of the men better at it than the women. Whoever was good at it did it.

In my time, when all the travellers camped together, I saw six or seven of us at home at the camp. We would sit at home and make baskets or make flowers, or else go out with the pony and gather old stuff (non-ferrous metals), gather rags and scrap and that, or go away looking for a swap or a deal with the horse to get a few pound. But the women still went to the houses. And if they got good clothes when they were collecting, if the clothes suited their family or suited their man, they brought them back. They would never sell anything that was good for their family. So these were the things I was learning, forbyes being there, at the Hoolet's Neuk.

While we were staying at the Hoolet's Neuk, it was not unusual for some of us to drive our carts for twenty miles in the morning and twenty miles home at night to shaw neeps on a farm. We brought back hay and tatties. Usually somebody would pick the fastest horse then and drive to the town and pick up the women, bring them home with the cart before it got dark. We were there all through Christmas and New Year.

Mostly all travellers in that time liked to sit down some place for the winter. I remember there were four or five weans going to school from the Hoolet's Neuk. And I remember some of them took diphtheria and the officer came up and fumigated the tents. But it was only mild cases. They took them to hospital, but they didn't stay in very long. There was no disaster like it was in those outbreaks earlier on. But the Hoolet's Neuk was a regular camping place. When we moved off, people who had been somewhere else for their winter moved onto the camp for their spring coming in. And they would stay there for a few months. That was the change! Well, people who had been at the Hoolet's Neuk for the winter moved up to Forfar and Angus, and had their spring in there, a new district. Even suppose the new travellers who moved in were doing the same thing, the same work.

One of the many jobs I learned to do there was the tattie baskets. At that time there were no tattie lifting machines, and all the tatties were gathered by hand. And there were no plastic tattie baskets. It was wire, chain-like netting baskets. And the carts went over them, people sat on them, tramped and flattened them. Well, the traveller men would go with their pony to the farm, collect them, ask the farmer, 'Have you any wire baskets needin fixed?'

The farmer would say, 'Oh, I've a great big heap o them.' And they would pack them all on their cart, drive them home. Then they would sit and straighten all these baskets out, put aluminium paint on them, and pack them into dozens. Take them back to the farmer and get three, maybe four pound a dozen for sorting these baskets. Now this was a great run, went on for years and years.

And then, they made a lot of laces. Travellers were great at making leather laces. Because you couldn't get leather ones during and shortly after the war. There were a lot of miners in places. And you know their pit boots, working boots, were hard leather. And the travellers used to go to the old dumps, old places where they collected all these old boots, maybe in the old shoemaker shops. And especially in farm places where the boots were hard; you needed hard leather. They cut these round circles off the side of the boot, spun them out and made leather laces with them. I've seen an old man sitting one night making fourteen dozen. Fourteen dozen pair of leather laces! And his wife sold them for a sixpence a pair. She never came back with one. But you see the thing about the leather laces – you could hawk anywhere with them – start off leaving home and walk to the town, hawk all the wee cottar houses along the roadsides. They were the best, because the cottar men needed the leather laces for their boots. And I learned how to make the laces, how to sort these wire baskets, and I gained a good education of traveller survival while I was at the Hoolet's Neuk. I was able to mend these baskets because I sat and saw it getting done.

And then watching the traveller men shoeing their own horses. They went to the blacksmith shop and they collected old cast shoes that would come off somebody else's horse. And they knew the size of their pony's feet. They would take them back. But first go to the man and say, 'Give me a sixpence-worth o nails, horseshoe nails.' And there were some travellers very clever at it. Willie Cameron was the greatest ever you saw, as good as any blacksmith. They had their own foot knife for cutting a horse's feet. See, they had to look after these horses, clean their feet, clean the frog at their foot and clean their hooves. That was an offence in these days. The police or the cruelty inspector of animals could stop you at any time, check your horse's feet. It didn't make any difference what kind of shoe was on, as long as the horse's feet were covered. But woe be to you if you were gotten going too far! It was all right to take a horse, say, two mile with its bare foot on the road, till ye walked him to the smiddie. But if you walked that horse too far, then its hoof would get so short that it wouldn't hold a shoe, because it wore down into the quick. Then you had to go and put it into a field. That was you left without a horse, till its hoof grew again.

Now, horses that had been running on the rough ground were very easily caught. A shoe could catch on a wire fence and get pulled off. I've had them pulled off with wires myself many times, pieces of wire lying on the ground and old fences the horse was stepping over. The least loose bit or loose nail would catch, and the horse's foot got stuck. Well, it had to pull, and it pulled off the shoe.

I remember me, a long time ago on the top of the Rest-and-be-Thankful. This was many years later. I came late at night with a pony and the kids on the top of the float. I was making to Dunoon. I rose up in the morning and my pony had cast a shoe – barefoot. And you know the nearest blacksmith from there was in the Cardross – twenty-eight mile away. Now I knew that horse was never going to make it with its bare foot. So I cut an old rubber tube, a trick I had seen done before, the inside tube of a tyre. I made a real complete shoe for a horse's foot. Not like a horse's shoe, but just a kind of boot, drilled holes in it and put a string and tied a lace round it, round the horse's fetlock. That horse went from there, that twenty-eight mile, and we landed at the blacksmith's shop, its hoof not even marked. That's the truth.

And the blacksmith says to me, 'I've never seen that done.'

'Well,' I said. 'I came fae the top of the Rest and Be Thankful wi that horse like that.' I was told how to do this there at the Hoolet's Neuk by some of the old travellers.

You learned all these things because you never knew in your life when they were going to stand you in good stead later on. I learned many's a thing. Like yoking horses and how to put harness on a kicking horse. You can put harness on a kicking horse, but if you get too near behind it, you're going to get kicked. Now you had to put on a crupper, a strap that goes under the horse's tail to keep the breeching and saddle in place. Otherwise, when the horse went downhill, the shafts of the cart shoved the saddle up over the horse's neck – there was nothing to hold it back from sliding forward. Now, horses didn't like cruppers on their tails. They didn't hurt, because they were padded. But if you didn't know how to stand in the right position, you'd get your leg broken, kicked.

Then you had horses that kicked the cart whenever you yoked them. We had a kicking horse there and it was a pantomime to see it getting yoked every morning! They could kick clean, kick the floor boards right out of the cart and never hurt themselves, because they knew how to kick with their shoes. They were dangerous, you know, very dangerous. Travellers didn't mind a good kicking horse. But they didn't like a biter! You could watch a kicker, but you could never watch a biter! I've seen in my time, dealing among travellers among horses, a man who owned a biting horse. A man asked him for a swap.

He said, 'No, no, I wouldnae give ye that horse even suppose you gie me ten times its worth. Because I couldnae sleep at night if I thought it would bite some o your weans.' But if it was an old man and woman who didnae have any weans, he would tell the old man, 'Mind, ye'll have tae watch it because it'll bite ye!' It would turn around and snap you. You could never trust them. If you went to feed them, especially if they were hungry, they didn't just nip you. I was bit often by horses. It's like getting a red-hot brand, like a piece of hot steel touching your hand when it nips you. They didn't break your skin. But a real biter can take a big lump out of your flesh with one bite because they've got powerful teeth, a horse. So you had to learn all these things.

Then you had to learn the tricks, the tricks among the dealing men. You saw it happening with them all, the things they got up to. The travellers in these days, only some could afford good horses, really good horses. When I mean a good horse, I mean one costing forty-five, fifty pound. Now I knew some travellers in these days who bought horses for twenty-five shillings, two pound ten and three pound ten. These were cast horses. Well, they got them off the pits, cast out the pits. And they got them off pig carts, men feeding pigs. Pigmen kept a lot of horses for carrying the swill. But you could never trust a pigman's horse! It didn't matter what kind of horse it was, he always kept it fat with feeding it the swill, cabbage leaves and everything he got. Even suppose it didn't have a tooth, it was always fat. The travellers would get them from pigmen, and oh, a horse was in beautiful condition. But after the travellers had it for about three weeks or a month, it would go in like a balloon because it wasn't getting the same meat. And it couldn't eat grass.

They called some horses a 'mummy', meaning mouth, bad mouth. Well, their front teeth grew too long in the front with age, and the back ones couldn't close. A horse's back teeth grind. It pulls with the front ones and chews with the back.

The mummy just half rumbled food around its mouth and tried to swallow the grass. It got poorer and poorer and poorer. Then they would take the horse to the blacksmith's shop and get their teeth filed down. But it was a sore thing on a horse, filing the front teeth down. It wasn't every smith would do it. It helped the horse a lot, but within another two or three month they just grew again. There wasn't a cure for it. It was just old age. You've heard the expression, 'You're gettin kind o long in the tooth.' That's where it came from, the horse gettin up in years. You never got a horse with bad teeth from the North, Inverness or any part of the Highlands. They ran on the moors and ate the heather, which kept their front teeth short. They were always good horses.

Then the Aberdeenshire travellers used to bring horses down from Aberdeenshire, and they all came to the berries at Blairgowrie. Then the Inverness Stewarts used to bring horses down. And then you had travellers coming up from the Borders, up from Ayrshire and Dumfries, and they fetched horses. Then you had the Irish travellers coming across from Ireland. They fetched them across in the boats. And they bought them cheap in Ireland. I remember a man telling me he bought five donkeys for twelve and sixpence, half a crown each. That was all the price of a donkey in Ireland, two and six. That was dear for a donkey there in that time! And they took them to the market. I learned all these things at the Hoolet's Neuk, went with the rest of the men and learned the trade. It was a great time.

Then it came the spring, about the middle of February, and the travellers wanted to shift, move on. I had been working at the turnips and managed to keep a few shillings by. I thought I would take a wee trip back to Furnace and see the old folk. I was nearly sixteen. I could have taken a bus or a train, but I didn't bother. I said I was going to walk and make my way back the way I came. So I bade goodbye to my auntie whom I had stayed with all the time there, and the rest of the folk, I bade them all goodbye. They were shifting on. But I waited till everybody was packed up in the morning to go their own directions. Some going away by Forfar, some going away up by Broughty Ferry and up the length of Montrose, and some were going back by Perth. Charlie Reid and his mother said they were going there.

I said, 'Well, I'll get the length o Perth bi youse.' So we all bade farewell to each other, and they all parted, said their good mornings and their goodbyes. They had their dealing and their swapping and they gave each other presents and things before they left, because travellers were very funny.

When they parted from each other they liked to part in good company. They believed they might never see each other again. And they wanted to remember the person – if they ever went to his funeral or somebody went to *his* funeral – they would remember him in good faith. I've seen it happen many's a time! I've been in company with some folk and bade them good morning, and never had the pleasure of seeing them again. Old travellers, sometimes young ones and all, maybe through an accident or through some other means they met their end.

So we left the Hoolet's Neuk. But first we cleaned up the place, shut all the gates, gathered up all the stones, gathered up all the rags. Because travellers had respect for the farmer there at that time. These were real good travellers. You wouldn't have got as much paper about the place or a bit of rubbish that would have lighted my fag when they were finished! Heaped all their stones and packed up all their sticks, burned up all the old straw and every kind o rubbish. Left the place neat and tidy. They knew that the farmer would come in and check on that the minute they left. And if they'd have left any kind of mess or anything, they wouldn't get back again. There were some crowds who would come in and just stay two nights, and move away. They never cleaned up the place. And it finally got closed through time.

THE TRAMP AND THE ANGEL

O the night been dark and the night been cold
And the rain'd been falling down
When an old beggarman lay down to die
Upon the cold, cold ground.

O he had no one to comfort him
No one who would understand
For he was just a lonely,
A dying old beggarman.

And then he saw a beautiful light
A-coming down from the sky
Such a beautiful light, such a wonderful light
To the bush where he did lie.

'O who are you?' the old beggar said,
'And why do you trouble me?
For I am just a dying old beggarman
As you can surely see.'

'O I have come,' the Stranger said,
'From my Father's home far away
And this long, dark, cold winter's night
I will keep you company.'

'But I am a beggar,' the old man said,
'Just a dying old beggarman
And why you'd come to comfort me
I do not understand.'

'In my Father's home,' the Stranger said,
'In the place from where I came
For the tramp and the beggar and the poor and the rich
There everyone is the same.'

'And I have come to comfort you
And with you I will stay
This long, dark, cold, wild winter's night
I will keep you company.'

'But I am a beggar,' the old man said,
'Just a lonely old beggarman
And why you'd come to comfort me
I do not understand.'

Next morning that old tramp was found
In the bush it's where he lay
There were a happy smile upon his face
For his soul had passed away, away
For his soul had passed away.

                              Duncan Williamson

Chapter Seven

What the Fairies are Playing

I made my way back the journey I had come with my brother Sandy over the hill, up through to Crieff and Comrie. I walked up to Lochearnhead one night late and I slept in a haystack. I made my way up to Tyndrum, Dalmally and into Inveraray and down into Furnace. When I landed back at the old camp with the old folk, they weren't very well off. My father wasn't working at the time, and they were after having the flu. I had a few pound to help them out. The next day I went down to the shop to get my mother some messages. This is a good tale, a good laugh.

Now I had grown a bit by this time. In the shop was this bakery kept by an old man. And when I was wee I used to run about with my bare feet, nae arse in my trousers and my knees all bare, a few cuts on my legs. And he used to come up with a batch, used to make these tarts, biscuits and things, all these fancy cakes. He put them in the window. And we were awful hungry, you know, and there were these wee rhubarb pies. We used to come and stand at the window, keeking in, staring at the cakes, my nose flat up against the pane. And he would come out. He wore one of these old white aprons, you know, a baker's apron.

'Get away ye wee tinkie fae there!' he would say. 'What are ye daein standin starin at my windae? Ye're breathin on the window pane and people can't see in with yir breath.' So he'd come and take his apron, clean the window. This was when I was about five year old. And he'd always hunt you away from the window. If you had a penny you would go in.

You'd say, 'I want a cake for my penny.' And he'd pick the hardest ones he could get. He wouldn't give you a fresh one. I didn't know then, but I know now what he did. He felt them with his fingers and picked the hardest ones, those he couldn't get sellt. He would give you that one for a penny or a ha'penny. But not would he give you anything unless you had a penny!

Now I land back. The same old man was still there. He was even still there when I was married with a couple of children. I get my mother's messages in another shop a wee bit further up the street. And I walk down to the shop, and I had this great big Western hat on. I stand at the shop window. And there's his tray, the same tray I saw when I was five year old. One of these wooden batches. It held about three dozen cakes.

I said to myself, 'I'm going to have some fun!' Well, I got the finest satisfaction – maybe it was a bad thing to do that day. But I walked in, I said, 'Can I have some o your cakes?'

'Oh yes, you can have some of the cakes,' he said. I think by that time they were about twopence or threepence each, up a penny or two. 'How many do you want?'

I said, 'I'll take the whole lot. Every single one.'

'Are you wantin them all? he said.

I said, 'I want them all.' So he went to the window and got them all out. He got this big brown poke and he placed them in all tidy, you know. 'Oh yes, I'll give ye them,' and he's cracking away to me. Gave me the good patter, never even remembered anything about me, when he used to hunt me away from the window.

And across from the door there was a wee path going up to another house, and there was a bit o green grass. I walked out to the green grass and I stopped. It was about four yards from the front of the shop. I took everyone of these cakes in my two hands, and I crumbled them all up like that, one by one. And I was laughing to myself and flinging them up in the air. There were rhubarb cakes and cookies and buns, I was flinging them up! And all the sparrows and starlings were gathered round me. He came out. And he stood at the front of this window with this apron on him, the same old apron. He walked across.

He said, 'What are ye doin?'

I said, 'I'm feedin the birds. That's yir cakes. But they're mine, aren't they?'

'Oh yes.'

I said, 'I paid for them didn't I? I'm feedin the birds with them.'

He says, 'What are you feeding the birds with them for?'

I said, 'Because you wouldnae give me one when you used to chase me – I'm the wee tinkie you used to chase awa fae the window. I've bought yir cakes, I paid for them and I'm gettin my satisfaction noo. I'm feedin the birds wi them.' And I had the best fun o my life! Because things were really bad for us back there when we were wee, back in those times. You remember, there were nine of us going to school at once. And my father wasn't working most of the time. My mother had to just try and keep us alive. There was little we could do, because there were no jobs to get. The wee crofts didn't have very much work on them. If we could have got sale for whelks, we'd have been all right. But all the sale we got for whelks was our stomachs, we had to just eat them. We lived on the shellfish. Times were very, very hard.

But I stayed back with my old folk for about a month. And I got the yearning to be on the road again. By this time my older brother Geordie had taken off. And it was just a case of the lassies and my youngest brother being left with my mother and my father.

So I took off again and this time took the bus to Glasgow. It was only six shillings. Now I'd seen many trains in Perthshire, but I'd never been inside one. I got to the train station in Glasgow and bought a ticket. I'd heard about first and second class. And I was walking up and down – the train's ready to pull away and I'm standing with my ticket – I couldn't get in, I didn't know how. And this old woman came to me. I said I was looking to get into this train for Perth. She got me in anyway, so I sat and cracked to her all the way to Perth. Then I took the bus out to the Knock Camp. And when I landed, there were about fifteen camps in the Knock Camp, fifteen gellies!

There were some of the Highland Stewarts, and by sheer good luck, my mother's cousin and her laddie Charlie were there. I stayed with them for a couple of days and then I made my way to Balbrogie. Because, mind, I had promised my brother Sandy I would pay him a visit.

I went up through Burrelton, Coupar Angus and went to Balbrogie. He stayed in an old mill and his wife, Betsy, was away in Campbeltown having a bairn. And, he was so glad to see me! He'd been there all that time since he'd left me at the Knock Camp the year before. He was just himself and the two kids there. Oh, it was just out of this world for me to come and visit him. Because I liked him an awful lot. And I stayed with him for nearly two months there at the farm. He and I had some great times. He wrestled with me, showed me how to fight and all this carry on. He was only a young man then, a hardy, great strong man. So he tellt many cracks and tales. Sandy was a good storyteller too.

When he was young like me he travelled among all the travellers before he got married. He kent all the roads, he kent all the travellers, but he made his living with a mouth organ. Well, he wasn't the world's champion but he was as good! And he kept this instrument wrapped up in a silk hankie and he played the houses. He played up in Skye. You never heard anybody in the world play a mouth organ like him. None of this classical stuff, but really good playing by ear. And he taught me. I never learned to play it very good but I could always get a bit tune out o it.

Sandy had this great big field of turnips he was shawing and I helped him. Sandy was a great cook. Oh, he could make anything. And he had the dog Jackie for fourteen years, reared Jackie as a pup. There never was a hare that rose Jackie couldn't kill! It was just great for me! Sandy would say, 'Well, brother, we're needin something for the pot again.'

And I would say, 'Come on, Jack!' We'd just walk out to the field. The first hare that rose [kchkch] snick and he was dead. He only took one at a time, you know. Two rabbits and one hare. I'm tellin ye, we had some rabbit and tattie soup then! They were great times.

And then Betsy came back from Campbeltown on the bus. She had this wee fat baby girl. So by this time, it was the spring. Sandy said he wasn't going to go away that summer. He was going to stay at the mill. He liked the farm. And they had this old shed, but he'd converted it into a rough shelter for himself and his family. Sandy liked these things, to be on his own by himself. He liked us coming about him for a while. But I knew by the time his wife had come back, he and the two kids were all right. He'd asked me all the questions about my mother and father and how it was at home. I told him about me shaking the old man's cakes. He and I had a good laugh about this.

And Sandy told me tales what happened when he was with

Granny and Grandfather in Tarbert years and years ago, my father's mother and father, when he was a wee boy. He told me these tales about his experiences travelling though the North with a mouth organ. He always went on his own, never kept up with anybody. The only person he liked to stay with was Uncle Sandy Townsley, my mother's cousin. Sandy learned the mouth organ from a wee buck gadgie* called Holl, so named because the man sellt holly for a living. He was a tramp who went on the road, played a mouth organ and sang in a canister, in the side of a tin to make an echo. And he sang the houses, was a great street singer. Sandy had met up with him. This man never had a wife, and he'd taught Sandy to play the mouth organ right, how to vamp it. Sandy told me about his experiences in Skye and all these places.

Sandy never had any interest in horses. But Jack, my other older brother, he was different. He was fond of a horse from the time he got married till whatever time his family grew up. He hardly ever went without a horse. But he wouldn't keep an animal any time. He always thought somebody else's horse was better. I've had many's a good deal with him myself.

But anyway, I left Sandy there at the old mill. I promised him that if he wasn't away by the harvest time, I'd come back about August or September and see him again. I said I was going into Aberdeenshire to see the country. And he tellt me what kind o places to look for, what kind o travellers there were, the good travellers from the bad ones, and how to conduct myself among them. You know, he was always that way, telling me how to take care of myself among the travellers – not to be too boastful, not to be too cheeky and all these kind of things – so I would get along with them and not cause any trouble. Oh, some of them were hard to get along with, aye. Sandy didn't mean the old folk, he meant especially laddies about my own age. Sandy was feart o me getting into fights. Not that he thought I couldn't take care of myself, but he was concerned about me getting into trouble and maybe falling in with bad company and stealing.

You know, my mother had sixteen of a family. Thirteen survived, and there were six brothers all alive together. Not one of these brothers ever got into trouble in their lives, except for

---
* buck gadgie – half-traveller man

camping. Just fined for camping. And none of the sisters were ever in trouble either. That was because of my father, discipline from him when we were young. So this is what Sandy was trying to knock into me when I was with him.

Anyway, I set sail into Aberdeenshire and I travelled up. I didn't know the country very well, but I just kept going on. And I landed, before you get into Aberdeen, I saw this tent off the side of the road. It was just a big bow tent among a bing o whins* at the roadside. I was needing a cup o tea. I walked over to this tent. And who was it? Uncle Sandy Townsley and Katie! The very folk I had left at the Hoolet's Neuk in the spring. I was glad to see them. I had got word they were up that way, but I had never known where. Katie was my mother's cousin too. And then they had the laddie Willie, Winkie we called him. He was younger than me, about nine. Then the lassie Isobel, thirteen. And wee Nellie was the baby at that time, about five. And Sandy didn't have a horse. It was a handcart he had, a barrow. And I stayed with him from there on till the berries in July.

We travelled all through Aberdeenshire. Every part we were in – Donside, Deeside, Speyside hunting for white heather in the hills and going to all the games. Sandy was saving up, seemingly, to buy a horse. He could have bought one many times. And he played the pipes. But he seemed to be enjoying it because I pulled the cart for him, so he had no need for a horse. We had a great time in Aberdeenshire. But I was going to tell you this wee story.

Sandy had this big bow tent, and he said, 'You're gaunna stay with me?'

I said, 'Aye, I'll stay wi ye for a while, Uncle Sandy, and I'll see a bit o the country. It'll save me hikin on my own. So I made my bed in the bow tent, picked up plenty of dry grass. They pulled down the door at night and I made a bed in the front. It was fine for me, summer coming in. But it must have been about two o'clock in the morning, the first night. Sandy got up, he sat up in bed. And he started to whistle. Oh, I thought this kind o queer. I wakened up, lighted a match.

I said, 'What's wrong wi ye?'

He said, 'Wheesht, brother! Don't say a word.'

* bing o whins – lots of gorse

I said, 'What's wrong?'

He said, 'There fairies!'

I said, 'Fairies! Ye been dreamin?'

'No,' he said, 'I'm no dreamin. There fairies in below my ear playin pipes.'

I said, 'Lie doon, man!" So Isa got up. She was lying away at the back of the tent.

She says, 'There's something wrong wi ma daddy, Mammy. Ye'd better get up and see!'

I said, 'The're nothing wrong wi yir daddy. He's jist sleepin.' But he swore as low as his father and as low as all belonging to him that definitely there were fairies in below his ear. 'Well,' I said, 'if there is – what are the fairies playin?'

And he whistled me the tune the fairies were playing. And he lay back down. He says, 'Come here. Haud yir ear doon there . . .' He had a wee pillow, just had his boots down and his pillow on top of them to keep his head up. I put my head across the bed there. Nah! I couldn't hear a thing! He lay back down. But no, he's back up again. He said, 'I'm tellin ye, man!' And he started to punch the ground with his hand to get rid of them. He said, 'That's them, that's them away!'

I said, 'Definitely, you're away wi the birds!' No, Sandy never drank anything. Travellers never bothered much about drink in these times. But he swore. He started to whistle the tune again.

He said, 'This is the tune the fairies played.'

I said, 'It doesn't sound like a tune to me.'

He said, 'This is what the fairies was playin, as low as my faither!' But anyway, he lay back down.

And I was always up in the morning early. It was clear about six o'clock. And with the rotten whins around the fire was just a pleasure to kindle. In two minutes I had a big fire kindled. And I got the can on to get the tea on. He got up. I said, 'Come here, fairy man! Come here a minute.'

'What is it?' he said.

I said, 'That was an awfae carry on* ye had last night, you and your fairies!'

He said, 'I'm tellin ye . . .' And I wouldn't tell you a word about

* awfae carry on – mad commotion

him, he's dead in the grave if God pleases, he said, 'Brother, the fairies was definitely under my ear last night in this moor. I heard the pipes as plain as I could hear onybody playin.' We were camped on a moor outside Aberdeen. The travellers called it the Twopenny Moor, because it used to be you paid three pence to stay on it.

So I said, 'What was the tune the fairies's playin noo you were tellin me aboot last night?' He and I were sitting at the fire. But if you gave Sandy a thousand pound, he couldn't remember one note of that tune. And never could to his dying day. No, that's the truth. I tormented him about it for years after that.

So we left there and went into Aberdeen, up by Bucksburn and then went up Deeside and Donside. Then we went to Old Meldrum Green and then to Huntly. I pulled the barrow, the handcart. It was made of bicycle wheels and was easy to run. We came to Huntly Green. So he and I were mending baskets. Katie went to the houses and she collected all these baskets that were needing mended, brought them back to the green. You could camp on the greens in these days right in front of the houses. Folk didn't bother. You just kindled a fire. 'No,' they'd say, 'it's only tinkies in their campin place.' And you could go to a house and get water. They didn't bother you. Nobody paid attention. It was a pleasure to see the tinkers coming in about. The Aberdeenshire folk thought the tinkers were lucky. They believed that there were no trouble or anything would come to the town if the tinkers came to the greens. It's when tinkers didn't turn up that they thought there were some bad luck attached to the town, especially in Aberdeenshire. A lot of that happened in Argyllshire too in some places. They never sent for police to shift the tinkers in these days, especially one tent or that. They wondered how the 'tinkies no turned up . . . there some'in bad aboot the place if you didnae come in aboot.' This was their idea. They thought there was some illness coming to the town, a plague or something coming. Like the birds no turning up in the spring, something queer was going to happen if they didn't turn up.

So, there was a great big tree. We were lying against it and we were sorting baskets. He said to me, 'I'm tellin ye, there fairies in this bit tae!'

I said, 'The're fairies in every camp wi you – how many mair places got fairies?'

He said, 'Ye see this tree?'

'Aye,' I said, 'it's a great tree.' It was a big beech. I was sitting with my back against it. I said, 'You and your fairies. I dinnae want nae fairies the night!'*

'Laddie, ye'll no believe me, but the're fairies in this camp tae here. This is Huntly Green and some folk says it's haunted, but this is the fairies in this. This is where the wee man lay below this tree when the elf queen cam and took him awa tae Elfland. And I'm gaunna tell ye the story about Thomas the Rhymer. He was a fool, a toll that wandered aboot the toon daein nothing, lyin here and there. And a bonnie woman cam tae him on horseback and took him away tae Elfland. My faither used tae sing it, sing bits o it.' And Sandy sang a wee bit o it to me.

We had a great time in that place and we must have stayed in Huntly for about a week. Then we moved back to Dufftown. I spent that whole summer with him right up till the berry time. I wanted to go to Blairgowrie because he had tellt me so many tales about all the travellers who went there. In that time it was a real heyday in Blairgowrie, they came from all parts and all over. They came with donkey yokes and they came with horses. And they came with carts and barrows, prams and bicycles, all to the berryfields. They had fights and they had arguments, they made love and they had marriages, they did every single thing under the sun. It was what you call a working fair. You could always make the price of your meat and have a good time. You could always go out, if you could pick berries at all and make two-three shillings to get as much as you could eat.

Then some of them went there just for the sake of swapping and dealing in horses. They never picked a berry. Some of them went without a pony and left with a good horse. Some of them went there with a good horse and left with a barrow. The horses were bought and changed hands – a horse could have maybe six owners in one day. And families went there with a barrow; maybe a father and mother and two-three sons and daughters with a pram, maybe a couple o prams, and they left with a good yoke. Anybody that had any kind o money could

---

* the night – tonight

buy anything. There were good dogs for sale, good canvases for tents, sets of good camp sticks for sale. There were no caravans then. And they swapped lums and chimneys and elbows – that was when the gellies started coming in. And everybody wanted this great inside fire, the tank and lum inside the tents. And it was a pleasure to see some of these Skye MacDonald folk sitting making these. They could make them themselves out of sheets of tin, their own chimneys. They came and showed the Perthshire and Forfarshire travellers the right way to build a good long gelly tent. But those were the stories I was getting from Sandy. So I wanted to get my own experience of the berries.

Sandy said to me, 'Laddie, you like runnin about the country – would you no be better wi a wee pony tae yirsel, a wee yoke?'

I said, 'Aye, the next time, uncle, the next thing I'll be needin tae masel will be a wife if I get that. I want to keep awa fae that! I dinnae mind havin a horse, I would like a horse. But I'm no wantin tae have nae horse yet.' But it was before the berries, and Sandy wanted to go to this wee place, Aberlour.

That was a great place on Speyside for pearl fishing. I'd never done this in my life, I'd never even seen a pearl shell, apart from pearls in clabbydhus back home in Furnace, saltwater pearls. I wanted to have a go at pearl fishing.

We put our camp up at the side of the burn and Katie and wee Isobel went away to hawk the houses. We were making baskets because it was the summertime and the wands were all peeling. You just peeled them with a split stick, and there was a good trade for baskets. I used to make the bottom, put in the upsets, fling it to Sandy and he would fill it up. I would set up another one, he would fill it. We made the one between us, got on faster that way. My father had taught me how to make a basket when I was wee, and the stuff was good then. You could really make a good basket. We were making them, and Winkie, the wee laddie was peeling the wands.

Sandy says, 'We'll have to go pearl fishin.' Old Katie came back and she had gone into the jeweller's in Aberlour. There was a jeweller who bought pearls, any kind. She had asked the jeweller herself, because traveller women were always doing these things: if there were a shilling to be gotten, they would sure try it! She says, 'I remember, Sandy, years ago the travellers used to get an awfae lot of pearls in this strip along here.'

'All right, Katie,' he said, 'we'll make a couple o pearl jugs tomorrow. Bring me back a couple of candles.' I was wondering what he wanted candles for.

So true to his word, the next day away he goes. He had his wee bike and he cycled along to the village. He came back with two panes of glass from the joiner. He sat down and got a wire, a piece of iron and made it red hot in the fire. And he made a circle with the hot iron right round the pane of glass, tapped it right round and it came out like the face of a clock!

Then Sandy went and got two tins and cut the bottoms out, but left a flange around the bottom. He placed the glass on the flange and he lighted a candle. Next he melted the wax around the top of the glass, right round the whole way till the candle was finished. He left it sitting till the candle wax got hard, and he polished the glass.

'Now,' he said to me, 'look through that!' I'd never seen this done before. I looked.

I said, 'It's clear, I can see through it. What are ye gaun tae do wi it?'

He says, 'Laddie, you dinnae understand. You've been reared in Furnace all the days of your life. You never kent nothing! You put that in the water and you look through it, and you can see the least wee thing. The glass magnifies the water.'

'Oh,' I said, 'fair enough.'

He says, 'I'll make one for you.' It was one of those big fruit cans. And he got a burlap sack, cut a bit off it and put a string on it. He says, 'Put that in your bag. Now, wade oot to your waist.' He got a long piece of stick, hazel, and he split it like a clothes peg. 'Now,' he says, 'all ye need tae dae is when ye see a shell, if it's too deep, tae save ye puttin yir hand into the water, just put this split stick on the top of the shell. Turn the stick roond and lift it up. The shell'll be stuck in the split! Because the shells dinnae have much o a grip.

So he's going out into the water, wading up to the waist and I'm wading beside him. 'We're picking up a shell here and a shell there and more shells. Putting them in this bag. Now when you think you have enough, what you can carry, you go out on the banking, sit down and open them all up. And you search the insides for a pearl. When you're finished you throw them all back in the water to feed the eels and the fish, keep them from wasting.

But I was unlucky that day, never got a thing. Sandy got a couple of miniatures, pure wee seeds, and wee barrel-shaped ones. We fished it for about four or five days. I never got a thing. I got plenty of shell, but I couldn't get a pearl. Sandy got a good handful. He had them in a wee box, not very big, the biggest one about the size of a head of a match. But saleable. They were bonnie and clear. Then we saw these two traveller men coming with a pony and cart. We came up, soaking to the waist. We stopped at the road. This was the MacMillans and they had a nice pony and a float. They kent old Sandy.

They said, 'You pearl fishin, Sandy?'

'Aye.'

'Hae you any luck?'

'No,' he said, 'we never got a thing.'

'Ah man,' he said, 'we fished that bit. It's nae a guid bit. There plenty shell but there nae pearl in it.' They had a droll way of speaking, these hantle, but they kent the good bits.

Sandy said, 'I got two-three wee seeds! And he showed the man. And this laddie sitting in the cart put his hand in his pocket and took out a boot polish box. There was cotton wool in it, full to the top. Some of the pearls were as big as green peas. There must have been about three dozen, and they were beautiful! Just like drops of water.

He said, 'We've been fishin all summer, cove, and that's all we got, about twa-three dozen.' Then that was about fifty or sixty pounds' worth. Now, it would get you three or four hundred pounds, maybe more.

Well Katie, I think she got about three pounds for the wee handful Sandy collected. These wee seeds were used for brooches and rings, mixed pearls. And I began to get the pearl bug! Like the gold fever. I wanted to stay on because I believed that I was going to get ... you see, every shell you lift you think you're going to hit it lucky. Like digging for gold, but it really gets to you! Through time some travellers get the fever. Once they get into a burn it's like drink – they cannae stop.

Because from morning to night they still believe that around the next corner they're going to hit the big thing. That man in Newburgh there, ten thousand pounds for one pearl the size of a pigeon's egg! Mr Abernethy, largest pearl ever gotten in the River Tay, ever gotten in Scotland, about five or six years ago.

But anyway. Sandy says, 'You've some nice pearls there, maister.'

'Aye,' he said, 'Sandy, but we took a lot o lookin for them. Well, we're gaun awa doon to the jeweller to see if he can gie us an offer for them. But he's no as guid as the man at Grantown. The man at Grantown-on-Spey is a better payer for pearls.'

So I said, 'Sandy, how about goin to Grantown?'

He says, 'Aye, well . . .'

Katie says, 'Aye, I like Grantown. It's a good wee toon.'

So we made our way to Grantown and we camped in beside a golf course. The next day we would go and fish for pearl. Sandy said, 'This is a good bit o burn, but ye've tae watch for these pot holes. A stone gets trapped and it runs roond, digs a hole and it gets deep. If ye're coming along a suddent,* ye cuid faa inta it.' So we fished the Spey for about four days and I got one good pearl, a nice barrel-shaped one, but Sandy got nothing. I gave old Katie this pearl and she sellt it. She was doing awfully well with her baskets and she was telling us it would be far better if we stopped fishing for pearl and went and made some more baskets, because hers were getting finished.

Now Sandy had sent for wands to some kind of factory, and he had them sent to the train station before him. Bought in stuff. And adding to this our cutting the wild stuff along the roadside, we had a good mix of wands. We could have made baskets. And we weren't getting very much off the pearls. So that night Sandy took awful sick, and he took lumps on the back of his neck.

He sat up in the middle of the night and got delirious. He was telling old Katie to rise up, burn the pain out with matches. He was in an awful state. So I went along to the police and they phoned an ambulance. Sandy was taken away. They put him to Elgin, the nearest hospital.

I was left with Katie now and the weans.

---

* a suddent – suddenly

So the next morning she says, 'There only one thing we can dae. We cannae stay here wirsels any longer. We'll have to make wir way back to Elgin. It's a long journey. Wait a minute. I think the best thing we can dae is pack wir pram, pack wir barra nice and tidy, put all the stuff in it and send it by train tae the station in Elgin. It'll save a long walk on the road and we'll take the bus.'

So I went down to the station and booked the wee handcart with the stuff in it to go to Elgin. And we took the bus. But I don't mind how many times we had to change buses along the way. It was late at night when we landed in Elgin. We went to the station to collect the pram, the barrow with all the stuff. There was nothing, not a thing there. Now the two lassies, Winkie, old Katie and me, we had nowhere to stay and not a thing with us. So Katie went and bought a kettle and something to make some tea. We walked out, and came to this quarry. I kindled a big fire. And there were these heaps of stuff, cloths that had been chucked out in the quarry, and they had tassels round them like things for covering a coffin, coffin covers. Winkie believed they were.

'No,' he said, 'I'll lie on the ground first before I'd use any o these things.' So I managed to make a shelter with these cloths, but none of them would sleep in it. They thought they were unholy things.

But it was the summertime, and I'd kindled this big fire. Katie and me sat and cracked all night till the daylight came in. The next day she and I walked up to the hospital. And here Sandy's sitting with a great big poultice on the back of his neck, a tattie poultice. The doctor told her Sandy had took four or five boils at the same time. And instead of coming out, they worked their way into his neck. When Sandy saw us he wouldn't stay in, he wanted out. So we took him and went to the station. His things still weren't there. Whatever happened to them, they didn't arrive. We waited till about six or seven o'clock at night. Another train came in.

The stationmaster tellt us, 'It's in that middle truck.' It was parked right in the centre of the track junction! There was railway on each side, and the trucks were parked for the weekend right in the middle. There's no way in the world we could have got that barrow out, because there was no loading bank to reach the trucks. But we had to! We managed to open the door of that truck, and we had some job. It was as high as a roof to get at it. Sandy was cursing and he was swearing and this neck of his was swelled out. But with all our strength and God's help we got the barrow out. We managed to get it on the road, and we went back to that quarry.

I put up the tent. We stayed there for three or four days till Sandy felt better. But he never went back to the doctor again. Then old Katie said she wanted to go to the games at Lonach. So we set sail for Lonach Gatherings.

And Sandy was always telling me, 'I'm fed up, brother, wi this pram. I'm gaunnae try and get two-three shillings and get a wee pony.' Every day he was was going to get money. But this pony was never coming – I was the pony – as long as he had me. He was always saying, 'Ach, we'll no be long noo, we'll get a wee pony. I ken where tae get them, I ken a man in the next toon who'll have a pony for me and a wee float.' He had two-three pound to buy it, but he never got round to it as long as he had me to pull this handcart. I wasn't getting fed up. I liked it.

I really liked Aberdeenshire, I liked the travellers there an awful lot. Their stories and cracks were good, and I liked the way they spoke. And they liked the way I spoke because I had the Highland tongue. There was a lot of Gaelic and Highland talk in Argyllshire, and I'd picked it up being around the country weans in the village and at school. I met a lot of the Aberdeenshire folk years later, the Whytes, Stewarts, Higgins and MacConnachies, and the Kelbies. I came to ken all the Aberdeenshire travellers, the MacAlisters and a big family of Lindsays. The Aberdeenshire folk were always nice, different travellers from the local ones about Perthshire and Angus altogether. Everybody was made welcome, 'Come on in, laddie, and sit doon and gie us yir news, man! Tell us wha ye come fae and tell us yir crack,'

They all kept horses, some of them had old cars at that time too. But they kept good horses and big carts. They never kept any floats. They had spring carts with high double rails on the sides. And they used to go to the games, travel there and sell heather. They collected rags and rabbit skins, rags and woollens. And they sold a lot of dishes. Most everyone you saw sold crockery. They had cups and plates and bowls of all kinds and went round the farms. They sent to the factories, and there were places in Aberdeen where you could get them. With their carts they hawked these dishes. And they gathered sheep's wool. And then they swapped and dealed among themselves.

In all these wee towns in Aberdeenshire travellers met, and swapped and dealed. It was a great place for horses. The Aberdeenshire travellers were good to deal with and I liked to see them swapping and dealing in a camping place. And the funny thing was, you could go in, maybe about fifteen or sixteen families in the one camp. Seven, ten or twelve men around the fire having a swap and deal through each other. And you'd never hear an angry word among them. Nah, never an angry word. They were very sociable folk to stay beside.

I gained a lot of knowledge from these travellers and I gained a great respect from them. The main difference I found between them and the Lowland travellers – the Aberdeenshire ones were hawking travellers. Every Aberdeenshire man in the morning yoked up his horse and went off to hawk – with dishes, scrubbers, baskets, whatever he could make. And he took his wife along, and maybe a couple of kids if he didn't have somebody to watch them. And they hawked all day, travelled for miles to make their livelihood. They weren't interested in dealing or swapping in any way unless somebody came along and challenged them for a deal or a swap. But they always kept a good horse. The Lowland traveller depended on the horse to swap and deal, but they bought a horse and all they wanted to do was just go out, swap and get rid of it, get another one as fast as they could, have a quick turn over and make money off the beast, you see! But the Aberdeenshire traveller, whom I loved and respected and still do to this day, had a different notion and a different idea. I wouldn't say the Aberdeenshire travellers were dealing folk, I wouldn't call them horse dealers or horse traders. But they used the horse in a manner to make their livelihood, which seemed fit to me.

And they tended their horse like one of the family. They had dishes and clothes pegs and baskets, they gathered rabbit skins and used the horse from day to day as a vanman would use his van. But they never forced it, never hurt it, never overdrove it. And they were kind to it, fed it and respected it. I said to myself, 'If ever I get tae have a horse in ma day, I would like tae be like Aberdeenshire folk.' And that I did in later years.

So as I was telling you, being along with Sandy and Katie in Aberdeenshire was fine. Because I liked it, I met all these travellers and enjoyed their company, had their crack and had their tales. I had their stories. But I had heard so much about Blairgowrie all the time.

Everyone said, 'Ye gaun tae the berries, Sandy?' Because everybody kent Sandy in there.

Sandy says, 'Nah, there nothing in the berries for me. It's all right for young folk, ken, wants tae have a carry on.' He said to me, 'Hae ye made up yir mind tae go to the berries?'

I said, 'Aye, I'm gaun.'

'Well,' he said, 'me and yir Aunt Katie's goin tae Lonach Games and fae there we're goin up tae Braemar. It's only a short trip ower the Devil's Elbow and doon to Blairgowrie. So if ye stick along wi us for a while till we get up there, ye ken have a bit trip ower the hill. It'll no tak ye, young man like you, nae mair 'n a day gaun ower the Devil's Elbow fae Braemar, and ye gae doon. Wonst ye land in Blairgowrie, I s'pose there be plenty o yir ain folk there. And I'm sure you'll no go wrong.

So I said, 'Okay, Uncle, I'll stick along wi ye.' So we journeyed to Donside and made our way to Lonach Highland Gatherings. Wooden flowers were all the go then.

So old Katie said, 'Sandy,' it being too early for white heather, 'the best thing I think we could dae is make plenty flooers. I'll take them and sell them tae the folk, stand at the gate o the games.'

He says, Wumman, naebody wants tae buy flooers – who's gaunna carry flooers when ye're gaun tae the games?'

She says, 'You make me some flooers!' Now by this time I was a good hand at making wooden flowers. So Sandy couldn't see how a woman standin at the gate of the games with bunches of flowers, especially wooden ones, was going to do any trade with them. He was thinking folk were there to to enjoy themselves, but he never thought about folk leaving the games and coming home.

So I said, 'All right, Auntie, if you want flooers, I'll make you plenty!' So her daughter Isa then was about thirteen. And every piece of elderberry along the way I saw, I stopped. I cut it, put it on the wee barrow.

So Isa, she was in her bare feet most of the days, she was only a wee lump o a lassie, and she would say to me, 'Here's another, another bit o flooer wood.' I pulled the barrow, stopped, cut the best bits, flung them on the top. By the time we got to near Lonach, there was an old place called Heugh-head, an old right o way road. We pulled in. But by this time I was loaded with elderberry! Sandy had an old bike and was away cycling along the road. He never did anything! I was the horse pulling the barrow.

When we pulled into Heugh-head Katie says to me, 'Dae ye see this camp, laddie?'

I said, 'Aye.'

'Well, I remember,' she said, 'yir auntie, aye, we were here years ago and we camped here on this auld road. We cam tae the games the same way, it must be twenty-five year ago.'

I said, 'I wasnae born then.'

'I know,' she said 'you werenae born. And she was expectin in this same place. And she had two wee babies on this auld road. Both o them died, twins, and they died here. Just because it was my sister, dinnae gae too far up the road: I want you tae just stay at the fit o the road. Jist for the rememberance's sake.' It was great about the travellers, they had a great respect for these things. She says, 'It would be awfae nice if ye didnae gae too far up, jist stay at the end o the road.'

'That's fine, Auntie,' I says.

Now this was about the end of July, the beginning of August, you see and it was great weather. The days were hot and long, beautiful. I did all the work, put the tent up and went for sticks, kindled the fire, and we had a sip o tea. I said, 'Auntie, I think I'll mak some flooers.'

So Isa said, 'I'll help ye.' Aunt Katie smoked a pipe, you see. Now Sandy, you never got him to stay in about. He was always away with his bike. He wouldn't give you a help to do anything! As long as he got on this bicycle and away, cracking to the old men, begging tobacco and begging baking soda, wandering here and there with his bicycle. He never came back till late at night. So old Katie used to tell me all these cracks and all these tales, you see, all the things I could get out of her. Talking to her about old travellers, about old stories, about the berries and how she never went, and all these things.

So she said, 'If youse two's gaunna mak flooers, I'm gaunna mak a basket.'

I said, 'Auntie, there a basket I made a bottom for last night. I'll jist put a couple o upsets intae it, set it for ye. Ye can fill it in.' So I shoved a couple o upsets in and pulled them, bent them over and tied the top. And I said, 'There's some wee wands. Fill it. Dinnae touch auld Sandy's wands, because I dinnae want him shoutin when he comes back.' You durstnae touch his – he had his own stuff for making his own baskets. Ye durstnae touch this! He left the rubbish – if he left you any bits o pieces that he didn't want, you could work with that. Even suppose Katie had to look for the living with what she made – if you touched anything belonging to him, he wasn't pleased. So I said, 'You pick that, Auntie, wee bits and pieces there, cast bits that he didnae want, and fill your basket.'

She says, 'Doll, I'm gaunna get some o that broom.' This is the God's honest truth! She says, 'I'm gaunna take some o this broom.' It was in bloom, beautiful yellow. And these long green strips of broom when it was in flower, She went and picked all the long strips. They were just like willows, but green. And after I'd set up the basket to her, she weaved and filled it with this broom. Now, Sandy had made two baskets the night before and I'd made two. And I always tied them behind the back of the cart, so's if anybody took a notion to them they could be seen. I'd tied these four baskets and we'd just turned in at the end of the road. There was the main road passing by here. I'd put up the bow tent. And I went to the hedge and gathered all these hedgeroots, put on a big fire. And I'm sitting on a bit canvas and making wooden flowers, sliping the wood. And Katie's sitting with the pipe, pipe stuck down the side of her mouth. There's reek blowing from her, and if you'd got this picture, you'd have a picture for life! Isa, she's sitting peeling the wood for me to start a new flower. When along comes this great big fancy car. Oh, I think they were Americans because they had the biggest car I ever saw! And they drove along and stopped. This young lady came out, oh, about twenty-five or thirty. And a young gentleman with her.

She said, 'I see you've some lovely baskets there. Are you selling any?'

Now by this time Katie had finished the basket with the broom. She wasn't very good at putting on the handle, but I'd put it on for her. And I'd hung it beside the rest. And you know how eager these traveller women were, If there was a sale on the go, she would have to get there just as fast she could, like lightning, you see! Suppose it was only for five shillings. And this Sandy never lived down till the end of his life the story I'm about to tell you. So I had made, I mean I could really make a good basket and so could Sandy. If you wanted to make a good one, you could if you put your mind to it. But if you wanted to make something sellable, just for a quick turnover, you just threw it up any way at all. But I'd made a nice couple of wee oval ones, and Sandy had made a hamper with a long handle, a bag basket. And Katie had made this thing with the broom. It was brown on the bottom, white on the sides and green the whole way up with a white top, with a white handle. It was the drollest looking basket you every saw in your life!

And this great car had pulled up, and the young lady had said, 'Oh, what lovely baskets! Do you sell them?'

I said, 'Katie, eh, bene mort; bing the mang tae the bene mort!'* I never spoke to the folk, but I was close to them.

'Yes, my lady,' Katie says. She's still got the pipe stuck in her mouth.

And the man says, 'Wait, wait, wait. Wait, wait!' He came out and he had the camera over his neck. 'Wait!' Katie's still got this pipe sticking, you know. 'Wait,' he says, 'I must have a picture! Can I have a picture?'

'Oh yes,' said Katie, 'take as many pictures, sir, as you want.' And this young gentleman's back up the road, and he's taking all these pictures. I bet you some of these are in America yet. I would give the world if I had one of them. So, he got his pictures.

The young lady came round and said, 'I would love to have one of these baskets.'

---

* bing the mang tae the bene mort – give the patter to the lady

'Oh, my lady,' says Katie. She was on the patter then and she tellt her all the stories. 'Take this one, ma'm, feel it, feel it in yir hand. Look, it's fine and strong. And feel the handle. It's strong. Ye can carry anything on it. And my laddie, that's my boy there – he makes all these baskets. He was disabled oot the Army.' This was the story. She always kept the story for me, how I'd passed my grade four. I hadn't yet at that time. But she'd say, 'This is ma boy and he's disabled.' My hand was abnormal due to an injury I'd suffered at the age of five.

'Oh,' the young woman said.

'This is my son and he makes all these baskets, he's busy makin some flowers. The Army wouldnae take him because he's got a paralysed hand.' This was an excuse! 'And this is all he can dae for a livin. It's my son. This is my wee lassie,' pointing to Nellie. All the patter! And Katie never touched her basket! She left it hanging on the back of the barrow. I think she was a wee bit ashamed of it because it looked kind o rough. She said to the woman, 'Try that one and try this one, and try that one.'

No, the woman, the bene mort would have nothing to do with none of my baskets or Sandy's. She says, 'That one there with the green on it – that's the one I want.' Katie's wee basket, made with broom, bits o broom! She said, 'I love that from my heart. I want that.' Well, five shillings then was a great price for a basket, great price.

'Oh yes, my lady,' she says, 'you can have that one.'

'Well,' she says, 'what is it?'

'Five shillings.'

'Oh!' The bene mort opened her bag in two seconds. 'I'll just take it,' she said. 'A pound. There you are, my dear, granny, and keep the change.' A pound! Now a pound in these days . . . Winkie was a wee totie laddie.

'Mammy dear,' he says, 'you're the best basket maker in the world, Mammy. You got a pound for your basket. Wait till my daddy comes back!' So the bene hantle* drove away in the car, and Katie's got this pound. Now this was messages for the next day, tobacco and fags. We didn't need to shift the next day at all. We could stay home and work baskets. Because all Katie needed to do, go along with that pound to Heugh-head shop

---

* bene hantle – well-to-do folk

and she could get as much that would have done us for three days. She was as happy as a lark.

But about six o'clock he came cycling back with his bike, and the white coat on him and the reek blowing, the pipe stuck in the side of his mouth. He pulled in, had a wee handful of wands tied along the bar of the bike, ken, with two bits o string. Pulled in. And two bits o bullwood, elderberry. See, this was an excuse. He came in, put the bike against the dyke. It was a high dyke.

He said, 'Hello brother, eh, you got the camp up?'

I said, 'Aye, Uncle, I got the camp up.' He'd never come near me. Once we got to the roadend, he just jumped on the bike and went away. I said, 'Did ye go far?'

'Ach, I was away alang,' he says, 'tae the other end o the toon tae see if there were any traivellers there.'

I said, 'Aye.'

He said, 'I got a wee handfu o wands.' I was sitting making flowers. There were a big heap lying beside me. And Winkie was peeling the wands. He said, 'Eh, was that the hornies I'd seen in the car pullin awa there?'

I said, 'No, that wasnae the police.'

'I thocht when I'd seen the car pullin,' he said, 'I thought it was the police.' You see, the police always came in and gave a check on you in these days.

I said, 'No, it wasnae the police. It was the bene hantle.' Noble people, you know, gentry. I said, 'They stopped tae buy a basket.'

He said, 'I ken they bocht a basket. That's the way I took a good job at mine, I made a good job o it, brother. I bet ye it was mine!'

I said, 'Uncle Sandy, look, me and you cannae make a basket.'

'What do ye mean,' he said, 'we cannae mak a basket, Rorie?'

He always called me Rorie – after my great-grandfather. 'What do you mean we cannae mak a basket?'

I said, 'We cannae make a basket, Uncle Sandy. What was the best you ever got for a basket, one o yours?'

'Oh brother, I got seven and six for a basket,' he said, 'five shillings, seven and six.'

I said, 'Did ye ever get a pound for a basket?'

'No, brother, I never got a pound for a basket. I couldnae make a basket,' he said, 'that ye would get a pound for.'

I said, 'Look, Aunt Katie – ye wouldnae gie her a handfu – a wee taste o yir wands tae mak a basket, would ye? Ye wouldnae let her touch the wands tae mak a wee basket. And she went to that bush and she filled it in broom, strips o green broom.' And you can't peel broom, the skin'll no come off it. 'And there a young lady and this young gentleman cam in here, I think they were Americans, and they stopped. They wouldnae look at your basket, nor they wouldnae look at mine. Noo, Katie filled it with broom and the bene mort gied her a pound for her basket.'

'Nah,' he said.

I said, 'Aye, he gied her a pound fir it. They wouldnae look at me 'n yir baskets.'

He said, 'Is that right, Katie hoy?'

'Aye,' she says, 'that's the truth.'

He says, 'Look, any wands you want, take the lot!'

I said, 'I should think so! Look, me and you we're wastin wir time. She, she can sell baskets; she can mak them. Me and you cannae mak baskets. Folk wouldnae look at wir baskets.' And from that day on to the day that I left him, he never stopped her from interfering with his wands again.

So Isa and I sat all that night and made all these flowers. Old Katie had got a couple of packets of dye. You got packets of dye in muslin bags, and you poured water into a pot and popped them in – yellow was a great colour. So we sat and dyed all these flowers.

Sandy says, 'Wumman, you're only wastin yir time gaun tae the games.' Next morning was Lonach Games. 'You're only wastin yir time gaun wi the flooers.' Now, she had a pound in her pocket, she wasn't caring. And we had plenty messages, because we had picked up a few things along the way. You see, that was the only thing the traveller women hated long ago, when they used to call the houses, they hated to go away in the morning to their hawking if there were nothing left at home for them who stayed behind. That was the only thing that bothered them. Because they didn't know how long they would be away.

So she says to me, 'Brother, if you come along in the morning tae the first wee shop, I'll get ye a pint o milk and a packet o fags. And I'll send it back wi ye. And then I'm no carin, I could stay the whole day.' It was a worry to them, you see. Honest to God, they were really good.

'That's aa right, Aunt Katie,' I said, 'I'll go along wi ye in the morning.' At the first of the wee toon, Lonach, there was a shop. And there was a hillside and a big field at the back. This was the games park. I told Katie after I'd made all this heap of flowers, 'There's nae privet tae put them on.'

'Oh, dinnae worry about that. I'll get privet tomorrow masel.' And Isa always went with her to give her mother a help with the flowers. She was an awfully clever lassie for thirteen.

She says, 'Aye, Mammy, I'll go wi ye in the morning.' And Winkie stayed with me. And Ningen, the wee totie lassie. But Sandy would just jump on his bike and cycle away, never give a thought to the weans. As long as I was there, he kent I wouldn't leave them. Sandy liked me being with them.

So the next morning I got up, picked all the hedgeroots and got a big fire on, got the kettle on and made a cup of tea. It was a beautiful morning, sun was scorching hot. They got a lovely day for the games.

And we were just having a cup of tea when I heard the patter of feet going along the road. This was a traveller man, his wife, two boys and two lassies with a donkey cart. And they came in. A big old, tall man. Oh, I came to know him, even work with him later when I was married. He was in his late forties. His two boys were about my age; one was younger. And he had this donkey.

I had never seen a donkey yoked before. With the big, old long ears, you know. I'd seen plenty in pictures and I'd seen folk swapping them, but travellers weren't partial to donkeys. I'd like to tell you the God's honest truth; the travellers felt ashamed, because they hated to burden the holy animal. That's what it's supposed to be. As far as they believed, if you were yoking a donkey you were insulting God by making it work for you. They believed it had already done its work. It wasn't needing anything else, just be a pet. Now this goes back a long way to the story from the beginning. The reason they didn't yoke and burden it was not that it wasn't fit for doing these things. It was the respect they had for the animal, back to the time when it carried Mary and Baby Jesus to Jerusalem. You see, travellers are very religious people. I know they curse and they swear and they take the Lord's name in vain. But when it comes down to earth, they really *believe*. Because they've got all the truth in their own mind and they've got all their own facts and their own ways and their own truth. They never go to church and they don't like ministers. But that doesn't mean to say they're not religious. It's hard to understand the idea, but this traveller was doing something another traveller wouldn't do.

The man tellt us later, 'Sandy, I'm ashamed that I'm burdenin the wee animal, poor wee cuddy.' It was loaded up and you couldn't put shoes on its feet, you see. 'But Sandy,' he says, 'I couldnae get nothing else. I hadnae got nae money or coppers.' Oh, he apologised, oh yes, definitely. Otherwise he wouldn't have been company to us. The man said, 'Sandy, I'm a wee bit sorry.'

Sandy says, 'It's aa right, dinnae worry about it.' Once the man said that, then he was okay.

He said, 'I ken it's no fair, but the first chance I get tae swap it awa fir a wee pony . . .'

'It's aa right,' Sandy says, 'it's okay.' I didn't know anything, I mean, I wasn't in the horse trade. But I knew in my mind the man shouldn't have been yoking a donkey in the first place. But it was all the man had. So in this way he was forgiven.

Mr Stewart was the man's name. This donkey was loaded with covers and camp sticks and wands and everything. And it was a female, that made it worse. If it would have been a wee jack, it wouldn't have been half so bad. And it was a bonnie wee cratur. Sandy was a wee bit upset in his own way. Every traveller was. But, not to be rude and not to be selfish, and not to be against the man, it was only against the idea.

After the man apologised yet again, 'Och,' Sandy says, 'it's aa right, dinnae let it bother ye! Put it up there, up the road. The laddie'll gie ye a hand tae put yir tent up. And tether it up the auld road there an gie it plenty tae eat. Are ye gaun tae the games?'

'Aye,' he says, 'wir gaun tae the games, man.' And he was after the cranberries!

This man was an expert in cranberries. He had these wooden

Furnace, in the early 1900s. Rising behind the houses to the right is Furnace Wood, where Duncan's family camped for many years. (*Scottish Ethnological Archive*)

The Township of Auchindrain, near Furnace. This is an old-fashioned, joint tenancy farm, now preserved as a museum and well worth a visit. Duncan's first job was with Adie MacCallum, building drystone dykes here. (*School of Scottish Studies*)

Travellers in Kintyre, with their pony and light cart, before the First World War.
(*Scottish Ethnological Archive*)

A typical travellers' camp in the West Highlands, c.1910. (*Scottish Ethnological Archive*)

A traveller family in Kintyre, Argyll, in the early 1900s. (*Scottish Ethnological Archive*)

Kettle Pot
Used for tattie
soup, any food
or drink.

SNOTTUM
Made holes
in the
ground
for sticks
and a
pot-stick
Home-made
from iron.

The kettle pot and snottum were basic requirements for a traveller's life. The snottum in particular had many uses: it was kept by the tent door, to keep it open and (occasionally) to ward off unwelcome visitors. It also suspended cooking pots above the fire.

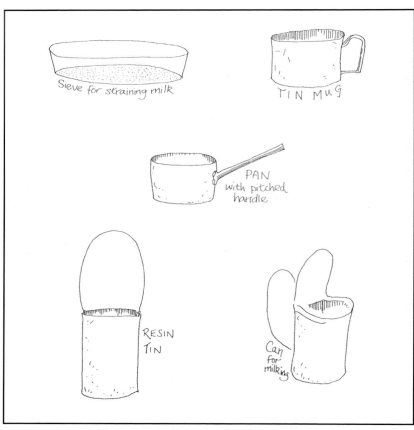

Some of the goods made for barter or hawking around door-to-door.

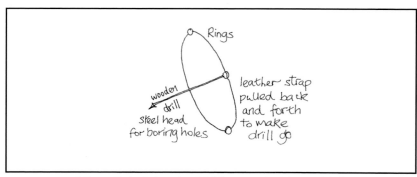

A Cheeny Feeker's (mender of delph or porcelain) bow and drill.
It works on the same principle as the early caveman's fire-starter.

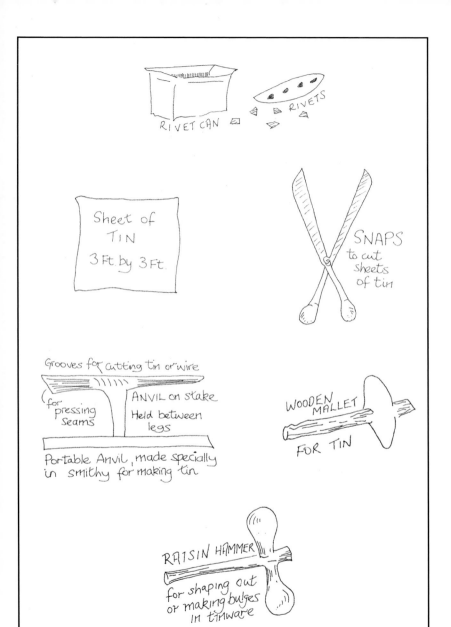

Tools of the trade for a tinsmith.

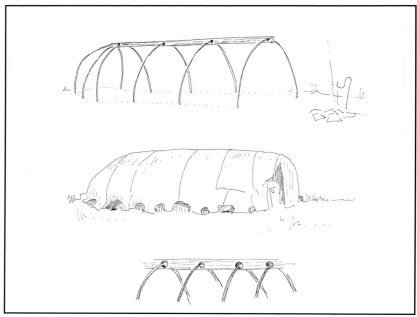

Traveller's tents. *Top:* Bow tent inside. *Top centre:* Bow tent outside.
Above: Rigging stick. *Below:* Gelly tent. *Bottom:* Barricade tent.

Heavy horses and ploughmen outside the Volunteer Arms, Forfar.
(*Scottish Ethnological Archive*)

Kirriemuir, Angus. As a young man, Duncan travelled all the country about here.
(*Scottish Ethnological Archive*)

A traveller's camp in Fife. Note the iron snottum in the entrance of the tent.
(*Scottish Ethnological Archive*)

Beauly, near Inverness. A typical Scottish market square, on a fair day in
the early twentieth century. (*School of Scottish Studies*)

boards with six-inch nails chopped into them, round like a horseshoe, like combs. And he and his family set sail every morning from June till the end of August, and all summer they collected cranberries. They grew wild among the heather in bunches. They used these steel combs and combed them off the top of the heather, and put them into sheets. They combed leaves and everything. On a windy day they held them against the wind and poured them into another clean sheet. The wind blew all the leaves away, and the cranberries were beautiful in red heaps. I'd never seen this done. So I gave Mr Stewart a hand to put his tent up. The man built a big bow tent and me and the boys carried up some sticks and his water.

By evening time everybody was back from the games and the donkey was up the old road. I made sure she was tied in grass to her knees. Everybody had their tea, so we all gathered round the one fire. I made sure I had plenty sticks. Winkie and I gathered all the hedgeroots that were rotten. We always called them 'auld gadgies', old men, meaning they were too old to grow any longer. We pulled them out of the hedge. They weren't good for anything. The farmers didn't bother you because you weren't doing any harm. You left spaces in the hedge right enough, where the sheep could go through. But they were the greatest things in the world to burn. So we got a fire of these old gadgies on, ken! And Mr Stewart was the greatest storyteller you ever heard in your life. Cracks and stories for evermore. But he was awfully fond of ghost stories, believed in ghosts. And we spent a fair night with him. They really were good company.

So next morning I was up early, put on the kettle and made the tea, shouted at Sandy. Sandy got up. And old Katie, the first thing she got up in the morning she had to get the pipe. Pipe before she tasted anything in the world, to get a draw. And Winkie and Isa, after they got their faces washed and their bit breakfast, they said they were going to the games. Now the games didn't open till about ten o'clock. So the night before Isa and I had packed all the flowers in Katie's square basket.

And Sandy says, 'Wumman, you're only wastin yir time gaun tae the game wi flooers! Different if ye had white heather or something, wumman!'

I said, 'Lea her alane, man. Wha' dae you ken? It's no you

sellin them is it? If she wants to stand at the game wi flooers it's aa right.'

So she said, 'Come along wi me, brother, and I'll get a pint o milk tae send back tae mak a cup o tea fir wee Winkie and yirsel, and I'll get ye a packet o fags. It was only two pence for a pint of milk and four pence for ten Woodbine. We came along to the wee shop. She bought me the fags and milk. On the road there we came to this wee house at the corner. And the privet was growing away up, beautiful. She went into the house and asked the woman.

The woman said, 'Aye, misses.'

She says, 'I'm only wantin tae put wee bits o privet, stick on ma flooers tae go to the games.'

'Oh!' the woman says, 'go and help yirsel.' So Katie chose three beautiful flowers and put three bits o privet in them. She gave them to the woman.

'Oh,' the woman says, 'thank you very much.'

Katie said, 'That's for the wee bit privet.' And they were beautiful!

I said, 'Auntie, I'll come along and meet ye at night-time after the games is finished.'

She says, 'Brother, I'm no gaun nae farther than the games.' It was only about half a mile from the games field to the shop. 'After I sell ma flooers I'll get some messages and come hame.'

So I had taken the bike with me, but I walked with it. After Katie had put the flowers on the privet and I'd said goodbye to her and Isa, I jumped on the bike and cycled back. When I got back to the camp here's Sandy and Mr Stewart, at the fire. Sandy was peeling wands and Mr Stewart was sitting cross-legged. His wife was away to the town, his laddies away to the hill. So I came in, put the bike against the dyke. Sandy's sitting, pipe going well and the pocket knife lying aside him. Mr Stewart's cracking to Sandy, he'd never seen him for months.

I said, 'I'll go and mak a cup o tea.'

'Aye, brother,' he said.

Winkie was running about making bows and arrows. So I got the tea on, good cup of strong tea and a full pint of milk. And the travellers didn't carry cups in these days, it was wee bowls. Katie wouldn't give you two pence for a cup. She loved these wee cheeny bowls. You could pack them into each other when you shifted, you see, they wouldn't break. Katie had about half a dozen of these. And while she was away I used to go for a can of water, roll up my sleeves and wash all the dishes, turn the barrow upside down and put all the clean dishes on the top for her coming back. I was really good about the place. Then I went for sticks and sat down beside Mr Stewart. Sandy and he were telling cracks about travellers and about ghost stories and burkers, cracking about horses, dealing the horses and the fast horses he had and the horses that wouldn't go and the anes that would! And the good deals he'd had and the bad deals, and the swaps he'd made and the good swaps he'd had and the bad swaps. Who had the best horses at the present moment, how far a horse could go in a day and driving up the glens, how much they could get in one day and all these things, the natural crack among travellers. So anyway, I came out with these two big bowls of tea.

I said, 'Mr Stewart, do ye want a bowl o tea?'

'Oh, cove,' he said, 'aye laddiekie!' That's what they called me in Aberdeenshire, 'laddiekie'. 'God bless ma sowl and body, man, that's a braw cup o tea.' He was kind of droll to me, ken? I gave him this bowl of tea and Sandy a bowl. So they sat and cracked and I helped Sandy peel the wands for a wee while.

Mr Stewart said, 'It's a wonder these laddies o mine's no comin back. It must be gettin round about evening.' And here his laddies came down, and they had bags on their backs.

'In the name o God,' I said, 'whaur were they, Mr Stewart?'

He said, 'They were awa tae the hill, man, cranberries!'

I said, 'What?' Now berries to me were juicy things you packed in a pail. I said, 'Ye cannae carry berries on yir back, Mr Stewart!'

'Oh aye, man,' he said, 'cranberries.' I'd never seen these because there were none in Argyllshire. You got blaeberries there. 'Oh, I'll hae tae gang and gie them a wee bit helpie,' said Mr Stewart. So I walked up with the man. And the man had the donkey yoked, the laddies had two bikes forbyes. They were cycling along, and they put their bikes lying against their father's tent. He said, 'Did ye get a wee puckle, boys?'

'Aye,' they said, 'Father, we got a puckle.' So he went to his

donkey cart and pulled out this beautiful, clean burlap sheet.
He spread it on the top of the ground and the boys cowped
about half a hundredweight of these things like red pellets out
of their bags onto it. And they had these combs and a string on
them around their wrists.

'In the name o creation,' I said, 'Mr Stewart, tell me a
wee bit about this. I'm a wee bit strange tae this, I dinnae
understand.'

The man picked up a handful, about half a dozen. 'Try two-
three, man. Ye no ken about these things?' They were a wee bit
bigger than redcurrants. I took one and burst it in my mouth.
Inside it looked to me like a boiled potato. They weren't juicy
in any way, just dry inside. The man said, 'They're cranberries,
man. We collect them and I'm takkin them tae a man up the
roadie a wee bit on the other side o Heugh-head. We stay here
for months at a time. We mak a wee bit o livin aff it.' They kent
what they were doing.

I said, 'Mr Stewart, what will ye get fir that?'

He said, 'I'm gettin six pence a pound.' Six pence a pound!
And they were pulling berries in Blairgowrie at a penny
ha'penny.

He said, 'We mak a guid livin at it, man. Ye've nae idea. Do ye
want tae try them? Look up the hill. The hill's red with them.'
But they were experts at it.

I said, 'No, I could never dae that.' You could see them in the
distance. The hill was dark pink with berries at the top of the
heather. They got ripe before the heather. So he shaked them
all out and against the wind. The wind blew the leaves away
and they were beautiful. He packed them in this big basket. He
jumped on his bike with the basket and away he went. Oh, he
must have had half a hundredweight on his bike. I went over
to the laddies.

They said, 'Aye, my daddy's away along tae see the man aboot
these berries. We dinnae hae too much. We dinnae ken, would
the man still be interested in them or no.'

Sandy and I had another cup of tea and we peeled some
more wands. I said, 'I think I'll go and meet Aunt Katie.' I was
just going to go out the road when here's Katie and Isa coming
in. Those flowers only stood them ten minutes at the games. It

wasn't the folk going into the games, it was folk in seeing the things coming out who wanted to take the flowers home with them. And the woman had plenty things, twenty fags to me, tobacco, the messages, everything.

So Sandy says, 'I think we'll stay here another couple o days.' But I was wanting to get on. Sandy knew I was wanting to go, but I didn't know my way up Deeside to Braemar. The Stewarts went back to their cranberries. They wanted me along but I said I wasn't interested. I stayed with Sandy and made some more baskets.

But I told him, 'I want to go to the berries.'

Sandy said, 'Brother, the berries is aa right if ye want a good time, but ye're no gaunnae make nae money.'

'I'm no makin nae money onyway,' I said. 'What difference does it mak? I'm no wantin tae mak nae money. My years'll come for makin money. I want tae see what's gaun on at the berries.'

'Well,' he says, 'I'll tell ye what's gaun on at the berries. There hunger and poverty, and starvation at the berries.' These are the words Sandy tellt me. 'And dirt and filth.'

I said. 'That's poor encouragement ye gie me.'

He said, 'I'm tellin you the truth.'

Aunt Katie said to me, 'Laddie, you're no wise gaun there tae the berries. You're better stayin wi me and Uncle Sandy. We'll go away back, up tae Braemar and we'll cut across, go back doon the other side, doon Deeside. We're thinkin o goin tae Fraserburgh for the wintertime. We're gaunnae work wir way up roond Inverness and back tae Fraserburgh, look fir an auld hoose for the winter.' Now I'd never been there. Fraserburgh to me was as well to be in America.

I said, 'Look, Uncle Sandy, I want to go to the berries. Whaur'll I get ye?'

'Well,' he says, 'I cannae tell ye whaur I'll be. Ye dinnae ken the road. But we'll shift the morn, go up the length o Crathie, across tae Crathie Kirk.' And the old man tellt me about Balmoral Castle and Crathie Glen. So the next morning we shifted from Heugh-head, and it was only a day's travel to Crathie Kirk. In the evening we landed there and the first thing I saw was a cart pulled close to the road. And a white horse.

I said. 'Uncle Sandy, there traivellers here.'

'Aye,' he said, 'I wonder wha it is.' So we pulled the barrow up and you had to leave your things at the roadend, go down the banking in beside the burn. And this wee man came up. Oh, he was about five foot two inches high, slim built and this great big moustache. But he had the bonniest blue eyes you ever saw in your life. And he only had one ear. Well, a bit o one anyway. And Sandy came up. I stopped the barrow at the roadside. Winkie was hurling the bike, Katie was walking behind smoking the pipe as usual. She and Isa were talking. And this cart was pulled right close to the roadside, just enough room for the traffic to pass. Down the banking was a nice camping place. And I could see a big bow tent and a big fire, and two or three folk round the fire. And this wee man came and shook hands with Sandy. Sandy introduced me.

He said, 'This is my Katie's sister's man, Katie's good brother.' He was called Hector Kelby. And he shook hands with me. We came down and put the tent up. The man had this white horse and he liked the way I spoke, you see. He asked me all about Argyllshire and he tellt me he was born at the Baton Farm, in Argyllshire. He had lived in Argyllshire but he hadn't been down in years. So he and I got on just like we had known each other for life! I never saw two people take to each other like me and him did. And years later we were to become the greatest of friends. The only regret I ever had in my life – when he died I never knew about it.

So Sandy said to me, 'That's wee Hector Kelby, a hardy wee gadgie. See that wee cratur, he can fight like big guns! There no a man in Aberdeenshire would speak tae that wee sowl.' He was no older than forty-five or so. Big moustache. Smart as a weasel. So after the supper was over we got round his fire. And then the cracks and tales started.

And ghost tales went on the entire night. Till about two o'clock in the morning with Hector. And then he wanted me to sing to him. And I had to sing. I sang the first song, that was it! He sat up and he made tea, and he made more tea and wanted another song, and he made more tea! And everybody went to their bed while me and Hector sat till daylight. It was summertime. This was the first time that somebody was really interested in me singing to them. And he had two lassies, two laddies and his wife Lizzie. Oh, he was awfully fond of country and western songs, Jimmie Rodgers. He had a gramophone and he had the records.

The next morning after Sandy and Katie and the crowd got up, they had a bit breakfast and a bit wash. Sandy said he was shifting on to Braemar. He was going to wait there till the games started. And Katie was going to sell heather.

So old Hector said, 'Well, I was thinkin o haein a run up tae Braemar wi yese. Prob'ly I'll no stay as long as that.' Because it was nearly a month till the games. 'But I'll prob'ly come back tae the games. I'll walk wi yese anyway.' So the man packed his cart and Sandy packed his wee hand barrow. Hector had this big white horse and a nice spring cart. He turned to Sandy, 'Sandy, look, I know that laddie's been wi you fir a guid while and I bet ye he's pulled that barra every road in Aberdeenshire. Come on wee Sappie, you'll get yoked in there, you take a shot o the barra!' And Hector says to me, 'You go ahead, laddie, and you tak ma horse. I'll walk wi him, I'll see he takes the barra.'

So we made our way to Braemar green. When we landed, there wasn't a soul, nobody. We stayed for a couple of days and the women did pretty well with baskets and flowers. But I had a yearning to get to Blairgowrie. So I tellt Sandy and Hector I was taking off the next morning. And Hector told me he was at the berries two-three times himself, but he wasn't going that year. And he tellt me a few things.

'Pro'bly my sister Lizzie and Johnie Whyte, they'll be there. If ye see them ye'll be okay.'

I said, 'I'll prob'ly stay two-three days and see how it goes. Then I'll push on tae Inveraray again and see the auld folk, and I'll prob'ly come back.'

'Well, I'm goin back tae Aberdeen,' Hector said, 'after the summer, efter the games is over. I'll prob'ly take an auld hoose about Aberdeen, if ye ever come in aboot, mind and look me up!'

I said, 'I'll keep that as a promise.' So the next morning I left Braemar and made my way over the Devil's Elbow. This is the first time in my life I'd been this road. I travelled on. It was late in the day before I took off – I'd promised Sandy I would come back again, and wherever he was I would look him up . . .

He'd tellt me, 'You're goin to Blairgowrie, eh? We'll prob'ly never see ye again fir a while.'

I'd said, 'I'll be back sometime.'

THOMAS THE RHYMER

O True Thomas he lay on a Huntly bank
Beneath an eldin tree
O when he saw a lady fair
Comin ridin ower the lea.

O Thomas he doffed off his hat
He got down upon his knee,
He said, 'Lady you're the greatest queen
That ever I did see.'

'O no, o no, o Thomas,' she said,
'That name does not belong to me
For I have come from Elfin Land
And I have come to visit thee!'

O her mantle it was of the forest green
And her tresses they were so fair
And from ev'ry tass of her horse's mane
Hung twenty siller bells an mair.

'O mount you up, o Thomas,' she said,
'An you maun come along wi me
For I am bound for Elfin Land
It is very far away!'

So they rode and they rode, and they merr'ly merr'ly rode
And it's merr'ly they rode away
Antil they came to a red river
That lay across their way.

'What river is this?' o Thomas he said,
'O please to me do say!'
'O this is the River of Blood,' she said,
'That is spilled on this earth in one day!'

So they rode and they rode, and they merr'ly merr'ly rode
An merr'ly they rode away
Antil they came to a crystal river
That lay across their way.

'What river is this?' o Thomas he said,
'O please to me do say!'
'O this is the River of Tears,' she said,
'That is spilled on this earth in one day!'

So they rode and they rode, and they merr'ly merr'ly rode
An merr'ly they rode away
Antil they came to a thorny road
That lay across their way.

'What road is this?' o Thomas he said,
'O please to me do tell!'
'O this is the road you must never lead
For that road it leads to Hell!'

Then they rode and they rode, and they merr'ly merr'ly rode
They rode for a night and a day,
Antil they came to a great orchard
That lay across their way.

'Light down, light down,' o Thomas he said,
'O it's hungry that I maun be!
Light down, light down,' o Thomas he said,
'For some fine apples I do see!'

'O touch them not,' the Elfin Queen said,
'Please touch them not I say!
For they are made from the curses
That fall on this earth in one day!'

Then reachin up into a tree
Into a tree so high,
She plucked an Apple from a tree
As they went ridin by.

'O eat you this, o Thomas,' she said,
'As we go riding by
And it will give to you the tongue
You shall never tell a lie!'

So they rode and they rode, and they merr'ly merr'ly rode
And they rode fir a year and a day
Antil they came to a great valley
That lay across their way.

'What place is this?' o Thomas he said,
'O please to me do say!'
'O this is Elfin Land,' she said,
'And it's here that you maun stay!'

So Thomas got some shoes of lovely brown
And a coat of Elfin green
And for seven long years and a day
On earth he was never seen.

                          Traditional

Chapter Eight

A Traveller Heritage

I wasn't really interested in picking berries, but in seeing for myself what happened in Blairgowrie. So I made my way, and it got kind of late. I slept in a haystack all night right on the top of the hill, near the Devil's Elbow. The next morning I made my way down the Spittal o Glenshee and into Blairgowrie, a place they call the Well Meadow. This was a green, a great big open space of ground where the travellers used to loosen out their horses. There was a pub across from it where the men made all their swaps and deals. If they couldn't swap at home at the tents, two or three men drove into town, and when they got a drink they went out in the green. When I came into the Well Meadow six or seven horses and carts were loosened out. Horses were tied up to the wheels and the harness flung on the carts. I said, 'There a lot o traivellers like masel I doot.' And a bunch of men were standing out on the green and some of them drunk. They were hitting hands [SLAP] 'Come on noo, come on then, I'll . . .' And I knew this was a deal going on. And the country folk in the village paid no attention because they had seen this often, 'Oh, that's jist the berry workers fae Blairgowrie.'

So I walked out a bit of the road. Uncle Sandy had tellt me, 'Ye'll see plenty traivellers. Ye'll be all right, jist jump on the first cairt ye see. Ye'll get a hurl oot to the berry fields.' And this man came along with a pony. The man was sober and he was trotting on. He stopped.

He said, 'You want a lift, laddie?'

I said, 'Aye.' He had a good bit o thick pony in the cart and he drove up to the berries. This was the first time I was in the Gothens. It was a moor at the other end of Blairgowrie just before you go to Meikleour. There were some large fir trees on this big heathery moor. And there was a big gate where the travellers could go in and put their tents up. You didn't need permission. Then there were dormitories, tin huts further back next to the farms. They were kept for the local folk who came from Dundee or Glasgow. In these dormitories were running water and toilets. And all the young folk used to come there and pick berries. Couples met and many were married. They had a great life just by meeting at the berries! Some non-travellers came at the time of the Glasgow Fair. When the really poor folk wanted a cheap holiday they came to the Gothens. Maybe they had two-three bairns and they just picked and earned enough money to keep them alive. They enjoyed the countryside. There were trees and fields for evermore, and they enjoyed getting away from the towns for a while.

But I had got a lift and the man said to me, 'You goin to the berries?'

I said, 'Aye, what kind o crop is the berries this year?' I had never picked berries before in my life, not domestic ones for sale. And there were these drills with raspberries hanging in clusters, and all these couples, one on each side of the drill picking the fruit with pails. They had these tin luggies tied round their waists.

So when I came into the camping place I looked round. I'd never seen so many tents in all my life: there were bow tents and there were barricades. There were gellies and there were home-made structures of all description. There were some travellers with horse-drawn wagons, ones with wooden tops and horse-drawn lorries with wee tents built on them. And all these ponies tethered up, I'd never seen so many in my life! Grey ponies and black ones and thin ones, all kinds of horses and dogs running about for evermore! Greyhounds, oh, big greyhounds! So I was lucky, one of my cousins was there and I stayed along with him for a few days to have a look at this berry carry on. But to me it was more exaggerated than what it really was. At night-time, oh, they gathered round a big fire and they started swapping and dealing. But you finally got sick of this through time, you got so used to it. It was a great thing when you heard about it, if you didn't know much. But after you'd been a time through it and had seen most of it, it didn't appeal to you the same. There were drunk men coming on stottering on top of fires, arguing with each other and pulling horses by the head, 'Come tae ye see this! Come tae ye see that!' And arguments would start and fights and women shouting, kids roaring, bawling.

But the best day among them all was a Saturday when the berries were finished for the week. It was time for everybody to go to the town. Everybody had a horse. And the man with the speediest one would wait till all the horses were strung out away along the road. Then he would jump on, he and his wife, and one by one he would overtake all these horses on the road. And it's an awful shaming thing to any person who has a horse – you're trotting on, sitting driving your horse on the road and all in a minute – another horse overtakes you. Then it overtakes the next one and the next one and the next! And a man would say, 'By God, that man's horse can fairly go!'

Now he was only giving them encouragement, for he had his own idea that everyone he'd passed would be at him for a deal. And he knew fine he could have his own way in a deal because he'd got the fastest horse and everybody would be after it. When he landed in the town the first thing he would stand and loosen the horse out. They'd all gather round and explain how fast this horse would be. 'Och,' the man who owned it would say, 'it's no nae faster than any other one.' Probably he turned down about six or seven deals till he got something that suited him, and then he'd swap. And this man who had got this horse faster than all the other ones would wait till the next Saturday coming, and he would do the same thing. Or maybe somebody had got it who wouldn't part with it; they did refuse to deal too.

But the thing that was most interesting of all was the dealing round the fires. Then they would take their dogs and all go out to the field. And the first hare that rose they would hunt it with their hounds. Then they'd come back and start swapping among dogs. My cousin took me round all these travellers and introduced me. Some of them I had met before in my travels, some I knew and some I didn't. He pointed out the horses and told me the ones that had complaints. My cousin had a good horse of his own, and he showed me ones he might swap for her and ones he wouldn't have. But the next day I was going to go out and pick berries. I said I wasn't going to come to the berries without picking any!

I went out and took a drill with my cousin. He got one side and I got the other. I picked and I picked and I picked on till about one o'clock. And I had this big pail. He was saying to me, 'Squeeze them doon, dinna be feart tae squeeze them!' And the juice was running over the side of the pail, running on to my leg. And I carried this big pail of berries into the weighing machine. The man took them and cowped them into a big bucket. He hung it up, weighed it. 'One and eight pence, a penny ha'penny a pound.' So I tellt my cousin, 'No, that's me finished. That's my berry pickin finished!'

So I never picked any more berries in Blairgowrie. But I did go back years later when I was married. My first visit to Blairgowrie I wouldn't say was a big success to me. I wasn't seeing anything that was really new. But the main thing that I enjoyed was two-three deals and swaps, and the two-three stories, you know, cracks, tales and sing-songs round the fire. When it got dark at night-time all these fires kindling, maybe about sixty or seventy fires going, all outside. Some of the folk had gellies, the folk from Skye or the Highland Stewarts had gellies with inside fires, tanks and chimneys. But most of the folk all had their outside fires at night-time and their horses tethered nearby. Then every cart and horse would drive away along the road, and the travellers would cut loads of grass because the feeding was very poor, eaten down to the quick. And the farmer wouldn't give them a field. Even suppose the farmer had, they couldn't turn all the horses loose together because there would have been murder made, horses kicking and biting each other. And travellers as a rule liked their horse close beside them. So the only thing was, you had to tie the horse beside the fire as close to your place as you could, go and cut grass and hand feed it.

So I waited for about three days and I saw the whole rigmarole, what went on. And I went into Blairgowrie a couple of times, saw the dealing and swapping going on in the Well Meadow. Other travellers I had been talking to, like Rabbie Townsley and Sandy and Hector and them, they probably enjoyed it. But I didn't. I did enjoy it later on. I was there at the last year of it. I think the farmer closed the Gothens in 1950. And then the travellers spread out to the wee local farms, maybe three or four camps, four or five at Marshall's. And they went up into Park Hill above Blairgowrie. But there never was the same amount got together after that. They always went to the berries, it's traditional, travellers still go back to the berries. But I said to myself, 'Prob'ly it's guid enough fir the folk that really likes it that way fir a wee while.' But you soon got very sick of it. I stuck it for about four days and then I left. I had the notion in my mind I was going to get a job somewhere, work and buy a horse for myself. I mean, it was all right standing by watching someone else dealing, but I had never actually had a deal myself. And I'd never had the pleasure of going to a man and asking him to buy an old horse, because I'd never enough money at these times. I was always on the move from place to place. I travelled round about Scotland for two years nonstop, never waited very long in the one place except in the wintertime.

So I made my way back into Perth, and from there I went back over Tyndrum again once more. I landed back home and I stayed with the old folk right on till October. I went to the old farm at Auchnangoul where I'd started to work, and I worked with Mr MacVicar for another couple of weeks. Then I took a notion I was to go on the road again. I remember saying farewell to my mother and my father. And that's the words my mother tellt me, 'Ye'll prob'ly be mairrit and have a wife the next time ye come back.' Those are the words she said.

I said, 'No, I don't think so.'

My father said, 'Why don't you go back to the farm where you were working? If you say that horses are so cheap, why don't you work and make some money on that farm? Then go back tae Perthshire and buy a horse there to yirsel?'

Well, it would have taken me a year working at the pay I was getting from the old farmer at Auchnangoul. I was seventeen past and he was only giving me ten shillings a day. It was too slow for me. So I saved up a few pound and made my way again to Perthshire, and landed back with my brother Sandy. By this time he had left Balbrogie and he had landed in Stanley on a berry farm. I stayed with him for a while and I got word that Rabbie Townsley was in Coupar Angus. It's not far from Stanley – in by Kinkell bridge and Meikleour. But he was at Burrelton, staying up in a place called Gallow Hill.

I went and saw Rabbie, and he and I had a great carry on, sat the whole night telling stories, cracks and tales. Rabbie had this sheep he'd got from a farmer; it had choked on a turnip. He and I sat with this big outside fire and we were cutting big lumps of mutton, holding it on sticks, roasting this mutton in the fire. So he tellt me his half-brother, Sandy, and Katie were in Fraserburgh. So I made up my mind I was going there.

I left Rabbie and went back to my brother Sandy, tellt him I was going off. And I made my way back into Aberdeenshire. From Aberdeen I went through Ellon right out to Fraserburgh. I got Sandy and Katie camped at a wee place at the roadside. Sandy had been in the town that day and he was mending baskets. This baker whom he'd met gave him a wee house and tellt Sandy he could have it for the wintertime. We moved in. It was a lovely house, oh, we liked it fine. And I got a job on a farm and I went and worked for MacConnachie's soup kitchen, outside work round about the place. And lo and behold one day we came back. Everything had been grand, when Katie said, 'I'm movin back tae Aberdeen.' Now this was January! And it was snowing. She went down to an old woman called Annie Mathieson, and she sellt all her furniture, bought two prams and packed all her things she could get into it. The next day they set on the road with these two prams to Aberdeen.

Now I had to go with them, I had no other choice. So we moved into Bucksburn and we stayed there for a couple of days. A traveller man Sandy knew whose name was Mackay, was one of the first travellers to get a motor. He had a wee Ford lorry He said, 'Sandy, cove, it'd be better if ye wad gang inta the toon and squatted inta some o the auld hooses.' In these days houses that were empty travellers could walk in, squat in them. And if you stayed long enough the councils never bothered you. So he took Sandy's stuff, packed it in his lorry and Sandy, he and I drove into Aberdeen. We drove right down the main street and came to this big building. We burst the door and went in. There were three flats. So Sandy and I picked one, put our stuff in and kindled the fire. The gas was on, we lighted the old gas lamps. Katie and the others came and we moved in. Next day the police came, 'Oh, yese is squattin?' 'Aye,' we said. 'Okay then.' and they took our names and addresses. 'Behave yirselves.' That was it.

So we hadn't been there a couple of days when who moved

in but Katie's sister Jeannie and her laddie Buggie! And he had
a horse. Now I was dying for this, it was a beautiful horse, half-
blood. He had no place to keep it and he wanted to sell it.

I said, 'Look, if ye hang ontae it . . .'

He said, 'I cannae hang ontae it.'

I said, 'I'll buy it fae ye if ye jist hang on fir a wee while, gie
me a week.' But he went down the street and gave the whole lot
away to a man for twelve pound – horse, harness and cart. That
was it. So he squatted in next door. Now the two flats were filled
up, but the bottom one down below someone had converted
into a boiler room. There was a great big boiler built inside. So
a couple of days after this, who comes in but wee Hector Kelby,
the very man I'd left in Braemar! And he shakes hands with me,
is glad to see me. He says, 'I'm lookin fir an auld hoose.'

'Well,' I said, 'it's only the boiler room doon there.'

'But,' he says, 'it would dae. It would be a guid place to stay
in if we could get that . . .' So he and I knocked the big boiler
out, broke it up in bits. And I built a fire into the space where
the boiler was. He got furniture, he papered and painted and
made it into the nicest house there.

Now fags were very hard to get, very scarce. So one night I
tried all the shops and I couldn't get a cigarette, no way. I'm
walking the street in Old Aberdeen. What was going to happen
in the next two or three minutes I didn't know, but this was
about to make a big change in my life. I see this man come
walking up. He had plus fours on, brogue shoes and a white
woollen sweater. He wouldn't be very old, about his late thirties.
I never noticed, but he had the white minister's collar under
the jersey. He was smoking. And I walked up.

I said, 'Excuse me, sir, I wonder if you could sell me a couple
o cigarettes. I've been huntin this village high and low, I'm
goin crazy for a smoke!'

He was very pleasant to me, 'Oh, they are very scarce, ye know,
tae buy. Ah, I won't sell ye any, but I'll give ye some cigarettes!'
And he took a packet of Players out and gave me five. 'Have
that packet. I have some more in the house.' He looked at me
for a long, long while and said, 'Have I not seen you somewhere
before?' Now I thought he was one of the doctors because the
college was just down the street a bit. And you had to be kind

of leery in these times who you were speaking to. There were some queer folk going about in the world, you know, and you had to keep an open mind!

'Well, sir,' I said, 'no, I just moved in.'

'Oh,' he said, 'youse are squatterin in the old house, in the old building.'

'I said, 'Aye.'

He said, 'Where are ye workin?'

'I'm no workin anywhere. I cannae find a job, I'm huntin fir a job.'

'Where do you come from?'

I tellt him, 'I come from Argyll.'

'Oh yes,' he said, 'ye come from Argyll. Do ye know Inveraray?'

'Yes sir, I know Inveraray well.'

'Do ye know Glen Aray?'

'Yes.'

'What's the name o the farmer in Glen Aray?'

I said, 'MacIntyres. John MacIntyre.'

'Oh yes, I see ye know the district well. And you know the MacIntyres are relations to my mother?' he said. And I didn't know who this man was. He was Reverend Iain Begg, the minister of Seton. And he says, 'Ye're lookin for a job?'

I said 'Aye, I could do with a job, sir, tell ye the truth.'

'Have ye registered for National Service?'

'No, I never.'

'What age are ye?'

I said, 'I'm seventeen past, goin on eighteen.'

'Oh, I see. And ye haven't registered for service?'

I said, 'No.'

'Well, I prob'ly could give you a few days . . . have you ever done anything in the wood work?'

'Oh well,' I said, 'I've swung an axe and I've cut plenty sticks in my day. And I've done a wee bit o this, a wee bit o that and a bit o everything!'

'Well, if you report to my house tomorrow morning about eight o'clock, I'll see if I can find ye a job.'

I go home and tell old Katie and Sandy, 'I've met this man,' and I explain to them.

Katie says, 'That's a doctor, he's a dodder! He'll burk ye – a burker. I'll bet ye it's some o the young doctors fae the college. If ye go to his hoose, laddie, that'll be the last ye'll ever be seen again! Ye've tae watch yirsel in Aberdeen because they burk bodies here.'

Sandy said, 'Awa woman, ye're auld-fashioned. The're nae such a thing as burkers here noo-a-days.'

She tried to persuade me not to go, but I said, 'Aye, I'm goin.' He had tellt me where to come to, it wasn't far. There was a big orchard way round the back and this big green door on the main street. So I knocked at the door and he opened it, took me into his office. This old woman came in.

He says, 'This is my mother.' And to her, 'Mother, this is the young man I was tellin ye about from Argyll.' And she was a good age, a woman in her late sixties.

She says, 'You are the one that knows the MacIntyres?'

I said, 'Yes, I know old John MacIntyre, I know him well.'

'How is old John?'

'Fine.' I tellt her all about Glen Aray and all the places, about Dalmally. She was fair taken away with this.

She said, 'It's been a long time since I've been there, ye know.' So we had a good crack. She brought coffee through, and Reverend Begg and I had a cup.

He says, 'It's about time tae get to work. Now, what I want you to do: I've got a sawmill and I want you to work in there. I'll give ye five pound ten a week.' That was a pound a day, sister dear! Then that was great money.

I said, 'What kind o line are ye intae?'

He said, 'I'm in the firewood business.' Well, that man was to become one of my greatest friends. That morning he went round the back and came out with an old Alvis car, and he took me down to the sawmill. There was an old man starting up the engine to drive the saw. And Reverend Begg says, 'The old man'll put ye to work!' And he went away. So old Arthur, as he was called, was very nice and he and I got along just like two peas. About twelve o'clock back comes Reverend Begg himself again with a big lunch basket, and he had a big flask of tea and a heap of sandwiches. He gave me something to eat. I worked on. But right where I was at the front of the saw I could see Arthur wasn't cutting the very good stuff. They had collected all the trees out of folks' gardens, dug them out. And the Reverend had two men who cut out the trees, loaded them onto a lorry and took them away, dumped them and kept the firewood. He had a big strip of wood at Alford, and he cut out there. But in front of the saw was an awful lot of knots, or blocks of wood, stuff you couldn't put through a saw. He must have had about four or five ton. And Arthur was cutting all the bits, and his men were filling their bags with this wee stuff.

I said to him, 'Reverend Begg—'

He said, 'Don't call me Reverend Begg anymore, call me Iain.'

I said, 'Right, Iain, look, I can see ye're kind o hard up fir stuff.'

He said, 'We are very short o stuff right now.'

'What's about that stuff lyin there?' There were about five ton of this beautiful ash, but it was full of knots. 'That's great firewood. That's the kind o firewood ye want.'

He said, 'We can never cut that.'

'Iain, ye can cut that! Why don't you split it?'

'You couldna split that!' he says to me.

'Ye can split that – that'll cut and split as good as anything. 'You split that, and you'll have about six or seven loads o stuff.'

He said, 'Dae ye think ye could do anything with it?'

'Certainly, I could dae something with it. Have ye got a hammer? A fourteen-pound hammer?'

'Yes,' he said.

'And some wedges, iron wedges?'

He went and got me this fourteen-pound hammer, and these iron wedges and a big axe. And I turned them over. It was like splitting ribbon. They didn't have an idea. So I got stripped to the waist and by night-time I had about three ton split, split right in four. And the men just carried them up to the saw and made these beautiful, big ash logs. He came and was so pleased!

He said to me, 'You have done a great job there, a great job! Man, I never gave it a thought that that could be done. Are you willin—'

'I'll do every single bit that was there.'

'Would you need some help? Have you not some o your pals could gie ye a bit help?'

Now Buggie was knocking about the house doing nothing. I said to him the next day, 'Buggie, ye wantin a job? The Reverend had said he would pay a pound a day. I'll gie ye a couple days work.' He was courting his future wife. They were just ready to get married. 'I'll gie ye a job.' He came down with me for one day. But night-time he went and drew his pay, drew his pound.

'No,' he tellt the minister, I was a slave-driver. He couldn't work with me. So I split every single thing that was in the place myself, never left a bit. Iain was so pleased that one night he came up to the house and he brought me jerseys, shirt and trousers. He handed them in to me. And fags, I never wanted for fags. I got kind o shan after that he gave me so many packets. He wouldn't take money for them. He had loads of fags, wherever he was getting them.

So one day he came for me and said, 'Duncan, we're goin downtown today. It's kind o queer, but we're goin to demolish a church.'

I said, 'No a church, Reverend, you bein a minister!'

He said, 'Yes, we're goin to demolish a church.' There were these big old-fashioned beams in the church, and the wood was good. He wanted them. So Arthur, Iain and I were stripping these big beams. And there were lumps of lead piping. I was gathering all this. And he said to me, 'What are you gaunna do wi this?'

'I'm gaunna take it home wi me, Reverend. I'm gaunna keep it, save it up and sell it.'

And every time he came across a bit – 'Duncan, another bit o lead?' He worked with us. So a couple of hundred yards down the road from where I stayed there was a wee scrap store, and I was nicking in every weekend. I was getting four pound, five pound extra with these pieces of lead out of the church.

But round the back of the church there were about fifty panes of glass, beautiful glass. 'Oh,' Iain said, 'I could do with some o that!'

I said, 'Take it!'

'Oh no, I couldna take that.'

I said, 'What are ye wantin it fir?'

'It's fir ma mother's lettuce. To make cold frames, put the panes o glass together and grow the lettuces in between them. No, I could never do that . . .'

I said, 'I'm no a minister!' So I packed every single pane o glass into the boot of his car. He never said a word to me. Right back to the house with them, I carried them all out, went into his mother's garden. I set up all these panes making a hothouse among the rows of lettuce. And he was so excited and so glad.

So he said to me, 'Duncan, I'll hev tae get ye a card, a broo card.'* He wanted me to work steady with him now, he began to like me so much. I wasn't registered. I was only working casual with him, but he wanted to take me on full time. And he had to pay my National Insurance stamp. So the next day he drove me down to Aberdeen, took me into the broo office and got me a card. Three weeks after that I got a letter, a summons to register for National Service. Now I'd tried to avoid this for about a year. I should have signed on when I was seventeen, and I was over the age. I was getting kind of fed up because the police stopped me wherever I went and wondered, 'Were ye registered wi National Service? Why are ye no in the Army?' The war was finished but you still had to do two years' National Service and I was always getting pulled up.

So I told Iain this same story, 'Iain, I've finally made up my mind. I want tae go into the Air Force.'

'Well,' he said, 'I don't want to lose ye. Ye're a great worker.'

'I have to go to register tomorrow.'

He said, 'I'll take ye doon.' So there was nothing to it. I just registered. About three weeks after this, another form arrived – a medical. He took me down to the office again. He said, 'Ye'll no pass.'

I said, 'How no?' But I had told him about my hand.

He said, 'That hand's finished, damaged. Ye'll no pass wi that. You'll be back home. I've got a job fir you. You'll be back!'

I said, 'I dinna want to be back, I want tae get intae the Air Force!' So I went in, signed on, stripped off and went through these doctors, got my medical examination. I came to the last old colonel at the end. I sat down and he talked to me a long, long while.

---

* broo card – signing-on book for National Insurance contributions

'What would ye like tae go into?'

'The Air Force,' I tellt him. He asked me, could I read and write and that. I tellt him, 'Aye.'

He said, 'Show me yir trigger finger. Put it against my finger. Now, push.' And I pushed. There was no force. He went away and came back in a wee while. 'You can go and put yir clothes on.' I put my clothes on. He went in his office and flung me a green card – Grade Four – unfit for National Service.

I came back. Iain was sitting in the car. 'How'd you get on?' I told him. 'I knew it,' he said. 'I knew you wouldna make it. In fact I'm glad!'

Well, I was with Iain for nine months after that. I made a few pound then and I had a good job. I wouldn't have left him, but he was going to get married. I even went back, when I went to Aberdeen in 1968, to his bungalow. I went round the back and there was an engine and some old wheels sitting by his car. He was still dabbling among old cars and things. But he wasn't in. I'd just missed him that time. So this was the minister who had taught me so many things and put me on my feet. I'd made some money with him. And we'd had some fantastic times together. He told me some great tales and some great stories, you know. We had a lovely time.

But to make a long story short, I began to get restless for the road again. I was kind o wearying. Now I was safe and I knew fine I could go anywhere I wanted to, I wouldn't be picked up by the police for the Army or anything. It was summertime again. This is why I wanted to get on the move. So I made my way back and I had a trip through Fife. I saw all the travellers there. I stayed in the Coaltown of Balgonie, moved down to The Firs* and from there I went to work on a farm on Kinglassie Moor. I worked there for a month digging drains and got some money, bought myself some clothes and took the bus to Glasgow. I walked right through Glasgow, right up to Arrochar and over the Rest and Be Thankful, walked the whole way.

When I came to the top of the Rest it started to snow. And it snowed and it snowed and it snowed. And I was very hungry. I was wet with snow. I came to the top of the Butter Bridge, and there were a lot of navvies' camps there, huts. They were

---

* The Firs – a camping place owned by Lady Wemyss

building a new road. I swore to myself, what I suffered coming over that hill in among that snow, I said, 'This is the end. This is the end o my wanderings. My wanderings is finished. Frae this time on there's no more wanderings fir me! I've seen it aa noo. It's about time I was tightenin my belt and tryin tae dae something better than what I'm daein.' I walked into the hut, went into the office. There wasn't a soul there. And I saw a light in one of the huts. I walked down and there was an old gaffer, and I told him I was looking for work.

He said, 'The're nobody here, everybody's away, jist masel. But come in. Where are ye makin fir?'

I told him, 'I'm goin to Inveraray.'

He said, 'Would you take a job? I'm lookin fir a boy to help me in the store.'

'I'll take the job.' And he and I sat. He gave me a couple o bottles o beer and we had a drink. He made me some tea, sang to me all night and gave me a bed. He fell asleep. But the next morning I got up. I was wearying to see the old folk, and I caught the Royal Mail* at six o'clock to Furnace. And I tellt my mother, 'I'm back. I'm no gaunna go away no more. I'm fed up wanderin, I'm stayin at hame.'

Mother says, 'Ye'll be lifted fir the Army.'

'No', I said, 'I'll no be lifted fir the Army any more. I'm passed, Grade Four.' So I stayed there with the old folk all that back-end, and who came in the wintertime but my brother Sandy and Betsy! He put a big tent up beside my father and mother in the wood. And he and I had a rare, good winter of it. We had a great time together fishing and going to the shore for shellfish, going to the hill for rabbits, and I was quite happy. But the spring following Sandy coaxed me, said he was going back to Forfar. And I went back with him to Forfar again.

Before we landed in Forfar we went up to Benchie Farm and planted tatties. From there we walked on to Forfar and right away up to Oathlaw. In Oathlaw we were camped at the burnside. Sandy and I were sitting beside the fire when we heard these feet on the road. This was my cousin John! He and his mother and his auntie were staying about two miles along the road. So I left Sandy the next day and went with John. I

* Royal Mail – post bus

stayed with John all that year and we went back into Fife, into
Dunfermline. By this time I was twenty.

Now I've said very little about my feelings towards the things
I had seen going on; which way I really fared, which way did I
want to go, which kind of life did I want to lead? After I went
back to Forfar with my brother again, back over the 'same old
story', the same old roads, seeing the same old things again,
I'd ended up with my cousin in Oathlaw. And then we'd moved
back to Fife. Now I'd known my cousin John's sister Jeannie
since she was about thirteen years of age, from the very first
time I had met John, when I went to the horse market in Perth.
And I had little thought of ever getting married, especially to
her, for she seemed to me just like a sister. And I could have
chosen many other lassies that I'd talked to along the way for to
be a wife. But a fate was to send me back to Fife with my cousin
and meet his sister once again.

By this time she was seventeen years of age and we had
both grown. I saw her in a different light from her just as my
cousin – now Jeannie was a young woman and I was a young
traveller man. Naturally, when young travellers get together
and they take a liking or a notion to each other there's no
time wasted, such as long courtships and planning for houses
and planning for everything else. It's just a matter of getting
together and get one thing understood between you – you love
each other. You might be penniless. Her mother might not be
happy, or my mother'll not be happy. But we didn't give one
thought to anything else. We just wanted to be together and
be on our own and start from the beginning. I didn't have a
ha'penny, I had no job, I had nothing. And we just made up
our mind that we were going to start out in life together. We
had nothing planned, we didn't know what to do, we just said,
'That was hit.'

I mean all travellers are like that. When you go back to the
beginning and see among these travelling people, the thing
that really means so much to them – it's not property or all this
great security or anything else – that doesn't have any *meaning*
to them. It's the actual partnership and being together that
actually has the meaning to travelling people down through the
years. And their stories and tales and songs going back for four

hundred years among the traveller people, how they eloped with each other, and they had nothing. And the amazing thing is, even though they had so little and they had planned so little for the future, they always managed to stay together and have a happy family. Some of them went on to become old together and die together. For hundreds of years this went on. And they never regretted one moment of it.

I had little thought or little knowledge of being married in any way, and neither had she. So I'd heard stories of how couples just eloped and built up a future together with each other. I said, 'Well, if they could do it so could I!' That was the idea, I mean it was a traveller heritage. I wasn't doing anything new that my forbears had never done before me. This was expected of me to do this. And her father and her mother had done the same before her, and her grandfather and granny had done the same before them, and she didn't expect anything else. She wasn't looking forward to marrying rich and she had no thought of security or anything. It was just the love of being together and being with each other, and fight the battles as they came. Of course we could have turned round and told her mother we were getting married, and her mother maybe would have been quite happy. Because in fact she was my cousin; and my auntie and I got on very well, and so I did with my cousin and his brother as well. But anyway, just to keep things on the right form and make it look as if we really meant it, we had to elope – we just called it 'run away'.

So we took the bus to Cupar . . . If I'd had said to my auntie 'Look, I'm in love wi yir daughter and I want to marry her, and me and her'll jist stay together with you,' she would never have had the same respect for me that way. We were breaking away, running away without a penny, just showing her mother that we could go on our own and do as we wanted to, like she had done before in her time and her father and mother before her. It might sound unnatural to you and the settled community, the non-traveller – if you run away you're doing something wrong. But in the traveller idea you're taking your wife with you to show her family that you can take care of her. You'll probably meet them three weeks, five weeks, maybe a year later. And you'll come back with a good horse, a good cart to show you had conquered the moment and had survived, were quite happy together. You had made a start.

Probably my brother-in-law, my cousin had searched for me and Jeannie that evening after we left. But never having an idea what direction I had gone, he had little success. But it was *expected* of them to search after the lost daughter. Like me, when my daughter went away in later years. I, too, searched for her. Not that I didn't trust the man she went with, but it was expected of me. The man who sits and lets his daughter run away is not regarded as a good father at all. Let it be brother, sister or father – you must do something to show face, even suppose it's only a half-hearted attempt. You kick up a stir, even though it's only a front, to show you're doing something. When my daughter Betty left she was only fifteen past. She'd worked beside me all that day gathering tatties. I'd seen them kissing and cuddling in the drills beside me. I was lifting the baskets. And I knew. I was happy and pleased, for the laddie was a good laddie. I knew him. And when she left, her mother was a wee bit upset. Now, she had to comply with the other women around the site, you see. And they would say, 'Oh, what kind of woman is she that would let her wee lassie at fifteen run away wi a man?' So, when Betty's mother went for the police and kicked up a row, she showed a kind of respect for her family. Even though it was only a half-hearted attempt and they knew that nothing would come out of it. This is the traveller idea.

So anyway, I had chosen that Jeannie and I should go into Cupar, and then cross the ferry to Dundee and take the bus to Aberdeen. We stopped in Cupar and I remember I walked into a shop and bought a large bottle of cider. None of us ever had a drink before, but I said to her, 'Would ye like something to drink?' And we'd only been together – I mean we had nothing in common. We had kissed but I'd never touched her or been near her in any way. I walked into the shop and I bought a large bottle of cider, and we walked out of Cupar. I knew that I had left Dunfermline – her brothers were well behind me. I said, 'Do you want a drink?'

She said, 'Yeah, I'll take a drink.' She drank and she said, 'Gie me some more o that cider.' And she drank nearly half this bottle. And I hated the stuff. I was going to throw it away. So she said, 'Let me carry it.

I said, 'I'm no carryin a bottle o cider. If you want to carry it, you drink it!' So she drank it, and it took a wee bit effect on her, you know! And she was so happy. I said, 'Look, I'm no tryin to make you drunk!'

'No,' she says, 'I like that stuff. It's like appleade.' She was quite cheery.

I said, 'I hope you have got nae regrets.'

'No,' she said, 'if I had any regrets I wouldn't be here.'

I said, 'I'm goin on to Aberdeen. Yir two aunties are there. In fact, ye have three aunties in Aberdeen.' Her mother's three sisters, Katie, Jeannie and Mary.

She says to me, 'I don't care where ye're gaun. As long as I'm with ye, I'll go anywhere you want to go.'

Now we only had our bus fares. No idea what we're going to do or anything. So I said, 'The best thing I can do is go back tae Aberdeen, and I'll go tae Reverend Begg. I'll take a job, I'll work and we'll save wir money and I'll buy a horse! There plenty auld horses knockin about Aberdeen and I'll have a deal. And me and you'll get a horse and cart. We'll go on the road like real travellers. And after we get a good horse and a good cart, we'll go back to Fife and see yir mother, tell her we're okay – she's gaunna be worried.'

But the thing was, I had spent about two years steady back and forward with Jeannie's mother, and I used to read Western stories to her and we used to go to the town. And I'd hawked with her, I'd sellt holly with her, and she knew me through and through. In fact, I was her man's sister's son and I was closer to her than a stranger. We had great respect for each other. And I knew, in her own heart she knew that as long as Jeannie, her daughter was with me, little would happen to her. But that wasn't her mother's worry. Every mother worries what happens to her lassie – it doesn't matter who she goes with.

So, as the story goes, we got the bus into Aberdeen. Then we walked through and out to Old Aberdeen, about a mile and a half, and we preferred to walk. When we landed back at the building where Sandy and Katie and Jeannie were, the roof was off of the building next to theirs. But the downstairs floor was still there. We walked in. Only wee Hector Kelby and Lizzie were there. He shook hands with me.

'Duncan, ye're back!'

I said, 'Aye, I'm back, Hector.'

'Is this yir wife?'

'Well,' I said, 'this is my wife. She's my wife noo and she's gaunna be the only wife I'll ever have.'

'Well, yir Uncle Sandy left two days ago. Buggie left the same day. They're makin their way for Perth.' So we had some tea with Hector and we cracked for a wee while. So, no place to go. Hector asked us to stay. 'Stay the night, there's plenty o room for ye.'

'No,' I said. 'Jeannie's never seen her Aunt Mary.'

'Noo,' he said, 'Jeannie and Mary are up the road in the huts.' It was a big Army billets. Jeannie and Mary are up there. Sandy and Katie left yesterday, but I was oot when they left. I dinna ken what direction they took. If you go to Jeannie and Mary,' who was Katie's and Hector's sister, 'they'll prob'ly tell ye where they went.'

So we sat and had our tea with Hector and we bade him goodbye. And you know this was the last time I was ever going to see Hector Kelby. He died shortly after that.

And old Lizzie says to Jeannie, 'You run awa, ye wee lassie, ye're only a wee cratur yet!' You know, Jeannie wasn't very big. She was young looking, but she was seventeen going on eighteen. She didn't look very old and I was taller than she.

'No,' she said, 'we only cam for a visit.' Jeannie was kind o shan. 'We only cam for a visit!'

And old Lizzie said, 'Aye, ye wee liar! Ye're awa wi a man.'

'No, Lizzie, I'm no awa wi a man!' And Jeannie had these blue eyes, and she'd short, short hair and it was curly. Her eyes were as blue as berries, you know. And she wasn't very big, only about five-foot-two or five-foot-three, and she never was stout, no way. She was only made like a lace, a boot lace.

She says, 'Aye, ye're a wee liar, ye run awa wi a man.'

And old Hector turned around, said, 'Look, Lizzie, if she ran awa wi a man, I'll tell ye something. She got a man that can look after her.' That was really true, till the last days that was really true. I looked after and took care of her, and it wasn't my fault that God took her from me. (She died in 1971.)

So Hector had said, 'If you go up to Johnie and Mary, ye'll see where Katie and Sandy went.' So we walked up, it wasn't far up to Seton. And there was a big place where the Army had huts. These were condemned. They gave them to the travellers rent free. Dozens of travellers were staying there. And some had horses tethered on the green, and carts up beside the Nissen huts. So by the time we walked up it would be about five or six o'clock. Now old Mary had five sons of her own and three daughters, and they all were with her. Not one of them were married, and there were some of them older than I, so we landed up at the hut, knocked at the door, walked in and they were all sitting at their tea. Old Johnie knew me from that time, because he used to love me singing to him.

'Oh,' he said, 'ye're back!' Johnie was awful dark. He was like the Whytes a lot, the same kind of eyes, the same kind of eyebrows. These were ay the markings – you could always distinguish the Whytes – their eyes never change.

And Mary says, 'Oh, it's you!'

'Aye, Aunt Mary, it's me, I'm back. Hae ye any idea where Sandy and Katie went? We cam fae Fife this morning.'

She says, 'Wha's this here wi ye, what lassie is this?'

'That's yir sister Bellag's lassie,' I said, 'Jeannie.

'Ah, it's wee Jeannie.'

'Aye.'

'Oh God bless hus, it's no a while sin I seen her! It must be years. What age are ye noo?'

Jeannie says, 'I'm eighteen.'

'No, ye're no eighteen! And ye run awa wi a man!'

'No, I only cam through wi my cousin Duncan here tae see yese!'

She says, 'Ye wee liar, ye're tellin lies, ye run awa wi a man! If I kent where yir mother was I'd take ye right back the night.'

I said, 'No! What about yir ain dochters?'

She says, 'All my dochters has no got nae men!' She was like old Katie, good at heart. 'Anyway,' she says, 'If yese are married, are yese gaunna be wi each other? Ye're no gaunna get Sandy and Katie the night! They left yesterday and bi this time they'll be makin their way to Stonehaven. Well, come in and get something tae eat.' So she gave us a good tea and we sat and cracked for a long while. 'Well,' she says, 'youse young couple'll be needin a bed. So, Jeannie, come on lassie, come wi me, you've got a man noo, dinna be ashamed. Come on and I'll tak ye and show ye where yese can make a lie doon fir yirsels.' So the woman made us a good bed. And the next morning she wanted us to stay for a couple of days.

'No, Aunt Mary,' I said, 'we have tae mak wir way back. We only cam fir a visit.'

'I ken ye only cam fir a visit,' she kidded us on. 'I ken the way yese is lyin wi a young woman aa night!'

'I ken! It's aa right, Aunt Mary,' I said, 'she's my wife and we're gaunna get married and that's hit.'

So they were very happy about it anyway, and old Johnie bade us goodbye, And he said to Jeannie, 'There, lassie, there's ten shillings tae ye. There a wee present for ye.' It's a good job he gave it to us because we had nothing.

We bade Mary and Johnie goodbye and we walked down to Aberdeen. I said to Jeannie, 'There's nae sense in stayin in Aberdeen. We'll no bother. The best thing we can dae is mak wir way, catch up wi Sandy and Katie. We'll stay with them fir a while. Wherever they go, we'll go wi them and somewhere along the way we'll get a job.' Now Jeannie was really very clever. She could sell flowers, she could do anything because she'd done it with her mother steady. I didn't need to worry about anything. She could get a shilling under other folk's feet, honest to God, she really could.

We took a bus from Aberdeen, only about half a crown each, to Stonehaven. But we came out the other side of a wee place called St Cyrus, and there we saw these barrows going along the road. This was Katie and Sandy with his newly built barrow, and Buggie with a pram and Winkie with another pram! They were all strung out. The bus slowed down and we pulled the bell. The bus stopped and Jeannie and I came out. Then there was a happy reunion. Katie, who had never seen Jeannie since the Hoolet's Neuk, said, 'Oh, what a big lassie!' And Isa, Katie's youngest lassie, was really jealous. Now by this time she was about fourteen. And we had spent a great time together that one summer in Aberdeenshire with Sandy and Katie. She believed I was going to marry her sometime. She was really upset, you know. Isa was a grown lassie, as big as Jeannie but younger. I said to her, 'Never mind, Isa, ye'll get a man tae yirsel sometime.'

So I said to Aunt Katie, 'Oh no, I'm no married! I just took Jeannie up to see ye. She's goin away back . . .' We couldn't convince them, you see! So we came along the road with Sandy.

He says, 'We're gaunna go tae Stonehaven.'

I said, 'Ye'll never make it to Stonehaven, Sandy.' So we came to this old house, a ruins. And there was a big garden, and the house was empty. I said to Uncle Sandy, 'Why don't we stay in there for the night?'

He says, 'Brother, ye cannae stay in there.'

I said, 'Come on, come in to the garden!'

He says to me, 'Ye got a mort?'

'Aye, it's my wife.'

'Well,' he said, 'brother, there no much I can dae fir you, but I'll gie ye half o my covers. So he had two big covers, and Sandy gave me a big canvas one. Then Katie gave me two blankets. Then Buggie's mother gave me another two blankets. That was four, all we needed. So Sandy put up his tent and I put up my tent on the other side of his. Now by this time Buggie had run away with Johnny and Mary's daughter.

Buggie said, 'I've got a wife tae!'

I said, 'I ken, I see that.' He had Mary with him. And they were only about four days together, but old Mary Whyte had consented to them before they'd left Aberdeen. Her daughter could go with Buggie because it was her cousin, you see, and they had been reared together. Old Mary didn't worry so much about her. So he and me, and Jeannie and Mary, we sat together cracking at the fire in this old ruins of this house. We made plans, oh, all these great plans what we're going to do.

So Sandy had given me a cover, but I couldn't get any camp stick – there was not a camp stick to be gotten in this garden. So I went into the house and I took a couple of pieces of raft off the door, and I built a bivi, a marquis tent with two poles. I put some stones round it, and I went and cut some rashes and made a bed. Jeannie was kind of shan, with other folk next to us. We were only about two nights together. I said, 'Come on, get the bed made!' And she was awfully ashamed. She was very easy shanned. I said, 'Come on, ye're a mairriet woman now, so get the bed made!' So I cut these rashes and made this tent. We sat, cracked and made tea for a long while.

Sandy said to me, 'Brother, you stay wi yir Uncle Sandy and we'll go to Forfar, to Rescobie Loch. The wands is growin like corn. Me and you, we'll cut wands, make baskets.' And Jeannie used to go and hawk with Katie and her mother, since she was only five years old. Old Sandy kent Jeannie was a really good hawker. And he said, 'Me and you'll make baskets together. We'll get a pony between us. We'll buy one horse between hus first. We'll buy it fir you.' This was the plan. 'Suppose it's only a wee Shetland, jist something to pull the cloots and pull the bits o camp. And me and you can hawk wi hit. You pay me back and we'll get another horse.'

I said, 'All right, Uncle Sandy, that'll dae.' So all the plans were made. I said, 'Sandy, I'm definitely needin a pony. All my days, all my life I've been lookin for a horse now. I could have had a horse a long time ago but I cam to the consideration, what was ae body daein wi a horse . . . folk would speak aboot me. Noo I've got a wife, I definitely cannae dae withoot a horse. Never mind nothing, a horse has got to be the first priority!'

He said, 'Brother, dinna worry, you'll get a horse. You stay wi yir Uncle Sandy, you'll get a horse!'

So we travelled on and I put my cover on top of Sandy's pram. I was pushing it. Jeannie says to me, 'Ye cannae keep yir bits o cloots,* hae other folk hurlin yir wee bits o cloots alang the road.' She was always like that. And we stayed at an old road beside the graveyard at Montrose on the way to Rescobie Loch. She and Aunt Katie went away to the town. And Jeannie came back. She had this great big double pram, oh, beautiful! This was as good to you as a horse in these days! And she hurled it up.

She says, 'I got this pram. It'll help hurl yir ain things.' It had big high wheels and there was plenty o room, you know, you could put a lot of stuff into it. A pram may seem little to you. But it was the entire means of life to these folk. They could pack their blankets into it, they could put their tent on it and they

---

* bits o cloots – old blankets and tent covers

could tie their camp sticks round the side and their dishes on the top. You could walk and just shove it easily. So she'd got this pram, and this was the start, the first beginning.

Sandy says to me, 'Oh. brother, that's a good pram, a real good thing. That'll hurl a lot o stuff.' Jeannie had begged it in a house. I've seen travellers hurling scrap, rags and woollens with a pram till they got the price of a horse. Many's a body today is well off who had started with a pram! So the first thing I did was take the hood off it, flung it away.

'Doll,' I said, 'that's fine, that'll just dae, the very thing!' Now she and I were on the road, see! We were on our own, we had our pram, we had our cover, we had our blankets. That's all we needed. We could build a tent, we could go on the road anytime. Nothing stopped us. We were free and easy, we could go as we liked.

The Broken Token

O a pretty fair maid walking in her garden,
When a handsome sailor came walking by,
And as he viewed her he stepped up to her
Sayin, 'Fair you' maid would you fancy I?'

'To fancy you, sir, it would not do, sir,
For I have a true lover of my own,
And he's but a true and a faithful sailor
And seven long years now since he's been gone.

But seven long years make no alteration
Another seven I'll wait for him,
And if he is wed, sure I wish him happy
And if he's dead, sure I wish him rest.'

He said, 'Do you see that big castell up yonder?
And do you see all those lilies white?
I will but give you its gold and silver
If you will be my true love tonight!'

She said, 'What do I care for your castell up yonder,
What do I care for your lilies white;
What do I care for your gold and silver
If my own true lover was here tonight!'

He put his hand all into his pocket,
His fingers were so genteel and small;
He brought out a ring that was broke between them
And when she saw it she down did fall.

He picked her up all into his arms
Then he gave her kisses one and two,
Sayin, 'I am your true and your faithful sailor
And I've come home, dear, to marry you!'

Traditional

CHAPTER NINE

BEGGARS, THIEVES AND STRANGERS

So the next morning I packed my pram and put the blankets in the bottom. Whatever bits o clothes Jeannie had, I put them on. And I folded the covers on the top, put the two poles o the camp on and I had plenty of room. Sandy's watching me like a crow. He had this wee bit o a pram, small wheels, and it was awfully hard to shove.

He says to me, 'Brother, I couldna shove that. That's finished, that pram.' See, this is the way o him. 'That's completely finished. Brother, you've bings o room. Why don't you pack all my wee bits o stuff on top o yir pram and we'll shove it between hus?'

'I'm game,' I said, 'that's all right.' So once you tie a lot along the side of a pram, it broadens the top and then you can build more stuff on. For all he had anyway, two sets of sticks and his two-three blankets, two-three dishes, pots and pans and that. It was nae bother. Because they were all packed up nice and easy. So we packed everything on the top of this big pram that Jeannie had got. And he flung his pram away.

So he said, 'Brother, there's an old road oot the other side o Stonehaven. We could stay there fir the night.' It wasn't far. So we made our way to this old road. We landed there and Jeannie and old Katie went away to the town to sell the flowers they had made. He said, 'I think I'll go to the toon wi Aunt Katie.'

'I thought Jeannie was away wi her,' I said. 'What are you gaun to the toon fir?'

'Ach, brother, I'll hae a wee walk tae the toon, get masel a bit tobacco. You go on to the camp with the lassies, wi Isa, Ningen and Winkie.' Sandy walked away to the town. I went on, put up his tent, put up my own camp for myself at the old road just above Stonehaven by the graveyard. Buggie put up his tent for his mother and the tent for himself. In a couple of hours' time Katie and Jeannie came back. Jeannie brought me a Western book and fags, everything, messages. We just made tea with Aunt Katie for a start. About an hour later Sandy came back, and he had a lady's bike. Here he's going on a lady's bike! And his pipe going, the reek fleeing from him.

'Aha,' I said to Jeannie, 'look! He thinks this is gaunna start all over again, the carry on. He worked me sore in Aberdeenshire a long time ago.' He thought in his own way, 'Ma blankets . . . an Duncan'll shove ma cloots an shift ma camp, and I'll get an old bike.' He went to the town to beg it, the bike from some of the houses. This is what he wanted! No bother, no trouble, I'm pushing the pram with his stuff and mine. I never said a word. I mean I was young and strong, I didn't bother. So he came in. Katie gave him his tea. Oh, and he has a wee oil pourie, keeps a wee box with tools in it and keys. He was like a weasel, a crow for keys. Out to the bike and he oiled it, turned the chain and tightened the nuts.

I said, 'What is this fir? Ye're not gaunna hurl much stuff wi that.'

'Oh, brother,' he says, 'ye've nae idea. This is fir me and you. I got this fir me and you! This is fir gaun fir the wands tae me and gaun tae the shop wi the baskets, gaun tae meet Aunt Katie. The handiest thing in the worl fir me an you!'

I said, 'Aye, oh aye. Fir you, no fir me! I'll no get much guid o it.' But I wasn't worried.

So the next day he said, 'I think we'll shift today. We'll go to Forfar.'

I said, 'All right.' We shifted to Forfar. We went out to the old road. And he never pushed the pram all day, never put his hand near it. All he did was cycle along with the bike. And, 'I'll have to go, brother,' he said, 'and get a wee taste baking soda, ye ken, fir my stomach.' And he cycled away on. It was night before you saw him! He was away begging his own tea and begging dry socks for himself. He would cycle to a town and mend baskets and get tobacco for himself. I was coming behind with the pram, see, with all the things in it. So we landed in Forfar old road, put up our camps.

He said, 'We'll stay here for a wee while. This was on the road to Rescobie Loch. So it was a God's blessing that there were only certain places on the old road that you could put your camps. You couldn't put them close together, so's to leave room on the road for folks passing by. It was a right o way walk. You had to put your camp up the banking apart from the others and not in a line. Buggie put his camp up. I put Sandy's camp up and further along I put my own tent up. I helped build them all. Sandy was away with his bike looking for tobacco, and Buggie couldn't build a tent by himself. Sandy carried his sticks with him and one of these rigging poles you just shoved the sticks in. You didn't need to tie them for a bow tent.

I didn't bother about a bow tent. I just had two poles, stuck them in the ground and made a cross bar, a bivi for me and Jeannie. The lassies went to the town, came back and we had our tea. So we started playing quoits. Oh, Sandy was good at this. He'd left his bike against the wall, but none of the weans should touch it! He's more interested in this bike than anything else. We played quoits on till about ten o'clock at night, Buggie, Sandy and I, while the women did other things about the place. But we stayed there for a couple of days and I always got up early in the morning, made a cup of tea. So one morning I was just finished my tea and Jeannie was washing her face. I had mine washed.

I said, 'I think we'll shift this morning, we'll leave Sandy and Katie. We'll make wir way back. I think we'll go to Fife. The're nae prospects, him wi that bike, me wi ma pram. As long as he gets me tae hurl his stuff, he'll never dae nothing, Jeannie. The best thing we can do is cut oot on wir own.'

'I think that's the best thing ye could dae,' she said.

'We've nae use tae wait on naebody,' I said. 'We'll pack wir ain pram and tell him we're gaun away across the ferry. We'll go intae Dundee and tell him we're leavin him.'

She said, 'That's all he can dae is cycle that bike. He jist depends on you every day.' Old Katie was all right and the weans were all right, but he wouldn't do anything. And I knew even suppose we landed in Rescobie Loch, all he would do is go away with his bike every day and I wouldn't see him.

And I said, 'We're only wastin wir time.' Now we weren't worrying anyway. So, we had just started when in came a policeman with a bike. And he was only about twenty-one. I said, 'Good morning, constable.'

'Oh, good morning,' he said. 'How long hae you been here?'

'Well, constable, I've been here about three days.'

'Where do you come fae?'

'I cam fae Aberdeen.'

'Is this your wife?'

'Aye.'

'Your name?'

I said, 'Duncan Williamson.'

'Where do you come from?'

'Originally I come from Argyll, but I've been in Fife fir a long time. And we're jist makin wir way back. We're intendin tae jist move oot.'

'That's all right,' he says. 'What's about the other crowd?'

'Constable, I don't know nothing about the other crowd.'

'They were in the town last night, late last night,' he said.

'Aye, I suppose they were.'

'And I had a number of complaints aboot them,' he says.

'No, constable, you never had nae complaints about them,' I said. 'The're more travellers in the district than them.'

'Well, I had complaints anyway about them bein in the town beggin.'

'Well, I'll tell ye something,' I said, 'if you got complaints about beggin, it wasna them. I'm no sayin they're any better than anybody else, but, constable, you can believe me! You wouldnae get any complaints about them beggin because my wife went to the shop in Forfar on the road through, and so did the rest o the crowd. I can verify that. There's a lot o tinkers in the district forbyes them.'

'Well, that's the complaint I got anyway,' he said, 'from the station tae move ye.'

'Ye dinnae need to move me on.'

'Oh,' he said, 'all right. If ye're shiftin, it's okay.' So I put out the fire, took down the tent and packed my pram. Sandy was still in bed and so was Buggie and old Jeannie and Nellie. Constable went up and he knocked on the top of the tent.

'Who's there?'

'Police.'

Sandy got up, flung the door up. He was lying with all his clothes on him right in front of the tent. Travellers usually did that in case they got up in an emergency. All they took off at night was their jacket and boots, especially the men. Maybe the women took off their clothes, but the men never. And he said, 'What is it, laddie?'

He said, 'Ye have to shift.'

Sandy said, 'We cannae shift. I've nae way o shiftin. How can I shift now?'

Constable said, 'How did ye get here?'

'It was only the kindness o the laddie,' he said. 'Ye have to wait, constable, fir a wee while till my wife gangs tae the toon and begs an old pram or something.'

'Look,' he said, 'I'm doon here tae charge yese fir beggin already! I've got complaints about youse beggin. You mean tae tell me ye're gae'n back intae the toon tae beg a pram!'

'Well, that's the only way you're gaunna get rid o me, when my wife gets back tae the toon and begs a pram tae shift me!' By this time Buggie got up.

The constable said, 'I'm here tae move youse on, and I'm no movin till I see youse on the road.' So Sandy got up and he started to curse, and he cursed at Katie.

And he turned to the policeman, 'Laddie,' he said to the constable, 'did ye get yir porridge this morning?'

'No,' constable said, 'I never had nae porridge this morning. But I had some breakfast.'

'Well,' he said, 'I never got nae tea yet! And I never got my fire kinneled. And that black woman o mine is lyin there smokin a pipe. She put me oot the tent wi reek! Can you no move on? I'll shift. Can you no move on till we get wir wee bits o things together?' He was kind o shan with the polis standing on top of him.

The polis said, 'Look, I'm waitin here till you shift!'

'I'll shift, but no the noo,' Sandy said, 'till I get my fire kinneled.' And then the polis moved to Buggie.

And Buggie started, and cursed, and he cursed at his mother. The things that he said to that policeman, I guarantee you, I would never mention in a hundred years! Well, that policeman stood for one hour till everybody got up and had their tea, washed their faces and packed their tents. And then he walked along to me.

He says to me, 'What kind o people is that ye're associated wi?'

I said, 'Constable, I'm no associated wi them nae way, no in this worl. I just cam in here late last night. I dinna ken nothing aboot them, nae mair than you dae!'

He said, 'They're thiefs! They're beggars and they're prob'ly murderers for all I know! I never in my life, have ever I suffered such an hour wi that crowd. I'll tell ye something, young fellow, you'd better get away fae that crowd o people. I'm tellin ye fir your own sake, you and your wife. You take a tip from me and get as far away fae that crowd as you possibly can! Because I'll tell ye something, if ye're with them, in another three days they'll definitely get ye intae trouble!'

I said, 'All right, constable!' So by this time my pram was packed. I walked with the polis to the end of the road.

'Well,' he said, 'ye have yir orders.'

I walked back and said to Sandy, 'Jeannie wants tae see her mother. She wants tae go back tae Fife.'

'I'm no shiftin,' Sandy says to me, 'I'm no shiftin.'

So I bade Sandy goodbye, old Jeannie and them goodbye. 'I'm gaun away back tae Fife,' I said. By this time we had been away about a week, and I was making excuses to get away. Because I knew fine I was all right when I was single, but now I had the responsibility of a wife, and I couldn't do the things they were doing. I had to take her into consideration because she didn't like the things they were doing, no that they they were doing any harm. They weren't drinking or anything like that, but she could see that it wasn't leading to anything. As long as I kept with Sandy we weren't going to amount to anything.

So we set sail from Forfar old road. And we cut down into Dundee and stayed a night in Hangman's Strip. Then the next day we cut in by Tealing. And the first thing I saw was this horse coming, a fast trotting horse. I said to Jeannie, 'Here travellers comin along the road. I wonder who they are?' Everybody was sitting on the cart. They were driving on.

Jeannie said, 'That's my brother John's horse.'

I said, 'Awa lassie, ye're mad! That's nae yir brother John.'

She said, 'That's my brother John's horse. I ken that horse frae the distance. I bet ye a pound it is!' We could see it coming in the distance.

I said, 'Never in a million years, that's nae yir brother.' So we

pushed on and sure enough it was, her brother John and her
mother, and they were all the way from Dunfermline to Tealing.
They must have got an idea that we were in Aberdeen. They
would have made their way there. And they stopped, pulled
into the roadside.

Old Bellag never said a word about us being together, but
only asked, 'Where are yese makin fir?'

I said, 'We left Forfar auld road. We were wi Sandy and Katie.'

She never said a word, but only, 'Where dae ye think the two
o youse is makin fir?'

'Well,' I said, 'Auntie, we're jist daein the best we can. We're
makin back tae Fife.'

She says, 'We cam lookin fir youse. We heard youse is in
Forfar.' Somebody had tellt her. And she said, 'I was wonderin
how yese were gettin on.'

I said, 'We're gettin on fine.'

'Well,' she said, 'what are yese gaunna dae? Are youse gaun
tae come back wi hus or are youse gaun on bi yirsel?'

'Ach,' I said, 'It maks nae difference; we'll go back wi youse!'

John said, 'Mother, there a lot o travellers in these huts in
there.' Now it was a big Army camp and all these beautiful huts
were lying empty. Anyone could walk in and take one. So John
said to me, 'How about me and you takin a hut in here fir a
while?' In this Army camp at Tealing.

I said, 'All right, John. That suits me fine.' So we pulled in
the horse. There was plenty o grass, meat for the horse. And
we took one big hut between us. There were these big stoves in
them. You kindled a big fire in the hut, you know. There was
plenty of room. And you could make all your beds on the floor.
I said, 'You take that side, I'll take this side.' He and I were fine,
happy there. The police came in but they never said a word.

John said, 'We'll stay on, see what like it is.'

But we were in there for two days. Who dropped in next?
Sandy and Buggie. Sandy had two prams, Katie had got them.
Buggie and his mother, and Mary his wife all came in. They
took the next hut beside us. So we stayed there for about a
week and there was a bus running to Dundee. The women
did pretty well. But they couldn't get any elderberry to make
flowers. Dundee was red hot for flowers, you could sell them

galore. So we searched all the district looking for elderberry.
There was none to be got.

So I said to Jeannie one night when she and I were sitting
together at the fire, 'It's all right, elderberry. But there bound
tae be other ways o makin flooers.'

'Aye, ye can mak flooers wi onything,' she says, 'but ye cannae
stick them on privet.'

'Well, wait a minute. Hoo can ye pit paper flowers on privet?
They've got nae heart in them neither.

'No, you've got to put a wee bit copper wire on them ta tie
them ontae the privet.'

'Well,' I said, 'copper wire's easy gotten here.' Because there
were lighting services all round the huts. the wires were all
broken. 'There's loads o copper wire,' I said. 'Wait a minute.' I
went and got a big log, a pine log. I split it into kindlings. And I
sat down and made three dozen flowers out of these kindlings.
Any kind of wood'll make the same flower, but the travellers
used elderberry because it was soft in the heart. You could shove
a stick up into it. But after I made my flower heads I went out
and burned a lot of copper wire, and put a twist of wire around
the end of each flower. I said to Jeannie, 'Twist that round, on
the top o the privet wi a wee bit copper wire, same as a paper
flooer.' And I made these beautiful curly flowers, you see. Sandy
was in the next hut.

The next morning Jeannie went away to the town with the
rest of the women, but she had three dozen beautiful flowers.
She always carried dye with her, packets. She dyed them red
and yellow.

'Oh,' Katie said, 'whaur're ye gettin the bonnie flooers?'

She says, 'Duncan made them.'

'Whaur's he gettin the wood? He never tellt Sandy. Where's
he gaun fir the wood?' And they had nothing, you see.

She said, 'He made them oot o kindlings, bits o board.'

And then they started. They stripped every bit of wood, every
piece round the whole huts. So when I saw that, my plan was
finished. So I went round the old huts at night and looked.
The huts were loaded with lead. I said, 'I'm no makin nae
mair flooers.' I saw all this lead hanging, lead piping and lead
wire. And then the gutters and the roans in the huts – the huts

were finished – but all the gutters were filled up with lead. So I pulled in this lead, pulled it all down. And I had a big fire in this hut. I got a big basin. I put it in the front of the fire. And all night when everybody was asleep, I was putting these big lumps of lead into the fire. And it came running out, and I filled this basin. I was making big ingots of lead, basins full! And I packed them in the bottom of my pram the next day and hurled it into Dundee.

I was making good money! Nobody knew what I was doing. Even the police that stopped me on the road couldn't say anything because it was melted ingots of lead. Nobody ever knew. I was going with the pram every day, Jeannie and I to the town. And I was doing fine. Then one night Buggie came in and he saw me at this. He watched me making this lead. I couldn't help it.

'Oh,' he said, 'this is what ye're up tae, wee man! This is what ye're daein. Is that why ye're gaun tae Dundee so often?'

I said, 'Aye.'

So that night he would go and he would do the same thing, see, he copied me. But he had no pram to put it in. Didn't he fill a suitcase to carry in his hand? And he made these square ingots of lead. And he walked out to the road to stop a bus. Who came cycling along but the police with a bike? Polis stopped, asked his name.

'Oh, Charlie Reid.' Now Buggie had made up his mind that day to leave his mother. He and his wife were going back to Aberdeen to see her mother. And he was taking this case of lead with him to sell in Dundee, and take the bus to Aberdeen. The police stopped him. I was there. I was standing at the roadend. There was a big wide drive going in, and I was out to see him off. He had this big heavy case packed with these ingots of lead. Now by this time I had saved a few shillings and I had two-three pound tucked away in my own pocket. I had this and I wasn't caring. I had buried about six hundred weight of ingots in the ground and covered it over with earth. I was working all night! And we had so much lead, in later weeks I left Fife and came back for it with a pony. John and I drove the whole night through, the whole farin night. This was how I got my first start. And I was stealing it right enough. But it was derelict properties.

We didn't think of it as stealing. We weren't hurting anybody. We had to survive.

Polis said, 'What's in the case?'

Buggie said, 'My claes. My wife and me is gaun off.'

'Oh,' he said, 'ye're movin oot?'

'Aye.'

'Open it, open yir case and let's have a look at it! It looks kind o heavy tae me.' A polis wi a bike!

Buggie said, 'It's only ma claes, man, that's in the case.'

'If it's yir claes, open it!' Buggie opened it, and there were these melted bars of lead. 'Oh, that's yir game,' polis said, 'that's yir game. This is what ye're up tae. Well, look, laddie, I'll tell ye something. Where'd ye get that?'

Buggie said, 'It's wee bits o cable I gathered roond the huts and I've melted it.'

'Well,' he said, 'tak it and go to Dundee and sell it, and get tae Aberdeen! And look, if ever I catch yir face aboot Dundee or aboot this district again, there nae charges fir ye – it's arrested on the spot! Now get!' It was a good policeman would do that, ken. Buggie jumped on the bus with his case of this lead. And the polis let him off, oh, he let him go. He couldn't prove it because it was melted, you see. And Buggie went back to Aberdeen. And two days after that John and I shifted across the ferry.

'Noo,' I said to John, 'I'm no leavin my leid.'

'Brother, it's a big risk,' he said to me, 'taking that.'

I said, 'I cannae sell it aa.' Because I had all these melted bars. I was melting all night making them, like mill wheels. 'I'm taking this wi me, John. I'll put it in yir cairt. If anything happens, I'll take the blame o it. I'm no sellin it in Dundee. We'll take it through to Fife tae Leslie.'

'All right,' he says to me. And he had a horse and a four-wheeled lorry. So the next morning we packed all our things. I packed my pram and I got John to give me a hand. I put these four bags of lead in the back of John's lorry. And I came behind him with my pram. His mother and his wee sister and his brother, we all walked on down through Dundee. John's horse was a wee bit afraid of the ferry, because horses didn't like it very much with the water on each side.

But anyway, we got across the Tay all right. It was only a six pence for the horse and cart, and thruppence for each person. We landed at Tayport, and a mile along from there was an old road where you could camp. John pulled the cart in, and he and I put up our tents. We had our tea. And we're just sitting at our tea when along comes the police with a car, an old-fashioned car, two policemen. Now these bags of lead are sitting in the back of the cart. Police come in, ask our names. We told them everybody's names.

'Where do you come fae?'

'Tealing.'

'Oh aye. Did you come across the ferry?'

'Yeah.'

'Well,' he said, 'we've got a search warrant tae search yir premises.'

'Oh well,' I said, 'constable, if you've got a search warrant tae search the premises, you'd better go ahead and dae it.' Jeannie had a wee case for holding her own bits of clothes. Not me. I just wore my clothes from day to day. I didn't have any extra. What I had was on my back, except an odd clean shirt now and again she washed in the burn when it got too dirty. So, she had wee bits o things for changing herself.

He said, 'Eh, can I look in yir case, hen?'

'Oh,' Jeannie said, 'you can go ahead and look in the case if ye want.'

So he opened the case. 'Oh aye, it's all right.' Shut the case. Into my tent.

I said, 'The're nothing but two-three blankets in the tent.' Into the other tent he went, round all the things.

'No,' he said. Up to the cart, looked all round the cart. And these bags are sitting in the back. And it was a sergeant, you see. He chapped the bag with his hand. 'What's in the bags?'

I said, 'Lead, lead in the bags.'

He said, 'Lead, my bloody arse 'at's in the bags! Lead, my bloody arse!'

I said, 'It is lead!'

He said, 'That'll be right!' You see, lead was a good price then. And he walked back.

I said, 'Constable, tell me the truth, what is it you're really lookin fir?'

'Well, seein we huvnae found what we're after, I'll tell ye: there were two lads' suitcases lifted off the ferryboat this morning. Someone lifted them and youse travellers cam across the ferry about the same time. We thought prob'ly . . .'

I said, 'If tinkers is there, they'll get the blame o anything.'

'Oh no, no,' he said, 'we never blamed nobody. Anyway, we had tae come and see.'

'Oh,' I said, 'ye're quite welcome tae come and see. But I'll tell ye something, we never lifted nae suitcases. We haenae got nae suitcases.'

So they went away. The next day John says to me, 'Me and you are definitely lucky.' So we shifted the next morning and we drove the way right to the New Inn in Fife, and that was a big whinny moor. We stayed there, and the next day John and I drove into Leslie and sold the lead. There was never a word ever said about it from that day on.

John and I spent two-three months in Fife and my one ambition, because he was shifting, carrying my camp in his cart, was to have a pony of my own. But that's another story! The most important thing I want to tell you about right now is the story which lives in my memory for evermore. It is one of these things you can just never forget.

One day we were camped at the New Inn where that garage is on the motorway to Kirkcaldy. We got up this morning and my cousin said to me, 'Brother, we've been here a while now; we've been six months in Fife. I would like tae have a trip back to Angus.' He was awful fond of Angus and Perthshire, but I had no time for these places. My life was in Fife because this is where it all began with me as a grown man.

I said, 'All right, cousin, it's up to you wherever you want to go. It disnae make nae difference to me.' We were young then. I had no children. I said, 'It's okay wi me. If you're fed up with Fife, I'll go wi you to Perthshire or Angus-shire, wherever you want, providin we can always come back to Fife in the wintertime.'

He says, 'Okay then.' It was only he and his mother, his brother and his wee sister. I was married to the other sister. He had a nice pony and I had a nice pony. How I got this pony is another story. Beautiful yokes we had. So Jeannie was expecting our first child and John wanted a trip back to Angus because this was his father's country. His father was a pearl fisher and he had spent many a time in Angus and Perthshire. I think the very first time John ever came to Fife was when he came with me. So the spring was coming in. It was about the month of March or April. The grass was just coming for the horses and we didn't need to feed them. I had this beautiful pony and so had he. But his pony only had one eye. It was a roan horse. But oh, sister, it could trot for fun! And he had refused many's a swap. It was fast, a really fast horse. This pony I had was a good one, but it was young. I was awful fond of getting a colt and breaking it in, making it my own so's it would grow into money.

I don't know what put it in my mind in these days, but I wasn't just a person who would go for any kind of horse. Probably it was going back to my own time when my father had tellt me, 'Laddie, if ye ever get a horse, make sure you dinnae get a thing that everybody else is finished with. Get something that's young and strong that you can dae something with.' That was his words. So they were always in my mind. Though I did have many's a deal later on to things that weren't worth tuppence. That, too, is another story.

But the thing I want to tell you now is the original tale, how my cousin and I set off from the New Inn in Fife. We travelled through Cupar and camped the other side of the town, and then we made our way to the ferry. There was no Tay Bridge in these days, in 1949. So we crossed on the boat. It was a day of rain and sleet and the waves were lashing! My horse was only about three years old. It had never been on a ferry boat in its life. So, the man on the ferry was really up to the way you could cross water: he always came with blocks to put behind the wheel so's the horse couldn't move the cart. There were a lot of cars and lorries on. My cousin's horse was about nine or ten years old. It was an old-timer to the road, but it was a good one. We paid our ferry and pulled our horses on to cross to Dundee.

Now I wanted John to go to Hoolet's Neuk. The old traditional camping ground that brings back memories to me. I said, 'Cousin, why don't we make our way up to the Murroes? We'll have a night in the Hoolet's Neuk. Ye remember?'

'Oh,' he said, 'I remember the Hoolet's Neuk, brother. But it's too far for my mammy and Jeannie tae come hame, because the bus run is awfae poor. We'll go to the Murroes for the night. And it's close for the women to go to the toon.' It was a wee wood on the other side of Dundee.

I said, 'All right.' But anyway, the waves were lashing across the ferry. The spray was coming over the side of the boat. And I'm standing holding my pony by the head in case it would carry on. It couldn't get off the boat because the sides were high. And out comes this old woman. She had an umbrella and a white coat on. She took off her coat. And I'm standing – there's no escape from the spray coming over the side of the boat. We had a rough day, really rough crossing. And the waves were splashing across the horse's feet. Some of the spray was coming on the horse's back. But my cousin's horse didn't seem to mind. He was standing with his back to the spray so's the water wouldn't go in the horse's face. He got it on his back. And this old woman came with an umbrella, a handbag and a coat. The deckhands did all their best to provide for you crossing the boat, especially with a horse.

And the woman said, 'Oh, I can't take this! A beautiful pony. All the spray.' And she came up with her coat, 'Put that over the horsie.'

I said, 'Missus, please! What about me? I'm standin here and I'm haudin the horsie,' and I'm trying to keep my back to the spray. It was splashing the horse's face and I was feared o the horse rearing up.

She said, 'Put my coat over the horse to keep it dry.'

I said, 'How about giein me the coat, granny, and put it ower me?'

'No, I'm no givin it to you! I want to give it to the pony.'

I said, 'Never mind the pony. The pony's all right. It's okay. Dinnae worry. Take your coat. Ye're no haudin—'

'Try and hold it up in front of the pony, keep the water from goin on the pony!' she said.

'Never mind the pony!' But I coaxed the woman anyway, I got her settled.

So we got across the ferry. My cousin's horse was used to it. We drove off and I got in behind John because he knew the road. We led our horses up through Dundee, and this pony I had was young, a quick stepper. The Murroes was about four miles from Dundee on the Forfar road. So we landed there and put up our tents. Jeannie and her mother stayed in Dundee, got their messages and came out on the bus.

So the next morning after we got things done, I said, 'Cousin, where are we makin fir?'

He said, 'We're makin tae Forfar, roond by Kirriemuir, roond by Alyth and in by Blairgowrie. I want to see my father's grave. And if you're interested we'll go back in by Perth and the Bridge of Earn, and land back in Fife for the winter.'

I said, 'That's okay. That suits me fine.'

So the next morning we packed up. We only carried a tent, some sticks for the camp and a few blankets, some dishes and two-three clothes for ourselves, which was very few. It wasn't hard to do. The part of the packing left to the man was taking down the tent, folding up the canvas, tying the sticks together. The other part was left to the woman, his wife. While the man was taking down the tent, the woman gathered her wee bit of cooking utensils together, her dishes, whatever bits of messages she had. She had small boxes to put them in and she packed them in the cart herself. The man put the camp sticks and canvas on last, because it came off first. The snottum for the fire and for making holes for the sticks went on, and this was all the man's job. We always put the float, or cart or maybe a lorry, a four-wheeler or a two-wheeler, up on a prop so's it was level. But the woman always put her dishes and kitchen things to the very back, so's if she had to stop along the roadside and make a cup of tea she knew where to get her things.

John and I yoked up, packed up our things and drove on the road. It was only Jeannie, her mother, her wee sister and her brother – they just jumped up in the carts. And the horse, sister, a trotting horse could trot for miles! You jumped up and the cart was like driving a motor. You sat there and the horse could just – 'gee up!' And that horse could go on, trot for mile after mile after mile at a good trot. You never chased it. It never walked. It trotted, doing about ten or twelve mile an hour, a real trot, round bends, up corners, up hills, the horse never stopped. Till it got tired and you knew when your horse was tired.

But we drew into Forfar. We stopped and Jeannie and her

mother got some messages. We made some tea. John said, 'Brother, it's no far.' It was early spring. 'We'll drive oot to Glamis Green. We'll hae a crack, maybe a game of quoits or something. There always travellers on Glamis Green.'

Glamis Green has been a camp back to the fifteenth century for travellers. Any travellers passing by through Angus, they always stopped in Glamis Green. And my cousin John's father had this as his favourite camping place, and John wanted to camp there.

I said, 'That's all right to me.' Now I'd never been on Glamis Green in my life before. I said, 'Drive on, I'll drive behind ye.' But my hand to God – his old pony could really trot. It only had one eye!' So I said to Jeannie, 'Jump up in ahind the cairt and we'll drive on.' So, John's sitting on the driving side, and his mother and his brother are on the other side. His wee sister is in the middle. Me and Jeannie, we're only the two of us. And my pony, I'm holding her back behind John's. We drove up towards Glamis Green. There's two gellies sitting! Tank and lums, and chimneys right through the centres. And there were two rubber-tyred carts, a gig and a float pulled alongside the camps. But no horses. We stopped a wee bit back the road.

John says to me, 'There travellers on the green.'

'Aye, they're travellers.'

'Gellies!' he said. 'It's some of the Skye MacDonalds, Inverness folk.' They weren't Perthshire or Angus travellers, because they weren't up to the gellies in these days. He said, 'It's Hieland folk. Look at that gelly!' And you want to see it, sister! It was built just like a barrage balloon – you couldn't even see a ripple about the canvas – it was built so tight. And it was straight and long, the chimneys coming out and they were reeking! Two of them right in the middle of the green.

So we drove in. There was plenty of room for everybody. The first thing we lowsed our ponies out, let the shafts down on the ground. And then we took the harness off and put it alongside the wheel of the cart, and got our tethers out. We gave the ponies a rub down with a bag because they were a bit sweaty. We looked for the best bit of grass. Now in Glamis Green there's an old road, an old pathway that goes down. The green was big, but the grass was poor and the travellers used to

tether their horses down the old road. But till we got the tent
out we just tied the ponies close to the site. And we started to
put the camps up.

Now it was the early spring and we didn't need anything
but a bow tent, just a half-hooped tent with a fire. John put
his up, and I put mine opposite, and we kindled a fire in the
centre. Just two bow tents and an open fire in the middle. No
gellies. Because we had no weans. John's youngest sister was
about seven. All we needed was a bed of straw. And then we
had our snottum for hanging the pots over the fire. He and I
gathered sticks and kindled a big fire. It was up to the women
to boil tea or fry ham, or do anything they wanted. It wasn't
our business – we took what we could get!

I didn't need a big tent. It was only me and her, just the two
of us. And I remember fine what I had for my tent. It was one
of the war barrage balloons, one of these things you saw up in
the sky to stop the Nazi planes from coming over, in case they
ran into them. It was the finest of canvas you could ever get!
Never was there a drip of rain ever came into it. And this tent
was silver, pure silver – I had it beautifully made. Everybody
admired it. I got this barrage balloon down in Fife at the docks
in Methil. Silver inside and outside. I tightened it with stones
and put it round, a real bow tent and a rigging stick across the
top. Just for me and her, two of us. And we hung a sheet on the
door at night-time right across the front. So we had our supper,
had a wash, washed our faces and hands.

John said to me, 'I wonder wha has this tent?' We weren't far
away from the gellies, about a hundred yards. But we never saw
a soul. The people never came out.

As soon as I had my tea Jeannie said, 'I've a wee bit dishes to
wash.' We never kept very much, two cups for her and a cup for
me, a couple of plates, wee bits of things the two of us needed,
very little. Travelling life was just like you were on a picnic.
That's what it was! You were never settled. She didn't build up
any hopes that we were going to stay anywhere for long. The
lightest things she could get she always kept, maybe a couple
of spoons, two knives. No tables, no chairs or anything. It was
a lifelong picnic from day in to day out. But we were happy.

After we had our tea John says to me, 'We'll take the ponies

doon the old road. There might be some grass. It's kind of
bare here.'

I said, 'Aye, that's all right.' I had this bonnie mare. John had
a mare too. John always carried a curry-comb and brush. That
was one thing about him – he always made sure that his horse
got a clean after its day's work. And a drink first thing, and they
were tethered out and shifted every three hours. So after we
got our ponies kind of cleaned up and brushed, checked their
feet and put the tether on them for the night, we walked them
down the old road. But we never saw any horses! Now this is
about five o'clock in the month of April. And the nights were
a wee bit longer. We tethered the ponies so they wouldn't get
fankled in each other's ropes. We came walking up.

John says, 'It's queer hantle.' Meaning, queer people, never
saying a word. But we came level to this gelly. This man stepped
out.

He said, 'I see youse come in.'

John looked at me and I looked at John. We knew. There's
nobody in the world knows better than the travellers where
another traveller comes from, by the traveller's language and
how he speaks. Travellers have got that gift. They know all the
travellers in Perthshire, all the travellers who met them before
and all the travellers they've seen. But we had never seen this
man before in our life. We knew by his tongue that he came
either from Caithness or Wick. Or in the faraway North. And
he was a stranger.

He said, 'Where youse come from, boys?'

'Ah, we come across fae Fife.'

'Oh, whereabouts is Fife, then? Is that a faraway place?'

So we tried to explain to him. 'Oh, it's away across in another
country. It's no this shire. The're a big river that separates it.'

He said, 'Is it a foreign country?'

'No, it's not a foreign country. Well, it's another country on
its own,' trying to explain to him.

What do they call you, boy?'

Oh,' I said, 'never mind what they call me – what do they
call you?'

He said, 'I'm Dealin Isaac MacPhee from Wick!'

Now I had said, 'Never mind what they call us. What do they

call you?' It's a wee bit umperant to ask people's name. I said
to him, 'We'd never ask your name would we?'

He said, 'Oh, you needn't ask me, boy! I'm Dealin Isaac
MacPhee from Wick. It's up North.' This is the way he carried
on. 'And ma boys,' he said, 'is in here. Come oot now boys and
meet the young men!'

He flung the door of the gelly up and these two boys came out.
They were about four foot high. They were young laddies! One
about eighteen and one about twenty-five, I would say. And they
were like gorillas. Their arms were longer than their legs. They
were cave-looking creatures. They weren't just the full shilling.
'This is ma laddies,' he said. But, sister, we came to love that man
like a brother. You have no idea. The first meeting we gained a
bad impression. Maybe we got off on the wrong leg. But he was
very civil. 'Where youse boys come fae?' he asked.

I said, 'I'm a Williamson.'

'Oh, you're a Williamson? The're a lot of Williamsons in my
country.' His accent was different from my tongue. I could
understand him, but I could not speak exactly the way Mr
MacPhee spoke. Inverness or Skye was me, or Argyll. But I'll try
to get as near to what the man said as possible. He said, 'Hev
ye horses, boy?'

I said, 'Aye, we've a couple of beasts there. This is my
cousin.'

'Oh, this is yir cousin, aye. Come in, man, come in.'

John said, 'No, we dinnae want to go in.' We felt kind o shan,
kind o strange. We'd never been in his kind of gelly before in
our life. Well, we didn't want to go into the man's camp. You see,
this is a traveller thing. If I had known the man before, we would
have went into his tent. And we weren't known to the man. You
see, it wasn't our policy! We didn't want to be friends with the
man and we didn't want to go into his camp, because we didn't
know anything about the man in the first place. No, it's not the
case o not being sure. I mean, the man couldn't hurt us in any
way. The man was in his fifties and he had two sons. But it was
too much too soon, too forward. As I'd said, 'We'd never have
done it with him.' I wouldn't tell him my name first, you see. It
was too forward. But that was his way in his country! We didn't
want to make the man feel bad. And then we didn't want to go

against our own tradition either. He was one of our own, but he was a foreigner. His traditions weren't ours and our traditions weren't his. We didn't want to feel that we were imposing on the man in any way. Up in his own place when he met his own type of folk it was expected of him to bring his people into his place, into his tent. We didn't want to see what was in the man's tent in no way! He wanted to treat us like we were his friends, but we couldn't be anything like that, because we weren't. We were paying him a respect in our own way, expecting him to respect us for what we were too. This is a code among travellers which is a very droll thing.

He said, 'Come in, boy. Sit doon, man, sit doon.' He was free and kind hearted. But if John and I had walked into that man's camp, then we would have destroyed all that we live for.

I said, 'No, mister, we've things tae dae!' This is the excuse we made. 'We've got horses.' The understanding was, you could talk outside the tent and talk at the outside fire until you became accustomed to him, till the man really understood what you were and what he was before you entered his premises. The thing that I was trying to do, you must understand, was to give the man the impression that he had no reason to ask me in. He didn't ask me in because he wanted me; but rather because it was his tradition, because I was a stranger. So in my mind I said, 'I dinnae want to go into the man's camp no way.' And he was pleased by me no accepting this offer! By him knowing me through that way, when I never accepted his invitation, we became great friends! Because deep in his mind he knew that I knew the same thing as he.

Now, if I had walked into this man's camp he would have changed, 'Oh, what kind o gadgie is that? This must be some kind o flattie or something,' he would have said. He had to ask, he was testing us. He had the same code as I had in his own way.

He said, 'They call me Dealin Isaac MacPhee. What kind o beasties youse got, man?'

'Oh, a wee bit o pony,' I said, 'It's no up to much.'

Man,' he said, 'I've a braw beastie! I've fetched her doon fae Inverness. I got it in Inverness. She's a braw beastie! What kind o beast youse got?'

'Ah, a Shelt,' I said. 'It's only a—'

Oh,' he said, 'it's only a wee Shelt.'

'Aye, I've only got a wee Shelt.' It was fourteen hands! If you had it today you couldn't buy it for two hundred pound.

'What kind o beast you got, laddie?' he said to John.

'I've only a wee bit thing. Ach, it's no much, it's a wee bit dottled. Just for shiftin the camp aboot.'

'Man,' he said, 'I've got a braw beastie. Youse laddies, young men like you in these days . . .' He was a bit forward '. . . man, you want to get a haud o a guid beast. If you want to keep a beast, a guid ane or a bad ane, it eats the same grass, ye ken.' He never saw our ponies. We never saw his. He said, 'I'm tellin youse laddies, if you want to keep a Sheltie or keep a bit o a beastie, man, you want to keep a guid ane. It eats the same grass.'

John said, 'I believe that, maister, but it's no easy gettin a guid ane.'

'Ach,' he said, 'guid anes is as easy tae get as bad anes. Never kept a bad horse in my life!'

'Oh,' John said, 'I believe that, maister!' Now John was very, very quick tempered. And he could fight like big guns. I had to control him many times, though he was in the wrong. If he thought somebody was trying to pull his leg, he just jumped the gun. And I had to try and control him.

I said, 'Stall, man, stall. The gadgie's no mangin naething at all, din ye jan?'*

'Man,' he says, 'I would like to have a look up at your Shelties.'

'Ach, we hev nothing tae look at, maister,' John said. 'Me and my brother, we have nothing tae look at. Only two auld ponies that we use.'

'Man, I've got a great beast! In fact,' he said, 'it's the finest beast ever I had in my life. And they tell me there an awfae dealin men aboot this country.'

'Oh, aye, I meet them every day, maister.' This was John's way. And he'd begun to draw apart now. Now he had come to his full course. John began to back out. Now Mr MacPhee was a nice old soul. But I could see by John's idea that John had had enough. When he cried the man 'maister' I kent he'd come his full score.

_____

* din ye jan – don't you understand

'Maister,' he said, 'if you're lookin for dealin I'm sure ye'll get bings. In Forfar or Blairgowrie, the berries and all the places. If you want and you've got a good beast, everybody's after good horses, maister. But we cannae afford good horses.'

'But there's only one thing,' he said, 'I'm worried about in your country, man – fleas.'

John said, 'What, maister?'

'Fleas, man,' he said. 'They bother our horses here. They eat their eyes oot, man, the fleas. And up where we come from there nae such a thing. The fleas eat the poor auld horses een oot, man, eat their een.'

'Oh,' John said, 'they eat their een oot, aye. Well, maister . . .'

'But,' he said, 'eh, you wouldn't mind me, haen a look at your bit Shelties?'*

'Oh,' John said, 'no!'

He said, 'Here!' he cried the two laddies, 'gang doon, man, and bring up the mare! Eh, the laddies here is a wee bit interested, and they've never seen a good horse for a long while.'

John said, 'I'm gaunna mar him!'

I said, 'Stall mangin! Stall, man. Stall, gadgie, nae mang!'

And Mr MacPhee was dark in the skin. His face full of blackheads, but he was a lovable soul! And his wife was a nice cratur. She had long, dark hair, and he had two wee lassies and two laddies. He had two gellies, built two camps for the laddies and himself. 'Hey boys!' he says. 'Gang doon and bring up the mare! Let these boys hae a wee bit show here o a guid beast!'

The laddies went away down. Now, when you went down the old road, there was another road down the other way. That's where me and John had bypassed. We went straight down the road when we'd tethered our ponies. But they had turned a quick left and took it further down in a clear bit, a branch off the road. John and I are sitting. I'm cracking to him. We never went in the tent, but sat with our backs against the camp.

'Wait a minute,' Mr MacPhee said, 'and the laddies'll bring up the beast, the mare. We waited a wee while. The two laddies weren't very tall. And were thin, as if poorly reared. Not for wrestling at all! We were fit, could have sprung over a seventy-foot fence. But they were lazy-looking, as if they lacked

---

* your bit Shelties – the small ponies

something. You could see it. They weren't stupid in any way.
We called it poorly brought up. But we never went in the man's
camp so we couldn't explain how the children were reared.

But here the laddies were coming with this thing. And one
pulled it over his shoulder on a rope. A cloot was tied on the
horse's face! And holes in the cloot for its eyes, and holes for its
lugs. A white cloot tied over its head for the fleas! There were an
awful fleas. And he pulled it up. It was about fifteen hands high.
And I'll guarantee you, there is more flesh on that poker for the
fire that what was on its body. If you could have went down its
ribs, you would have went rick-tick-tick-tick-tick! It couldn't eat,
it couldn't chew your finger. A mummy! He brought it up. And
it had every complaint under the sun. Its two eyes were sunk
in, and it had two holes at the top of its eyebrows, the temple
holes, sunk back in.

'Ower here, laddies,' he said, 'bring me the beast! Bring ower
the beast.' But he had a beautiful cart and harness. Oh, the
man had a beautiful cart. But he had this mummy. Now he was
trying to take us for mugs, trying to get one over us, 'wee young
laddies', ye see! And he thought he was in the score, thought
he had a couple of fools at hand. And he brought up this thing,
a 'crocodile', that's what John called it.

'Stall yir mangin,'* John says to me. 'Stall, man, stall, laddie!
Stall!' We were mangin cant to ourselves, so he couldn't hear
us. Aye, he would have understood, but we didn't let him hear
us. 'Stall yir mangin. Me and you're gaunna have good fun
right in a minute!'

The horse had two white feet in the front. This made it look
worse. And its throat pipe stuck out. Now this is a complaint.
And you know, there was nothing on the chest bones. You could
see the throat pipe going right through between its legs. It
was a knacker's case! And every step it took, the laddies pulled
it over their backs. A crocodile! Its hip joints were sticking
out. It couldn't chew your finger. The tinkers called a horse
that couldn't eat a 'mummy' because its front teeth were too
long. But he brought it up. And it was chestnut-coloured. That
made it worse. Red chestnut. If it had been black or any other
colour it wouldn't have been half so bad. Travellers hated a

---

* stall yir mangin – hold your tongue

chestnut horse of any description. The're no traveller would take a chestnut horse, suppose it was like gold. It was the colour, you know . . . the burkers were red headed. The chestnut was unclassed, supposed to be unlucky. And when Mr MacPhee saw the laddies come with it he rose to his feet.

Well, man,' and he stuck his fingers in his jacket. 'Well, boys, what dae ye think? Isn't that a beautiful animal?'

'Oh, maister!' John was keen. John was a master of horses. The laddie was born and reared with horses, since he could creep. His father had horses before he was born. And when his father died he worked with horses, broke them in, bought them and swapped and dealed. He was moich on horses! 'Oh,' John said, 'maister, it's no a bad auld beast. It would do onybody's turn, maister.'

He said, 'Isn't she a beauty?'

'Oh aye, maister, a beauty,' he said. I never said a word. I never spoke.

'Eh, you wouldnae be feelin like a bit o a deal, man?' he says to John. I'm Dealin Isaac MacPhee. I swap and deal and fight like big guns!'

'Oh, maister, I believe you can!' Now I knew John. Since he was sixteen, and I knew he had taken enough and he wasn't going to go anymore. 'Oh well,' John said, 'maister, the horse I've got, maister, I dinnae think you'll have much interest in it. It's no nae better than yir ain.'

'Oh man,' he says, 'a strange face is ae worth a bit o difference, man!' He was dying to get rid of it, you see. And he's treating us like mugs. But I knew. I was ahead of him, a hundred years ahead. He said, 'Eh, you wouldna mind me seein your bit animals?'

'Oh no,' John said, 'maister. You can see wir animals if you want.'

'Laddie, tie it up to the fence, man!' Mr MacPhee said. 'And we'll gang doon and we'll hae a look at this beast.' So he walked down with us. And it was Woodbine he smoked, and he gave us a fag. 'We'll go doon and see yir beasties.'

I said, 'Aye.' And I had this pony. It was three years old and you could have poured a dish of water between its shoulders, and it would have run down between its back, its tail. Its hips were that bowed. It could have drained down its back, it was that fat. It was chocolate brown, and as quiet as a mouse. Its feet were broad. The weans could go in between its legs, any wee wean could.

And John had this other pony called Tootsie. She was a good old horse. He'd had it for two years. She wanted an eye, but, oh Jesus, she could trot for fun! You could never yoke her wrong. You stopped at the door of a shop and said, 'Tootsie, sit there!' She would sit till you came back. And his mother could take it any place, or anybody could take it. It was an old friend.

Mr MacPhee came walking down. And John was making up his mind to hit him. I had to stop John from hitting Mr MacPhee. I stopped. My horse was first. She was tethered first on the old road. And the laddies came with us. Mr MacPhee said, 'Is that yir bittie o a pony, man? Is that yir Shelt?'

I said, 'That's my Shelt. That's mine. A thing I got fae an old man in Fife. I dinnae ken much aboot it. I dinnae ken much aboot horses, maister. In fact, I never had much horses in my day.'

'Aye,' he said, 'It's no a bad bit cuddy. It's kind o fat. It's bound to be lazy.

'Ah, maister,' I said, 'to tell you the God's truth, it's no very fast. It definitely is lazy. You hit it nail on the head.' (It wasn't lazy at all!) So he wasn't interested.

He walked down to see John's pony. John's was about fourteen hands, fourteen two. Aw, a beautiful roan. A strawberry roan, but it had one eye. And it had a habit of looking round at you. The horse had to turn its head. Now John had a bad eye himself. In later years he got his eye taken out. But from birth John had this bad eye and it was coloured, and bigger than the other one. He was only a young lad, unmarried. Oh, a beautiful man, a handsome laddie when he was young! He had this bonnie curly hair. But he had this bad eye. And oh Jesus, he could fight! Mr MacPhee came down. And John's pony had a wild way of looking at you. It had to turn with its full head round when you came up to it, because it only had one eye. The four of us came down. John kent the pony. It never bothered with him. But when it saw the strangers it hurled round its head.

Mr MacPhee said, 'Is that yir pony, laddie?'

And John said, 'Aye, that's my pony, maister, aye.'

'Well, it's no a bad bit beastie. That is a good beastie. Laddie, son, I'll tell you something, that's a good beast!'

John said, 'Aye, maister, it's no bad.'

'Are ye no better,' he said, 'tyin a cloot on its ee! If the fleas gets in there, man, they'll make an awfae mess o it!'

Now if anybody, if you mentioned 'eye' to John, because he had a bad eye, he couldn't take this. Every laddie who knew John, and everybody knew John, had this thing – you never mentioned 'eyes' because he hated this eye he had. He was only seventeen. But he was completely blind in this eye. If you joked with him or anything it was all right. But when the gadgie said to him, 'Ye should tie a cloot, man. That's only got one, a bad ee, man. Its ee is nae good, don't ye see? Ye'd better put a cloot on it for the fleas!' The man meant no harm. John couldn't take this.

He said, 'Maister, I'll tell ye something. You get up that road! Look, and take that object, braxy, you've got, that thing up there, that crocodile! That mummy, maister, you've got up there, and that thing with the cloots on its face.' John says, 'Look, you go and tie that! Tie as many cloots on its een as you want. Dinnae try and tell me tae put nae cloots on my horse's ee. And tak that crocodile you've got up there, and tie as many cloots as you want on its een, but dinnae tell me what tae dae wi mine!'

The man never said a word. Never said a word.

'Come on!' John said to me. We left him. Walked up. He came back and he was fuming at his mouth, fuming! His nerves were up. He was raised up. That was him started for the night. John. There was no satisfying him. You couldn't talk from then on. Oh, many's a fight he and I got into – he got me into many's a fight just for this carry on. This was him raised. His mother tried to satisfy him, but it was no good. 'I'm goin down to kill him. I'm goin down right noo,' he said. I'm gaunna tear the tent atop of him. I'm gaunna mak him . . .'

I said, 'Man, calm yirsel, man! The man wasnae referrin tae you at all!'

The next morning on Glamis Green – we never went out of our camp till then. But when we got up Mr MacPhee was away, packed up and gone. There were three of us, including John's brother. The man thought when John went off so quick, off the fan, the man thought we were looking for trouble. But the man didn't mean any harm.

JOHNIE O MONYMUSK

Johnie he got up one fine mornin
Cauld water to wash his hands,
Say'n, 'Gang bring tae me my twa grey dogs
They are bound wi iron bands-o
They are bound wi iron bands.'

'O Johnie, O Johnie,' his mother she cried
'Tae the green woods dinna, dinna gang!
O Johnie for yir mother's sake
Son, a-huntin, son, dinna, dinna gang!'

But Johnie buskit up his fine broad bow his arras ay sae lang
And he paid nae heed tae his mother's words
Tae the green woods he would gang- o
Tae the green woods he would gang.

And then he spied a grey dun deer
Comin doon by the green wood-side
And he fired on the grey dun deer
And he wounded her in her pride-o
He wounded her in her pride.

And then there comes a silly auld man
Comes doon by the green wood-side
And he is awa tae the king's foresters
The seven foresters for to see-o
The seven foresters for to see.

'What news, what news, you silly old man,
What news do you bring today?
What news, what news, you silly old carle,
What news do you bring to me-o?
What news do you bring to me?'

He said, 'As I cam doon the merry green wood
And through thon peat and bog,
There I spied a handsome man

He was a-huntin wi his dogs-o
He was a-huntin wi his dogs.'

Then up and spake the first forester,
A man amongst them aa,
'If Johnie is a-huntin in our merry green wood
Nae further dare we draw-o
Nae further dare we draw.'

Then up and spake the second forester,
An eldry man was he,
'If Johnie is a-huntin in our merry green wood
We'd better let him be-o
We'd better let him be.'

Then up and spake the third forester
A brother's son was he,
'If Johnie is a-huntin in our merry green wood,
We may gang and we'll gar him dee-o*
We may gang and we'll gar him dee.'

Then up and spake the fourth forester,
A bright young spark was he,
'Gang get yir bows my brothers bold
And come along wi me-o
And come along wi me!'

Noo Johnie placed his back against an oak
And his fit against a stane,
And he fired on the seven foresters
And he slew them aa but ane-o
And he slew them aa but ane.

But then an arra it pierced him deep
Comin doon through the green wood-side
And betwixt the waters and the wood
It was there O Johnie died-o
It was there O Johnie died.

Now Johnie his great big bow lies broke
And his twa grey dogs lie slain,
And his body lies in Monymusk
And his huntin days are gane-o
And his huntin days are gane.

Traditional

---

* gar him dee-o – cause his death

CHAPTER TEN

SILVER AND THE SHAN GURIE

My cousin and I always returned to Fife for the winter months, about the beginning of the harvest time in August. Life was hard in Fife in 1948 for the travellers, because there were so many families, about forty-fifty, wandering through the country, everybody after the same thing trying to make a living to the best of their ability. But the only pleasure they had in those days was that camping was easier gotten. You could camp any place, on any old road, any old piece of wood, any old quarry, any old layby. And it was all mostly horses; travellers didn't have any cars in that time.

Things were really hard. The price of non-ferrous metals, which the traveller depended on was just rock bottom. And rags were very poor (when we collected and sold them for recycled wool). Then the advantage in Fife was the settled community of non-traveller folk kept ponies. There were dealers in Kirkcaldy, fishmen in Kirkcaldy, coalmen, rag-and-bone men, stick men and a lot of pig farmers – all these folk had horses. Well, they all needed to change their horses back and forward, and there was a blacksmith's shop in every small village you came to. It was no bother getting an old horse shod. And then there were so many rag stores in Fife: one in Leslie, three in Methil and two in Cupar. These were the merchants who were non-travellers, who had a settled base and bought stuff that the travellers collected.

But you had to hawk it; then you had to collect it, then sort it, then take it to these stores, and you got very little for it when you got there. It was all done by horse – you needed a horse, without one you couldn't do these things. Only other thing was, you had to go and take a job on a farm till you got the price of a horse. Horses then were cheap. But even a little money was hard to get. And if you had a decent horse of any description you wouldn't have it very long, because so many folk wanted horses back in the 1940s. You only got a certain distance along the road when you were stopped, maybe four and five times in the one day by the local dealers asking you, 'Would you like a swap?'

Well, you would naturally swap and deal with them. You got maybe a pound about, maybe two, and every time you got a swap you got a poorer horse till you were back where you started, till you had something that was worth nothing! And then you had the Inspectors of Cruelty to Animals who were down upon the travellers and horses. They stopped you along the road, and the police were authorised to stop you if they saw your horse was bad and they thought it was lame, or thought it was maybe cut under the saddle. Because some travellers hardly ever looked after a harness, and they did get wet. Travellers never polished their harness every day and kept them soft, so sometimes the horses did get cut. But the travellers had their own way of curing these things – that's another part of the story.

In Fife in the 1940s there were dealers who could drive from the Coaltown o Balgonie, about nine miles from Kirkcaldy to catch the fish markets in Anstruther with a horse, and drive back in the same day. Now that's a good journey! And they hawked fish off their floats and carts with these horses. If you had a pony that was kind of fast, a trotting horse of any description, then they pestered the life out of you till you came and had a deal. And if you had a horse that was thick and strong, then naturally the pig feeders who carted broch and these big bins of swill for the pigs were after it from you. But it was all in the trade. Everybody was trading among each other with horses. You swapped and dealed, maybe three-four times a week, maybe twice a day. But you didn't always get the good deal. There's nobody alive always got the best of every deal!

But the main thing the travellers like myself did, when I got a wee bit o knowledge about horses, we went after the unbroken stuff, the young horses that never were in carts, or something that was wild. A horse that wouldn't stand or one that would maybe kick the cart. And especially the unbroken two-three-year-olds that nobody had bothered with. We got them, broke them in and taught them how to stand, and we trained them with the best of our ability. Then we swapped them away to the local folk about the district.

The very first good horse I got was during the winter of 1949.

My daughter Edith had been born. Money was awfully hard to get. I mean, you were lucky if you worked on a farm all day taking in the harvest from seven o'clock in the morning till five at night for fifty pence a day, ten shillings. Now that was barely two-pound-ten a week. You had to keep yourself off that and your wife, that's if you were working. If you weren't working and you were away doing the hawking and you sellt paper flowers or wooden flowers or made baskets or collected rags, if you didn't use a horse you had to carry the rags on your back and walk with them. Now you carried a hundredweight of rags on your back in these days, and you were lucky if you got three shillings for that hundredweight, the equivalent of fifteen pence today.

Now if somebody had a horse and you tried to buy it, especially among travellers, they would say, 'Well, I would sell it to ye, but ye ken the position I'm in – I'm the same as yirsel – I need it because otherwise it's like cuttin aff yir nose tae spite yir face. So if ye had something I wad gie ye a swap!' But ye had tae have a horse o some description.

So anyway, the first good horse I ever got in my life, I'd managed to save up fifteen pound after a long struggle. Two-three times I had attempted to buy one, but every time something else was always needed. I had kept putting it off because my brother-in-law used to shift my bits of stuff along with his. But I had made up my mind I was going to buy this yoke come hell or high water! I would do without anything else, I was going to buy this horse. And we were staying out at a place they called The Rosie down near Buckhaven.

My cousin says to me, 'I know where there's a wee yoke we could buy fir ye. It's no very big but it might dae ye a turn till ye get something else.' So we drive up to a place they call the Star o Markinch. And there's an old man who kept pigs. He'd sold off his pigs and he had his wee yoke that he had used to gather the broch, the buckets of swill. We walked down and the old man was in his garden. We told him what we were wanting.

'Oh yes,' he said, 'I've got a pony and a float and harness for sale. But I'm needin a good lot fir hit.' He took us round and we had a look at it. The horse was standing in the stable in beautiful straw. But it was fat, very fat. And it wasn't very old, a

mare about seven or eight years old. I asked him how much he
wanted for it. He wanted fourteen pound for the whole yoke.

Now I really knew in my heart I was going to get it. But there's
no way in the world I was going to give him fourteen pound
for it. Because if you ever had any deals with horses or listened
to any dealings, and you had got the same experience I had
being among dealing men for a while – you knew no man ever
gets what he asks for – especially when it comes to a swap or a
deal! And he knew in his own mind he was asking me fourteen,
when I knew he would maybe take twelve. This was the idea,
you always ask more than what you're expecting.

'Well,' I said, 'Is it quiet?'

'Oh, it's quiet, very quiet,' he said.

So I said, 'Is it a good worker?'

'Oh, it's a good worker. I was usin it. I've had it fir about a
year.' And it was terribly fat. He showed me the harness. I was
pleased with it. And he showed me the wee float and I was
pleased with it.

My cousin said, 'That would do ye a turn, that would shift ye
till ye get something else. It looks all right to me.'

'Bring it oot,' I tellt the old man.

So the old man went in the stable, and the horse was in a
wee loose box. He brought the horse out. It was made like an
Aberdeen Angus bull, short tail, a mare. It was only about twelve
and a half hands high. But it was that fat it would barely come
in a barn door!

'Well,' I said to him, 'tae tell ye the truth, old man, I dinnae
hae much money but I would like to buy yir wee yoke.' I checked
its feet, and they were all right. It had a bit of founder, but it
had went kind of dry and wouldn't do it any harm. Its feet were
a bit curled at the front, but were well shod. I said, 'What's the
least you would tak fir it?'

He said, 'I told ye I want fourteen pound fir it.'

'I'll gie ye eleven pound fir it,' I said. 'Come on, hold yir hand
then, I'll give ye eleven pound. That's all it's worth – what is yir
auld harness worth? Ye can buy the old straps o harness like
that fir a pound a piece in any dealer's in Kirkcaldy.'

'I know, laddie,' he said, and then he got on with the patter.
'But ye see it fits the pony, it's jist the ideal thing fir the pony and

the wee float's nice and handy. It's a good wee yoke and I wis jist considerin in my mind whether to sell it or no. Maybe I'll get another pig or two at the back end o the year and I'll prob'ly need it.' Pig men collected cabbage leaves in the shops and old tatties, and the swill to keep the pigs in meat. They fed the pig all winter, and when it got fat they sold it in the market for a big profit. You could buy young pigs cheap. And there were dozens of these pig feeders round about the district on small-holdings. But he hemmed and he hawed and said, 'No.'

'Well,' I said, 'I'll tell ye what I'll do with ye. I'll go another pound, I'll give ye twelve.'

'No,' he said, 'ye'll hev tae come a wee bit more than that.' Now if that had been a traveller having a deal it would have been a different story. Or a horse dealer. We would have been spitting and slapping hands, but this old man had never done much dealing in his life.

So I said to him, 'Well, I'm gaunna give ye one more offer. Before I go. In fact I've no made up my mind. But seein I've seen it, I'm no much interested. It looks kind o slow to me, kind o lazy.'

'No, it's no lazy!' he said. 'Noo it would be very handy fir ye!' He went out with all the patter.

'Ach,' I said, 'no. Forget it. I'm no wantin it. I winna bother aboot it.'

'Well, come here noo, dinnae gae awa like that, laddie! Come on back here and I'll tell ye what I'll dae wi ye. Ye'll gie me thirteen pound fir it, fir the yoke! Noo I'm droppin a pound.'

I said, 'No. I tellt ye what I offered ye. I offered ye twelve. Well, just fir the sake o a deal, I'm gaunna give ye one more bid and one more bid only. I'm gaunna give ye twelve pound ten, take it or leave it!'

He said, 'Well, I'll take it, and ye're gettin a good bargain.'

So I paid him his money and we yoked it up. Now we had to go back to the Rosie Row, a camping place for travellers for many's a year. And this was summertime. We had bought this wee pony from him at about three o'clock in the afternoon. By the time we got it yoked up and out on the main road, half a mile away, it took exactly four and a half hours to get home. It was the laziest thing you ever saw in your life! It would walk at a snail's pace, It wouldn't trot or wouldn't gallop. It would do nothing. This was my first real horse and I'm pulling it over my shoulder. Now I had to walk into Kennoway, down into Windygates and from there to the Rosie Row. By the time I got back it must have been seven o'clock at night.

Well, I came in and a lot of travellers were there, and they all had horses. So they gathered round. This was a strange face. And my first horse, everybody knew. Some said, 'It's no a bad wee pony, ach it'll dae. I've had worse many's a time. Okay, laddie, it'll dae ye a turn, it'll shift yir camp,' and all this patter.

'Ach,' I said, 'it'll dae fir a wee while,' but I wasn't pleased with it. I was far from being pleased. So I said to my cousin, 'It's definitely lazy.'

'Oh,' he said, 'it's past bein lazy.'

'Well,' I said, 'tae tell ye the truth, it's no gaunna be much good tae me. I couldna keep it. It'll have tae go.'

So the next day everybody was packing up to shift their tents and their horses. They pulled out on the road. We were all bound for the Coaltown o Balgonie, another old road. So they all set sail and I had to walk. I walked, bit by the head, and by the time I got into the Coaltown everybody had their tents up and their fires going. They'd all had their tea. But I managed to get there and get the tent up. My cousin was there, gone long before me for hours. And I was cursing myself for buying this thing. It wasn't its fault it was born lazy, but there was nothing in the world you could do, hitting it wouldn't have made any difference. By the time I'd got in, got my tent up and went for a bit coal and got the fire going it must have been eight o'clock at night. But I staked it out on a nice bit of green grass and gave it a bit clean up.

I said to my cousin, 'I'll have tae get rid o this, swap it away.'

He says, 'Take yir time, dinnae be in a hurry. Wait till somebody comes. If ye go and try to offer it to somebody, ye'll get nothing fir it. Somebody'll make a fool o ye. The wee harness and the wee cairt's aa right.'

But two-three days passed and I'm getting sicker as the days go with this thing, this pony. So it was a Sunday and we were having a game of quoits. Travellers always played quoits on Sunday. When up the old road comes this man on horseback and he had on riding breeches and long-legged riding boots. And he was riding this Arab mare about sixteen hands, snow white it was. It was that white it was kind o silvery, and it was prancing! It was reining, passing the tents and blowing at the tents with the fright.

John says to me, 'Look at that horse! Isn't that a beautiful animal?' And all the traveller men were out to see this horse.

So the man jumped down and he was leading it, and it was prancing. He was a non-traveller man from the town. All the traveller men came up, admiring this big horse. A beautiful horse and its skin was that smooth from being inside a stable. It had funny eyes; they were red. I think it was off the Arab strain and about ten year old.

'That's a beautiful horse you've got, mister!' I said.

'Oh aye, it's a nice pony,' he says. Youse hes got some nice ponies yirsel there.'

I said, 'Aye, some nice ponies.'

So this man said to me, 'I bet ye this horse o mine could give ye a hurl if it was in a cairt.'

'Aye,' I said, 'I believe it would!'

But he said, 'I'll tell ye something. Hit's never been in a cairt in its life. And it wadnae be much use to youse kind o boys. I'm lookin fir a pony.'

So some of the men said to him, 'What are ye gaunna dae with a pony when ye've got a pony there? That's a guid enough horse, what ye're usin it for, your job.' He was very civil to talk to, this man, because he knew a lot of the travellers, dealed with them before. He was only a young man in his thirties. I was to become well known to him, Mr Sinclair, later after that. But this was the first time I'd met him.

He said, 'I'm lookin fir a pony fir my wee sister.'

It was my cousin spoke first, 'Well, there's only one pony here that would suit yir wee lassie; that's it tied tae the fence doon there.'

So the man took his white horse and he took the reins and tied them round the fence. 'Come doon, let me have a look at it!' he says.

So we took him down and this was my fat Sheltie. My cousin said, 'How would that do yir wee sister?'

'Oh, that's a nice wee pony, very quiet.' He petted it. He went round about it, looked at it up and down and up and in.

I said, 'There's a cairt and harness tae go with it if ye're interested.'

'Well, I'm no really interested in the cairt and harness,' he said, 'but I suppose it would come in handy in case I ever need to yoke it for something roond aboot the place.' He had a wee pendicle in Thornton. So he said, 'Would ye sell hit?'

'Well,' I said, 'we never usually sell them and lea wirsels stuck. We usually swap. Hae ye nothing I could gie ye a swap tae?'

He said, 'Aye, I'll gie ye a swap tae my mare, my big white mare.'

John says to me in cant, 'Bing the prank fae the gadgie! Tak it! You tak it, tak that horse.'

So I considered it a wee bit. I said to myself, 'What would I do with that?' I gave it a bit of thought. I couldn't put it in a cart. So while the gadgie was talking to the other men and admiring the wee horse, John says to me, 'Look, if you could swap fir that, you get that! We'll put that in the cairt, we'll break it in. It's quiet as a moose, the horse is fresh. I bet ye put that in a cairt, ye've nae trouble,' he says to me where the man couldn't hear him.

So I said to Mr Sinclair, 'Right, what kind o swap would ye need?'

'Well, I need a few pound aboot wi ye.'

'Aha, ye'll no get nae pound aboot wi me!' I said. 'That's a complete yoke. I was thinkin I need a bit money aboot fae ye, fir a complete yoke tae a ridin pony. A ridin pony, ye ken, is no much good tae hus.'

'Well, what would you think?'

I said, 'Well, gie me yir horse and five pound and I'll gie ye the yoke!'

John says tae me, 'Stall, stall, man, canny, stall! The gadgie, ye'll sicken the gadgie.'

I said, 'No, I'll no sicken the gadgie.'

He said, 'I wouldnae gie ye five pound, but I'll gie ye three pound and my pony fir yir yoke.'

I said, 'Haud out yir hand, it's a deal! I'll tak yir horse.'

He takes his saddle off and his bridle off, and I get a rope

and tie it round this big horse's neck. Now I had to tie it up to
a tree, because there's no way in the world you're going to put
it in a tether. We yoked the Sheltie to Mr Sinclair, and away he
went with it, leading it.

Cousin said to me, 'You got yirsel a good pony now. That was
a quick deal ye got from him! Ye got money aboot?'

'Aye, I got money aboot. I got three pound. You would rather
me gied him money? Is it no better tae gie me the money?'

Well,' he said 'there's something wrong wi that pony, when
he would gie ye money alang wi it.'

'Well, I dinna ken if there's something wrang with it or no,
but it's mine noo. And I'm gaunna get harness fir it and I'm
gaunna put it in the cairt.'

'Well,' he said, 'I'll gie ye all the help I can.'

I didn't have any cart and harness; I gave the wee man the lot.
So all the rest of the traveller men gathered round and some
said, 'That's a good pony.' They checked it up and down. We
couldn't find a fault with it any way. It had the most beautiful
feet that you ever saw and it was fat, and it wasn't lazy. It was
prancing when you took it on the rope. Some of the men were
saying, 'God bless me, if that was on a cairt, that wad gie ye a
right hurl.'

I said, 'It's goin on a cairt and I'm keepin it. I'm no sellin it
till I get a cairt fir it!' So I tied it up to a tree and hand fed it.
I cut grass for it and I did everything with it I could. The next
day I borrowed my cousin's yoke and I drove into Kirkcaldy,
the Gallatown, and I went to this old dealing man. And I tellt
him, 'I got a pony. I'm needin a set o harness fir hit.' The old
man had lots of sets hanging up. He sellt and dealt in harness
and ponies forbyes.

'Well,' he said, 'there a set there that might suit ye.' But it was
a van harness, a co-operative harness. Travellers didn't like
them very much. It wasn't a padded saddle, but a small saddle
that just sat on the horse's back. But it was good for the horse
because it let the air in below the horse's back. They were less
expensive to buy. But everything was complete, the reins, the
bridle, the breeching, everything, and it would just suit this
horse I had.

So I said, 'What will ye need fir that?'

He said, 'I was wantin two pound fir them.'

'I'll gie ye thirty shillings fir them, aa the money I've got.'

'Gie me another croon, thirty-five shillings, and you can have them.' So I gave the old man the thirty-five shillings and I flung them in the back of the cart. I got some messages and drove home.

So I landed back in the Coaltown and everybody saw me coming in. And the travellers were after their tea by the time I'd got back. They all came up. They saw this good set of harness. Everybody said what a nice harness they were, how strong. I said, 'Dae fine, it'll suit me fine.' So we cracked away for a while and I said, 'I'll go and see my horse.' I'd led it up the roadside, let it pick here and there. But it was awfully feart of things that were sitting at the roadside. Some of them were saying, 'That horse would run away wi you suppose it was yoked.' Some horses took the idea, if they got the bit in their teeth, they would set sail, run away.

So the next day was a Sunday. My cousin said to me, 'What do you think? We'll put the harness on that horse, see what happens.'

I said, 'The best thing we could dae!' So I went up, took the bridle up with the blinders. And I had this rope around its neck. I pulled it up. And as soon as it saw me with the bridle, it went right up in the air above me, stood up on its hind legs. So we put a loop on its nose and pulled it down, and got the bridle on. Then we got the saddle on it and we put on the britchen, put the cripper on. It wouldn't kick, that was one thing about it. So we walked it up and down, let it hear the noise of the harness rattling on it. But it didn't seem to bother about that.

Cousin said to me, 'That horse has been harnessed before.'

I said, 'No.'

He said, 'What do you say we put it on the float? We'll take a shot o my cairt and we'll yoke it up. We'll get some o the rest o the boys tae gie us a hand in case it rears up and flings itself.' Horses have a habit of flinging themselves on the back of the cart and breaking the shafts, you know. You had to watch them!

I said, 'No, the best thing we can dae is put it on a log first, let it pull a log, drag it on the ground.' So I went and we got a couple of logs, big sleepers that were lying down the old railway. We carried them up, put a bit rope round them and made a swingletree, a crossbar, so's the rope would keep it off the horse's legs. Got it yoked up on this log, and I took it by the head, led it. It had the weight of the log to pull. It started to pull. So I did this every time I yoked it: up and down that road, and I gave it two good days on this log till the sweat was coming from it. By this time it wasn't as good looking a horse as when I'd got it! Its coat was all ruffled and there were spots of dirt on it. Its mane was all fuzzy and its tail was all fuzzy. It was silvery-coloured, and we called this big mare 'Silver'. When she was lying down she was laying on the wet ground, and you could see the big wet mark on her hip.

I said to my cousin, 'It's gaunna be an awfa horse to keep clean.'

'Dinna worry,' he said, 'the horse'll clean itsel through time. That'll fall aff it.' But I had to get a curry-comb and brush and keep this horse clean, because it was so beautiful when the man first came and gave it to us.

But the next day John says, 'We'll put it in the float, yoke it up. We'll take it to the bing fir coal. I'll sit in the cairt and take the reins, and you lead it. We'll see how it goes and then you can gradually let it go, and I'll work it frae the cairt.' But the only thing that was bothering it was blinders on its eyes. But it went easier with the bridle, because a riding bridle hasn't got any blinders. So down we go to the old coal works. This is where they cowped all the rubbish out of the pits, and good bits of coal were in among it. We used to gather this for our fires. So he and I put a good load of coal on the float, and I was leading it.

He says to me, 'Let it go! Stand back fae its head and gie me a shot o the reins. jump on the other side! If anything happens I'll jump aff and catch it!' So we jumped up and he gave it a slap with the reins on the hip, and off it went at a trot, this big beast. And we drove right into the camp, past all the travellers right through the muck, right in the road, this big horse in the cart. It was a beautiful animal, and it was going as if it had been in the cart all the days in its life! And I was as proud as punch with this horse. No way in the world was I going to part with this!

Some of the men came up and said, 'By God, that horse is goin well with you, laddie!'

I said, 'Aye.'

'Never thought I would see that animal in a cairt.' Some said this, some said that and some had a notion to it, you know. I knew I could have had a swap in a minute. But no, I wasn't going to put it away.

So I went out with my cousin and we hawked about with his yoke. I kept Silver tied and began to learn her on the rope, on the tether. The next day we shifted and went right down the coast to Anstruther. We collected rags, woollens, scrap (non-ferrous metals); along with our tent stuff, you know, we just gathered a puckle here and there. So John and I had got a good load each. It took us three days going down and about three days coming back, because in these days you couldn't travel far with a horse. You had to camp along the way. You could hawk a wee while at night. And the next weekend we returned once more to the Coaltown o Balgonie, and by this time Silver was as if she had been in a cart all her days.

I said, 'We'll go inta Kirkcaldy tae the scrap store tomorrow.' We had some brass, some copper, some rags and woollens, horsehair. John had put all the camping stuff in his cart. What we used to do, when we were far away from the stores and two travellers were in partnership, like friends of each other, father and son or brother-in-law or two brothers, and they had two yokes: one would take the camping stuff and the other would load the other yoke with all the metals to be sold. So I yoked Silver in this float I'd bought before I'd shifted from an old man in the Coaltown. And we packed up these two carts in a wee place called Upper Largo. We came to the Coaltown back to our same camping place, because I wanted the same tree I had tied my horse up to before! We got our tents up and the next morning we would go to Kirkcaldy with our stuff to sell. This was our week's work, our collection.

While we were saving up the old stuff over the week the women were selling flowers and baskets and things to keep us alive. So we took big Silver in to Kirkcaldy to have a sell-up, and we sat up, drove the whole way in, right through Thornton. And the first man we met was Mr Sinclair, the man who had given us the horse. He stopped us on the road. I jumped off and caught the pony by the head.

He said, 'Dinnae tell me you got that beast yoked?'

I said, 'Aye, I got it yoked.'

'How long ye got it yoked for noo?'

'Since the day after ye gied me it.'

'Man, man, I'll tell ye something, laddie! If I could hae done that wi that horse, you would never hae got it.'

I said, 'Ye regret—'

'No, no, I'm no regrettin my deal. I'm only sayin, if I could hae done it. But tell me something, how did you manage to get that horse yoked?'

So my cousin spoke up, 'That horse was the easiest yoked horse ever we've had in wir life! We've had some bad anes in wir day, but I hope every ane we get is as easy as that.' So we go into Kirkcaldy and the first man I meet is the old man who sold me the harness, Jimmie MacLaren. He came out and stopped us. Because these dealers, you know them, you couldn't mistake them! They wore the polka-dot hanky round their neck crosswise. If he had a whip in his hand, old brown boots and this polka-dot hanky, you knew – a dealer right away! But he was standing cracking to another man when we came up, and I was leading the pony by this time. We were making for Robertson's in Kirkcaldy.

Mr MacLaren said, 'Hello, boys, yese is busy makin yir way on?'

I said, 'Aye.'

'Tell me something, would I be wrong sayin that's Sinclair frae Thornton's pony you've got there?'

'Aye, that's it.'

And old Jimmie MacLaren said, 'Nah, it's no! That's no the same horse. I've been among horses all my days, lad, and I'll tell ye something. The're no a person in Fife could hae yoked thon horse! Because I could hae bocht it, but I couldnae even get it intae the stable the last time tae get in near it!'

'Well,' I said, 'I'll tell ye something. He must have changed a lot. There's the harness ye gev me fir thirty-five shillings on its back. That's what I wanted it fir!'

And this man, a Johnstone from Leslie, whom I was to have

many deals with later said, 'I'll tell ye something, if these boys cannae dae nothing with a horse, there little chance fir me and you doin anything with it!' So we drove in and sellt our stuff up. That was about the month of April, because the grass was just beginning to come in. You know, Silver was a great horse to me.

So I had a longing to go to Argyllshire because I had never seen my mother and father since I'd got a wife. Now I had a wife and a baby and a horse. I was wanting to show them that I was getting on fine, and I was going to take this big horse back with me. I said, 'The're no way in the world that anybody's gaunna make me swap till I go to Argyllshire and back.' I liked it a lot, and I knew along the way from Fife into Perthshire and all the road going back I was going to meet many's a traveller, and prob'ly I would be needing to have a deal with it. Because I knew I wasn't going to be very rich. Things were hard on the road; it was for all travellers in these days when you were travelling – you would be forced to deal sometimes when you weren't wanting to. But I'd made up my mind there was no way in the world I was going to part with big Silver!

We left the Coaltown o Balgonie on our road to Argyll. It was the end of April and we made our way into Perthshire. Now this horse of mine always kept in the front, and John had a mate too. His was a white one forbyes. My cousin was with me. His horse was a kind of garron he'd swapped for in Fife with an old man Whyte before he'd left. It was a heavy thick-set horse, an old one but a good worker. But it couldn't keep up with my big horse. When we used to get tired walking, we could all jump up because there was only me and the wife and the bairn. And John and his family could jump up on their cart, and we could drive on making the speed, seven or eight miles an hour setting on the level, and walking on the braes.

We made our way into Perthshire and we stayed at the end of Perth. There were some travellers camped there with horses. Two or three folk were at me for a swap, but no – I wouldn't swap this horse away. I was going to take this horse to Argyllshire. So from Perth up to Crieff, into Comrie, up Lochearnhead, we stayed there. Then made our way right over the hill down into Inveraray and back to Furnace where I was born. Now I

couldn't camp in beside my father and mother, so we camped
on the Furnace shore, the place where I was born. And by
this time Silver was tether-broke and I could tether her out. I
wouldn't need to worry about her, she wouldn't get her legs
caught on the rope or fankled up or anything. And by Silver
getting a wee bite o green grass, it began to get bonnier again,
getting away from standing in its own dung during the winter
and the rough muck in other places. All the camping places
were clean – it was summertime coming in. I used to comb
Silver's mane and tail. It was a real picture to look at. But it
had this funny red nostrils and red eyes, like a ferret. It was
off the Arab strain.

So my cousin and I landed back. I didn't go up to see my
mother and father that night. I went up the next day. I took
Jeannie with me and the bairn, and we had a good time with my
mother and father. And he says to me, 'Oh, ye're married?'

I said, 'Aye.

The old man said, 'Ye got a wife and a bairn?'

'Aye.' Edith had been born in October, six months before.

And he said, 'Ye got a horse? Ye finally managed tae get a
horse?'

'Aye.'

'What kind is it?' I tried to explain to him. 'Aye, is it a good
worker?'

'It goes fine, aye.'

'I'll come doon on a wee walk tomorrow and see it.'

I said, 'Daddy, it's a white horse. Ye remember auld Princie
we had a long time ago when you were workin on the road?'

He said, 'Aye, I mind on him fine.'

'Well, he's a white horse, the same kind o horse as thon one,
no as heavy made.'

'Aye, thon was a good horse.' So we went away home and we
got our tea. But true to his word, the next day he came down.
And we had a crack to him. He admired this horse. 'It's a bonnie
animal,' he said to me.

'Aye, it's a nice animal.'

He said, 'It would cost you a lot o money fir that.'

'No, Faither, tae tell ye the God's truth, it didna cost me a lot
o money. It cost me exactly, no coontin the cairt and harness – I

gied twelve pound ten for a wee pony, swapped it away and got three pound aboot – that horse has cost me aboot nine pound ten.'

'Nah,' he said, 'ye're makin fun wi me.'

'No! I'm no makin fun. I'm tellin ye, that's what it cost me, about nine pound ten.' That's what the horse was standin me at.

'Well, I'll tell ye one thing, ye got a bargain!' So we sat and cracked for a long while about all kinds of things. He said, 'Will ye go any further doon by Lochgilphead?'

'No, I don't think I'm going to Lochgilphead. I'm gaunna mak my way back. My cousin John wants to make wir way back to Barrhead, up by Glasgow fir the thinnin o the neeps. Because you and my brother Jimmie and my sisters, and my brother Jack – there no enough neeps doon that way by Lochgilphead fir everybody. So the wee puckle that's doon there, you've got yir fairms.' He and my mother used to go to the neep thinning every year. They just stayed in the farm shed and thinned during the days, and he came back to Furnace when he was finished. I said, 'We'll go wir way back ower the Rest and Be Thankful, ower the ferry at Erskine and up into Barrhead and Neilston where my cousin used tae thin neeps years ago. And I was there tae before Edith was born. I liked that part, but I didnae hae a pony then.'

'Well, I'll tell ye something,' he said, 'ye'll no go far wi that pony till somebody'll be wantin it aff ye.'

The're a lot o folk wanted it aff me already!'

'Ah but jist you watch yirsel,' he said, 'and dinnae gie it awa tae onybody the first chance ye get. That's a good beast!'

'Aye,' I said, 'it's a good beast.' So he went away home. And the next morning I went and saw my mother before we left. And my cousin and I shifted the next day. We made our way back up by Inveraray.

Now, there were no smiddies on the road over the Rest. So John and I checked our ponies' shoes in Inveraray. Two blacksmiths were there at that time. We got our ponies checked, and their shoes seemed to be all right, and we made our way round the head of Loch Fyne into Cairndow. We stayed there for the night. The next morning we made our way up the Rest and Be Thankful. But we were only half roads up the Rest when it started to rain. And it rained and rained and it came down in torrents!

So I said, 'John, the first place we come to we'll have to pull in and get a camp up or everything's gaunna be soakin.' But we landed half-roads down the other side of the Rest, and there's a wee bit of an old church, or an old school. And the door was lying open. I said, 'Here's the very place fir hus. We'll no bother puttin the tents up, we'll go inta the auld school.' There was a fireplace in it, just a ruins, but there was a roof and windows, doors and a floor. I said, 'We'll gie it a sweep up, make wir beds on the floor, and we can kindle the fire.'

He says, 'Fair enough! That'll be better 'an puttin the tents up when the canvas is wet. It'd be a hell of a job.' So we tethered our horses out in front, kindled the fire in the old grate and made our wee bite of tea. We weren't very long there when in came a car. This was two gamekeepers, and they would have us moving out.

'Ye'll hev tae shift, ye've nae right bein in here. This is private property. This is no a campin place fir youse folk.' And it was still raining.

I said, 'I'm no movin the night, fir nobody breathin under the sky. We're stayin.'

'Well, we'll go fir the police.'

'Well,' I said, 'go fir the police if ye want to go, but I'm no shiftin. I've a young baby here seven months old, it's needin the shelter. You can go fir the police. We're not doin any harm, only shelterin fir the night. We cannae get wir tents up because it's too wet.' So they hemmed and hawed and away they went. But they never came back and the police never came.

So, it wasn't a place to stay for long, only a night's stop. Because there was nothing in the world we could do for ourselves there. So the next morning I got up. We made some tea and things began to dry up. We spread the covers out on the ground to dry and I went to have a look at my horse. I looked at its front foot and I said, 'There's something wrong.' Its shoe was gone, the front shoe. It had got pulled off in some fence, an old wire that was stuck in a bit of old fence sticking in the ground. And the nail holes were burst and it took a good part of the hoof off with it. I said, 'John, my horse is bare-fitted. What am I gaunnae dae noo?'

'Well,' he says to me, 'brother, there's no a blacksmith's shop in Arrochar. Nor there's no one in Luss. I believe the nearest one fae here is doon by Helensburgh in the Cardross, and it's a long way tae Balloch.'

'Well, what am I gaunnae dae with this horse?' So, I had a spare wheel for the cart. We took the spare wheel and took out the rubber tube of the inside wheel, and we made a rubber boot for the horse's foot. We opened the tube up. I cut a round circle and put the horse's foot standing on the tube. It was opened into a big wide strip and I put a line of holes, and put a rubber string on, made a draw string like a wee baby's bonnet, you know. And I pulled it up tight round the horse's fetlock. Then I padded it with some rubber inside. I yoked her up and we went on our way down Loch Long, in by the Cardross, into Helensburgh. And there's a camping place beside the old cowp. We put up our camps and the next morning I checked my horse's foot. And this rubber thing was still round it, never moved. I lifted and checked the boot, and the rubber wasn't even worn through. John had told me, 'I saw ma father daein this years ago in Aberdeenshire.' It saves the horse's foot. If this horse had gone with its bare foot for too long, its hoof would have worn down to the frog, into the quick. And then it would have went lame. We would have had to put it in some farmer's field where its hoof would grow again, and I would have been left without a horse.

So that night we stayed at Helensburgh and the next morning I said, 'I'll take the pony along to the blacksmith.' I didn't have much money, very little. We never had very much money then, just a few shillings from time to time, unless we were working or staying in the one bit. So I go along to the blacksmith's shop and it was a nice old man in the smith.

'That's a nice beast ye've got there, laddie,' he said.

'Aye, it's no bad.'

'Where'd ye come fae?'

'I cam up fae Argyll, over the Rest and Be Thankful,' and I told the old man the story. 'My pony cast its shoe right on the top o the Rest.'

'But goodness gracious, laddie, how did ye get here? All that distance – I cannae put a shoe on its hoof if it's worn doon wi walkin that distance. Is it no goin lame with ye?'

I said, 'No, it's no goin lame wi me.'

'I cannae believe this. I'll hev tae see fir myself.' And he came out to the door of the smiddie. 'Oh,' he said, 'that's a nice animal!'

'Aye.'

'What's that ye've got on its foot, a poultice?'

I said, 'No, that's a rubber boot, home-made boot. And that pony walked all the way frae the top o the Rest and Be Thankful. It never even put a mark on the rubber.'

Well, he stood and he scratched his head. Well, I've been in horses all my days, and I've never seen that done before! Bring her inta the stable.'

'Noo,' I said, 'afore ye start, I dinnae hae very much money. I cannae buy a new shoe. Ye'll have tae put an auld shoe on fir me.' (You know, cast shoes that he takes off somebody else's horse, just like a traveller wearing a cast-off boot.) It was good enough, because the blacksmith made a good job of it. He heated it on the fire again and drilled new holes on it. But it was still a second-hand shoe.

I brought her into the stable. He measured the horse's foot with the ruler first, and then he measured her hoof. He picked through all the big heap of shoes till he got one about the right size and he took it, flung it in the fire. He blowed the fire up with the old bellows and he heated the shoe. He shaped it, punched new holes in it and put it on the horse's foot, nailed it on. And he gave it a rub down with the rasp. Oh, it was nice, fine, you see! 'Well,' I said, 'look, as I told ye, I dinnae hae much money.'

'Aye,' he said, 'ye'll have as much as I'm gaunna ask ye.'

'Well, what'll that be?'

He said, 'Two and sixpence, half a croon. And it's worth it tae me.'

'How?'

'Well, ye learned me a good trick!'

'I hope ye'll never need tae tie a rubber on a horse's fit!'

'Ye never know what I might need tae dae yet,' he said, 'afore

I'm aff this worl.' I never saw that old blacksmith again. A new shoe would have been about seven and six, a right good shoe about ten shillings. You got a good horse shod for about two pound.

So we made our way further down and we came to a place on the shore outside of Helensburgh. There was a traveller woman and her son staying on the camping place. Jack was his name. And his mother wanted to buy him a horse. He was only about seventeen and I wouldn't sell mine. So John sellt his tae him. the whole complete yoke for him and his mother. I think he sellt the whole yoke for seventeen pound, a lot of money then. She had one of these old-fashioned pockets that my granny used to wear around her waist, and she paid him out of this pocket. I remember her fine, God rest her soul now, old Maggie.

And John says to me, 'Ye'll take my stuff ower tae Barrhead tae the neep thinnin place. Once we get inta a fairmer's field fir tae thin his neeps, I'll gae inta the horse market in Glasgow. And here, you've never been in the Glasgow market!'

I said, 'No, I've never been in the Glasgow market.'

'Ah well, this is better than Perth,' he says. 'Ye've been in Perth with me.'

'Aye, I ken, I've been in Perth wi ye.'

'But wait ti ye see the bonnie ponies that comes aff the Irish boat!' Now the tinkers in Ireland used to go round and they took horses across on the boat the day before the market. Some of them sat out all night with them on the greens and parks to catch the sale the next day. It was every Wednesday, all day, horses in the market. And there dealers came from all over every place to buy and sell and swap. It was the same kind of market as Perth, but a bigger do, and it went on longer. And you believe me, there were some dealing o horses round about Glasgow at that time! There were men selling brickets, men selling coal, fish merchants, fruit merchants, tattie merchants, dairies, co-operative horses, you name it, everybody had a horse – fishmen, folk selling and dealing in second-hand furniture – all with horses, ponies of all description! And this was the day to look forward to, coming into the horse market, to see their friends, have a deal, have a swap, have a change of horses.

So I shift my cousin's camp on my cart to Barrhead, and

we get a field of neeps, because we'd thinned neeps to this farmer before, Mr Young at Newton Mearns. So we thinned the whole field and got paid for them. It didn't come to very much, two-three pound apiece. But my cousin and his mother had a terrible argument the next day. And instead of John going to the market, away he goes, clears out, off on his own. This was about the first time he's left his mother in his life. And he goes to Aberdeen! Now whatever kind o money he got for his turnips and his horse, he took it with him in his pocket.

So his mother says, 'That's him away. We'll prob'ly no be seein him again fir a while.'

'Well,' I said, 'there one thing fir sure, we'll no need tae worry about another horse anyway, because there naebody tae look after it!' Because John's other brother wouldn't bother about horses. So we made our way from there down to this wee place the other side of Glasgow. It was late on in the summer now, and by this time mostly all the neeps round about Glasgow were finished. I said, 'The best thing I can do, because I was the man that had the horse then, I'm gaunna make my way back tae Fife.'

So my auntie says, 'There's nae sense o hus stayin here wirsels when John's awa. The best thing I can dae is jist go back tae Fife wi yese. He'll prob'ly come back sometime.' Because he wasn't married. He had no wife or anything, and just stayed with his mother, looked after her all the days of his life since he was a wee laddie. And we made our way to a place called Bellshill on the outside of Glasgow, on our way back to Fife. We stopped at the roadside to make some tea. And I looked over the hedge and saw this big field of turnips. Oh, they were growing past the common and never were thinned.

So I said to Charlie, John's brother, 'You watch my pony a minute. I'm gaun doon tae this farm and see if I can get these neeps tae thin.'

He says to me, 'They're too big. Ye could never work wi these turnips.'

'I'll work wi them. I'll dae them some way.' But they were an awful size. Now, I was a bit upset because I'd never got to the horse market in Glasgow. John had promised me, and I was upset. So, I went to the farm, not far down the farm road.

This old man was in the dairy washing milk cans. And he had a rubber apron on him.

He says, 'What is it, laddie, you're wantin?'

'Well,' I said, 'tell ye the truth, I'm on the road, I'm after comin over fae Barrhead way. I've been up there all summer thinnin turnips fir some o the fairms, and I go there every year. I was makin my way back tae Fife and I stopped up at the shop there tae make some tea, and I see you've got some turnips in yir field that's needin done.'

'Oh, laddie, I've tried ma best tae get them done, but we had a bad spell o rain there fir a while. I used tae get some women oot o the village there, but they never cam the year, and I dinnae ken what I'm gaunna dae with them neeps. Ach, I'll jist let them grow and it'll be a loss tae me fir my dairy coos in the wintertime, but I'll jist have tae let them grow wild. What was it ye wanted?'

'I'm wanting a job fae ye tae thin yir turnips.'

'Do ye mean to tell me you want tae dae them fir me?'

'Aye, I'll dae them fir ye and make a good job o them to ye.' It was beautiful weather.

'What were ye gettin fir yir turnips up there in Mearns?'

'The man was gien me a shillin a hundred yards.'

'Well, if you do that fir me, I'll gie you one and sixpence a hundred yards.'

'I'll need that because they're kind o dirty and kind o big.'

'You make a kind o fair job fir me even suppose you only pull oot the doubles and lea them single. I'm no worried what you do wi them, dae yir best wi them and I'll pay you one and six.' Now that was the best money ever was gotten for thinning turnips up till then from any farmer!

'Well,' I said, 'I'll need a place fir my camp.'

He says, 'The fairm's big. I'm sure you can find a suitable place.'

'And a field fir my horse.'

'Oh,' he said, 'there plenty fields. Ye jist put it in among the coos there, among the milk cattle, it'll get plenty to eat.' Nice old man. Hamilton was his name. And he says, 'Bring up yir pails, ye'll get plenty milk.'

Now there was only me and Charlie to work. The lassies and

their mother didn't bother because they had been working all summer with us, and we didn't want to bother them with those big neeps. I said, 'We'll work away at them and we'll sit here jist in case John ever turns up again from where he went away on his journey. If he turns up he'll no hae far tae find us. He'll trace us oot some way.' But we worked away. It was a Thursday. Charlie and I worked Friday, Saturday, Sunday and Monday. Tuesday we finished them.

Now it was Wednesday and my auntie says, 'I think I'll take a trip into the horse market in case that laddie does turn back. He might go there.'

And Jeannie my wife says, 'Ach, I'll go in wi my mother.'

'Well,' I said, 'away youse go if youse want tae go. I'll no bother gaun in. I dinnae ken much about it.'

She says, 'We'll just go and have a look roond. And we'll see – if he's no there, we'll take the tram car oot.' The tram went right into Argyle Street to the Gallogate, where the horse market was. So away they go.

Charlie goes up to the farmer, comes down with a big pail of sour milk. And the sun was hot. He's sitting with this cup drinking this sour milk. So this woman steps in off the road, a young woman about in her twenties and she had a long coat on, and high-heeled shoes. So Charlie says to me, 'Shan gurie.'* He always spoke in cant, you see. 'Shan gurie, dinnae mang tae the shan gurie.'

She said, 'Excuse me, boys, I was wonderin, boys, if yese could gie me a wee cup tea.' Oh, a real Glasgow tongue too.

'Oh,' I said, 'certainly missus.' Now I always kept the can, the kettle full of tea at the fireside. It was bow tents we had and the outside fire. It was a beautiful day and we were staying in the corner of this field, and there were plenty of rotten sticks. I had this good fire going.

She said, 'Is it aa right if I sit doon?'

I said, 'Aye, sit doon, missus.'

'And eh, are youse married?'

'Oh yes,' I said, 'aye, we're married, both o hus is married. We've got women and bings o weans, we've got a dozen weans. They're only awa up to the shop there.' We were kind o eerie,

---

* shan gurie – prostitute

feart o her, ken, because we didna want tae cause any trouble. So we gave her a cup of tea, and she starts speaking about what happened to her, how she went in hospital, how she went to the British Legion and what they did for her.

But after she had tea she said, 'I'm awfae tired. I think, could I hae a wee lie doon in yir tents, one o yir tents? It looks awfae comfortable in these tents. I would like to have a wee sleep.'

I told her, 'Ye better go, missus, cause I've got a wife and six weans and this man's wife is wicked here. If they come back and get you asleep in wir tent, you'll never live, they'll kill you dead.' We had to do something to get rid of her. She wasn't wanting to go. I said, 'Missus, we're very sorry. Look, we've got work tae do. If we're no oot on that fairm at twelve o'clock, we'll get shifted here. We're only in here to work. We're sorry we'll have to go.' So I pulled down the flaps of the tents, put a stone on them and put out the fire and walked away.

So, we finally got rid of her, and away she went. Charlie and I kindled the fire back up again. In about an hour's time we hear this horse, horse's feet on the road. Charlie says to me, 'I hear a pony on the road. Maybe it's yir pony got oot.'

I look up the road and here's John and his mother and Jeannie coming! She had the bairn in her oxters. And John had this beautiful pony, about fifteen hands, a trotting, chestnut pony. He had come on the train from Aberdeen on the Wednesday morning and was there early, in the market and had his horse bought by the time his mother had come in, thinking we were still in the same camp where he'd left. John didn't have any harness or anything, but he had this beautiful horse he'd bought in the market. So he comes in and has his tea.

He said, 'What do you think o that ane?'

I said, 'It's no bad. Had ye tae go to Aberdeen fir that ane? Did ye go to Aberdeen market wi that ane?' I was laughing.

He laughed and said, 'No, I didnae go to Aberdeen market wi that!'

I said, 'What's about the promise you made to me, you'd take me to the Glasgow market? You never took me!'

He said, 'Look, the summer's no finished yet. You'll prob'ly be back in the market before the summer's oot yet.' And true to his word, I thought it would never happen, but I was to go to the market before we landed back in Fife.

So I said, 'Were there many horses in the market today?'

'There were dozens o horses! I bought this pony for sixteen pound, a beautiful horse.' It was young and a real fast trotting horse, a cross blood and hackney. 'And I'll be all right once I get a cairt and harness. We'll shift up to Baillieston old road. There's some travellers on it and I saw them at the market today. They tell me my Uncle Johnie and my Uncle Sandy are up there. They've got yokes and there's other travellers. A man Townsley frae Edinburgh and he's got a horse, so they might have an old cairt and harness I could buy fae them. If you shift my stuff up to the Baillieston auld road, I'll prob'ly get something before we mak wir way back to Fife.'

So it just shows you how things take a twist. We shift up to the old road and my two uncles were there. One was old Sandy Reid, who told me so many good stories later on in my life. Another was my mother's second oldest brother, Johnie. They were great horsiemen. And they had gotten in with the Irish. There weren't many Irish travellers in Scotland at that time, but they were beginning to come over. And this is how I met Ned Cash, the big, big, tall Irishman.

My Old Horse and Cart

O the summertime has come again, but it surely breaks my hairt,
When I think on the happy days I spent with my old horse and
    cairt;
The roads they were nae lang for him, nor yet too lang for me,
It's on the road I used to gang, oh my old horse and me.

Frae Aberdeen tae Galloway we tramped the country wide
Fae Edinburgh doon tae Stranraer and roond the banks o Clyde,
The roads they were nae lang for him, nor yet too lang for me,
It's on the road I used to gang, oh my old horse and me.

O many's a time on a winter's night he stood tied to a tree
Wi no a bite to gie to him or no a bite for me,
With a wee bit cover across his back to shelter him from the snow
And I ken it's in the morning on the road I'd have to go.

Noo many's a time upon the road my old horse he'd cast a shoe
Up to the smiddie I would gang, to the smiddie man I'd view,
'I cannae buy a new shoe,' to the smiddie man I'd say,
'O pit me on an auld ane, I'm sure it will have to dae!'

Noo those happy days are gone and past, I've bocht a motor car,
Sure I go drivin on the road – I'm sure I travel far!
I drive past all those places, but I'll turn to you and say,
'I'll never be as happy as I was with my old horse and me!'

Duncan Williamson

CHAPTER ELEVEN

BY GOD, LADDIE, YOU'RE GAME!

So I came in, put my tent up, put the horses up – there was plenty of room on the old road for the horses. Oh, we had to go and crack, and get a big fire going. Everybody got round the big outside fire and the tents. All were cracking and speaking about this thing and that.

So this man Townsley says to me, 'That's no a bad lookin pony you have there.'

'Ach,' I said, 'it's no nae better as nae other horse. I see a good lot o horses on the road here.'

'Man, I've a notion to that horse! I bocht a wee gypsy wagon. I've never had ane before and I was wantin, fir the sake o me and the wife in the wintertime fir tae stay in this wee wagon.' It was a caravan, a bow-topped wagon. And he said, 'My pony is a good one, but it's no big enough to pull my wagon. I thought maybe, I was up here on the auld road tae see what yir Uncle Johnie had, but his is nae much bigger than mine, nor yir Uncle Sandy's. That ane John's got is kind o light in the leg. I could dae wi yir pony.'

I said, 'Aye and I could dae with it tae. I need it fir masel.'

'Come on up and see my horse,' he said. 'Look, afore ye see this horse, I'm no tellin ye nae lie about it. This horse at one time could do a mile in three minutes. It cam off the trots in Musselburgh.' Well, you've seen an Appalusa horse. This was a different way round about, a pure brown horse with white spots all over its body, as if somebody had taken a pail of whitewash and just cast handfuls here and there. It was a beautiful animal, fat, and it was standing in long grass.

So I said, 'Well, it looks a nice pony.'

He said, 'I'm tellin ye, it is a good pony. But that's the only way I'm puttin it awa, I dinnae think it'll pull my wagon. It could pull it right enough, but it looks kind o shan wi the wee horse bein in the wagon. Even though yir horse is bigger, it might no be nae stronger. Yir horse'll no look so bad, haen a big horse inta a wagon, especially gae'n through the toons with all the Cruelties and that. If they see a wee horse overloaded ye're pulled up every minute.'

'Well, I'll think about it.'

'Aye, tak yir time. ye'll no be gaun awa fir a day or two.'

'No, I'll no be gaun awa fir a day or two.' So I had a crack to John on the sly. 'John, what do you think o that horse belongin tae Willie Townsley up there?'

He said, 'That's a good pony, a trottin horse. I heard my Uncle Johnie and the rest o the boys speakin aboot it – that horse can trot!' Oh it could, no mistake.

'Well, he wants tae swap me.'

'Well,' he said, 'do you no think you've had that white horse lang enough, you've had her since ye left Fife.'

So it was Jeannie, the wean's mother, I tellt her. She said, 'Look, I'll tell ye something about that horse – that horse is lame.'

I said, 'You're lame, no the horse!'

She said, 'I'm tellin ye it's lame! I seen the man takkin it fir a drink, it's goin lame.'

'I was up at the horse and I seen it and I looked . . .'

'You seen it standin among long grass. I'm tellin ye, that horse is lame.'

'Well,' I said, 'I'm no carin if it's lame or no, I'm swappin fir it.'

'Well, dinnae complain tae me about it if ye get a bad deal.'

So the next morning I go up to the man, come a-crack to him and I swap with him, three pound about, his horse for mine. Horses and harness we swapped. So I wanted to shift that day.

I shifted on the road and I said to John, 'I think instead o goin back to Fife, I think I'll go back up to Barrhead.' Something tellt me to go back to Barrhead. I was on my road going to Fife, too, for the winter. But it wasn't far back the same distance I'd come, about twenty miles.

So he says, 'Ach well . . .' John didn't get a cart, but he got an old set of harness from some of them. 'We'll go away back up that way. I might manage tae pick up an auld float or something.' So back by Barrhead we made our way right enough, and we go right out to a wee place called Neilston. And it was hell of a bad for a fire. Now this horse was definitely going lame with me when I got on the road a while. But once it got heated up, it went kind o sound. But it was definitely sore. One foot had ringbone and there was nothing in the world you could do with it. This was a sinew that turns into a bone, gets hard through time. You can patch it up, poultice it, make it go sound for a day or two, but it never gets better. It's an overstrained tendon in the front foot. Anyway, I only had it that day and the next. And it was a hellish place we were staying for sticks.

So I said, 'I'll have tae go fir some sticks.' I yoked this pony up and away I went. I must have went about four miles down this road, and I loaded the cart. On the road back I jumped up on the top of the sticks. I said, 'If you can trot, I want to see! Lame or no lame, if you can trot!'

But when the pony went about a mile the lameness went away from him. And I looked behind me. Here's an old-fashioned Army lorry coming. (The Army sellt a lot of lorries after the war.) Two men were in the front of it and they're keeping behind me. I waved them on, but they wouldn't pass. And when I turned into the camp they followed me up. The two men came out and I could see it was a father and son.

He said, 'That's a guid goin pony you've got there, laddie! We were follaein you wi the lorry there.'

'Aye, I seen ye.'

'Well, we cam frae Saltcoats and after I seen that pony trottin, I want tae buy it frae ye. Is it for sale?'

'Oh, it's for sale aa right. It's fir sale, mister, all right! I'm sellin it first chance I get. I'm lookin fir something a wee bit bigger.'

'What would you be wantin fir it?'

'Oh well,' I said, 'it cost me a good lot masel.'

'Aye, put a price on it and I'll buy it fae ye.'

Now this horse has cost me six pound ten . . . the white horse had only cost me nine pound, because I had got three pound in the swap. The price is getting wee-er. This horse I'd got was only worth six pound ten to me. It had cost me that much. And this is the way the travellers worked it out, till the horse they had cost them nothing. I said to these two men, 'Twenty pound for the yoke. It's yours, no a penny less.'

'By God,' he said, 'you're game! Haud out yir hand, I'll tell ye what I'll dae with you.' I held out my hand. He said, 'I'll gie ye eighteen pound in yir hand, cash!'

I said, 'Get it paid, and it's yours.' So it was a deal. The man paid the eighteen pound to me.

He told the laddie, 'You yoke it and mak yir way noo. Nae chasin it on and walk it hame! And I'll drive hame with the lorry. I'll gae hame and hae a bite tae eat. I'll yoke up my other pony and come back and meet ye.' So away goes my horse and that was the end of it.

Now here are we left in Neilston. John has got a pony and harness and no cart. I've got eighteen pound and no horse. And it was a Monday. I said, 'John, ye're gaun . . .'

He said, 'I cannae tak ye to market. I'm goin to see a man about a cairt. I have tae see him on Wednesday.'

So I said, 'Well, I'll go to market masel, and I'll get something before I come back. I'll take a tram-car in myself,' He tellt me where to go.

So on Wednesday I get a bus in a bit of the road, and then I get a trammie into the market, right to Argyle Street. And I come off. I asked everybody to tell me the road to the market and it was no bother. The first body I met in the market was my Uncle Johnie. Also my Uncle Sandy and a big bunch o travellers. They're all standing with ponies and carts right at the front of the market. And two Irishmen. This one Irishman had the biggest horse I ever saw in my life, a grey horse about seventeen hands. But I walked up and down and up and down and looked at all the horses, and I couldn't see anything worth my money. Horses began to get dearer then. And this Irishman was cracking to Uncle Johnie.

He says to me, 'Ye looking fir a horse, son?'

I said, 'Aye, I'm lookin fir a horse, mister.'

'What kind o money would ye be gaunna pay fir it?'

Now I had given Jeannie two pound to get messages. And I'd paid my bus off it, which wasn't very much. I think I had fifteen pound odds left in my pocket, and I bought fags. This is why I couldn't buy anything in the market, because they were a wee bit more than I had in my pooch. If I had kept my eighteen pound I might have had a chance. I said, 'I havena got very much money. I've got nae way o gettin nothing.'

He said, 'How much money do ye hev?'

I said, 'Tell the God's truth, mister, all the money I've got between me and God is fifteen pound.'

He said, 'I could get ye a pony fir yir fifteen pound, boy, on my road back where I stay at a place called Harthill. But it means a long walk for ye.'

'Oh mister, I'm no carin about a walk.'

'Well, I'm goin oot this way and I know the old man that owns it well. And I'm sure I could buy it to you fir yir fifteen bar.' So by this time the horses began to get sold in the sale and everybody was moving out. 'Well,' he said, 'wait till I get this auld woman o mine, fling her in this cart an we'll drive out. I'll show ye this pigman has this horse!'

So I jumped in the cart with the man and I'd never been out this road before in my life. His name was Ned Cash. He stopped at this shop. His wife came out, and she had this great big box of messages. She put them in the side of the float. He jumped up. And he drove that horse all the way out, never giving it a stop, never a chance to draw a breath till it landed where he was staying.

Now, sister, when we landed there – I've seen rough travellers in my day, real rough ones, and I've been among a lot o travellers – and God kens I was brought up kind o rough myself! But never in my life have ever I seen a rougher place than this. These travellers were fresh from Ireland, Irish travellers. They treated Scotland like I couldn't tell ye. But the law didn't mean anything to them – they camped in any farmer's field, they camped any place, and if they wanted something they just went and helped themselves to it. When the police came, 'Oh, we're just from Ireland – we don't know any better. We thought . . .' This was an excuse! They pleaded ignorant.

So this old woman said, 'Come on up to the fire, boy, and hae a bite o tea!' The man took me up to the fire. The woman made a kettle o tea and she gave me some. This old woman was sitting at the fireside making a loaf o bread. She had a big metal pot, and the loaf into the pot. She had a fire kindled under the pot, and the lid of it was turned upside down. Another fire was kindled on top of the lid. That was heat from below and heat from above. She was baking a home-made Irish loaf. I'd never seen this before in my life. I'd seen my mother making bannocks at the fireside, scones and that. But these were the freest people you ever saw in your life! You could have stayed with them all your days! But questions – they asked you questions about this, questions about that, and they were very inquisistive. They wanted to know everything. What are old coal bags a dozen? They collected everything, you see, old coal bags, rags, bottles and bones, anything they could turn into a shilling. I'll tell you, some of them are well off today with big new trailers and lorries. And they got their start here in Scotland.

Ned Cash said, 'We'll yoke the old pony again and I'll drive ye down to this pig feeder, and we'll get you that pony.' He never said 'buy it; well get you this pony,' he said. So he yokes the big horse up again. 'Jump in, son!' And he jumps in, drives away back the road a bit and then down this side road. And he comes to this wee old croft. He says, 'I was down here the other day and I got some old bags from him, and some old scrap. And I seen the wee bit of a pony he's got. I think it would do you a turn. You hold the pony and I'll have a speak to him for ye.'

I said, 'The're the fifteen pound to ye. If you can buy it fir that, keep the rest.'

'Oh not at all, boy! What are you gae'n to do for a smoke or maybe a sup o tea when you go home to your woman? You couldnae gie it all tae him. Gie me thirteen and you keep another two, because you might need it, you know, tomorrow.'

'All right.' I gave him the thirteen pound. He took the reins of the horse and tied it to the gate post.

'Come with me,' he said, 'and we'll see him.' We walk in and out comes this old man. He said, 'I was down yesterday and bought that puckle scrap frae ye.'

'Aye,' the man said, 'so you were.'

'And I was tellin the young boy here – this is a friend, a mate o mine. He's just new married and he's just tryin to make his way in the world. He disna have very much money. I thought maybe I could buy that old teat from ye. It would maybe give him a start in life. He'll prob'ly get an old bit o harness fir her.'

'Well,' the man said, 'there it is there, she's fir sale.'

'Come here, boy, and have a look at this teat and see what

you think!' I looked at it. And oh, a nice wee pony. A mare it was, beautiful wee brown pony, a long tail and mane. He said, 'Would it do you, son?'

I said, 'God bless me, aye, mister, it would do me aa right! That would suit me fine.'

'Well,' he says to the old man, 'and what would ye sekkin fir it?

The old man said, 'I was wantin twenty pound fir it.'

'Och not at all,' he said. 'I'm sure now he was offered one there now just afore we left at my own place for fourteen pound. He could have got a nice wee pony, and he hadna the money tae pay fir it. I'll tell ye what I'll do wi you, I'll give ye ten pound fir her and ye're gettin a good bargain!'

'Oh,' the man said, 'no ten pound. I would never dream of it!'

'Now, I'm sure it's no good to you now. Would you no be better now, maybe you could buy a couple o pigs fir the ten pound, you see, and it's far better tae you. Now it's only standin there and it's eatin all yir meat, and it's no doin you any good.'

Man said, 'I've plenty meat fir it, plenty food fir it. I'm no going to gie it awa fir ten pound anyway.'

'Well, I'm sure now a biddin man's a buyin man! Now hold your hand: I'll tell ye what I'll do with you now. If ye hold yir hand I'll give ye a right deal. There's [SLAP] six in that hand. Now hold that, I'm gaunna give ye more – now this is the last penny and there's seven in that hand! Now there's thirteen pound to ye. Am I no givin ye a good bid now? Now be sure, let me see ye puttin that in yir pocket and sayin it's a deal!'

Well, I think the old man began to agree with him. 'Ach well,' he says, 'seein this is fir the laddie, you can have it!' The old man put the money in his pocket.

'Now ye'll gie the boy a bit bridle fir tae put on it tae lead it back!' The old man went into the stead building, got me a nice working bridle. I had the bridle for years after that. 'Now I'm sure you'll gie the boy that bridle now fir a luckspenny! I'm sure it'll bring him luck! Take yir pony, boy, and tie it to the back of the cart.' And he had a ring on the back of his cart for tying other horses to. 'Tie it there and we'll drive home. We'll get some more tea.' Oh, this wee pony could fair step up behind the other cart. It was going fine. He drove back. All the people gathered round it.

'Ach, it's just an old teat fir the young fellow here,' he tellt them. 'It'll give him a bit start.' He says to me, 'Will you manage to make yir way back noo?'

'Oh, I'll make my way back.'

'Look, you can't go wrong. Sure I know the way to Barrhead all the way fae here. Now if you take the way I show ye, it's a quicker way.' He gave me directions, 'Ye'll go back the tram car rails, follow the rails ti the end. It'll save ye gaun down the main street now. And fae there on you've a straight road home. But I'll tell you something, it'll be late before you get home so you better fill yir belly before you go!'

I had a nice cup o tea with Ned Cash and his family. My main interest was watching this other old Irish woman making this bread in a pot on the fire. I said to Ned, 'That's nice. I bet you that tastes good.'

'Well, son, you should know if it tastes good or no. You're after havin a bit of it!' I never knew I was eating the bread his mother-in-law had made. It was delicious. Great I thought! So he said to me, 'Now, son, after you've had tea – did you fill your belly up?'

I said, 'Aye, I've had enough to eat. Thank you very much.' They were awfully nice folk.

'Now you remember the directions I'm sendin ye?' This was Harthill, past Bellshill a good bit. 'You'll have to go straight back through Glasgow, right through Argyle Street and go over the Jamaica Bridge, straight out to Carnwadric, Pollokshaws and on to Barrhead. Now that's not a bad little teat you've got. It'll prob'ly do you till ye swap it away for something bigger. Where dae ye come from?'

I told him, 'I come from, well mostly I come fae away doon in Fife.'

'I've heard a lot about that country. But I've never been there.'

'Well, if you're ever down that way, look me up. We'll have a good time o it when ye get there.' It was nearly three years later before I was to see him in Fife. And I did have a great time with Ned Cash, but that's another story.

I was quite pleased to get this wee pony and I didn't mind the walk. I was really young, in my twenties, and walking to me was nothing. So the old man had given me a bit rope, a bridle. I put the bridle on the pony and started to walk. It was a beautiful day. The funny thing is, if you're walking with a pony leading it by the head you seem to walk better, faster, because you keep time with the horse. You never feel the time passing because you're aye speakin to the horse and watching the horse and the miles seem to pass on. But I walked on till I came to the tram car rails. And I said, 'I hope it's no feart o traffic. It cannae be feart if the old pig man used it in the street often enough.' A lot of horses were feart o tram cars with the 'ssshhhhhtt' and the sparks fleeing off the wheels, and the overhead sparks off the wire. But this wee pony didn't seem to bother.

So I walked on and on and on and I was well into Glasgow making my way for Argyle Street. When I came along there was a big building, and just as I was coming level with this building there were two or three kids playing in the road. This wee lassie, about three, she ran straight out in the front of this tram car! I just let go the horse and ran out. I snapped the wee bairn away from in front of the tram car. And the horse being loose set sail, galloping right down in front of the tram car. All the cars are stopped and the horse is loose! It hadn't run far, maybe a hundred yards when a policeman on patrol stopped it. And, with the help of some of the folk he caught it. He walked back with it towards me. Now I'm standing and I've got the wee bairn, and I'm shaking with the fright I got. And this woman came out of a close. She was just coming out when another man in plain clothes came across, and he, too, was a policeman, or a detective. This other one came up who had the horse.

'What's the meaning o this?' he says to me. 'Lettin your horse go in traffic! Lettin it go. You know, it could hae been killed. You could have caused an accident. What's your name?' I tellt him my name. 'Where do you stay? Well, we'll have to see more about this.'

This other policeman or detective came up. 'Constable, wait a minute! It's not the young fellow's fault. He's after savin that kid frae the front o that tram car.' And the tram car stopped. The driver came out and he tellt the police.

'It ran right in front o the car,' he said, 'and the young fellow here, he had to let go o the horse. He let go of the horse to save the child's life. I never really seen her.' You know, because in tram cars you sit up high and you could hardly see right down in front. But I'd snapped her and saved her life. And then her mother came out. She snapped the wee bairn! She gave it all the scolding you could get!

And the policeman said, 'Come here you!' To the mother, 'You take the tellin off you gied her. You could have caused the bairn's life, and this young man could have been killed. And the horse could have run away in the road, caused an accident! All through you neglectin your child. Now never let that happen again!' He gave her a terrible scolding.

So the two policemen pulled me aside, asked me where I was going. I tellt them I was going to Barrhead and I said, 'I bought . . .'

'Where'd you get the pony?'

'I bought it away up oot at a tinker's encampment.' I never said I got it from a pig man. 'And I drove oot with him in his cairt tae this Irish tinker's campin place. He got me this horse, and I have to walk to Barrhead.

'Well,' the policeman said, 'I see you're on the right side of the road anyway.'

I said, 'Oh aye, I've walked horses a long way.' You've got to face the traffic. You always keep yourself next to the traffic because if the horse shies, it'll no shy towards you. It'll shy up to the pavement.

So he said, 'It's okay then.' So I never got charged. The policeman gave me the rest of the directions to take, told me two or three shortcuts. But I didn't want to get lost. I just kept on the way Paddy tellt me.

So I travelled on. I followed the tram car lines over the Jamaica Bridge and right out to Carnwadric, Pollokshaws, right to Barrhead. And we were camped on an old road. It was about ten o'clock at night when I got back. So, the next day we shifted. Now I had no cart and I had no harness. John had a gig he'd bought. We called it a 'machine', a governor's car.

He said, 'We'll try wir best to pack it up and you just walk your pony, and we'll make wir way back to Fife.'

So we did make our way gradually back to Fife. We cut away in by Glasgow, in by Larbert and in by Kincardine Bridge, and into Dunfermline. It was at Halbeath where I bought this wee cart and harness from an old man. I got myself a complete yoke once more. And I swore that no more was I going to break up my yoke. I said I would never sell out again! It disna matter what I had, I was going to keep it. If somebody offered me a swap, they would have to swap me a complete yoke.

So we landed back in Fife anyway. And we started gathering the puckles o scrap and stuff and trying to make our living the best way we could, hawking flowers and that. But we got word that there were travellers making a lot of money at the tatties at Muthill by Crieff. It was coming up now about the end of September. The travellers were gathering at Muthill. This man, Sir Dembey Roberts, had opened up a big place for the travellers to camp there, an old Army billet called Hell Fire Corner.

My cousin says to me, 'I think the best thing – we should go for a while to the tatties.'

Now it was only me and Jeannie and Edith. She was only about eleven months old. So I said, 'Okay by me, that's fine. We'll go to the tatties. So we left Fife. But I said, 'Look, I'm comin back to Fife in the wintertime. I'm no stayin in Perthshire in the winter.' I liked Fife because in these days you could camp any place and you got plenty of coal. There were plenty of coal bings. And there was a scrap store in nearly every wee village. It was good for making a living. Money wasn't very plentiful but it was a poor day you couldn't go out with your cart and make something.

When we finally got to Crieff and were at the tatties, we were working for ten shillings a day. Well, I was lifting the tattie baskets and getting thirteen. That was twenty-three shillings a day between the two of us. Now when I was back in Fife I could go out and make a couple of pound for my day gathering a wee puckle scrap or non-ferrous metals, or suppose it was only selling flowers. But you got bored doing the same thing steady, every day. And you soon hawked a place out. Say, you were staying at Markinch for about a week. With a pony you only had a small district to hawk. And you soon got cleaned up round there, so you had to move on to get some place else. The further you moved away from the scrap stores the further you had the stuff to take back. And there weren't many travellers had cars then. All the travellers were flocking to the tatties because there were some families with six and seven gatherers. A father and mother and six weans would draw about five or six pound a day. Now, you could buy a good horse then for twenty-five-thirty pound. And travellers were just beginning to get a start in motors. The tatties is where you could buy a cheap tent, you see! Somebody ran out of money, and they were selling a tent. Or maybe they were selling a horse or a cover for a camp. It was better than the berries, because the folk out for the berries were only out for fun. But the tatties was reality – you had to really work.

We had made our way to the tatties. And when we landed there I never saw so many camps in my life! There were gellies and barricades, but not a caravan among them. Some had big tents with bits of barricades at the front. All had chimneys and fire cans in now. Different from what you would have today. There's people running about the country now wouldn't even go there. But that's where they were born, some of them. Even suppose such a place was there today, some travellers wouldn't go, disgrace themselves and do a day's work in such primitive conditions.

At that time you didn't need to go and ask for a job; you just came in and put up your tent. The next morning they sent a cattle float with the big doors. An odd traveller had a car, and they would drive to the field themselves and take their own family. But there were only half a dozen motors there. Everybody had horses, and it was good fun because the farmer gave you a big field. You could turn your horse loose and forget about it. There was a burn where you could poach plenty salmon. There were plenty of rabbits and you could take home as many tatties as you wanted. And firewood past the common. You had company; you could play quoits at weekends and go fishing. And there was a wee train passed by where you stayed; it took you into Crieff for a sixpence. You only had four or five hundred yards to walk to the wee station to get a train. And it went four and five times a day by Auchterarder and right through by Crieff. The women used to go in on a Saturday for their messages. They were no time away! Things were all right there. Folk liked it!

And this cattle float, you would have got a laugh with it coming in! The driver would say, 'All right then, there such and such is goin to one field, and I want twenty off at this fairm. I'm droppin off some in the other field . . .' And some farmers worked you harder than others.

It was a pantomime. I saw about sixty workers on this cattle float and bairns. They were all carrying these bundles, baskets and some with pots and frying pans. Pots of soup for their dinner and cans for their tea, baskets full of messages and wee bairns rolled up in shawls. Some with prams, and all on this cattle float. And the driver lowered the back door, and some of them would 'moo, moo' when they went in, same as they were cattle! So the travellers talked among themselves, if they got hard work on one farm.

'Oh, I'm no goin back there nae mair!' And when the man let down the back door he said, 'Right you, here!' Some didn't want to go to this field because they were worked too hard, and they'd tellt each other. And I've seen the driver standing at the door and the farmer standing in the field, and nobody would come out! They all wanted to go to the farm where they got it easy. And the farmer would go round welting the bloody float with a stick trying to get them to come out. But he finally got some of them coaxed. Some would go just to keep the peace. Maybe they went there that day, and they got it easy; and maybe the next farm they went to they worked harder! Then they went back to that first one the next day again! It was a real pantomime.

But anyway, a lot of horses were there. Dealing and swapping every night. Never a night passed but somebody was out, men standing, and you'd see them nodding and cracking to each other. Two of them [SLAP] hitting hands, 'Well, that's hit then.' That's another deal, another swap. I'll tell you, you could have had a horse there, had it four or five times, swapped it away and got it back, swapped it away and got it back. And the same with dogs. And the same with tents. And motors too! They were out in the road pushing these old cars. Some of them had no self-starters, but a starting handle on them. And then there were travellers playing pipes and playing the accordions. And the patrol car was there every night from Crieff. But the funny thing was, with such a crowd and so many folk being there, Saturday night was different from the nights nowadays. You couldn't put a crowd of folk like that together now and have the same peace. Maybe an odd one was away to the pub having a wee drink. He came back and there wasn't a word; if he did the same thing now there'd be fights and arguments and the police would never be away from the place. The folk's better off now and they've got everything they want. But in these days you had maybe twenty-thirty families in the one camping site. There never was trouble. The police came for a wee look around and that was all. Playing pipes and accordions and playing quoits and swapping and dealing – the police didn't have any trouble with them.

I stuck it for four or five weeks. And I was no better off. Day out and day in we weren't making very much. You maybe saved a couple of pound or that, but it just went away as quick as you got it. So I said to myself, 'I'm gaunna have a horse before I leave here. Ane a wee bit bigger than mine for carryin my scrap.'

So I got word, one of the men gave me a tip-off, 'The're an auld man and his wife ower at the wee toon o Madderty, and he's looking for a wee horse for the wintertime for him and his old woman. The ane he's got's too big for him to keep.'

I said, 'I'll take a drive over and see him on Sunday.' And now my pony's been running in the field among clover to its knees and it was really fat, good condition! I cleaned my harness, yoked my wee float. Oh, it was a real tidy yoke. I jumped up on the float and drove over to Madderty, about six miles from where we were staying. I knew the place where the old man stayed because I had worked on the same farm with an old woman, Katie Johnstone, years before when I was single. My pony wasn't too fast, but it was a nice wee trotter. I was no time in going over. So there were two families, a man Johnstone and this other man, MacArthur. I drove into the camping site just as if I were in for a crack, as travellers usually did on a Sunday.

The man Johnstone came out and said, 'Oh aye, ye comin in fir a crack?' He had a big gelly up.

'Aye.' I tied the pony to the fence. This man had four or five sons and he always kept a good horse. But this man MacArthur next to him was the man I had come to swap with. So after we'd had a cup of tea, we sat and cracked for a while. I asked Davie Johnstone, 'I heard that auld Davie was lookin for a wee pony for the winter . . .

He says, 'That's a nice wee pony you've got.'

'Aye, but it's too wee for me. I could dae wi something bigger.'

'There's your man across there, auld Davie. He's got a pony, a bloody guid pony. It's big, a lot bigger 'an that. It's a white horse, a good thick-set horse for your job.' He meant it was heavy in the bone. And I went over. When I came out the wee man was standing at the cart.

'That's a nice wee pony, laddie,' he said, 'ye have there.'

'Aye.'

And he says, 'I'm lookin for a wee pony for the wintertime.'

'So they were tellin me. And I'm lookin for a bigger ane.'

'Well, come ower and see my horse. Maybe me and you could hae a bit deal?'

'Oh well,' I said, 'the best we could! I'm sure it will stand a look, it disnae matter what like it is.'

'Oh, it's no a bad horse. But it's no a youngster like masel! Past its best – but it's a good horse.'

'Ah, as long as it's got four legs and a tail and can walk, and it's strong, it'll dae me.'

'Well,' he said, 'that's all right if that's the way ye see it.' So he took me over to the field at the back of his tent and here was this pony, a white horse about fourteen two. Thick set horse. I looked at him. He was white but he had wee brown spots on his skin, brown dapple through his coat.

And I said, 'Davie, it's a nice pony you've got.'

'Ah, it's no nae youngster.' But I knew it wasn't as old as he was letting on. Because all these white horses, when they get up a certain age, after ten–twelve year old they go completely white. He still had some of the brown spots through his coat. I took him to be at least ten year old, a good age for a horse. Some horses live till they're twenty–twenty-one. Good strong bit o horse. And I was really interested. So just to kid on and show him that I knew what I was doing, I opened his mouth and had a look at his teeth. Just for show! But I was really interested in the horse. I lifted his feet. He was well shod, beautiful hooves on him. His feet were fine and strong. I pulled him up and forward on the rope.

I said, 'Aye, he's okay.'

He said, 'Come and see my harness.' I looked at his harness. Now when you're swapping horses, it was no sense o me giving a man a wee horse and him keeping his big cart and harness. 'No,' he said, 'the best thing me and you can dae is, we'll have a complete swap o yokes, if mine suits ye. Because yir wee yoke would definitely suit me and the auld wife for the winter. It's fine for tae feed and the harness is fine. It's just the ideal thing.'

'Man,' I said, 'it's no fast. It can go, but it's no fast.'

He said, 'It'll suit me if mine'll suit you.'

'Well, come on, let me see your harness, let me see your float!'

'Well, the worse thing aboot it is the float.'

'Ach well, it'll no matter!'

'Oh dinnae think I'm sayin onything against it – it's a good float. But laddie, it's no like yir wee float. It hasnae got rubber wheels. It's got iron wheels.' Some people didn't like the iron tyres because they began to get too old-fashioned. But they were good because you could never get a puncture with them. On soft ground they sunk, cut in. But on the farm roads where I used to go hawking scrap and that, maybe away miles up a farm, with rubber tyres you could get a puncture. The horse then had to pull a flat wheel. For the old man and woman knocking about the towns and that, they could go to a garage and get a puncture sorted.

'Oh,' I said, 'old man, that disnae bother me. I'm no worried about that – in fact, I like the iron wheels.' They were good and strong.

He said, 'Some folk likes the iron wheels. But I like the rubber tyres. It's no so noisy on the road. The iron rungs is awfae noisy.' Because the roads weren't as good as they are now with a lot of gravel and chips on them.

'Well,' I said, 'me and you can hae a swap!'

He said, 'What's the deal goin to be?'

'You've seen mine and I've seen yours. Look, you've got a big horse and I need it.'

He said, 'That's right.'

'And I've got a wee horse and you need it. What do we say, one for the other? A level swap through!'

'By God,' he said, 'laddie, you're game!' And he spit in his hand. 'Haud yir hand! I hope me and you'll deal again.' Well, I never did deal with that man again. And we clapped hands and we had a deal. 'Come on then,' he says, 'and get some mair tea before ye gae hame.' So he took me in and gave me a good cup. He came out and gave me a hand to yoke this pony. And I yoked it up. 'Billy' he called it. And his float was a good one. Big, oh, plenty of room and a high back door on it, and it had beautiful shafts. The man's harness was fair. So, he was pleased with his wee yoke. And I jumped up.

'Oh,' I said, 'this is the thing for me!' And this horse was as quiet as a sheep. And it was a gelding. Some people didn't like a white horse. They said a white horse was only worth white money, ye know, among travellers. But to me he was worth a lot of money. Well, I had that horse for three years after that. So I said, 'Billy, you're a good old horse.' But he wasn't fast. Not a fast trotter, but he was a good walker. And if you get a good walking horse, it'll go further than any trotting horse. A good walking horse was better to you, in those days. So I took my horse home to Muthill.

And everybody came down to have a look, a strange face in the camping site; and 'Oh aye, you got old Davie's horse.' Some folk had their own opinion. 'Oh, that's a good horse, laddie. I'll tell you one thing, that's a guid beast that. That old man gied a few pound for that horse. You haen a deal wi him?'

I said, 'Aye.' So I took it home and tied it up to my camp.

Jeannie said, 'That's a good old horse that.' They knew a horse! You couldn't fool a traveller – they just had to look. If they saw it on the road, if they saw it walking, they knew. The wife's mother could hear a horse at night on the road and tell you if it was a good sound horse or not by the way it walked. And not only her, but other travellers as well. They could distinguish the difference between horses just hearing their feet on the road at night-time. I've seen me camped in a camping place with my cousin John, having our two horses tied. And we heard a horse's feet on the road. Sometimes they got loose. And Jeannie said, 'Laddie, that's yir horse 'at's in the road.'

I said, 'Mebbe not.'

She says, 'No, it's no John's horse, it's yirs.' And I would go out and sure enough it was mine. They knew the certain noise of the horse's feet with the certain size. A light horse would have gone 'pitter-patter' on the road. It was the rhythm. Travellers knew every single noise at night-time. If it was only the cracking of a stick, they could tell you if it was an animal that cracked it. If somebody was walking through a wood, they could tell you if it was a beast that tramped on a stick and broke it or a human being.

But anyway, I was quite happy with this old horse. I said to Jeannie, 'I'm goin away back to Fife.' And I tellt John and his mother. We were there about five weeks but we'd managed to save six pound for the last week. 'We'll shift on Sunday. We're no so bad noo, we've got two-three shillings that'll keep us on the road.'

We landed back in Fife and I went away down to Anstruther. We were doing fine there and we used to go every weekend to the store, sell our stuff. We weren't getting much, maybe eight or nine, ten or twelve pound a week working, to keep yourself living. Get a wee sell-up, sell old non-ferrous metals and rags and woollens and that. You saved up for a week and you took it into the big stores and sellt whatever you had, a couple of old car batteries and things. You worked hard all week till Saturday morning. Well, the wife kept herself and kept the messages going by hawking flowers and baskets. We made an odd basket at night-time. And she collected old clothes and sellt them round the poor houses, folk who couldn't afford to buy new ones. She only had Edith and she could put her in the pram and go away hawking all day. Well, I could yoke my pony and I could go away hawking all day. What I got I fetched home with me. She went to the wee village and I went out to the country. I dropped her off and picked her up at night with the pony. She only had the one bairn with her, so the two of us could get out.

I would say, 'Well, I'll pick you up about two or three o'clock in the village.'

Well, she would hawk that village all day. She would give maybe a dozen flowers away to some woman for a bag of clothes.

She would pick the good stuff out, what was wearable again
and she'd keep them in a bundle. Then she went to some poor
woman, a woman with a big family maybe who would buy some
second-hand clothes for her weans. She would sell them for
seven or eight shillings or so. That was plenty for us! Because
food was very cheap. And with her two-three shillings she would
keep the messages coming, keep us alive. And I would always
get tatties on the farms and I could get turnips when I was out
hawking. And I did my share too round the houses. I always
collected. If I came to a house the woman would say, 'Well, I
have naething tae gie ye. But there a bag o clothes here if ye
want tae take them.'

'Aye, I'll take them. I'd be quite happy. And I'll gie ye a couple
o shillings for them.' And I would take them home. Jeannie
would pick the good stuff she wanted out of it, and then I would
get the rest as a sell-up of rags for the weekend. But we worked
away that way.

SIR PATRICK SPENS

O the king he sits in Dunfermline toon
He's a-drinkin the blood-red wine,
He said, 'Whaur shall I find a skeely skipper
For to sail this fine ship o mine?'

Then up and spakes an auld eldry knight
Wha sits by the king's right knee,
He said, 'Sir Patrick Spens is the finest sailor
That ever did sail the sea!'

So the king he takes his quill in hand
And in a letter he did say . . .
'You maun tak this to Sir Patrick Spens,
You maun tak it right away!'

O the first words that Sir Patrick read
O a loud laugh laughed he,
And the next words Sir Patrick read
O a tear it blindit his ee.

He said, 'Wha has gone and done this thing
And tellt the king on me?
That I maun sail through storm and gale
That I maun gang to Norway?

But I'll sail my king, I will go my lord,
I'll sail right through the fame,
For I'll make my way to Norway
And I'll bring young Margaret hame.'

So they sailed away from Burntisland toon,
They sailed right through the fame
For they were bound for Norway
Just to bring young Margaret hame.

Well they hadna been in Norway
O a week nor scarcely three
When the highest lords in the king's court
Did turn around and did say:

'O those Scottish men they drink our wines
And they spend our gold
And they have come to Norway
And they've brought nane of their own!'

'O you leears aloud,' cried Sir Patrick Spens,
'You leears aloud!' cried he,
'The're twenty thousand of gold and silver
And a dowry I've brought with me.

But I'll sail this night, this very night
I'll sail right through the fame,
I'll make my way to Scotland
And I'll bring young Margaret hame.'

So they sailed away from Norway
They sailed right through the fame
For they were bound for Dunfermline toon
Just to bring young Margaret hame.

But in the Firth of Forth they ran into a storm
And the waves around them they did sweep,
Now Sir Patrick Spens and his gallant crew
Lie sleepin in the deep.

                                        Traditional

CHAPTER TWELVE

DO YOU BELIEVE IN EVIL?

You see, life in these days was very hard for the travelling people, and they could not depend on anybody. The only friend they really had was the horse. This was the only means of survival for them, and they could trust it to carry their burden, make their living and do anything they wanted. It was the only thing they could really trust. Travelling life was situated around the horse. Even when it came night-time, when their day's work was done and their chores were finished, when they gathered round the campfire, the subject was the pony, the horse. They didn't only deal among it, they told stories about it. Everything that meant really much to them was the horse.

It took me a long time to get settled into the horsie business. You didn't get the knowledge of horses easily. I mean, I wasn't even accepted with these travelling people: when you came from another part of the country, from people who never had horses in their lives, such as my family; and you came among people who were born and reared with horses, you weren't really accepted as a person who could understand the horsie trade! So I had to gather my own knowledge and make my own way so that my word might be taken – when I said something that really meant I knew what I was talking about. It may sound queer to you. But it took me nine years before I really could be accepted among these folk as a 'horsieman', after I'd had many deals, many swaps, many's a bad deal and many's a good deal. I bought my first horse at the age of twenty-one, and I would be thirty by the time I was really accepted. You had to gain your understanding of the people by having deals and swaps through the years with the travellers. It wasn't the horse. But it was the talk – so that I could sit around the campfire and listen and be able to communicate with the persons and explain the troubles that a horse took, explain the diseases and the cures. And when it came to buying a young horse or breaking it in, my opinion was accepted. Because they knew from past experience that I knew what I was talking about.

A horse maybe looked beautiful. One man would say, 'That's a beautiful animal.' I would say, 'Okay, it's a beautiful animal but he's standing a wee bit bent in the front,' meaning he's a wee bit tight in the skin. His skin's tight on his body, meaning he might have had a touch of hidebone. These small things you said were accepted and passed through the other travellers when they talked. They would say, 'Aw, that's a nice horse that Duncan's got right the now. Well, that laddie knows what he's talking about. He knows. He's no fool.' This didn't happen in months or years. It took a long time. And then they'd say, 'Oh, he's a good man to have a deal wi. He kens what he's talking aboot.' One man would say, 'I tried to deal him, but I couldnae dae nothing wi him.' The other one would say, 'Well, by God, I'll tell you one thing, he's the gamest ever I met!' These are the small things that meant the world among travelling people. These were things said when you weren't there, but were told to you later by people who'd heard them.

And then it came to the time – the stories round the fire. And if you could tell a good tale, even something that you heard told to you by somebody else, and capture the audience; then this was accepted that you knew what you were talking about. You see, the main thing that travellers were really interested in was your own experience. And they could pick up a lot from that. Somebody might tell stories that were a bit far-fetched, you know, unbelievable. But if it was entertaining, it was accepted. Not that they actually believed in it, but it was entertainment. So even suppose the story wasn't yours; they thought if you believed it, and they had a good word for you and *you* accepted it, then . . . If he believes it, well, there must be something in it! This is the way the travellers worked.

I heard a story, and it was told to me by an old man. I came to Blairgowrie in 1948 and we all gathered round the campfire. And stories passed down, stories about this and stories about that, stories about ghosts and about good deals and bad deals among the horse trade, stories about bad horses and good horses, stories about fast horses and slow horses, about lazy horses and stories about kicking horses and biting horses, you know what I mean! And then stories were told about, eh, the belief that horses could see evil and about ghost horses that were fed by unknown spirits right through the evening.

And this old man I remember, called Angus Stewart, he said, 'Well, people, you're probably no gaun to believe what I'm gaun to tell ye, but this is the truth. Now I'm no askin you to believe it, or if you were tellin me the story I wouldnae believe it, but I'm tellin you the truth. And it's up to yirsel if you believe it or not. I was in Inverness, me and my old woman, and I had a good yoke.' What he meant by a good yoke was a good pony, a good set of harness and a good cart. And he said, 'I went on the drink and I drank weeks out and weeks in. I swapped and dealed and swapped and dealed for the sake of gettin a few pound for money for drink.' Which travellers do when they go on the rampart,* they just go the whole way. 'But,' he says, 'one thing I would never do is leave myself without something for tae shift my camp and my old woman,† because I would never ask her to walk. But after about three weeks on the drink I finally realised I'd had enough, and I ended up with a Shetland pony, a wee set o harness and a wee float, and no money.'

Now this was the most interesting story you ever heard! And around the campfire you could have heard a pin drop. Now there were men there who had good yokes and men who had good horses.

'So,' he said, 'we didna have no money or nothing. So I told her, "The best thing we can do is clear out away fae aboot wir relations, or we're gaunna end up wi nothing." So the next morning we packed up and we left the lot of them.' That was the Stewarts from Inverness. Now when these people get together, it's just a whole session that goes on for months on end, a drinking spree. And then it comes to a stop and they split up, they disappear. They all go their own ways for months at an end and never touch one single drink! They collect money and swap horses, deal and sell and they beg and do everything on their own way, and they accumulate a good few pounds. Maybe after six months they'll say, 'Well, it's a while since we've seen wir relations. We'll drive back to Inverness.' And there's a camp

* on the rampart – rampant
† old woman – dear wife

called The Longman which is a strip, a wood at Inverness, where they all gathered before the wool fair. I don't know if it still goes on at the present moment, but the wool fair did in that time; and there they all met, swapped and dealed and drank and they carried on. Now this is where old Angie had been among these folk. It was all his own relations, cousins, brothers, sisters, friends of all description. And naturally when you meet your own crowd you've got to either join them or be an outsider. So, as the old man was telling the story.

He said, 'After, oh, I'd been on the drink for about three weeks, I finally felt it comin to an end. Me and my old wife, after I'd swapped and dealed . . .' He'd had good horses he'd swapped away. He'd got money about in the deals and drank it till he was left with a wee Shetland pony about twelve hands and a wee float that was just fit for a bairn! But good enough for him to carry his camp and hurl his old wife if she got tired. So he said, 'I finally had enough.' And we're all interested in this, you see. He said, 'I could take no more. So I told my old woman, "It's about time we're gaunna split up fae the family because they're going to put us to ruination if we don't." So next morning before anybody was up we packed wir wee tent on wir wee cart and we took to the road. Now I've been down through Perthshire and Angus many times before and it being the summertime I told the old woman, "We'll go to the berries in Blairgowrie. We'll make wir way there." No that I could pick berries very much, but we always could make the price o tobacco or a smoke or a cup of tea for wirsels. And maybe I could have a wee bit deal and get a bigger horse.' They didn't have any family, never had any in their life. So he said, 'By the time we left it was late in the day. We travelled doon Loch Ness. We came to Fort Augustus. And the old wife had begged along the road and tried her best to push the fork and get as much that would make a wee bit supper for us. She finally got as much that would do us down the loch, which was – I think it's twenty-four or twenty-six, I'm not sure, down Loch Ness.' But it was enough food for the old couple to keep them going, because there were no shops or anything down that way.

So he said, 'We came to Fort Augustus and we passed by, and then there's a wee campin place at the shoreside. There was only a wee bit o grass, no very big, and a place for my wee tent.' Now these people could make a bow tent, sister, past the common! I'll tell you one thing, there never was any rain or sleet or snow would ever come inside a tent made by the Hieland Stewarts. They were masters o making a tent or a gelly. Even to this day if they want to do it. Not the young generation, but the old – they were masters at the art of building a tent. Never would they get flooded with water, in no way in this world, and they carried the canvas and their sticks with them! They never cut any sticks, but carried the boughs for years. But as I was telling you, being their two selves they didn't need much of a tent, just a wee bow tent and this wee Shetland yoke. He put up his tent and went for some sticks, kindled his fire and tethered the wee pony as close to the tent as he could, in case anything should happen to it during the night. There was no place else he could tether it, but close to the tent, because there was only a wee piece of grass, enough that would do it for a night. And he said, 'We had a cup o tea. We sat and cracked and talked and said, "It's a lang way tae Blairgowrie."' But they were making their way there and they were in no hurry. You know, just an old elderly couple. This man would be at that time in his fifties. His woman would be about the same age. And he knew there were more relations to him there in Blairgowrie.

And he said, 'This story I have never told a single soul. Men, you're listening to something that I've never told to a single person in my life. And I'm no askin you to believe it. If you were tellin me the story, prob'ly I wouldna believe it. But I swear on my mother's grave that this is the God's honest truth.' Now sister, that man is dead and gone in these past years, and if it's a lie from me it's a lie from him, right? He said, 'After we had wir late cup o tea we went to bed. And you know in a bow tent there's little room. We jist made a small bed as if you were laying down a single mattress.' The small bed wasn't much bigger than a sleeping bag, ken, in one of these small bow tents. And the old wife always put her basket with her messages in the back of the tent, and whatever she needed, clothes for him and her and things at the back of the tent. And the old man tethered his wee pony right at the front of his camp. And he went to bed. He smoked a pipe, you see. So in a bow tent they always kept a flap in the door in the front. And the old man, for the sake of the smoke for his old woman, flung the half of the flap up, see, and it was the summertime. But by the time they went to bed it was late, maybe twelve o'clock. He flung the flap up and he had a smoke. Now the old travellers had a terrible habit, you know. They wore these peaked bonnets, peaked scoop bonnets as we call them. And when they went to bed they took off the peaked cap and left it in front of them, put the tobacco and the matches in the cap so's it would be easy to get.

So he said, 'I lay smokin my pipe for a wee while and the auld wife she was asleep at the back. And I took my pipe and I put it in my bonnet, and the matches and the tobacco.' If he felt the bonnet during the night, if he needed a smoke he knew where it was. 'But,' he said, 'whatever happened, I must have dovered off to sleep.' But he forgot to pull down the flap on the door. It was half up. So he said, 'I must hae fell asleep at least for a couple hours, and it must hae been about between two and three in the morning. And it was a beautiful night. Cle-e-a-r as could be! In the dusk.' They were making their way for the berries so it must have been about the month of June. In July the berries started. And it never really got very dark. 'But,' he says, 'something wakened me – it must hae been the wee pony. It started tae carry on, and blowin and "whooh".' You know when a horse gets feart at night it blows! So he said, 'This must hae been what wakened me up, the wee pony blowin through its nostrils. Now it was only about twenty-five yards to the shore o Loch Ness and there were a break in the trees where the pony was tethered. And naturally, when a pony has etten its grass it'll lie down to sleep, lie down in front of the tent.'

And we're all sitting round the campfire, putting on sticks. This was in Blairgowrie, the same place as he was making to, right in the middle of the berry centre! And everybody else in their tents were all asleep and there must have been about fifteen of us sitting round the fire, and every man there was a horsieman. We all had horses. And the old man wasn't telling us anything out of the way. And he still had his Shetland pony that he'd come all the way with, and it was a beautiful wee pony.

He said, 'You believe it or not, men, I got up. And I pulled on my trousers, and in my bare feet I went oot the door o the tent. And it was kind o dusky clear.' And he said, 'There's my wee Shetland pony and it's standin and it's lookin out into the water – Loch Ness! And the loch moon was shinin in the water cle-e-a-r as could be. And the loch was as c-a-al-m as you could ask for. And I went up to the pony and I petted the pony. And I said, "What's a-dae wi ye, pet, what's a-dae wi ye?" And I petted it and I put my arm roon its neck. And the pony says, "ogcch-cch-cch-cch," blowin like that. I says, "What's wrong? Settle doon! What's wrong wi ye?" And the pony, its ears was pricked forward like that – and it's looking out intae the water. Now I never in my life ever gev a thought tae any o these stories or tales. I heard people speakin aboot things, there were animals in the water that would scare ye and frighten ye. But it didnae mean nothing tae me. And I was born and reared in Inverness-shire. But anyway, I put my arm aroond the pony's neck, which wasnae very big.' Now a horse is the only animal that can work its ears in any direction it wants. It's the only animal that's gifted with that ability. Cattle can't do it, cows can't do it, neither can a bull or a donkey. So, when you see a pony that pricks its ears up and puts them straight forward and its nostrils turns out, then it's really tension there – it's really afraid. And this is the way the pony was. He said, 'I could see the red in its nostrils, its two ears was pricked straight forward and it was lookin straight out into the water. Me in my bare feet had made little noise. And I stood wi the arm roon the wee pony's neck and I looked out in the water. And the first thing I seen was this head comin up oot the water. A big, long head and a long neck like a goose and a long forehead. And I thought it was like a giraffe. But it was black. And it looked this way and it looked that way, and then there was a splash! There were a hump on its back and it cam up and it went down. It put me on mind o one o these things I'd seen away doon on Loch Fyneside travellin through Argyllshire, like a porpoise! And when it went down again there was another bend in its back, and it went down again a second time as if it had two humps on its back. It stared me in the face for about two minutes! It had a neck and a head like a giraffe and two humps on its back and it disappeared. It broke the waves and it disappeared in the water! And the funny thing was, it swam under the water and I could see the circles in the water as it went out. It only swam about inches under the water and it was still breakin the foam . . . till it disappeared in the distance. That was my experience of the Loch Ness monster. And you know, men, I never told a single soul about this because they thought maybe I was asleep and dreamin. But I swear I'm tellin youse the God's honest truth.'

Now that old man, sister, his old wife died many years later, and he fell down a stair and broke his neck. And I swear that I'm telling you the God's honest truth. And I believed him. And so did everybody there, really believed him.

So, I landed in Aberdeenshire a while before that. And I met in with this old man called Hector Kelby and I was telling him two-three stories of evil, you know. And how a horse could see evil.

'Well, I believe,' he said, 'that animals can pick up evil faster than anybody else. 'Specially horses. Because it's been proven to me.'

Now this old man was a great friend of mine. And I said, 'Eh, how do you think an animal can see evil better than any o us?'

'Well,' he says, 'they've got a better sight and they've got a better hearin. And if evil exists about the place, it's the first animal that can pick it up is a horse.'

I said, 'How do you think that?'

'Well,' he says, 'listen to me, laddie. I'm gaunnae tell ye the truth. I'm goin tae tell ye a wee story what happened tae me. And I swear on my dear mother's grave this is the God's honest truth.' And when people told you that, sister, you'd better believe it, because they weren't telling you any lie.

He said, 'I was only seventeen years of age and I ran away wi my wife in Aberdeen. And my father, God rest his soul, had an auld white horse, an all-white pony.' Now travellers hated white horses every way in the world, you know. I don't know the reason why. You could get a white horse cheaper and better, even suppose it was good. I've had eight of them in my time, white horses. They had no disregard to the animal. The animal was just as good as any horse, but it was a stigma attached to the colour. Was it the fright of the travellers – that they believed a white horse attracted evil more than any other kind o horse?

For there's a legend saying that the devil could appear in the form of a black horse or a black dog, or in the form of a black stallion. But the only tales I could tell you in my experience of travelling among the traveller people for many years, I found more in common attached to the white horse. And I don't know the reason, but they had a belief in their own minds that white attracted white. You see, ghosts were meant to walk at night-time after twelve o'clock in their shrouds, you know what I mean, from the graveyard. Now you can take it with a pinch of salt, but you can believe it or disbelieve it. It's like a moth being fascinated by light, do you understand what I mean? A white horse at night would attract attention. If burkers were passing by on the road, and they saw the white horse, they knew that somebody was there – it's like waving a white flag. And they believed that if spirits were walking about in their shrouds at night-time, and they saw something white, they got curious. And they would come and investigate, you understand what I mean? And you could be feeding your horse when this white thing comes up and scares the life out of you. But a black horse on a black, dark night couldn't be seen so much, or a brown horse. But they had this belief, and you couldn't change it to them. And there's many's a traveller wouldn't even swap for a white horse. So to get my story squared up.

He says, 'My father had an old white horse and to tell you the God's honest truth, laddie, I wasnae very fond o taking the auld white horse. Me and her were only young things. I went to my father and I asked him, "Father, would you lend me your old horse for a week to go up in the glen?"' You see, that's what the travellers did. When a young couple got married, maybe the son or the second oldest son or the third son, if they had no money and didn't have anything, they came to their father and asked for a wee shot of his pony and cart for a week. They would never swap it away. But they could gather scrap with it, collect rabbit skins or sell baskets with it. They could travel for weeks with it and camp around the district, maybe be gone for a month, and they saved every penny. They came back and gave their father back his old horse, and they took good care of it while they had it, seen that its feet were all right and fed it well, gave it plenty to drink, brushed it and looked better after it even though it wasn't their own, but because it was their father's, see! And I've known travellers, sister, to have horses in the family for ten to fifteen years, one horse. And that horse was never parted with. The woman could take it, it was tender, quiet, good. I knew a man who had five sons, now this is the truth. And everyone of these sons had borrowed this old horse and got his start, got his beginning by getting a loan of it for a week!

So he said, 'Me and Lizzie borrowed wir father's horse. And I got her a basket of clothes pegs and two-three bits o swag for masel, like laces and pins.' Because the both of them hawked, you see. They didn't depend on each other. If she didn't make a shilling or two, he could do it. And the main thing then was rabbit skins because they were light. A hundred rabbit skins is only two or three pounds. And there was a great demand for them in Aberdeenshire at that time. In Aberdeen these furriers needed rabbit skins.

So he says, 'The father lent us the old pony and we just took a bit o canvas to make a tent.' And what they did at night-time, being in the summertime, they just put the shafts of the cart up and pulled the bit of canvas over the shafts, covered the whole cart and made their bed under the cart between the wheels – enough for a young couple – which I've done myself many times. So their destination was up Glen Muick. And it's a long, long glen, a weary, weary glen, you know! So, they'd been up Glen Muick for three days and they were getting on fine, oh, doing well! She was selling and getting two-three shillings, and he was getting rabbit skins galore! And they were collecting non-ferrous metals, copper and brass and that. It wasn't worth much, but you got it for very little. And they stayed in one part – a bend on the road and an old bridge. Across from that was the ruins of an old chapel or an old mill. So, being there for two or three days with the pony tethered every night, the grass was getting kind of short. But the idea was you always kept the best bit of grass for the last, the day before you shifted. Because the horse had a journey to make home. You never took the horse and tied it straight to your tent the first night. You tried to get the horse to eat all the grass round about the part where you could see it, and keep the last wee piece of clean grass close to the tent for the night before you moved, if you were only on a journey. Different if you were staying for a long time, or a one-night stay. You would put the pony beside you like the old man in Inverness did. But anyway, the pony had eaten all the grass round the place.

And this night Hector said, 'We'll take the pony, we'll shift in the morning.' So they brought the pony in close to the tent – well, it wasn't a tent, only the cover over the shafts of the cart. And they had an outside fire of sticks which they cooked on. And Hector smoked a pipe, even in his younger days. Lizzie, she smoked cigarettes. He said, 'I must hae fell asleep. And the first thing I heard was the horse's feet on the road. So I nudged Lizzie wi my elbow. "Lizzie, I'll have tae rise. The pony's awa doon the road and prob'ly it'll go a long way." ' If a pony got on the road it wouldn't stop, because the glen was fenced off and all the way down were dykes. And it's a hard thing if you waken up in the morning and your pony's gone. You've got to walk miles to collect it. Now a horse keeps going when it gets loose. It'll travel for miles during the night till it gets to an open gate where there's a good field of grass. It'll probably go in. But if there's no gates or anything, it'll keep going on. That's why travellers used to keep a bicycle. If your pony got loose you could jump on the bike, follow it and try and turn it. But Hector didn't have an old bicycle of any kind. He knew he had a long walk if his pony got on the road that night.

So he dug into Lizzie with his elbow again and said, 'Lizzie, the horse is on the road. I'll have tae go and catch it! I hope you'll no be feart till I come back.' 'No,' she says, 'I'll be all right.' So he said, 'I got up. And I pulled on my trousers, and I oot tae the road. The pony was loose, it was away. Now I heard its feet in the distance, and I ran as hard as I could but I couldnae catch it. I couldnae overtake it! So I wis a wee bit feart that Lizzie would be feart by hersel, because it was a waste glen away oot o the district. The nearest hoose was miles away. So my love fir Lizzie overcome the love fir catchin the horse. So I hurried my way back and said, "If I'm gaun after the horse I'm takin her wi me!" So I hurried back tae the wee campin place and I said, "Lizzie, the horse is awa doon the glen. You'll have to come wi me 'cause I'm no leain ye." She got up and put on her claes and I took her by the hand. Me and her follaed doon the road. We heard the horse's feet in the distance and we ran and we ran and we ran and we ran as far as we could go. But we couldnae catch up on the horse. Well, we must hae went for two or three mile.' Now I swear, sister, this old man told me this for the God's honest truth, and he's dead in his grave, for God pleases, and I wouldnae tell the lie aboot him.

'But,' he said, 'we couldnae catch it. So the best thing we could do is turn back. So we turned back and we cam hame tae the wee place where we were stayin. And I was angry, really angry, see! Lizzie says to me, "Hector, we'll never gaunna get awa fae this place in the morning. God knows how far that horse'll go. It'll prob'ly go all the way back tae the main road which is about fifteen mile tae the foot o the glen! And God knows where it'll go tae!" And I was real angry! Noo I had an auld knife in my pocket fir makin baskets, a bit o a table knife. I put my hand in my pocket and I took oot this auld knife. I said, "Lizzie, look, dae ye see that knife? *If I could get that white wanderin spirit the night, the spirit, that wanderin spirit o Glen Muick, I'd pit my knife intae it tonight!*'At's gaunna gie me a lang walk in the morning." And I lookit roond and Lizzie couldnae speak. She – the hands was going. But I said, "What's wrong wi you lassie, what's wrong wi you lassie?" Her hands was goin like that, shakin. And she was dumb, couldnae speak. I said, "What is it? What's wrong wi ye?" And I took her and I pit her sittin doon. She pointed tae me that way, but she couldnae speak she's so terrified. And I lookit roond and there it was comin – the spirit. It was dressed in a white robe from head tae foot and I couldnae see nae face or nothing. And it was floating that way and its feet wasnae touchin the ground and it was comin, comin close and closer and closer. Right tae where I was standin. Well, the fright I got when I seen this thing – I ran in alow the float and I gathered all the blankets and I wrapped 'em roond my heid. And I cuddled Lizzie and buried my face, cuddled her in and buried my face in the blankets. My body was goin like that, shakin. And I shakit fir the fright till God's daylight in the morning, till it was clear. And it was aboot two hoors before Lizzie got her voice back wi the fricht she got.

'She says, "Hector," when she did come tae hersel, "Hector, dae ye no ken, I heard my faither tellin me lang ago that

Glen Muick is haunted. And you said that, you called the spirit oot!"'

'But when God's daylight cam again I was a man again, I wasnae feart nae mair. The birds was whistlin, it was God's daylight, I wasnae feart or nothing. I'm no heedin aboot nae spirits or nothing. But I wis still thinkin aboot the fricht I got, my heart was still beatin with the fricht I got. But in the morning we kindled the fire and made a cup o tea. I said, "Lizzie, come on, we'd better go and look for the old horse. This'll be the last time I'll ever be in Glen Muick as long as I live!" So after we made a wee cup o tea, me and her made wir way down the road and we were expectin to go a long way tae catch the old horse. But we hadnae went two hundred yards and there was the auld horse grazin in the corn inside the farmer's field! It went through a gate in the field. And we took it back.

'She said, "Hector, look, did you see onything last nicht?"

'"Lassie, what do you mean, did I see onything last night?"

'She said, "Do you remember when you said if you had that wanderin spirit o Glen Muick, you'd put your knife in it? Hector, I seen it comin, it was floatin towards ye!"

'"I seen it, lassie! What do you think I buried my head in the cloots for?"

'She said, "Hector, that's the thing my faither used to tell me about. That was the Wanderin Spirit of Glen Muick."

'So we made wir way back doon the glen and I got my father on Old Meldrum Green. And I gied him his auld horse back. And frae that day to this day never again did ever I hae a white horse, or never again did I go back to Glen Muick.'

And the old man's dead in his grave for God pleases, sister, and I swear that's the God's honest truth the old man told me. He called the horse the 'Wanderin Spirit o Glen Muick'. He was angry with the old horse. He didn't know a word about the legend, never knew about the Spirit of Glen Muick, no way in this world. Now people don't believe that there are such things in this world as the supernatural, that really happen to folk. And you never even give it an understanding until it happens to you! And the thing is, when it does happen to you, you don't think you're going to get anybody else to believe it. And when it happens to somebody else, you really think they're only telling a tale. Now I remember my auntie who was my mother-in-law. She told me this wee story.

And she says to me, 'Brother, you've got to be careful about horses.' You know, she was a good horsiewoman! Because she'd had horses all her days, and her man was a great horse dealer. He was known far and wide. He just looked at a horse and he could see through it. This was the father of the cousin who had taught me so much. He was a great horsieman. Big Willie Townsley could make a set o harness from an old wellie boot, a fisherman's wader. And he was unique in horse trade of all description. Everybody knew big Willie for his horse dealing. You know, he was as game a man that ever you met. And she says to me, 'Do you believe in evil?'

'Ah well,' I said, 'Auntie, it all depends what you mean. Everybody gets an experience o evil through time.'

But she says, 'Some things are hard to believe. But I'm goin to tell you a wee story. Your uncle had many experiences. Because I believe that only certain types of people that these things really happen to. When they tell you about it, you think that they're only making up the story, but it could really happen. He went to the market and he bought this horse. It stood all alone and nobody was interested in it. And it was a beautiful horse, a beautiful animal. It was a mare and about fifteen hands high. He was stayin in Madderty just outside o Crieff.' Now the people wouldnae go ahead and tell you the exact way it happened if it didnae happen. 'And,' she said, 'it was in a stall in the market. And he bought it for very little. It was cheap.' Why other people didn't buy it, sister, nobody really knows. And he fetched it back. He didn't have any cart to drive it home. When you bought a horse in the market you didn't get a harness or anything. So It was a long walk to Madderty, about fifteen or sixteen miles. But if you've got a good pony you don't mind walking with it to fetch it home. You couldn't hire a truck in these days. You had no money. You just had to walk it like I've done myself many's the time.

When he came back to his wife, my auntie, God rest her soul, he says to her, 'Ha-ha! I got a guid ane the day. A right guid horse the day. And I got a bargain.' He had his supper, had his tea, whatever he had to eat, maybe little or muckle, nobody knows. But it was in the wintertime, sister, and in the wintertime travellers had to find meat, food for their horse, and it doesn't matter where he got it. Suppose he had to steal it or walk for miles at night to a farmer's shed or take a bite, hay, for his horse. No traveller would go to his bed, he couldnae sleep if he thought his horse was hungry. Because this is what he depended on. His horse was his life.

So he says to my auntie, 'I'll have to go and look for some meat for this horse.' The travellers always kept a bag and they would go to a stack, a farmer's haystack in the field. In these days when the farmers cut hay there were no balers or anything, and they built big haystacks, left them in the field. It was a simple matter o just walking in and pulling the hay out and filling your bag, taking it home to your horse. I've done it hundreds of times. It was stealing, but it wasn't stealing to us. Because we knew we were doing good for the animal. Because the animal couldn't steal for itself, so we had to do it for him. In fact, we were only getting food for the beast which we thought was no sin. And big Willie knew the horse was hungry. And he gathered this hay and took it back, a nice bag of beautiful hay. He tied the horse up beside his tent, filled a nice pail of water, left it beside the horse, and left the beautiful hay beside the horse.

And he's always bragging all night about this horse to his wife, you know, 'Ah, I'm no gaunna swap this one away for a while. I'm gaunna keep him, hang on to this horse. This is a guid horse. And I got it cheap. Noo I dinnae know why people couldnae hae bocht it.' But the next morning he wakened up. The hay was still there. The horse had never touched one single bite, not one single bite! And it was fat. And the water pail was still full.

So he said to his wife, 'Funny, that horse never ate nothing last night.'

Auntie said, 'It's prob'ly strange. It's prob'ly a pet or something, and it's used wi folk feedin it. Prob'ly in a couple of days, in a while, when it gets hungry it will eat.' But he had that horse for three weeks, and that horse never had one single bite. He wouldn't accept one bite from old Willie. Now this is the truth I'm telling you. I'm no making up any stories. And she's gone, would God please her, and this is what she told me. He had that horse for three weeks and he coaxed it every way in the world tae get it to eat. But no. It wouldnae.

So he said to her, 'woman, hoo is that horse livin?' Now it wouldn't even eat grass. Through the day it wouldn't even graze with the wee bits of grass it got. Any horse will eat something when it's hungry. But it wouldn't take a bite, no way. So he says to the woman, 'I doot there evil attached to that animal. *Evil* attached tae it! How it lives I don't know.' But they left Madderty and they shifted to another camping place. And they landed at Cat's Corner before you go to Crieff, before you go to the smiddie. They landed in thon wee corner yonder, and there was no place to tether it out. He tied it close to the tent as he could. So he says to himself, 'There's nae use o gaun for meat to that. It'll no eat nothing.'

Now by this time the old man had got himself a float. And he'd pulled it in close to the tent. With no other place to tie the horse, he'd tied it to the wheel of the cart, close up to it, to give the horse enough room to lie down. And God rest Willie, he smoked a pipe, my uncle, my mother's youngest brother. And he was an awfae man to smoke during the night. If he wakened up through the middle of the night, the first thing he had to do was have a smoke. Now he had two wee boys at the time and they were sleeping at the back of the tent. And my auntie tellt me, 'He got up and he gied me a dunt with his elbow.'

He said, 'Listen, woman! Listen! Listen!'

She says, 'What is it?'

He said, 'Listen to the horse!' The horse was chewing now! Crunch. And if you hear a horse eating at night-time, I don't know if you've ever had the experience, it's the nicest sensation in the world. It crunch, crunch, crunch, crunch, crunch. If you're close to it, sister, and you hear a horse chewing with his back grinders, it's the most lulling sensation in the world. Travellers used to love to listen to it, lying at night-time with your horse beside your tent. It's like somebody singing you a lullaby. But the minute he spoke it stopped. It stopped.

'Well,' he says, 'upon my soul. I never fed it tonight. But I'm gaun oot to see what it's eatin.' And as low as your father, sister, I'm gaun to tell you the God's honest truth. The old woman told me 'He got up, and he went oot. Close to the cairt and he cam back in. [GASP] And he couldn't speak. He was gasping. He couldn't speak to his wife when he came back in.

She says to him, 'What's wrong?' He-he-he lost his voice. It was a wee while before he came to himself.

He said, 'Sh—, sh—'

She says, 'What is it?'

'The mort,' he said. 'The mort.' Meaning, the woman.

'What woman, what's wrong with you, man?' she said. 'You gaun aff yir heid or something?'

'No,' he said. 'When I went oot to the horse she was standin with an oxterfu' o hay and she was haudin handfuls tae it and it was catchin it fae her and eatin it – oot o her hand.' The horse was taking handfuls of hay and chewing them. And the minute they heard the voice, it stopped, like that. The next day he said, 'That's the end!' He took it to Perth the next day and sold it.

Now that was the story from her. Whether this really happened or not, sister, I'm telling you the God's honest truth. And she swears that that's the God's honest truth. The story was among travellers that this horse was a favourite, and this lady fell off. She'd had it for years. She fell off it and broke her neck, and she'd loved it from her heart. The horse wouldn't eat from anybody but her. Her ghost came back and fed it at night. No traveller would buy it. That's why it stood in the sale.

Travellers tied their horse close to their tent at night-time, and a horse then was as good as a dog to you. It was a guard because a horse has got the finest hearing in the world of any animal. A horse can hear things that nobody else can pick up. And this is the truth, you'd better believe it! So the travellers knew from experience the actions the horse went through and they could read these actions. If they heard the horse groan, 'gnorroach', this was the horse flinging itself down to go to sleep. Suppose it was a young horse or an old horse, it groaned when it laid itself down. And if a horse was lying peaceful, all was well. But if the horse got up in a sudden, and gave itself a shake, the horse was disturbed. Now the people in the tent heard this. Now they knew, it was like reading a book. A horse is not feart of small animals like squirrels or rats or wee rabbits passing by. A horse would never pay attention to it, anything like that they wouldn't bother. It has to be something bigger or something evil that would disturb the horse.

So, naturally when the traveller heard the horse getting up fast, he got up. He looked all around and he couldn't see anything. But the horse, it was watching something. The horse pricks its ears forward and it focuses, just like radar, on this thing listening. And it could see! So, naturally the traveller had the belief that all he needed to do was walk up, put his arm around the horse's neck and look between the horse's ears. And if there were anything o evil around, he could see it – like looking through a magnifying glass. This was the belief and they believed it! It meant so much to them, sister, that some of them wouldn't do it. Because they were afraid. Now just imagine a full-grown man afraid to look through the horse's ears at night-time! Now I can tell you this, some people were afraid to look in case they saw what the horse was looking at.

Now I can tell you about this, what happened to me. I left Strathmiglo and I travelled round by Kinross. I had a young pony, a three-year-old, oh, it was a high stepping hackney. So I'd left Cupar the day before, the wife and me and the three bairns, Edith, Jimmie and Willie. We were on our own and we landed out in the Crook o Devon, about four miles the other side of Kinross. We came to the Yetts o Muckhart, and instead of cutting over by Crieff we thought we'd make our way back by Dunfermline, back around through Bowhill and round there. I was collecting non-ferrous metals, but I wasn't selling up every day, just collecting and saving them up for a while. The wife was hawking two-three baskets and flowers. So it was a gate camp I had. And the three bairns weren't very old. So I had this beautiful pony, and he wasn't very broken to the rope, for the tether, because you had to train a horse to keep his legs from getting fankled up. It's very easy to get a horse choked with a rope. So it was late at night when we landed at the Crook of Devon. It was about the first of May. And Jeannie was expecting another baby. I wasn't going to go to Argyll this summer, but I was passing my time round through Fife because she was expecting. We wanted to keep close into the district. The camping place at the Crook of Devon is not a layby, but just a piece of grass at the roadside, a square about a tenth of an acre. And there wasn't much meat for the pony, but there was as much to keep him going. I put up the gate, came and we had our supper, got the kids to sleep. And I pulled the float up beside the door of the tent. I tied the pony to the wheel. We lighted the candle inside the tent and I read a couple of chapters of a story to her. She liked me to read a bit of a book for her.

Then a car pulled in, an old-fashioned Morris shooting brake. And it wasn't as far from here to the buildings there, about a hundred and fifty yards, and there was a gate going into a field. He pulled into the gate. And he was heaped up with carpets and all kinds of stuff in the back of this car. Like a commercial traveller. And he switched on the light inside his car and he's working inside it. An old man, maybe in his forties, grey hair. Oh, the man never bothered us. But he must have been making a bed. He must have seen our tent and thought he was going to stay there for the night. Then he came out and he lighted a cigar. I could smell the smoke coming on the wind.

So Jeannie said to me, 'That's a shan old gadgie* 'at's there.'

But I was young, twenty-five years of age. I wasn't worrying that any old gadgie could do anything to me in these days! I wouldn't care, suppose there were three like him! So Bobby, this pony I had, he was about fourteen hands and built like a hare, you know. Very fast. And I really loved him. I said, 'I'll tie him close to the tent as possible.' If anything happened to him, I would hear every sound. I was a very light sleeper at night-time. Even to this time, I am a very light sleeper. You had to be when you travelled in these places. Because you had to protect your wife and your family. And you never knew; you never know at any moment – I mean you couldn't even take your trousers off at night when you were a traveller because you had to jump to attention at any moment. You couldn't even undress yourself. You were never secure. A naked man getting out of a tent would never have a chance with any intruders.

So the kids were asleep. I was lying at the front of the tent. I always lay at the front of the door. Then the wife lay next, and then the three kids right at the back. Bobby was tethered. I didn't have a dog of any description. Travellers usually always kept a dog, because a dog would bark if it heard a footstep. But I tethered

---

* shan old gadgie – dirty man looking for a woman

Bobby right at the door. And it must have been about twelve o'clock. I heard Bobby going down for the night. He 'ruarrgh, ruach', groaned. And I knew that he was down. I said, 'He's okay, as long as he goes doon.' So I lighted a cigarette and I had a smoke. I always kept a wee part of the door open at the front for the smoke, for the sake of the kids, to let some fresh air in.

But I must have been lying for about an hour. Just kind of dovering off to sleep when I heard Bobby getting up. And he 'bowoopoochk' – now this was a warning to me. So I threw the blanket off. I was just lying fully clothed, my shirt and my trousers on, in my bare feet and my belt even on. I got up, but when I got up I never moved. I just got up on my knees and I keeked through the split in the door. I saw the red cigar coming, the man from the car with the red cigar blazing in his mouth. And he's coming, pit-pat, crawling on his hands and knees, crawling right to the tent!

So I waited and waited and waited, and he came up close. But the horse was standing, you see. And then the horse whirled round, and turned its backside to the door, got its nose on him! Now the horse was direct at the front of the tent. And I think the man was afraid of the horse. I think that's what put him off. He thought maybe I was asleep. So the man came up canny and then the horse started to blow, 'bpwooo-oophp', and its ears got up. Now I'm sitting here, keeking through the hole, the split in the doorway. And he came up as close as he could, till I could smell the cigar smoke. And then when the horse started to blow, he went away back again. Back to the car. And I heard the door of the car shutting.

So Jeannie said, 'What is it?'

I said, 'That old man in the car. He's comin creepin up to the tent.'

She said, 'He must be a shan old man.' The bairns were asleep.

I said, 'Dinnae worry yirsel. Dinnae let it bother ye!' But there was nae rest for her then mair the night. She wouldnae have it no way. 'I wonder what he wants,' she said.

I said, 'I dinnae ken what he wants. But whatever he wants he's no gaunna get it! But that's no miss out for me the night.' I just pulled the blankets over her and I lay on the top, stretched

my feet out and lighted a cigarette. Lying back. Oh, sister, as fit
as a fiddle! And the pony started to pick and graze, picking wee
bits of grass round the door because he was up now. The time
would be about two o'clock in the morning. And the pony was
chewing and chewing the wee bits of grass, you know. Then I
heard him stopping.

And he started to, 'whoochk, hoock, bwoo-oochk'. I opened
the flap. here the man's coming again! So he came as far to
here as the door of the old house there, within twenty yards,
on his hands and knees, crawling, the cigar going. So the horse
started to carry on.

I says, 'This is it!' I flung the door open, gang oot in my bare
feet. And I walked up and I patted Bobby on the neck, said,
'What's wrong wi you, boy? What's wrong? What's bothering
ye? Did something disturb ye?' And he's off like a shot, fweet!
The man's back and he shut the door of the car, banged it. But
he never came near us, never spoke. And the light inside the
car went out.

I said, 'What's bothering you, boy? Is something disturbing
you?' And I petted the horse and then I went back to my bed. I
lay a-top of the covers, and a wee while after that I heard Bobby
going, 'ahnnnnnng', down again in front of the door. And I
must have fell asleep. But when I wakened up it was daylight. I
got up and kindled the fire. And the car was still lying there.
So I wakened the others, made some tea, made some breakfast
to the bairns, got the bairns ready. But we were just packing
up when in come the police with a wee old Ford car. And two
young policemen came in.

One said, 'How long you been here for?'

I said, 'Constable, we just cam last night.' And this was a
regular camping place. Everybody camped here.

'Aye,' he says, 'it's aa right. I'm no botherin you for campin,'
He took my name, wife's name, the three kids.

'Aye.'

He said, 'Where ye makin fir?'

'Well, I just cam up fae Cupar and Milnathort and Kinross.
I'm making my way back, right round through the Crook o
Devon and back by Scotlandwells, and round back into Leslie,
back into Coaltown o Balgonie. We've been here for years.'

'Aye,' he says, 'it's aa right. I'm no worried about that. What age is the kids?' I tellt him. 'No in school?'

'No,' I said, 'well, they go to school. But they're oot for the summertime.'

He said, 'Who's your friend?'

I said, 'He's nae friend o mine. I'll tell ye something, constable, I didnae get much sleep last night wi, as you call, "my friend" here.'

He said, 'What happened?'

Well, I told him, 'Every time I went to bed I couldnae get peace for lyin. He came a-crawling on his hands and knees to the camp smoking cigars.

He said, 'Did he speak to ye?'

'No, he never spoke to me. But he disturbed the horse. I don't know what we would have done if we didna have the horse in front.'

'Aye,' he says. Do you know what the police said to me? This is the truth. He said, 'Sometimes a horse is a good guard. Is it wicked?'

I said, 'No, it's no wicked.' And he went up and put his hand on the horse's neck and he petted it. He said, 'Hello, boy. How are ye?'

I said, 'I'm just moving out, constable.'

He said, 'That's aa right, I'm no shiftin yese. We'll go and have a talk tae him.' And honest to God, sister, the two of them went away doon to this old man in the car. And they talked to him and he came out. He had plus-fours on and buckle shoes. He took out these papers and was handing them to him, letters. And the police were reading them. But we never waited to see what happened. Because I yoked Bobby in the cart, lifted the three kids onto the top of the cart and Jeannie and I walked away on our way to Dollar. But the old man never spoke . . . I wonder what he really wanted.

You see, the horse wasn't only a means of survival to the traveller. The horse was his friend, his watchdog, his means of livelihood. It was everything under the sun to us, as experience had taught me through the years. As I was telling you, when you were sitting round a campfire discussing these trades with the travellers, when they brought up a subject of any description, let it be the simplest subject of all, suppose it was only a horse disease or a horse seeing evil and all these things that were attached to the horse – if you couldn't explain and speak about it to them, they thought you were lacking knowledge and then you weren't classified as being a good horseman. You had to be able to talk on every subject from horse dealing to horse shoeing, horse disease, horses that wouldn't work, horses that would work and all these things. Once you learned all that, then you were accepted as a horseman among the travellers. You were a 'horsieman'.

Now there were some travellers who were the finest travellers in the world and the finest company in the world, and the finest crackers and storytellers who never owned a horse in their life. And the thing was, when these kind o people came to your fireside and had a talk, you never indulged in the subject o horses in case you would embarrass them. It's like the Gaelic-speaking folk not speaking Gaelic when non-speakers are about. Now I've camped with travellers who never owned a horse in their life, and when they came to sit by your fireside and crack, tell tales, you never started speaking horsie talk, knowing that the people didn't have any interest in horses. You could never talk horse to my brother Sandy, no way in this world, even after years, after I got into the horse way and was married. He moved back to Argyll when his family was grown up, but he still never owned a horse. And I'd had maybe nineteen or twenty horses by that time, the mid-1960s. When I moved back to talk to him and camp beside him, I never even brought up the subject o horses.

I've seen fifteen horses in the one camping place. Fifteen traveller men, when the women and kids went to bed, all sitting round the campfire. Now that night in Burntisland, as I was telling you about, when we sat so long, old Johnny Townsley had had a few horses in his time, but he didn't have a horse then. There were seven men with horses there that night. And I'll bet you there wasn't one word mentioned of horses as we sat under that elderberry bush, just because he didn't have one. They had respect for the old man, this was their way. But if he hadn't been there, it would have been all horse talk all through the night.

The Tramp's Dream

In his bed in a bush by the wayside a tramp lay fast asleep.
And as he lay deep in slumber with his coat over his head
O sweet were his dreams of a can of tea and a loaf of lovely
    bread.

And in his dreams he tossed and turned so weak he could
    scarcely stand.
He saw himself in his dreams a very wealthy man.
As he stood and gazed at his orchard where his fruit was
    turning red
His thoughts would often wander to his lovely feather bed.

And then he would look at his coal shed and his pile of pitch
    pine logs
And of that sign he had nailed on the tree that said, 'Beware of
    the Dogs!'
And then as he looked from his window as the night was
    drawing late
He saw the form of an old tramp man come walking to his gate.

His beard was long, his coat was torn, his boots had once been
    black
He carried a curled stick in his hand and a little bag on his back.
And as he walked up those marble steps that led to the great
    front door
Those beautiful steps of marble where no tramp had walked
    before.

And then to the sound of snarling dogs and a cry of fear –
'Get to the road,' the rich man said, 'there's nothing for you
    here!'
'Just a crust of bread,' said the tramp, 'or a bone you have kept
    for the dog,
For I am cold and hungry and wet with the freezing fog.'

'Get to the road and don't come back! I need all I have for
    myself!
Not a crust of bread you'll get, not even a drink from my well.'
Now that tramp in his dream was happy, now that tramp in his
    dream was bold
For in his dream he did not feel the freezing bite of the cold.

Then morning came to that tramp and he awoke with a start,
And what he had done in his dream had chilled him to the
    heart.
Now that tramp as he goes his way and meets other tramps like
    himself
Whatever he's got, he shares the lot, and to them his dream he
    does tell.

Duncan Williamson

Chapter Thirteen

The Secret of Traveller Trade

People, even dealers, had a disrespect for travellers. When they swapped and dealt with a traveller they thought the traveller was going to ill-treat the horse, or it would be driven all day in its cart gathering rags, bags, bottles and bones. There was a stigma attached to the traveller – that when you gave a traveller a horse it was going to be treated poorly, unfed, run down to the earth – and when travellers were really finished with a horse they sent it to the boneyard. The wives of the non-traveller people were worse than the actual dealers.

You take a wee pony belonging to a pigman or a coalman. It was standing in its stable in dung up to its knees and its feet got heated up with the dung. Its hooves got bad. And they probably fed it on wee bits of corn and wee bits of chaff mixed up with sawdust. This horse was in real trouble. And along comes a traveller and he wants to buy this horse. And the wife of the horse's owner said, 'Oh, we don't want to give that horse to the travelling people.' Not giving it to understand that when the travelling people got a horse, it went to a life of luxury.

I myself, from my past experience, and the other horse dealers whom I know of among the travelling people have picked up horses from the non-traveller people who were just about their life's end, their feet burned standing in their own manure; they had never seen a blade of grass, they were poor, had hidebone or maybe some disease that the non-traveller couldn't cure. I, along with many of my dealer friends and horse traders, have bought horses from the non-traveller people that were really only fit for the knackery. And *they* were the people who condemned us, that we were the bad people to the horses, never knowing in their own mind that they were causing the suffering to the animals.

Our attitude, if we saw a horse suffering in a stall, maybe it had founder or its teeth were so long it couldn't eat anything; we would take this horse and do something for it. We would

make his life last for another five or six years. When a traveller
bought a pony of any description, all he wanted to do was show
it off and bring out the best in it. Say, the traveller bought a
pony from a piggery. The first thing he did when he brought
back the pony that was a bit under the weather was inspect his
feet. Then he would inspect his mouth. And the traveller would
know by his coat if he was well fed. They would know what he
was needing and would say, 'Oh, this pony has been fed on hard
food. All he needs is a touch of grass.'

Now to even the smallest child in the tinker's encampment,
maybe only three or four years old, the daddy would say, 'Look,
son, I bought this pony today and it's your job. I want you to
take that pony and lead it along the verge side, give it enough
grass. Feed it on as much green grass as it can get.' And the
boy would enjoy this. Now the man knew that this pony had
never seen a bite of grass for years because there was no way
he could get any. And then after the horse had his fill of grass
the man would say, 'Bring him back and I'll inspect his feet.'
He would look at his feet and say, 'Oh, he's stood a long time in
hot manure in a stable. His feet are overhet. We'll have to get
him in a damp place.' And I've seen a man going to a puddle,
a pool of water and telling his son, 'You'll take that pony and
stand there and hold that pony in that pool of water two hours,'
till his feet got soaked with the water, soaked through and
through. And that traveller boy would stand by that pony's
side for two hours till it got its feet completely soaked. The
pony's feet had never seen a taste of water and that's why his
hooves were so bad.

That was the secret of traveller trade: if the non-traveller
people or non-traveller dealers were selling something, 'Oh,'
they said, 'we'll keep it and we'll sell it to the tinks.' Now the
tinks hadn't got very much money in these days and they had
to buy all the cast-off things that nobody else wanted. And if
a pony was lame they had to make it workable. And a traveller
was ashamed of a lame horse. There's no traveller in the world
would ever take a lame horse to a dealer or to a market. So he
had to make this horse as sound as he could really be. According
to the travellers, if you owned a lame horse and you couldn't do
something about it, then you weren't fit to have a horse. Because

the travellers had their own cures. And they stood by these cures. They stood by their idea that they could do anything for a horse. They would take a horse in *any* condition, and they always had a way that they could make this horse comfortable in his complaint.

Travellers were animal doctors in their own right, and a good doctor is a good man. I've cured my own horses. I've bought horses with grass sickness, horses that were bone-spavined, ring-boned, that had founder, callous pastern, drawn tendons in their fetlocks, and they had all these troubles. Foot rot, cancer in the hoof; but we had to treat them for these troubles, because if we didn't then we could never sell them again.

Now I would buy a horse with hidebone, with a bed of worms in his stomach that nothing could cure. And it doesn't matter how much he ate, his skin was tight on his bones, and you couldn't get him to fatten in any way. In other ways he was healthy, but his skin was sticking to his bones. So we would pull his skin a wee bit back from his ribs, touch it and say, 'Look, this horse is hideboned.' We looked at his teeth. Maybe he was six years old, eight years old. Now there was no reason in the world for that horse to be hideboned at that age. It was a mistake of the people who had previously owned him. Now they had given him to us and said, 'Oh, he's poor; we're jist fed up wi him.' So we have to cure him.

We went and gave him a dose of broom. We cut the tops off the broom, boiled it till the bark disappeared and there was nothing left but the centres, the tenions inside the broom. We boiled it till it came into a thick mixture. Then we added some oatmeal to make it tasty for the horse. And if he wouldn't drink it, well, we had to make him. So we cowped him and bottled him. This idea about bottling a pony is a thing that the country hantle had never known about. We took a lemonade bottle and filled it full of this boiled mixture of broom and oatmeal. This was a secret among the travellers. The broom was boiled till the twigs were completely clean, and the mixture was black like tar. The bottle was filled with the mixture and some oatmeal shaked into it. The oatmeal didn't do any good, but made it palatable for the horse. Then we put it in a pail and added a couple of spoonfuls of treacle, in case the horse would take it straight from the pail. But if he put his nose over it and he, 'hunnnng', blowed his nose and didn't want it, we said, 'You're gettin it!'

We put a rope round his front feet. Never mind his back feet! We tied his front feet close together. And then we put our shoulder to his and gave him a shove. Now he tried to separate his front feet, but couldn't, so naturally down he went on his front end. So we sat on his head and we got one of our legs over the back of his neck, pulled up his ears between our legs and laid him on his back. Now he's lying on his back, and I'm sitting on the side of his neck. The idea behind this is that any other animal, a deer or a cow, for example, rises end first. But a horse rises front end first. So if you've got his front end conquered, then there's no way in the world he can do anything. He can kick his hind legs, but he's not going to do any harm.

So we would get a leg round the back of his ears and pull up his head right to our belly, and put our hand at the back of his neck. And then with this bottle full of boiled broom and oatmeal, we'd pull out his tongue through the side of his mouth and shove the bottle down the back of his tongue, empty it. He would drink that! We gave him maybe three bottles of this material. Then we would loosen his legs and let him up. I've done it many times because I had to!

It was like you wanting to sell something and you are going to paint it up. This was all I had. You had to make it good, take care of it and make it bonnie.

Now we came across some beautiful animals who were suffering from neglect of the previous owner, neglect from the people who had said we travellers destroyed animals, neglect by the non-traveller people who were 'supposed to know it all': the pigmen, the farmers, the horse dealers. And we could only buy them when they were finally finished with them. And they ended up with the traveller and the traveller doctored them. The traveller led the horse along the roadside, fed him on the tiniest grass and only walked him every day on his cart. Pulling the cart was good exercise for the horse. And that horse grew! And he cast his coat, he got fat, and two months after that the owner would never even recognise the same animal. And we were the persons who weren't fit to take care of a horse, the tinkers who couldn't look after an animal, who cowped the pony and bottled it.

I've seen me buying a horse that was loaded with lice, lice boiling off it. At that time I was only young and had no understanding. After I'd bought this horse and led it along the roadside, my jacket was crawling with lice. I was only newly married and had to gain the experience. But I thought these lice were going to attack me because my jacket was plastered with lice, in the thousands. I threw my jacket away and led the horse in my bare arms.

My mother-in-law said, 'Laddie, what did ye dae with yir jacket?'

I said, 'Granny, I threw it away.'

She said, 'What for?'

I said, 'It was lice. That horse I got is loaded.'

She said, 'Their lice'll no do ye any harm. They couldnae live on you.'

I said, 'Granny, what am I gaunnae dae?'

She said, 'I'll get ye something fir yir lice. I'll go and buy ye some pooder. You take the horse and make a strip doon the horse's back, right doon from the horse's tail. Shake it along the horse's back in just one single line. It doesn't matter what he does, he cannae shake it off. During the night these lice will try and cross, cross this line o powder. And they'll never get across. And I'll bet ye within two days there'll not be a lice left on yir horse.' And that's what the horse lice did: they crossed from side to side and all got caught in the centre. This was a beautiful white pony I'd swapped for in Kilmarnock. And the wife wasn't very happy about it because it was poor, very poor.

But I had looked at its teeth and saw that it was only about seven years old. And I'd said, 'There's no way in the world that a seven-year-old horse should be as poor as this.' I knew there was something wrong, something that could be cured. Traveller people bought these poor horses and bought them cheap, and they knew they could cure them. Ringbone is a sinew that gets hard. In the fetlock of a horse there are about twenty-one bones, and the main sinew that leads to the movement of the hoof gets hard. For no reason, or no one understands, there's no cure for it.

Now I've seen in the market myself this bonnie pony come up. It was going kind of shan, kind of lame. And the dealer would say, 'Oh, that's ringbone.' There never was a bid. This pony was suffering and it was limping. The other dealers walked round, pressed their fingers round the horse's fetlock and said, 'Oh, he'll no mak much the day.' They were not going to bid on it. But the travellers didn't worry about this, you see. They couldn't actually cure it, but they could soften it. They could make it easier on the pony. The travellers had something to cure it.

So this beautiful pony, maybe it was a hunter, it could be anything. The travellers bought everything in the market that was cheap. A traveller man bid seventeen pound on this pony. She had a touch of ringbone. This horse is worth fifty pound if it didn't have this complaint. The man bought it.

After the sale the travellers met together and said, 'You got that pony? Ah, Jesus, it's a bonnie cratur that. Pity she had that complaint.'

'Ah,' he said, 'I knew what she had. That's why I bocht it. But she'll no be goin the same the morn. She'll no be gaun very lame the morn when I get her hame.' Now all the travellers knew the pony was suffering with ringbone. It was a certain kind of limp, a certain kind of twist in the foot. Once she was heated up and had a run, you would never hardly notice it. The traveller man said, 'I paid seventeen pound for it.'

'Well,' another traveller said, 'look. I'll gie ye three pound profit onto it.'

'No,' he says, 'no. you'll no! You'll no gie me three pound profit the night onto it. It's going back to the tent with me and when I'm finished working on it, and I take it back to the market next week you can gie me ten pound on it if you want to!'

You see, this was the idea. They would take it and put a hot poultice on it, right? And they would take a stocking . . . now this was a secret you never tell in your life! Travellers always kept things that were needed for their horses. You've seen old women's stockings? Not the nylon ones, but the old woollen ones that come to your knee. They would fill this stocking with baking soda and oatmeal, and they would put the horse's foot into it. And they would pull it up to its knee, pad it right to there and tie it tight. That pony was never allowed to move one bit! Food was carried to the horse with a pail and he was fed with cut grass. He was treated to everything, cleaned and brushed and a hap put over his back. But he was never allowed to walk one single bit. And this old-fashioned granny stocking filled with oatmeal and baking soda, more soda than oatmeal, right to his fetlock and tied under the knee. It stood there for three days.

And the man who owned the horse would take it off, take the horse for a walk and see the horse was a wee bit better. Then he'd say, 'Get it on again!' Back on again, the same thing for another three days. This time he would make it a wee bit stronger, maybe put a wee touch of washing soda into it. The soda would take a wee bit of the hair off, but this was the softening of the ringbone, the softening of the tendon, just up from the coffin bone a wee bit. Now the old farmers took an iron and they burned the tendon, but the travellers would never do that. The travellers' cure was easier. After another three days with the soda and oatmeal poultice on the horse's foot, the man would take it off.

Ringbone only happened in the front feet, never in the back. You got a callous pastern or a spavin in the back, but these things were never very hard to cure. You rubbed them with horse linament and made them go sound. So the poultice for ringbone was put on for six days. And when the traveller man took the stocking off the pony's foot, he said, 'I'll take you out today.' He groped the foot up and down. The hardness was gone from the tendon. It would be gone for three weeks or a month. The heat from the baking soda and oatmeal had completely softened the tendon, so when the horse pressed his foot and lifted his hoof there was no pain, and he could lift it right tidy. It would be that way for a month or so. That's what the traveller man wanted. He had relieved the horse of its pain. After he sold the horse it was none of his business. But he didn't do it for profit. He did it to prove that he could really do it. If he kept the horse, he would put the poultice on every three weeks. I've seen people keeping a horse for two years with the same complaint.

Now I've seen a traveller buying a horse from a pigman that was foundered. Its hooves went completely soft and you couldn't put a shoe on because the nails wouldn't hold. This is being too good to the horse, too kind. The people fed it all these scraps and things, and its feet began to curl up, turn up in the front. And the poor beast was in agony. After the traveller man dealed for the pony from the pigman, he would take it back to the camp. Its four feet were rocking with founder and it couldn't go another step. He'd tie it close to his tent. Now this pony had never been out of the piggery for weeks, months, maybe a year; it had never seen a taste of grass in its life. Now he wouldn't let it get too much grass because that would do it an injury. So it would be tied short.

The man would have his tea and go back out. And all travellers always kept a good knife. After his tea he'd say to his woman, 'I'll have a look at this pony, this wee pony I've bocht.'

She would say, 'Oh, it's a bonnie wee cratur. What's wrong wi it?'

'Oh,' he said, 'it's feet's foundered. I'll have to do something about his feet. It's a sin that the non-traveller folk who condemns us for being cruel to animals would keep a wee animal in that state, and mak its feet like that. Its feet's nearly boiled.' They were curled up, back and front. He took his knife and he pared its feet. Then he went to his wife and he said, 'Put me on a pot of oatmeal for a poultice.' And he took four wee bags and tied them on the horse's feet, filled with oatmeal and salt. And he said to the horse, 'You'll stand there!' It was tied right close to the door of his tent. 'You'll stand there the night!' These things like muggins or snowshoes were tied round the horse's feet. There was no way the horse could kick them off. But the hot porridge and salt were covering its hooves, and it stood there for maybe four days. It softened the feet completely. And then after four days were up, the traveller man would take them off. He would take his knife and trim the hooves right till they were short, as close he could to the frog, the quick.

And he would say to one of his weans, 'You tak that pony doon and walk it doon the old road, keep it in all the soft gutters and everything you can get. Keep it in all the soft water you can get. Every night take and walk it in the muck, in the gutters.' And all this muck on the horse's feet, and all this water, being far apart from the hard dry dung that the horse stood on in the piggery; in four or five days the horse's feet were clean. And he would take it to the smiddie.

He'd say to the blacksmith, 'I want to shoe my pony.'

'Mmm, shoe your pony? What kind of pony have you got?'

'Oh, this is it here.'

'But,' he says, 'it's got a wee touch of founder on its feet.' Oh, the blacksmith hated to shoe a foundered pony. Because when you chopped a nail on, it was like putting a nail into dry rot. There was nothing to hold it. Now the blacksmith could put a type of shoes on, what you call clamps. The shoe had a clamp on the side that was folded over and pressed down on the top of the foot. He had to be a special blacksmith to do this.

So the traveller man said, 'I want you to put on a set of clamps!' Now when the old blacksmith put on the shoes, he never put one nail in the horse's foot. He made his shoe and left a wee bit steel on the top of the shoe and wee pieces of steel stuck up around the shoe. And when he heated the shoe and put it on the horse's foot, he tapped these wee clamps into the side of the horse's foot. So the traveller man took his horse back. And I guarantee you, when that pony walked the road it was going just as if it had come out of a circus! There was no pain in its feet. Its hooves were soft and it had new shoes on, and no nail holes in its feet.

He'd take it back and say to his wee lassie or laddie, 'Tak it doon and lead it among all the muck and gutters you can get!' And they led it among the soft ground and all the muck they could get. And all the wee cracks in the hooves would get filled up with earth and muck. The pony enjoyed this because it was like you walking on a spongy sole, ken, if your feet's sore. The horse was going as level as could be! And he gave it a good grooming. The next day he would take it in behind his cart. Or maybe it was the market day. And you could defy anybody to know that that horse had founder! The horse was going as sound as a shilling. It would stay like that till the pony's feet grew again, about three months. If it was eating all right it would be fine, providing it got plenty of moisture and no dry food. And the travellers knew this. As long as it was fed on green grass it would be right.

But if you took that pony and put it back, sold it to a piggery or back into a farm where it stood in its own manure and the heat got it again, naturally the feet would just go back worse. If the travellers saw this, they wouldn't buy it the second time around. But if the traveller man sold the pony to a man who hawked fish on the street, he would tell him, 'Keep it tied in some place where its feet wouldn't get in any soft manure.' Then that pony would go on for years.

Why I want to talk about this is to give you an idea what the travellers had to face. It wasn't that they could go and buy a pony like buying something from a shop. They had to compete against people who really thought if they sellt something to a traveller, they were giving an animal to a cruel person. There were those who hated to give a horse to a traveller, even suppose they needed the money. There was a stigma attached to the traveller.

I went to this farmer once in Argyll on Poltalloch estate. He was the manager for Robert Malcolm Poltalloch. And I had sold my horse in Argyll and I was looking for a horse. This was 1966. And the man who was manager for Robert Malcolm Poltalloch was Mr MacKenzie. He became a high councillor for Argyll in Strathclyde. And this what I'm telling you is no lie. So, he had a couple of ponies for sale.

I walked up to the big house, I rang the bell and said, 'I want to speak to Mr MacKenzie.' He was English.

He comes out and he says to me, 'What is it?'

'Well,' I said, 'sir, I'm looking for a pony.'

'Oh,' he said, 'ye're looking for a pony are you? Where do you come from?'

I said, 'Well, I come from Lochgilphead.'

'Where do you stay?'

I said, 'I stay at MacCallum's Quay.'

'Oh,' he said, 'you're one of the travelling people?'

I said, 'Yes sir, I'm one of the traveller people.'

'And,' he said, 'do you mean to tell me you want to buy one of my ponies?'

I said, 'Yes sir, why not?'

'Look,' he said, 'I don't own the horses. Robert Malcolm owns the ponies. They're his.'

'Well,' I said, 'sir, I'm no worried who owns them. Look, I'm needing a pony. I heard you had some for sale.'

'Yes,' he said, 'I've got some for sale. I have a mare for sale and I've two geldings for sale. A two-year-old and two three-year-olds. But I'm not going to sell them to you.'

'Why not, sir?' I said. 'I'm willing to pay you for the pony.'

He said, 'I've been reared down in England.'

'Hmmm,' I said, 'you've been reared down in England, have you?'

And he said, 'I know what youse tinker-gypsy people do to horses. Youse drive them from daylight to dark gathering bones, rags, bottles and scrap. And you take them and tie them to a tree.'

I said, 'Oh? Well, that's your idea.'

'And the poor animal,' he said, 'hasn't got the life of a dog with yese. There's no way that I would ever sell one of Malcolm Poltalloch's animals tae the likes of you.'

'Oh,' I said, 'I'm sorry, sir, if that's the way you feel.'

Now life has got a funny story and has funny ideas. Not far from Robert Malcolm's place there was an old farmer by the name of MacColl. And he came from Orkney. He had a mare called old Jeannie. He had her for years. Malcolm Poltalloch kept these pedigree stallions, and he ran them on the moor not far from where Balnakeil Farm is. Now this what I'm telling you is the God's honest truth, as I have proof to prove it.

So I said, 'Well, Mr MacKenzie, thank you very much. Thank you very much. I'm sorry I cannae buy your horses.'

'No,' he said, 'I would never sell these to youse kind o people.' So I walked away from the castle. And I walked past this Balnakeil Farm, and I saw the mare in the field. And this young horse with the mare.

I walked down to the old farmer and I said, 'I'm looking for a pony, sir.'

'Oh,' he said, 'you're looking for a pony. Well, I've no ponies for sale. This is old Jean I've fetched with me from the Orkneys.'

'I know, Mr MacColl,' I said, 'you took this farm last year. I know Mr Turner who used to be here.'

'Oh,' he said, 'you do?'

I said, 'Yes. I was up at Malcolm Poltalloch and I tried to buy one of his ponies, and he wouldnae sell it to me.'

He said, 'Why?'

'Well,' I said, 'because he said I was a tinker and a vagabond and we were cruel to the ponies.'

And you know what old Mr MacColl tellt me? He said, 'Look, as far as I believe, if I were selling a pony, I would rather give it to youse kind o people before I would give it to anybody else under the sun. And I do have a pony. She's only two years old, a filly.'

'Well,' I said, 'Mr MacColl, I'm willing to try and buy it from you if you want to sell it to me.'

'Well, we'll have a look at her.' She was running on the moor. He said, 'Look, before you ever say a word. Robert Malcolm Poltalloch's pedigree stallion jumped the fence and covered my mare. And this is her foal.' Now it just shows you how things work out. 'And this is the half-sister to Robert Poltalloch's horses he's got for sale at the present moment.' So we hemmed and hawed.

I said, 'Mr MacColl, what would you want for your pony?'

He said, 'I'd want fifty pounds for her.'

'Well, it's a wee bit steep for me.'

'In fact, I'd want fifty pound for her, but I couldnae sell her right at this moment.'

I said, 'Why not? You want fifty pound for her?' Now I had this fifty pound in my pocket. But there's no way in the world he was going to get fifty pound from me. 'Mr MacColl,' I said, 'what's the price of a cow? A young cow?'

'Oh,' he said, 'maybe forty pound.'

I said, 'Are you no better selling me the pony? It's no good to you! And buy another cow with what I give ye for it. You can buy a calf for it. You rear it up, you've plenty of grass to feed it.' We steered away from the pony all together. 'You buy a good calf to yourself for twenty-five pound.' You could buy good wee heifer cows for ten pounds at that time. 'You could buy two calves for twenty pound apiece. You can grow them up and you've plenty to feed them. You've got two cows. That pony's no good to you. You'll never do nothing with it. It's wild, it never saw a cart. It's never seen a motor and you've never handled it. It runs with its mother.' He never was about it. I said, 'You've never put a halter on it. And prob'ly I could never do nothing with it. But I'm willing to buy it from you.' Now it was wild, really wild. But it was a beautiful creature. So we hemmed and hawed, hemmed and hawed.

And he said, 'Come back tomorrow. I'll talk it over with the wife.'

So the next day I went back again. And he was in. 'Well, Mr MacColl,' I said, 'I'm back to see about the pony.'

'Well,' he said, 'I'm no keen to sell it. I've had another offer from somebody else.'

'Oh well, that's too bad. You've had another offer from somebody else.'

He said, 'I've had an offer of forty-five pound from somebody else. They're goin to use it for the wood. They're going to drag trees with it in the wood.' Now this horse was fourteen hands and it was as broad as a barn door!

I said, 'Mr MacColl, no way in the world the man who's gaunna buy that horse is gaunna drag it in the wood! It's never seen a car or anything. You'd better sell it to me.' So we hemmed and hawed.

'And look,' he says, 'I wouldnae take nae less than forty-five pound fae ye.' Now I knew I had it. I knew it was mine. But there was no way I was going to give forty-five pound straight off for him. I would at the end, because I didn't have a horse. I was sitting at MacCallum's Quay. I had a cart and I had harness. I was in Kilmory for the neeps. And I had sellt my pony to old Jack. And I knew Mr MacColl was going to get the forty-five pound; even suppose it was like a raging lion, I was going to bring something back to the wife and tell her I bought a horse! And it was the most beautiful animal. This is the last horse I ever had. And we hemmed and hawed.

I started, 'Forty-two pound.'

'No.'

'Forty-three pound.'

'No.'

'Forty-four pound.'

'No.'

I hit his hand – now he didn't have any sense o dealin. He didnae ken what dealin was. I said, 'Mr MacColl, to tell you the God's truth, I'll give ye the fourty-five pound if you give me a luckspenny back!'

He said, 'What is a luckspenny?'

I said, 'A wee piece of silver tae give me luck with the pony I'm buying.' And I counted the forty-five pound in his hand. He went into the house and what did he bring me back? A sixpence. He handed me a silver sixpence and I spit on it [SPIT] and I put it in my pocket. Now I never knew what to do with this pony. I had to go and catch it. It never was inside a stable in its life. It never had a halter on its head in its life. So we rounded it up in the field and we brought the old pony, Jean, the old mother in. And we brought the pony in. I said, 'What do you call it?'

He says, 'Trixie.'

I said, 'Come on then, Trixie, get you in the stable! You're mine noo and I'm gaunna look after ye. And it had a silver tail and mane. It was a cross Arab and garron. It was about fourteen two and as fat as a barn door. There was a drain down its back. We got it into the stall and we crushed it in beside the mother against the wall.

He says to me, 'You'll never go near it.' And I put my hand on its hip and when I gave it a good clap like that, it pulled its backend into it.

I said, 'Look, you'll no kick!' I knew I had a pony. I had given it a skelp on the hip and it had pulled its backend into it, as if it was afraid of me. I said, 'I've got a pony! Come on, doll!' I put my arms round its neck. I said, 'Doll, I've got you. I've got a pony. It's mine noo.' And I walked up to his barn and took a rope halter down. I put it on its head and I led it out the door. And its bare feet were as broad as that, two handfuls. Its hooves were immaculate, back and forward. I said, 'I've got myself a horse this time. I'll never part with you!'

And I led it out. He shaked hands with me, bade me farewell. 'Noo,' he says, 'take good care o her.' Now wait till you hear this: it shows you what can happen!

I walked up from the Balnakeil which is in the canal bank in Cairnbaan crossroads. And I walked down past the hotel on the main road going to Lochgilphead, and a big private car came along and stopped. Right beside me. Who was this? MacKenzie. The Poltalloch's manager. And he came out.

He said, 'Eh, hello.'

I said, 'Hello.'

'You got yourself a pony?'

'Yes, I got myself a pony.'

He said, 'You know, eh, I tried to buy that pony. That's a half-sister to my garron ponies. And the half-brother o this mare, which is not half as good looking as her, took the prize in the Highland Show in Lochgilphead last year.'

'Well,' I said, 'I'll tell you something, Mr MacKenzie. This is no going to take nae prize in the Highland Show.'

'No,' he said, 'it'll be going to gather rags, bags, bottles and bones in yir tinker's cart!'

I said, 'It's got nothing to do with you what it does! It's mine, I paid for it.'

He said, 'If it was mine, you couldnae buy it for a hundred pound!'

'Well, Mr MacKenzie, it is not yours, it is mine. And I'm going to take it home and I'm going to yoke it in my tinker's cart. And I'm going to take it to Fife and I'm going to gather scrap with it. And I'm going to gather rags with it. And it's my pony!'

'Well,' he said, 'look, if it was mine you could never look at it.'

'But it is not yours, Mr MacKenzie, It's mine.' And he jumped in his car and he went off. So I walked Trixie back to MacCallum's Quay and my brother Willie was there and my brothers Jack and Jimmie. They had ponies. They all gathered round me.

Jack said, 'In the name of God, laddie, whaur did you get that animal? That's the most beautiful animal in the world.' And Jeannie, the weans' mother came out.

She said, 'That's a bonnie pony.' And everybody loved this pony. So the turnip thinning was finished and we're all going back to Fife.

Jack said, 'I'm gaun away, brother. I'm shifting back to Fife.'

And brother Jimmie, he had the big garron, big Rosie. He says, 'I'm going to Fife.'

'Well,' I said, 'boys, look. I'll have to get this pony broken in. It never was in a cart in its life.' So I took it up to Kilmory Farm. And Archie came out. Archie MacArthur looked. And I'll no tell you a word of lie. If he was here today he would tell you.

He says, 'How much do you want for it?'

I said, 'It's no for sale. But I'm needing a cart frae ye. That wee float I've got's too wee for it.'

He said, 'I've got a milk lorry round the back, a four-wheeled lorry I used to go to the milk with.' He had bought his first car to deliver their milk in 1966. His lorry and his harness were in the back of the shed. So I bought them. And I'm left with Trixie. I lifted her feet. Travellers lifted the feet of a new horse, and chapped them with a stone, like a blacksmith would do. If the pony carried on they knew the pony was wild. So I got Trixie's feet between my legs as if I were a blacksmith and I picked up a wee stone. I chapped her hoof and she stood like a lamb. I picked up the other back foot, and I chapped her hoof with a wee stone. She stood like a lamb. And then I picked up the front foot, and I chapped her hoof, and she stood like a lamb.

I said, 'You're a darling!' Next day I go into Lochgilphead, into Mr Neilie Crawfurd, who was a piper in the Argyll band. He was the blacksmith. I said, 'Neil, I want you to shoe my pony for me.'

He said, 'That's MacColl's pony.'

I said, 'Of course, that's MacColl's pony.'

He said, 'That's wild.'

I said, 'Neil, it's no wild. That's a darling! It's the quietest thing you ever seen in your life. I want a set of shoes on it.'

He said, 'It'll cost ye.'

'I'm no caring what it'll cost me.'

'It'll cost you two pound fifty for a set o shoes.' It was a lot then, but it was nothing! I could afford it. 'What do you call her?'

I said, 'Trixie.'

'Whoa, lassie!' he said, 'Trixie, lassie.' He put a hand up her neck, right down her hip. Lifted her leg, clapped her like that and he clapped her belly. He said, 'That's a quiet pony.'

I said, 'Right, mister. Nellie, put a set of shoes on her!' Nellie put a lovely set of shoes on her, right. And once she got her feet pared and a set of shoes she looked different. She was a different horse all together. She liked the click-clock of her feet on the road. So I came walking back and old Jack, my brother and my brother Willie and Big Jimmie thought I was never going to get this pony shod because she had always run on the moor and she'd never seen anything on the road. But she didn't bother about cars at all. She never bothered! She was a natural horse. I'll tell you something, if I hadn't gone into cars, I would have never parted with that horse in all the days of my life! So wait till you hear this.

That evening I went up Kilmory Road and I said to my brother Jimmie, 'I think I'll throw the harness on Trixie, see what happens to her.' So I put the saddle on her, bridle, breechen on, put the cripper under her tail. She never bothered. So I go up the old road what did I get? I took a big bath with me, and I filled it full of stones. I yoked her in this bath. With the noise of the stones coming behind her, she pulled it along the road, me leading her along. And with the rumble and tumble, the rumble and tumble of the stones in this bath she never even looked over her shoulder at it! I said, 'That's it!' And she never was in harness in her life. You'll no believe this, but I swear on my mother's grave this is the God's honest truth.

So I led her back down to MacCallum's Quay to the shore. And she was sweating. I loosed the harness off and I rubbed her down and dried her off. But she never was in a tether, you see. So I tied her up and I cut some grass for her. The next day old Jack shifted and big Jimmie shifted back to Fife. My brother Willie didn't have a pony.

He says, 'Brother, I couldnae go and lea youse.' Old Sandy Cameron had a pony, brother Jimmie had one, Jack had one and Pipe Empty had a pony. They all took off that morning from MacCallum's Quay and left me sitting there with this half-broken horse, me and my brother Willie. Now Willie had two wee kids, Christine and Duncan. I'm left with this horse. My lorry is lying up at Kilmory Farm. I had the harness down with me. So we're sitting.

I said to Willie, 'Brother, we'll never get shifted.'

'Tsst,' he said, 'there naebody to stop us. We'll go up and we'll yoke her in the lorry and we'll shift the morn.'

I said, 'Are ye game? Look, brother, it never was in a cart before in its life.'

'Never mind it,' he says, 'you get one side and I'll get the other side. She disna kick, she disna bite.' We go up, fling the harness on Trixie. Oh, she was a beautiful animal. God that I had her the day! I wouldn't take a million pound for her. We walk up to Kilmory. We lead her up, back her into the cart shed, put the shafts of the lorry down on her. It was a rubber channelled lorry. I pass Willie the reins.

I said, 'You take the reins. I'll take her by the head.' So we led her right out by where the caravan site is now, right out to the old post office down by the main road by Lingerton and right back to MacCallum's Quay.

Willie said, 'That pony's going nice, man, no bothering itself.' We pulled her into MacCallum's Quay.

I said, 'Tomorrow we'll shift.' Now this is truth, I'll swear to you on my mother's grave, I'm telling you the God's truth. We tied her up, cut her some grass. We got up the next morning. I said, 'Willie, we're shifting.'

He says, 'Okay.'

I said, 'Pack yir stuff on the lorry.' He had only a wee tent and two wee kids and a pram. I said, 'Pack it on!' And Jeannie got the weans ready, we packed everything, pulled the cover and happed everything. Yoked Trixie on. Where were we that night? Cairndow shore at the other side of Inveraray. Everybody was sitting on going along the roadside. Wait till you hear this now! As we pulled into Cairndow shore, old Jack and Pipe's fire was still going!

Willie says, 'They're ahead of us. And they left you, brother, they left you wi yir wee pony. They thought we couldnae go.' We stayed that night in Cairndow. Willie and I went up and we poached two salmon from the back of John Noble's big house. We had a feed of salmon that night. The next morning we packed up, packed the cart. Down Loch Lomond, into Balloch. Where did we catch up on Sandy, Pipe, Jack and Uncle Jimmie? In Drummond old road outside of Kippen. Were we going! And everybody was sitting on the lorry driving along the road. Trixie was stepping out just taking it easy doing about twelve mile an hour. We're sitting on. I drove into Kippen. I was the hero! And Trixie's stepping to her chin. Sandy Cameron's pony was turned out, old Jack's was turned out, and Big Jimmie's was turned out – all at the camp watching me coming up Lomond strait, coming into Kippen. And Trixie was going like the lamb of God, just taking it easy, these big strides in this lorry. I was only a day behind them. Pulled into the camp, lowsed her out, patted her, tied her to a tree. And they all came down. They swore in their life they wouldnae believe it.

They said, 'Look, that pony was yoked before! That pony was broken in when you got it.'

I said, 'Look, that pony never was broken in. It never was in harness.' But to this day they wouldn't believe it. So we drove on to Fife and I left Uncle Jimmie in Dollar. And I left Uncle Willie and he made his way back to Stanley for the winter. I came up here to Kincraigie Farm. I turned my horse loose in the field and I put the harness in the old house. Jack went down to put his camp up in the wood. And I took this old house, and we settled down for the winter.

Then one evening old Jack said to me, 'Look, why is it we have got to go on with horses for the rest of wir days? Everybody's takin motors. Why in the name of God can no one of the Williamsons get a car? The're nane of the Williamsons have got a motor.'

I said, 'Brother, tomorrow morning I'm going to the School of Motoring and I'm going to sell my horse and get a car.' And that I did. And Trixie was still running in the field here. I advertised Trixie in the paper for sale. But that's ahead of my story.

THE MAXIE RABBIT

O I am a maxie rabbit
And I sit here on the green
My body's full of trouble
And there's maxie in my een.

So now my story you will hear, and you will agree
Of what those greedy farmers have gone and done to me;
When first we came upon the land no man was King but one
The greyhound was not thought of and neither was the gun.

Then man he came, he ploughed, he sowed with harvest for to
    reap,
He needed all the grass for his greedy cows and sheep;
They killed us for our skin, they killed us for our meat
But no matter what they did, still we had them beat.

And then at last they found a way to beat us at the fight
They called it myxomatosis, some said it was not right;
They injected us with maxie, then they turned us free
For to wander round the green to spread disease and dee.

So here I sit upon the green, my eyes are shut and sore
My body full of maxie and I can hop no more,
But before I go I hope some day below this very green
Will walk some greedy farmer with maxie in his een.

So if there is a heaven and a rabbit will ever gang
I hope I will be there before very lang,
For I have suffered plenty, I've had my share of pain
As I sit here blind and hungry among the sleet and rain.

Now man is just a creature made by the hand of God
And just like me he will dee, us both will get the sod,
My bones will lie upon the grass and his beneath the sod
So why not leave the rabbits to the work of God?

If nature did not want us, why were we born?
For I am sure we are not to blame if farmer he grew corn,
So if you see a maxie rabbit, don't you be vexed
You too could take maxie, it could be your turn next.

But man I am sure will suffer
I am sure you'll all agree
For what those greedy farmers
Have gone and done to me.

Duncan Williamson

Chapter Fourteen

A Great Horsieman

In 1954 I had a wee piebald pony I'd bought from an old man down in Methil. Just before that I had this big chestnut with a silver tail and mane, and it was awful wicked – it would kick you! But this wee man with a piebald pony was selling sticks and he wanted to swap with me. The chestnut I had was the laziest horse you ever saw in your life. The man met me in the street and asked me for a swap. So he and I had a deal. I asked five pound about from him and a swap. He gathered rags and sold sticks and that. No, but we hemmed and hawed and then we managed to make a deal. He would give me three pound and his horse and harness for mine. So I swapped him.

And I was staying at the Fife shore away down at a place they call Macduff, right down at the beach where old Macduff Castle is. There are a lot of great big caves you could turn a double-decker bus in on the shoreside. And we used to kindle a fire in them on the wet days. The shore is a walk for people coming along from East Wemyss. One day it was a terrible day of rain and these two old women passed with dogs. They stood and looked at my pony. And I had my gelly up and I had the fire going, you know. They never spoke. But they walked away up the road. About an hour after that down came the police.

They said, 'I'm led to believe, eh, you've got some ponies down here.'

I said, 'Yeah, I've got a pony.'

'Well,' he said, 'eh, I've had a complaint that the pony is sufferin doon here wi the cold. Why youse people . . . people like youse ought to have more sense. When youse keep horses, why could youse not take care o them?'

'Well, officer,' I said, 'look. There's the horse there. You go and look at it.' Now this wee man who had had this horse only walked it when he sold his wee bits of kindlings and sticks. He'd fed it on all kinds of meat and broch and corn he could find.

I guarantee you, it just took me to put it between the shafts of the cart – it was that fat!

He said, 'How long have ye had that beast?'

'Och,' I said, 'I've had it fir a while.' I never said how long.

'Well,' he said, 'It's in good condition. But youse people are kind o daft. Youse build a tent fir yirsels – why don't youse build one for the horse as well?' He never had a clue!

Ours was such a different way of life, see what I mean. Because you take these people in the villages. You've never seen five families on the road at one time and all these horses trotting on, just like cars driving past you. And maybe five in the one cart, six in the other cart, four in this cart. Now these village people believed that the travellers drove these horses all day like that! But we didn't. We only drove these horses for a mile and then walked them for three, and drove another mile.

In the 1950s and 1960s I used to leave Fife here and go to Inveraray, go right down to Lochgilphead which is exactly, from here the way I used to go, a hundred-twenty-five, maybe a hundred-thirty miles right there. Now I used to leave Fife, Leven or the Coaltown o Balgonie and make my way into Perth. Now that would take me at least five days then. But I had certain times of the year for going. I wouldn't go when there was no grass because I knew fine the horse couldn't travel without food, and I couldn't carry enough corn to feed the horse on the journey. Once you got up there among the sheep farms, up in the hill country, they had no hay to sell you! Or none you could steal. And when you landed in Argyll, there was no grass because grass is late coming over there. You see, after a certain time, when the grass really came in the month of April, the travellers didn't have to feed the horses; they just had to tether them out in a picket line and the horses could take care of themselves. All they needed was a drink of water. They never got corn during the summer. But they fed them on corn in the wintertime and hot drinks and that. Now I used to leave Leven and make my way right to Lochgilphead. And when I landed there that horse of mine was as fresh and as fat as the day that I started. The only thing that troubled us in the 1960s along the roadside was these people with their cameras wanting pictures and photos, stopping you along the road.

It was really annoying. I was coming down Loch Lomond with Trixie, the last horse I ever owned. And just at Luss this Rolls passed by, and there were two ladies in it, an old gentlemen and a chauffeur. So when we came to the layby we stopped. And I had my four weans, Edith, Jimmie, Willie and Betty sitting on the top of the float – their hair as white as driven snow and curly. The pony was so beautiful, you know, and I kept my harness clean. It really looked nice. I was just walking it slowly leading it by the head when they stepped out in the road with all these cameras. And the chauffer had leggins on. This old gentleman, he looked foreign, like a German or a Jew or a Greek to me. I walked up to him.

I said, 'Look, did anybody give you permission to take my picture? If you want to take a picture of this part of the road, you move past till I get by!'

He never spoke to me, but the chauffeur came to me. He said, 'You shouldn't have done that!'

I said, 'Why no? If you want him to have any pictures, then you stand in the road and let him take pictures. It's no right . . . if he had asked me to take pictures . . .' And these ladies were flabbergasted. They thought that we should have stopped and let him have all these pictures.

So, another time I was coming back this way from Crianlarich. And in these days, sister, the roads were very bad. You know, it was up hill, down hill, bends and turns. There were no good roads at that time. And you had all these wee ditches, for letting the water off the road.

So we came round this bend and here was this lady, an old lady with a camera. And she's standing, ready to take pictures! But we're all sitting on the cart and the pony was just trotting on slowly, taking its time. And when she saw us coming she took out this camera. I put the stick to the horse, just touched it, and the horse started to trot!

She ran along with the float, 'Wait, wait, wait!' she was shouting. 'Wait, wait, wait!' She was holding the camera and she went into one of those wee trinks head over heels! Oh aye. They thought, you know, that you should agree every time. If they had come to you and said, 'I wonder would you let us take a picture of you and your horse?' But in the early sixties they were all after you and they were more torment than anything else. Because you pulled into a camping place and you were making a wee cup of tea, then two or three cars pulled up. Before you could say 'Jack Robinson' there were half a dozen round you with cameras trying to take pictures of your tent. You couldn't get peace up in the West Coast at that time, you know. And it was really embarrassing! It was hellish. Different if they would have given you something to help out the situation a bit. Times were really hard, really hard then. You only depended on what you could find along the way.

As I was telling you, if it wasn't for the horse or a pony, the traveller would never have survived so long. He couldn't have survived so long because he had no other way. In these times there was no social security. They only depended on a few shillings they could make, a few shillings they could get from a deal, swapping and dealing. And there were people who had horses, who swapped and dealed every day. They would travel miles just for the sake of having one deal to get that day's wage, even suppose that horse could hardly stand. And I've known a man to swap away a dead horse! You'd hardly believe that.

Travellers who knew each other had what you'd call 'sicht unseen deal'. You never saw my horse and I never saw yours. We were staying in different parts of the district and I would say to you, 'Well, what kind o beast hae ye got noo? I haena seen ye for years.' You would say, 'Och, I've got no a bad kind o beast.' 'Oh well,' I would say, 'come on then we'll hae a pint.' This was the start off for their dealing. They had a pint and then they would start talking.

So this man had dealed his way out, and he's left with a mummy horse. That was a horse with teeth too long in the front and its grinders wouldn't close at the back. It could pull the grass but it couldn't chew. This horse was just able to stand and no more, just about dead. But the man, Johnie Macdonald was his name, a cousin of my mother's; he wakened up one morning and there the horse was, down and out. It had died during the night. Now he had five of a family, and his wife and his cart and nothing to pull it and nothing to shift his camp. Well, the only thing you could get then was five shillings for a dead horse from the knackery. If you phoned the knackery

they would come and pick it up, give you the five shillings for
the skin. But he wouldn't have this.

He said, 'I'm gaun to the toon, and I'm gaun tae get a deal!'
So away he goes and he meets this man he knew well. But he
never picked a traveller. He picked a country horse dealer, a
non-traveller man who thought he knew everything! And they
had a wee drink together.

He says, Well, Johnie, how many beasts you got aboot ye the
noo?'

'Well,' he said, 'I've ane auld horse but he's jist a wee bit on
the big side for me. He's kind o poor. Well, come on doon to
the stable. Mebbe me and you can have a deal. I've a couple
here – I've mair 'an I can feed.'

'Well,' Johnie said, 'I'll tell you what I'll dae wi ye.' He picked
out a nice wee pony, beautiful wee horse. Now this is the truth
I'm telling you. He said, 'I'll gie ye a swap tae that ane there,
providin that the money's right.' So he swaps the dealer and
draws two pounds on this nice wee fat pony for the one that's
lying back on the old road.

He says, 'Well, I'll come oot for that pony in the afternoon,
Johnie.'

He says, 'You dae that.' He takes the pony home, ties it to the
fence. And in the afternoon the dealer drives out with his gig
and pony. They usually drove out with a gig, and if they came
for a loose pony they just tied it behind and drove it back in. So
they cracked for a while. Johnie says, 'Come on, I'll show you
your pony.' He took him up the old road and there the pony
was lying. Dead. So Johnie says, 'It was livin when I left. It was
okay. I dealed it to ye; I was fair enough.'

And the dealing man, 'Well,' he says, 'that's in the trade.
That's all in the deal.'

There's no way to know that Johnie swapped away the dead
horse. And that's the God's truth. Och, they all knew each
other, and the dealing man had trusted him, you see. They
had their certain clients whom they could deal with, some they
wouldn't deal with and some they wouldn't give a swap to and
some they would.

Now, there were no bills of sale. In horse trade there was
no such a thing as 'comeback'. If you got a bad deal, there's

no way in the world you can turn round and say, 'Look, I want my own horse back.' Once you had the swap made, that was it. And woe be to you if you rue, 'a rue bargain'. If I had made a deal with a man and said, 'Look,' and I'd swapped with the man, hit him fair [SLAP] and square and [SPIT] had spit on my hand and said, 'Right, [SLAP] I'll take four pound and yir horse aboot in a swap.' And the next morning I wakened up and that horse was lame. If I had said, 'I'm no havin this. I'm gaun back. I'm givin this back to him.' And I'd walked back and said, 'Look, you made a fool o me last night, you gied me that horse and it's lame.'

'Well,' he'd say, 'laddie, it's your ain fault. You swapped wi me didn't ye?'

I'd say, 'I know you swapped wi me, but look, I cannae dae nothing wi that horse. It's lame. Ye gied me four pound. There's yir four pound. Look, I want my ain horse back.'

He'd say, 'All right laddie, there you go. Go and tak yir horse back, go and take it back. But dinnae come back here nae mair!' You see what I mean. 'Dinnae think ye'll ever deal wi me again. You made a rue bargain. Dinnae think ye'll ever deal wi me again, because that's, as far as I'm concerned, you are no a dealer at all!'

If you couldn't stand the crunch, you shouldn't have been in the trade in the first place. And even suppose I had went back again and offered to sell that man a horse worth twenty pound for ten pence, he wouldn't have taken it. That was the way of them. It was the same among travellers.

I've seen many's a good deal. The man dealed. They had a swap with each other and then the next morning the woman came. And there's nothing worse a traveller man hated than dealing with a man, and the woman came in the morning saying, 'Look, my man swapped wi you last night.'

I'd say, 'Aye, your man did swap.'

She would say, 'Ah, well, I dinnae think you had a very good deal and it wasnae his horse onyway, because he didnae work for it aa. Half of the money that bocht it was mine.'

'Oh,' I'd say, 'missus, go and take your horse back. Oh, no, no, no, no. If that's the way you want it, take your horse. I'll take my ain. I'll walk doon and take my ain horse back.

Look, there's – he gied me a couple o pound – there it is back to ye.'

If a woman cocked the bargain it was the most shaming thing the man could suffer. The man wouldn't even look at you the next day! It was the most hurting thing that a person could ever do on a human being, on a dealer, was for the woman to interfere. For the woman to interfere the next morning was the most shaming thing you could ever ask for.

For a woman to come and try and deal with a man was out of the question. Even though he had a horse, if the woman had a good horse and she was wanting a deal. Even though he gave her the best of the deal, the travellers would say, 'Och, he would deal with that poor cratur, that poor widow-woman. He took her wee beast fae her, and look what he gied her!' Even suppose he gave her the best in a swap, the story would pass round.

But two women could deal and that was okay. The man might say, 'Look, I cannae deal with you, missus. But if the wife wants a swap with you, it's up to her because that's her horse. I gied it to her onyway.' This is the acceptable way to back out of it. But he couldn't deal with her himself 'Oh,' he would say, 'no, I got that wee horse for her. It's her horse onyway. She can dae what she likes wi it.' He'd say to his woman, 'You go and deal with her. Look, I gied that horse to you.' Even suppose he never actually intended that; suppose it really was his own horse. If his wife then made a bad deal, well, it was up to the two women involved. But the funny thing was, if two traveller women dealed and they made a bad deal, they would never back out, no. And they became good friends. But I've seen some fights, too, among women with the horses.

What the traveller horse dealers especially liked was buying young horses, you know, colts. They went to the islands, like Skye and the islands off the West Coast. They bought these unbroken horses in the crofts and farms, and they broke them in, fetched them back. Then any dealer who looked at them would know what he was looking at. He couldn't make a fool of the traveller and say, 'Och, it's auld. It's wind-broken, got bad feet.' The dealer would have to say, 'That's a nice pony you've got, laddie.'

And the traveller would say, 'It's only a two-year-old, two-year-old garron.' Well, there was no way in the world a dealer could try and take the traveller down.

The dealer would say, 'Well, I'll gie ye a swap tae two o these for yours.' The traveller would get two old ponies, and maybe six or seven pounds. Well, he'll naturally go home to his own place, maybe he'll swap that two old things he got for another young one from somebody else. This is the way it went on.

Because the traveller was no fool among horses. Their forefathers might not have had much knowledge about horses, but the travellers who were reared up with horses were the real dealing travellers. They were the ones up to all the tricks of all the trade. And they could outwit any non-traveller dealer. Because clever as the non-travellers were, and there were some crafty and good dealers among them, it doesn't matter how cute they were; the tinker would always go one better! But that was one thing about them; if a tinker got a trick played on him, he would never say he was 'done'. No, he would try his best the next time and get his own back in his own way. He would never complain.

So, this man I was telling you about, Johnie Macdonald, the cousin of my mother and my mother-in-law's brother, he was a great horsie man in the 1930s. He was well known for his deals, you know, and his swaps. They called you 'game', if you were game for a deal, game for a swap. So, one minute they were down and the next minute they were up. They never really got rich. If they hadn't got it one day, they might have it the next day! And the traveller was never really down, because if he was that low that he couldn't get the price of a horse, then he would build himself a handcart or go back to a pram or something, use that till he got the price of something better. So Johnie had dealed himself as low as he could possibly get, till he was left with a mummy. It got thinner and thinner till its ribs began to stick out. There was nothing more shaming than having a poor horse. Especially if you're going to pull into a camping place among more travellers, and everybody there has a good horse.

So, in case they met with travellers, they tried to keep out of other travellers' ways when they had bad horses, till they could pull themselves together and get something better. Johnie, he cut away up here through Fife. He came to this old road before you go into Cupar called the Sandy Old Road. That was a camping place. He pulled his cart away up the old road to camp for the night. And he comes to this tent. Nice wee tent and a governor's car, a kind of wee trap, but it was light. Johnie lowsed his old horse out and let it go. It wouldn't go anywhere, it was that sick and thin it couldn't.

He says to Jeannie his wife, 'We'll stay here for the night. There must be somebody who's got horses here. I see a camp there and a wee gig. Maybe I could get a swap!' See, always swapping in mind. So after he has his camp up and has a cup of tea, or whatever he got, and got a bit fire for the wife, he wanders up to this camp. And here is an old man and woman. Johnie starts to crack to the old man. But he noticed by the old man's tongue right away that the old man wasn't a real traveller. He was a 'buck' as you may call him – half traveller – just a flattie or a country man who went on the road. But his wife, she was a traveller woman. But they were pretty old, up in years. They had a lovely wee tent and this gig. So they sat and cracked and talked about many things till it came round . . . Johnie was waiting to speak about horses. So he said, 'Dae ye hae a beast, old man?' That's what he called it.

'Aye,' said the old man, 'I hae a beast. I have a guid beast.' Johnie's ears began to cock up, you see.

'This is a deal here,' he said to himself. So he cracked away again and he cracked away, but he was wanting to get back to the horse. He said, 'Whaur is yir beast, old man?'

'Och,' he said, 'it's jist roond there the back o the tent.'

Johnie's thinking to himself, 'It must be an awful wee horse if it's . . . I cannae see it over the back of his tent.' So they cracked away a wee while.

'Wait a minute!' he says. 'I'm gaun to feed the beast and I'll let you see it.'

Johnie said, 'All right. I've a beast doon there tae, and maybe me and you could have a deal.'

'O-oh no!' says the old man. 'I'll no; nae such a thing wi me as that! I dinnae dae these things. I wouldnae pairt wi my beast for nae other beast.'

'God bless me!' says Johnie.

The old man goes round the back and he takes a wee box with a bit of netting wire into it, and he puts it sitting in the front: a black crow with a broken wing! He says, 'The're my beast. I've had that beast fir two year noo since ever it had a broken wing.' He roared to it and it came out and sat in his hand. A big, old, black crow. He says, 'That's my beast.' He was pulling the gig himself. He didn't bother with a horse. Well, Johnie couldn't help but laugh! He came back down and tellt his wife.

She said, 'It serves you right! It serves you blinkin right!' He was a great man, big Johnie Macdonald, for horse dealing. He was a great horsieman.

A good traveller horsieman knew the situation, how the deal was going to go, even before it happened. Because they knew from past experience what kind of man they were going to deal with, right? They had probably dealt with him before. They knew the money he was going to take, right? And they knew what they were going to accept. They knew how much cash they had in their pocket and how far it would go. They knew the value of what his horse was worth and they knew what their own horse was worth. The traveller man knew what his horse was costing him: he'd probably had four deals with this horse and he'd probably got two-three pounds along the way all the time. He counted off that to find out what the horse had cost him. Look at it this way: he went into the market and he bought this horse, for, say twenty pound. Now he brought it back and took care of it. Maybe he had to break it in. They were always fond of buying young horses and breaking them in, because they'd always grow into a good horse. Then, along the way he would probably meet somebody and they would say, 'That's a braw beast you've got, mister!'

'Well,' he would say to him, 'I'm no married to it. What – hae you got onything?'

'No, I would like to buy it.'

'No, I hardly every buy, eh, sell oot. But have you onything I could swap tae it?'

And the man would say, 'Well, come doon and see mine.' Now he would go down and see the other horse. He would look over this other horse and he would know what the other man was thinking in his head, see what I mean! And he also knew what he was thinking himself. The other man would say to him, 'Well, hoo could me and you have a deal?'

And he would say, 'Well, we can deal the best we can!' Now he would say to his ownself, 'I'm going to gie him the swap.' But then he would 'kid on' after the first offer that he wasn't, that he had no intentions of dealing at all. And the further they went away from the deal the more keen they were, see what I mean! If they were really keen, then they kidded on they didn't want anything to do with it! This was the idea.

Say they saw this good horse and they said to themselves, 'I'm gaunna get this horse come hell or high water.' But the minute he gave away a clue that he was interested, then the dealer would come down on him like a ton of bricks, sting him for the last farthing. You see, the dealers couldn't afford to keep too many horses because they survived by dealing in horses. It was like a shopkeeper or a merchant – they had to keep a steady movement of horses. Say he had eight, maybe nine. Well, they could only afford to feed three or four.

Now a traveller would come in and look around the horses and say to the dealer, 'What about that one?'

'Oh laddie, that! That's nae guid tae ye. That would kick the cart in. It would run awa wi ye.' Now the traveller knew that man was only telling him that because he didn't want to put it away. Well, this is the one he would go for! If a dealer had one that he wanted rid of, he would say he didn't want it away – trying to deceive the traveller that he didn't want to part with it. These are the kinds of things that went on. He could read the traveller's mind just as good as the traveller could read his.

When it came to the actual deal the traveller would say, 'I'll take twelve pound and your horse,' knowing he was going to have to accept three or four. He would give himself plenty of room to deal, to come and go on. Now the dealer would know fine that no man ever gets what he asks, never in a swap or a deal. Otherwise you wouldn't be in the trade, you wouldn't be a dealer.

So he would say, 'Well, you asked twelve. I'll gie ye six. That's half.' The traveller was only expecting four. Now he'd got six.

He would say to himself, 'Well, if he's willing to pay six, why no try him for another two?' He would say to the dealer,

'No, come on, I'll split the difference wi ye – I'll gie ye seven!' [SLAP] He was still going to make another pound. This is the way it went on. They had it all set up. They weren't deceiving anybody. Because your eye was your merchant and your pocket was your guide. That's all you had. And they had no written words between them, nothing on paper. And there were no comebacks. If you were 'burned', it just went as a bad deal and you had to live through it and maybe make up the next time.

It was really fantastic when you think about it. And it still goes on today, the same thing. There are a lot of horses down in England yet and in Wales. I know a traveller lad who used to camp with me and he's got fourteen horses, but he's got three brand new lorries along with them. He only keeps the horses just for trading and swapping and selling.

From the First World War until after the Second World War was the heyday of the horses in Scotland. There were horses in the coal pits, the pigmen had horses, the fruit men, the fish merchants, the rag-and-bone men, the scrap men, the horse dealers. This was the horse's time. And I'm not counting the horses on farms, just the local people and travellers trading in horses. After the 1914 war all the young men came back from the Army who had been using horses, pulling guns and that. When they came back to their way of life, they made sure they were going to have horses, and this is when the horses really got among the travellers.

But the younger generation at the present moment, and anybody that was born since forty-nine, among the travelling people, I don't suppose could yoke you a horse, would know how to put a harness on it. They'll take a car to pieces and build it as you see yourself within a couple of hours, and they'll do anything with cars. But I'll bet you if you took a set of harness and loosened them down, threw the harness down and asked them to put that set of harness together for you, they couldn't do it. Horses started fading about 1945 or '46, and after the war, when the boys came back from the Army. With a few shillings' gratuity money, instead of buying a horse they bought a car. It was the war that really made some of them, because they learned to drive in the Army. When they came back as young men to their families, their children were maybe school age.

They bought cars, and the children of these servicemen were born with cars.

The beginning of the sixties marked the beginning of the end of the horses, especially among the travellers. The thing that hurt the travellers worse than anything else was that cars began to come in. Small cars, small lorries, and the farmers began to buy these new-fangled threshing machines, combines and things. And they didn't need so many hands to work at the harvest. It was only then, near the middle of winter, when the travellers could get an odd job on the farms, at the tattie time. By 1961 or '62 the horse markets began to change from every week till every fortnight, and then to every month. The young generation of the travellers growing up, like my two oldest boys, Jimmie and Willie, by the 1960s were in their early teens, and they had little interest in horses of any description. A horse was no fun to them anymore, although they were born and reared with them.

But it helped the horses that cars came in. The horse with the travellers was well enough done to, but it was only a horse. And it was used every day in the week. Travellers worked them hard, drove them some days on and on for hours at a time. They weren't cruel to them in any way, and they fed them and took care of them. But they really worked them hard because they had to. I think all the old horses in the country sighed with relief when the travellers finally stopped working with them! Then your fishmen and your fruitmen and your coalmen and your pigmen whom the travellers used to get all their swaps and deals with began to buy wee cars and wee lorries to sell their fruit and sell their fish. They could travel and hawk farther, and get more done in a day.

The travellers who had cars in the 1960s were little company to the ones who had horses. The ones who had horses were little company to the ones with cars. With a car you could travel and hawk further away. An old lorry or an old car was cheap to buy in these days, and the restrictions on them weren't half as bad as they are now. There were no MOTs or anything like that. Travellers just got an old car, put a pair of Ls on it, learned to drive, got a licence and that was it. They began to travel further distances between their camping places. Where it used to take

them a week to travel with a horse, they could travel in a day.
It was more economical to the traveller to have a car, and they
could keep their stuff dry. If it was a lorry, they could get a
canopy on it and shift even in wet weather, for their stuff and
their weans were always dry. And if they got a van, their stuff
and their weans were always dry when they travelled. And
petrol was cheap.

But gone was the comfort of five and six horses, five or six
travellers being round the one campfire and having a good
time! Things had completely changed in the sixties. The going
of the horse left its mark in many ways. By 1962 or '63 a lot
of the good camping places along the roadways got closed up.
People began to get hungry for land and greedy. The Forestry
Commission started taking over a lot of the places the travellers
used for camping; they closed a lot of these right o ways, planted
them with trees.

The travellers' horses disappeared very fast. When I went
to Muthill for the tattie-howking in Perthshire the very first
year with a horse in 1950, there were about twenty-five horses
belonging to travellers in that field. When I went back in four
years' time there were only about eight horses. And three years
later there was only me with a horse and my brother Jimmie.
But it was another ten years before I put my last horse away.
Within the space of thirteen years, from 1951, the horses on
farms where I worked were wiped out completely. When I went
to old Sandy Kerr's in Kennoway first, there were twelve horses
and not one machine on his farm. When I left there in 1964
there were three tractors and not one single horse.

I never was born with horses, and my father never owned a
horse. But the idea that put me to horses was that I had worked
on a farm with horses with my father when I was only five years
old. And then before I left school, at the weekends, I went and
worked on the farms with horses in Argyllshire. Then, seeing an
odd traveller coming to the West Coast with a pony; and leaving
Argyllshire and coming and travelling through Perthshire with
my brother, meeting all the travellers and seeing how handy
it was – eventually I became a good horsieman myself. But I
really liked horses! I still like horses. In fact, if I could afford it,
I would have two horses. For the horse goes back a long, long

while among the travellers . . . back to the time when travellers really began. If they hadn't had horses, they could never have survived to this present time. For myself and for many it was their only means of survival. It was the horse that really made the travellers from the start.

THE HAWKER'S LAMENT

O come all youse hawkers, you men of the road,
Youse hawkers who wander around,
My story it is sad, for it saddens my heart,
For they've closed all our campin grounds down.

Though we fought for wir country and we fought for wir king
An some gave their life for this land,
It's out there in Dunkirk it's many they fell
With their blood mixed up with the sand.

But what did they fight for and why did they die?
For freedom to wander around!
But where can we wander? We have no place to go,
For they've closed all our campin grounds down.

They say we are not wanted, to keep movin on,
Though it be rain or be snow;
For where can we move to when we move along,
For we have got nowhere to go?

So listen, my boys, if another war should come,
Just you keep moving around:
You have nothing to fight for, you have no house nor home,
And they've closed all your campin grounds down.

But maybe some day, when we've gone from this world
An we're buried deep down in the ground,
Will God make us welcome, will He give us a home,
Or will He tell us just to keep movin on?

Duncan Williamson

GLOSSARY

Note: Traveller Cant indicated by (C), Gaelic words by (G)

aa	all
ae	one; the same
ain	own
ane	one
antil	until
auld	old
awa	away
awfae	awful; great many; extremely
ay	always
back-end	October month
bairn	child
barra	barrow
barricade	peaked tent with inside fire on the ground
bene	fine (C)
bi	by
bing(s)	plenty; come; go (C)
bis	is
bit	piece of
blindit	blinded
bocht	bought
braw	fine
broch	scraps of meat; bread; leftovers
buck	half-traveller (C)
bund	bound
burk; burker	murder for medical research; body-snatcher, *cf* Burke and Hare
cadger	itinerant dealer
cam	came
camp	tent; place for tents
cannae	cannot
castell	castle
catcht	caught
ceilidh	get-together for songs and stories (G)

chap	knock
cheeny	china
chuik	chuck! cry to gather animals, *cf* diug! (G)
clabbydhu(s)	horsemussel, *cf* claba-dubhaidh (G)
claes	clothes
cleek	hook
cloot	cloth
couldna	could not
country	non-traveller
cowp	rubbish tip
crack	talk, news
cratur	creature
croon	crown, five-shilling silver coin
cruisie	small paraffin lamp
dae	do
daurstnae	dared not
didna	did not
dinnae	don't
disna	doesn't
div	do (emphatic)
dochters	daughters
dodder	doctor (C)
doon	down
doot	doubt; rather think
dottled; dottlin	in a state of dotage; enfeebled
dovered	dozed
droll	strange, queer
drooky	dripping
ee(n)	eye(s)
eerie	afraid (C)
eldin; eldrin	very old; old-fashioned things
faa	fall
fae	from
faired; fairing	cleared; entire
fankled	ensnared; tangled
feart	afraid
fir	for
fit	foot
flattie	dim-witted town dweller
follaein	following

forbyes	as well
founder	disease of the hoof
frae	from
friends	relations
gadgie	man (C)
gae; gae'n	go; going
gaun; gaunnae	going; going to
garron	small, sturdy horse; Highland pony
gav	town (C)
gelly	bowed tent with inside firecan and chimney
gie; gied	give; gave
greet; gret	complain; cried
guid	good
haben	food (C)
hae; haena	have; have not
half-blood	part thoroughbred
halflings	half-grown young
hame	home
hantle	folk
harlin	trailing
haud	hold
hecks	racks for fodder
hissel	himself
hit	it
hoo	how
hornies	police (C)
hoors	hours
hurl	a ride; push
hus	us
huvnae	haven't
jeelie	jam
kail	curly cabbage
[kchkch]	non-lexical vocable: dog's lethal snap
keeking	peeping
ken; kent	know; knew
kenneled	kindled
kist	chest
laochan	hero, boy (G)
lea	leave

leears	liars
leid	lead
lowsed	unyoked
loss	lose
luggies	small pails
mair	more
mairrit	married
maister	mister
mangin	intimating; speaking (C)
mar	kill
marlech	hare (C)
masel	myself
maun	must
mebbe	maybe
messages	groceries
moich	rotten; crazy (C)
moose	mouse
mort	woman (C)
muckle	greater
mushfeeker	umbrella mender (C)
nae	no
neep	turnip
neuk	nook
no	not
noo	now
o	of; non-lexical vocable
oot	out
orra	odd
ower	over
oxter	armpit
piece	sandwich
poke	small bag
polis	policeman
pooder	powder
pourie	small oil can with spout
prank	horse (C)
proochen	horse or cow caller, *cf* pruigean (G)
puckle	small amount (of)
puggy	little steam engine for shunting wagons
rags	woollens for recycling

raggie	ragged
reek	smoke
scholar	school pupil
sekkin	want, hope to get
seo	here (G)
shakit	shook
shan	ashamed; bad (C)
shaw	cut shaws off of
sister	the narrator's female listener
skeely	experienced
skelp	hit
[SLAP]	one slaps the other's hand to seal an agreement
slipe	cut at a slant; wooden tool for cutting
slutter	sloppy mixture of food
smiddie	smithy
snottum	wrought iron crook for hanging pots over outside fire (C)
soond	sound
sowl	soul
spate	sudden flood
sprach	beg (C)
stall	stop (C)
static	friction
stook	a shock of cut sheaves
stuff	scrap metals
tae	to
tak	take
taste	savour
tattie	potato
tellt	told
tenions	pith
there; the're	there's; there are
thes	these
thon	that, those
Tilley	manufacturer of pressure, paraffin lamps
tinks	travellers (derogatory)
toll	a tell-tale
totie	small child; puff, *cf* totaidh (G)
touching	harming

trinks	ditches
tuppence	twopence
two-three	a few
waste	unused, remote, forgotten
welting	hitting
wha	who
whaur	where
wi	with
windae	window
winna	won't
wir; wirsels	our; ourselves
wonst	once
worl	world
wumman	woman
ye(se)	you
yersel	yourself
yir	your
you'	young